PARIS

The Musical Kaleidoscope

1870–1925

PARIS

The Musical Kaleidoscope

1870–1925

ELAINE BRODY

George Braziller

NEW YORK

First published in the United States in 1987
by George Braziller, Inc.

The following essays have appeared in slightly different form:
"The Russians in Paris" in Malcolm Brown, Ed., *Russian and
Soviet Music: Essays for Boris Schwarz*, published
by UMI Research Press; "The Legacy of Ida Rubinstein" in *The
Journal of Musicology*; and "The Americans in Paris" in *Musical
Quarterly*.

For information address the publisher:
George Braziller, Inc.
60 Madison Avenue
New York, New York 10010

Library of Congress Cataloging-in-Publication Data

Brody, Elaine.
  Paris—the musical kaleidoscope, 1870–1925.

  Bibliography: p.
  Includes index.
    1. Music—France—Paris—19th century—History and
criticism.   2. Music—France—Paris—20th century—
History and criticism.   3. Art and music.   4. Music
and literature.   I. Title.
ML270.8.P2B93   1987   780'.944'361   87-6633
ISBN 0-8076-1176-X

Printed in the United States of America
First Printing, August 1987
Second Printing, October 1987

For David

Acknowledgments

All those who have helped me are indeed too numerous to mention. Several special services were performed by the following persons: my most able research and editorial assistant Asya Berger; my first mentor who encouraged me from the start, Jan LaRue; my good friend and adviser Joaquín Nin-Culmell; my patient and enthusiastic editor Deirdre Mullane; my colleagues William Austin, Martin Bernstein, and Jean-Rémy Julien; Carl Schorske, Aileen Ward, and the members of the biography seminar of the New York Institute for the Humanities of New York University; Colin Denis, Easy Klein, Eric Canepa, Mary Anne Shea, Jill Cusmano, Marion Green, and Alex Schlesinger who helped en route; my European friends and colleagues Elvira Viñes-Soto, Nina Gubisch, Olivier Delaigue, Yves Gérard, and Jean-Michel Nectoux; my long-time teacher and friend Alexander Lipsky who taught me the essence of French piano music; Dr. William R. Grace who granted me the time to write; my daughter Sue Shapiro for her counsel and support; and last and most of all my husband David Silverberg, to whom this book is dedicated.

Contents

Preface

Many years ago I decided I must tell the story of this fascinating period in French cultural history, but I was uncertain where I ought to start, and how to integrate the many and various trends of the panoramic tapestry that reflected the period 1870–1925. Would a continuous narrative be most appropriate or discrete essays? On which trends to focus and in what sequence? In time, a confluence of events yielded the approach I needed to review in depth and in breadth cultural Paris of this epoch.

I have had a longstanding involvement with French music of the late nineteenth and early twentieth centuries. It began under the tutelage of the late Harold Bauer, the pianist who had personally known both Claude Debussy and Maurice Ravel and was also a splendid interpreter of their music. It continued through my graduate work in musicology, when I wrote a thesis on the piano works of Déodat de Séverac, a contemporary of Debussy, and in my more recent efforts to accumulate material for a monograph on Ricardo Viñes, the foremost interpreter of the piano music of the three composers just mentioned, and the first to perform in Paris, and elsewhere, much of the new Spanish and Russian music of his time. Articles I wrote on the literary figures Catulle Mendès and Judith

Preface

Gautier brought me in touch with comparativists, scholars who sought to answer musical questions first faced by the writers they studied.

My interests and energies converged on an era in French history that began with the collapse of the Second Empire and the defeat of the French in the Franco-Prussian War, that included the establishment of the Société Nationale de Musique and also the eventual development of French music to the point where, by 1925, Paris became the musical capital of the Western world, having at last wrested leadership from the Germans who, throughout the nineteenth century, had assumed complete musical domination of Europe.

A study of this chapter in French musical history must discuss the masterpieces that emerged once the yoke of Wagnerism was cast aside; the growth of a specifically French musical nationalism; the significance of performers such as Viñes and others; the new importance of the ballet and its function as a focus for musicians, artists, writers, dancers and even impresarios. This was a time when poets animatedly discussed and sometimes even wrote music, when musicians regularly attended literary events, and people like Cocteau not only wrote but also illustrated their own works. In literature and in art these were the last years of *la vie de Bohème*, *la vie de café*, of occultism, mysticism, spiritualism, and exoticism—"isms" all present in the musical experience of composers of that day.

Russian music, too, was just being introduced to the West. Modest Mussorgsky's *Boris*, for example, heard in Paris for the first time in 1908, had a profound impact on that city's composers and performers. Spanish musicians, among them Isaac Albéniz, Joaquin Malats, Enrique Granados, Ernesto Halffter and Joaquin Nin, as well as the Catalan pianist Ricardo Viñes, all resided in the French capital at that time. (Arthur Rubinstein's memoirs, *My Young Years*, which closely parallel the material covered in Viñes's unpublished journal, only suggest what Parisian cultural life was like in the early twentieth century.)

Certain pieces composed during this era are seminal works of the twentieth century. *Pelléas et Mélisande*, that remarkable example of Wagnerism carried to the extreme, deserves recognition as a turning point in French operatic, indeed *all* operatic history. Charles Gounod and Jules Massenet were important, but what of Ernest Reyer, Emmanuel Chabrier, Alfred Bruneau, Ravel and others? In the 1920s, Sergei Prokofiev, Arnold Schoenberg, Paul Hindemith, and the group

known as "Les Six," of whom the most important are Arthur Honegger, Georges Auric, Darius Milhaud, and Francis Poulenc, were
all in Paris experimenting with musical ideas that would provide
the tonal language of the next few decades.

After "La Belle Epoque," when Diaghilev and the Russians made
Paris their home, specific works like *Le Sacre du Printemps* became
exceptionally important to all artists, not just to musicians. Another
landmark was Ravel's forward-looking piano piece *Jeux d'eau*. Erik
Satie's ballet *Parade* called on the resources and assistance of more
than composer and choreographer. Exoticism, mysticism, jazz elements and modality appeared not only in the music of Debussy but
also in that of Ravel, Alexander Scriabin, Chabrier and, later, Albert
Roussel.

Ballet and modern dance, the new piano music, the programmatic
orchestral pieces that grew out of the symphonic poem, the chamber
works for voice and instruments, the new treatment of the voice in
general in the twentieth century—one fantastic example is the Ex-
hortation Scene from Milhaud's *Les Choëphores*—the new use of
the pedal, in sum all kinds of things that relate to performance
practice or the way the music sounded at the time it was written;
the new forms of music criticism practiced by men like Henri Gau-
tier-Villars (Colette's husband) and M. D. Calvocoressi; the old style
of instruction at the Conservatoire and even at the newly established
Schola Cantorum; the battles between the d'Indyistes and the De-
bussyistes (whose support Debussy himself loathed and renounced);
the musical reviews of the period and also the numerous literary
reviews like *La Revue indépendante* and *La Revue blanche* that included articles about music; the newspaper magnates Thadée Natanson and Alfred Edwards and their mutual wife (in sequence, of
course) Misia Godebski, who afterward married artist Jose Sert; the
portrait painter Jacques-Emile Blanche and the Symbolist artist Odilon Redon, who sketched so many musicians; Picasso and Gris,
Frank Haviland and Stuart Merrill, Verlaine and Mallarmé, Apollinaire and Mendès—this is what the fifty-five years from 1870 to
1925 are all about.

In the 1950s the British critic Martin Cooper wrote *French Music
from the Death of Berlioz to the Death of Fauré*, a chronology of music
from 1869 to 1924, that took the "great man" approach, dealing with
individual composers and their compositions. Unfortunately it lacked
the excitement conveyed by similar studies of art and literature of

the period. Still earlier, L. Rohozinski edited *Cinquante ans de musique française* (2 vols.) which discussed various musical genres: the *mélodie*, the symphonic poem, piano pieces, opera, operetta, and so on. At about the same time, Julien Tiersot, a prolific French writer, reported on *Un demi-siècle de musique française, 1870–1919*, a short survey of the period. More recently, Laurence Davies's *The Gallic Muse* attempted to bring the period to life through an account of the lives and music of six composers: Gabriel Fauré, Henri Duparc, Debussy, Satie, Ravel, and Poulenc. James Harding, in *The Ox on the Roof* (1971), deftly describes some musical scenes in Paris in the twenties, but fails to disentangle the threads that together made this era extraordinary not only for those who lived during that time, but also for us who have inherited its aesthetic values. Most of these authors communicate awe but not enthusiasm for some of the most exciting years in French cultural history!

As part of a series devoted to the culture and society of various nations at different times in their histories, Scribner's published *Culture and Society in France 1848–1898* by F. W. Hemming. Incredibly, the author cites Baudelaire, Hugo, Verlaine, Mallarmé, and Rimbaud among poets, Flaubert, Maupassant, and Huysmans among writers, Rodin in sculpture, but only Debussy among composers. Just as rich musically as artistically, this epoch needs careful exploration and explication. That this has not yet been accomplished is astounding.

Roger Shattuck wrote about the period, or at least a portion of it (1885–1914), but he did so, as he says, through four studies of different personalities: Alfred Jarry, Henri Rousseau, Erik Satie, and Guillaume Apollinaire, assuming that the cross currents in this "irresistibly attractive era would then fall into line." They don't, and it is for this reason that I have taken another approach.

The first chapter included here, "The Death of Berlioz and the Birth of the Société Nationale de Musique," describes the state of French music that prompted the need for the establishment of the Société Nationale. Without it, French musicians would have waited even longer for their works to be performed. "Wagner in France and France in Wagner" offers two sides of the same coin. All his life, Richard Wagner had a love/hate relationship with the French. He needed to please them; he felt driven to meet their aesthetic standards, yet these obsessive goals caused him to despise the French. The French view of Wagner is a different story altogether. French musicians resented the incursions of all foreigners on their cultural scene, so they had no sympathy for Wagner, and certainly none for his arrogance and hostility. But the artists and writers who first discovered Wagner through his theories and prose writings—without having heard a note of his music—were overwhelmed by his concepts and were determined to put them to practice in their own country. The impact of Wagner on music, art, and literature in France is probably the greatest single phenomenon of this fifty-year period. The rise of *le wagnérisme*, commencing in 1870 and reaching its apogee in the 1890s, declined only with the advent of the First World War.

"Le Japonisme and l'Orientalisme" describes trends readily seen in arts and crafts movements of the period, but they also appear in music. A need for fresh sources of melody and rhythm was met by "Music at the Great Expositions," where the music of non-Western nations first accosted the ears of contemporary French musicians. "Café Concerts, Cabarets, and Music Halls," discusses the ways in which productions were aimed first at the working class and later at the bourgeoisie, musical compositions grew out of popular chansons, and political, social and familial scenes were depicted in the witty lyrics of entertainers.

"Music and Art" suggests the relationships between artists and musicians, how and why they became acquainted, and what influence, if any, they exerted on each other. Similarly, "Music and Literature" gives an account of the inevitable concern of musicians for and with literature and the occasional apathy of writers about music.

The Spaniards arrived early in Paris, one of the first groups of cultural immigrants, having left home for political and professional reasons. They settled in an enclave in Paris and arranged for the welcome and resettlement of those of their countrymen who followed. The Russians made their greatest impact through Diaghilev, but their arrival had been prepared for long in advance, and certain individuals, like Ida Rubinstein, continued their successful careers for decades after Diaghilev's death. The Americans in Paris bring to mind the doughboys of the First World War, and it was in the period immediately following that Americans came to Paris in droves. But earlier, too, the Gallic muse had made an impression, and the French-American connection can be seen from the 1880s onward.

When Paris refused to accept the avant-garde among artists, writers, and musicians, Brussels welcomed them. The story of "Les Vingt," unknown even to many Frenchmen today, merits more attention. Finally, the "Masterpieces of French Music," preceded by a discussion of what precisely characterizes genuine French music, offers a selective list of orchestral, chamber, vocal, and keyboard music of the period that has stood the test of time.

Each chapter is a discrete, distinct entity and can be read separately from the others. Together they present a summary of various trends, movements, people, and places which comprise the cultural and musical kaleidoscope that was Paris 1870–1925.

1

The Death of Berlioz and the Birth of the Société Nationale

Hector Berlioz died on the afternoon of 8 March 1869. As always, his timing was poor. The event took place too late for the reviewer of the *Guide Musicale* to include more than a short statement in the necrology column for the issue of March 11:

> A Paris, le 8 mars, M. Louis-Hector Berlioz, né à la Côte-Saint-André (Isère), le 11 dec 1803, compositeur et critique eminent.[1]

His passing mattered little to the French musical establishment and even less to the public. The greatest French musician of the nineteenth century went to his death with less pomp and ceremony than that accorded a few weeks later to Albert Grisar, a tenor at the Opéra. Berlioz's music was unpopular, his writing sarcastic, his wit caustic, and his personality unyielding. He had few friends—although those like playwright Ernest Legouvé and poet Humbert Ferrand remained close to him throughout his life—and no end of detractors. He also had an irascible nature, a tendency to exaggerate, a passion for gigantism, a cultivated belief in isolation from the crowd, stubborn integrity (about his own music and also about earlier music he deemed worthy of reviving), and an abrasive intelligence calculated to arouse animosity. Physically he was of medium height with an abundant head of fiery blond hair (not red, as some of his portraits seem to indicate) that often fell over his forehead; he had deep-set blue eyes that darkened as his thoughts changed; his sharp nose was his most prominent feature; his mouth was wide, but with thin lips, suitable for a flutist.[2] Barbey d'Aurévilly described him vividly when he said, "He had the beak of an eagle, the mane of a lion and the strange aspect of a heraldic animal."[3]

Unfortunately for Berlioz, his waning reputation paralleled a period of rising fortunes for Wagner, at least in Germany. As if this injustice were not enough, the decade had also been a good one for Rossini, the leading representative of the Italian school Berlioz detested; for Giacomo Meyerbeer, whose gifts Berlioz recognized but whose willingness to cater to the masses he deplored; and for Jacques Offenbach and Daniel-François Auber, who both seemed to wallow in the insouciant frivolities and endless entertainments of the Second Empire.

What is Berlioz's legacy? What did he gain for France?

A prototype of the romantic artist—it was Théophile Gautier who first grouped him with Delacroix and Hugo as the originators of the romantic movement in France—Berlioz possessed boundless energy. Even as a young man he saw greatness in his own future, admittedly more often in fantasy than in fact. His physician father in Côte-Saint-André, where he was born, expected his son to follow in his footsteps. Berlioz planned otherwise. In Paris to study medicine, he bolted from the dispensary and headed instead for the Conservatoire. On his first appearance there, director Luigi Cherubini threw him out of the library for having entered through the wrong door. Eventually he enrolled at the institution, studied there for four years but, as might be expected, did not endear himself to many. Jean-François Lesueur, that master of classical *tragédie lyrique*, warmed to him, surprisingly, and encouraged the young man. Also, Anton Reicha, who some claim initiated the harmonic experimentation of the nineteenth century, taught him composition for a time.[4] Essentially, however, Hector Berlioz was self-taught, and learned through trial and bitter experience.

Profoundly aware of his surroundings, irrepressibly curious, with a voracious appetite for the cultural diversions not to be found in the provinces, Berlioz rushed to sample everything. Fortunately for posterity, he left us his impressions. When conductor François-Antoine Habeneck presented the premiere of Beethoven's Fifth Symphony in 1828 at the Conservatoire Society Concerts, Berlioz was there. When Fanny and Charles Kemble brought Shakespeare to the Odéon, Berlioz attended the performances. Demonstrations in 1830 found him on the front lines. Concerned with politics, literature, and art— Gustave Courbet, J. D. Ingres, Emile Signol all painted portraits of him—Berlioz epitomized his age. Besides Shakespeare and Goethe, both of whom he placed on Parnassus, he worshiped Schiller, Byron, Scott, and James Fenimore Cooper. He displayed far more vision and more perspective than most of his eminent contemporaries.

Gluck, Mozart, Beethoven, and Weber stimulated his musical sensitivities; but he also enjoyed the music of Schumann, Mendelssohn (whom he met in Rome, but who did not reciprocate his feelings), Liszt, and Wagner. When editor Louis Bertin finally appointed him critic of the prestigious *Journal des Débats*,[5] Berlioz was in a position to assist those whose works he regarded favorably and also to chastise those who merited his displeasure. He wrote for thirty years for the *Journal* (1834–64), and during the same time he was also critic on a daily paper and on the weekly *Gazette musicale*. Although he liked the power he had thus acquired, he resented that these obligations left him less time for his own compositions.

Cosmopolitan to the core, Berlioz made five visits to London, and managed to conduct several operas at the Drury Lane Theater.[6] He also paid several visits to Germany, one of six months' duration in the company of his mistress Marie Recio, a less than talented opera singer whom he eventually married after the death of his first wife, Harriet Smithson. On two trips to Russia, one in 1847 and again in 1867, he made a strong impression on the leading Russian composers in St. Petersburg.

Flaubert corresponded with him; Pissarro discussed Berlioz's work in a letter to his son; Heine described him and his music (if incorrectly) in reports from Paris. Liszt had faith in him and scheduled a "Berlioz Week" in 1852 in Weimar, to which he invited the composer. And the Russian Princess Carolyne zu Sayn-Wittgenstein[7] became one of his confidantes, probably because she distrusted Wagner and thought Berlioz a lesser rival for her lover's time and attention.

Berlioz broke with musical tradition and established his independence at about the same time that the literati and fine artists did. But he acted alone, not in consort. Musicians were more isolated and had less impact as a group than writers, like Hugo and his followers, or painters, like Courbet and his adherents. Berlioz's music abounds in contrasts, in orchestral colors, in rhythmic innovations, and in long-line romantic melodies. He favored mammoth, large-scale compositions whose performance required the colossal interiors of the Invalides or St. Roch. Whether he worked in church music or in symphonic music, his sense of theater never left him. He had been involved behind the scenes in theatrical productions and all his work seems geared to the drama. Despite the extramusical titles of many of his pieces, Berlioz expected the music itself to appeal to his audiences. This most literary of composers anticipated Stravinsky's later declaration that music alone could not tell a story, but should nonetheless provoke interest, soothe temperaments, or incite patriotism.

Because Berlioz was prone to exaggerate, and also because he was overly sentimental, he tended to dwell in his writings on the bad times and often neglected to mention some of the good. Through his observations we have learned about the Opéra, the Opéra-Comique, the Théâtre Lyrique, the Théâtre des Nouveautés, and the Théâtre-Italien. From him, too, we discover much about the theater, about the nepotism and backstage chicanery that characterized the musical scene in Paris in mid-century.[8] We can empathize with his continued criticism of the Conservatoire, the free, national school of music established in Paris by the Convention Nationale in 1795. We note that even by 1869, the year of his death, things had not changed very much. Rules were rules and only somebody like Berlioz could break them.

The establishment, however, took its revenge. When the Conservatoire denied him its resources, concert preparations fell to Berlioz himself. He had to hire a hall, engage the musicians, arrange to print the programs, placate the managers and agents of his artists, order the tickets, and plan the publicity. All this entrepreneurial work exasperated him. He undertook most of his tours to other countries simply to gain leverage in Paris. Here, too, he failed. To the French, even the minority who believed in him, he remained unclassifiable—a veritable sin against the Gallic mentality—situated on the periphery, a genius, but mad. Camille Saint-Saëns liked him; Ernest Reyer adored him; Paganini and Liszt, two foreigners, encouraged him; critic Jules Janin fought for him; editor Armand Bertin supported him. Few others did.

Hector Berlioz achieved for French music close to what Wagner had attained for the German music of his time. He freed it for the future, untying the bonds of classicism and academicism that shackled the imagination of so many French composers. A nationalist, but not a chauvinist, Berlioz could see beauty outside of France and also in classical antiquity. His homage to Goethe in *La Damnation de Faust* and his reverence for Virgil in *Les Troyens* confirm this free-spiritedness. Posterity benefits from his lack of technical competence at the piano. Instead of composing at the keyboard, he wrote for the orchestra, often combining timbres and mixing the sonorities of unusual instruments.

Berlioz taught himself to conduct out of the sheer desire to hear his works as he felt they should be performed. He notated his experiments and thus produced both the *Grand Traité d'instrumentation et orchestration modernes*, the most impressive theoretical treatise of the century, and *Le chef d'orchestre: théorie de son art*, a primer for conductors. Among the first of his generation of composers to befriend the leading poets and painters in France, he set to music the texts of both Victor Hugo (*La Captive* and *Sara la baigneuse*) and Théophile Gautier (*Nuits d'été*); orchestrated Rouget de Lisle's *Marseillaise*; and wrote his own exquisite poetry for *Les Troyens*, *Béatrice et Bénédict*, and *L'Enfance du Christ*, on a level that makes some of Wagner's texts sound amateurish.

Whether rewarded with the Légion d'honneur (he would have preferred a post at the Conservatoire or an orchestra to conduct), or caricatured by the humorous illustrator Cham and book-illustrator Gustave Doré (who simply reflected the opinion of the public), Berlioz stubbornly continued to prick the conscience of the musical world through his perceptive musical criticism, his obstinate refusal to accept less than the best in any performance, vocal or instrumental. A titan among pygmies, he died unaware of the effect of his own crusade, never knowing that he had laid the foundation for the renewal of French music for the next fifty years.

Does Berlioz's music invite description? Is it a reflection of its creator? More than most composers, Hector Berlioz introduced his life into his works. A prophet without honor in his own land, his music, too, remained foreign to his countrymen. Yet in Germany, in England, and more than anywhere else in Russia, the music of Berlioz took root, flowering abundantly in the music of Mussorgsky, Rimsky-Korsakov, and Borodin, and returning to France via Debussy and Stravinsky, that gallicized Russian.

Like its creator, Berlioz's music cuts a wide swath, makes a bold impression. Even the earliest of the large-scale works, the *Symphonie fantastique* (1830), resembles a maelstrom of sound as it thunders through space. As unique within its category as the Ninth Symphony of Beethoven, Berlioz's first programmatic orchestral piece consists of five movements, with a program initially meant to serve as an explication for listeners. (The program appeared in six different editions between 1830 and 1836 before the author decided it was not essential for the audience to have it in front of them.) The mammoth orchestra requires, besides the usual complement of strings, woodwinds, and brasses, four bassoons, four horns, two cornets, two ophicleides,[9] cymbals, two harps, two bells—and if bells are impossible to obtain, several pianos.

Berlioz casts each movement in a separate, traditional, almost classical form with just enough deviation to make it singular. The first movement, in quasi-sonata form, opens with an exceedingly long introduction, and the principal theme, when it finally appears, could only have been written by Berlioz. Its extended serpentine profile introduces the new romantic melody: long-line, yet all of a piece, unsuited to fragmentation. The second movement, not a min-uet or scherzo, is in Berlioz's words "Un bal." In what other sym-phony can we find a waltz as the second movement, in 1830 or later? A scene in the country, out of which Berlioz builds his third move-ment, derives from Beethoven's *Pastorale* Symphony, as its creator was the first to admit. Berlioz handles his instruments with exquisite taste as he fashions a dialogue for flute and oboe, suggesting pan pipes in a bucolic setting. In the fourth movement, "March to the Scaffold," the music depends on the traditional French delight in military music for its effect. (This despite the originality of the spe-cific program affixed to the movement.) This patriotic composer recalled the marches scattered throughout the works of his forebears Etienne-Nicolas Méhul and André Grétry. In the "Dream of a Witches'

Hector Berlioz achieved for French music close to what Wagner had attained for the music of Germany. He freed it for the future, untying the bonds of classicism and academicism that shackled the imagination of so many French composers. He died unaware of the effect of his own crusade, never knowing that he had laid the foundation for the renewal of French music for the next fifty years.

(Above) Gioacchino Rossini, the leading representative of the Italian school Berlioz detested, had become "the first musician of Europe." England, Germany, Russia, and Italy clamored for his works and his presence.

(Left) Further competition for Berlioz appeared in the person of Giacomo Meyerbeer. Rossini staged the German composer's first Italian operatic success, Il Crociato, at the Théâtre-Italien. It is not inconceivable that Meyerbeer learned from Rossini how best to comport himself in Parisian society.

The Théâtre-Italien acted as a magnet for Italian composers who fled the political instability in their native land and sought a better life. Usually, they found their way to Paris.

While Paris continued to be the mecca for foreign composers, the capital was hardly hospitable to her native sons. The Opéra-Comique, slightly less rigid than the Opéra, nevertheless held to a policy of producing works with a successful past history.

But the birth of the Société-Nationale and the inauguration of Charles Garnier's magnificent new opera house in 1875 would ultimately be responsible for the revival and the efflorescence of French music.

Sabbath," Berlioz writes a finale that suggests a French counterpart to the Wolf's Glen Scene in Weber's *Der Freischütz*. In a single work he has blended Beethoven and Weber and seasoned them both with a dash of his own flavoring. For the first time, too, he offers a new means of musical unification in his choice of one theme, an *idée fixe*, which purports to represent the artist's beloved in the successive stages of their courtship.[10] The recurrence of the *idée fixe* throughout each of the five movements, sometimes alone, at other times in counterpoint with new themes, supplies both unity and variety to this expansive work.

Berlioz, a man of sharp contrasts, could also compose delicate music. The "Queen Mab Scherzo" from *Roméo et Juliette*; the love music from that same work, written in 1839 and providing Richard Wagner with the exact pitches for the love music in *Tristan und Isolde*; the finespun "Ballet des Sylphes" and the gossamer texture of the "Menuet des Follets," both from *La Damnation de Faust*; the exquisite flute and harp solos in *L'Enfance du Christ*; and the yearning viola melody that recurs through four movements of *Harold en Italie* all demonstrate that Berlioz could be tender.

How sad that Berlioz was forever denied access to the real theater! Considered a maverick by the Opéra administration, he could not get funds for his projects. *Roméo et Juliette* and even *La Damnation de Faust* could well have been written for the stage, but not after their creator had suffered repeated rejections at the hands of the establishment. Virtually barred from the Opéra, he took an alternative route, invented another genre—the dramatic symphony—an apt description for the pieces inspired by Shakespeare and Goethe. The two compositions served as models for Wagner, who merged the symphony with the opera to produce his own musical dramas.

Even as Berlioz lay dying, public attention in the French capital centered on the forthcoming first anniversary of Rossini's death. For a celebration scheduled for Sunday, 28 February 1869 (to coincide as closely as possible with Gioacchino Rossini's birth date),[11] the authorities planned a performance of his *Stabat Mater* at the church of St. Roch, the scene of one of Berlioz's earlier triumphs. Rossini's widow, Olympe Pélissier, in broken French that proved a constant source of amusement to the journalists who interviewed her, made her intentions clear. "A liturgical work," she insisted, "must be played in appropriate surroundings." What she had forgotten was that the maestro had composed it for the theater, the Théâtre-Italien, where it received its premiere on 7 January 1842 (with Giuditta Grisi, Mario Tamburini, and Emma Albertazzi as soloists). Not unexpectedly, the piece was a huge success, and by 16 March 1869, close to the day that Rossini's personal effects went on the block at Drouot's auction house, it had already been heard four times in concert.

Rossini had the Midas touch, and his French colleagues fumed. They were consumed with jealousy, but try as they might, they seemed unable to determine the secret of his success. From the day he first stopped in Paris en route to London—9 November 1823—Rossini's name was enough to send agents and impresarios scurrying for contracts. Theaters featuring his operas expected double and triple their usual receipts, and they were not disappointed. Not only did they sell out the house, but tickets printed to sell at 10 and 15 francs brought as many as 150 on the black market. (Before Paris and London, Vienna's famous Kärntnerthortheater had held a Rossini festival from April to July in 1822.) When he arrived in the French capital—he had already been represented there by more than a dozen operas—the rousing welcome he received astonished the composer. Not the first to cross the Alps to make his fame and fortune in Paris, he became—and by all accounts remained for almost half a century—the brightest star in the Parisian musical firmament.[12] Before him, in the seventeenth century, Jean-Baptiste Lully, who accompanied the Chevalier de Guise to Paris in 1646 as a page to Mademoiselle d'Orléans, a young cousin of Louis XIV, managed by dint of his talents and shrewd business tactics to establish and become the head of the Académie Royale de Musique, eventually known as the Opéra. Luigi Cherubini visited Paris for a year in 1786 and took up permanent residence there two years later as director of the new Italian opera. When the Paris Conservatoire was founded in 1795, he was appointed one of three Inspecteurs des Etudes. After a year's visit to Vienna, where he was invited to write an opera for the Kärntnerthortheater in 1806, he returned to Paris and reigned there with few interruptions from 1821 to 1841 as the de facto head of the Conservatoire.

The Théâtre-Italien acted as a magnet for Italian opera composers, a number of whom became restless in their native land as political instability and the false hopes generated by Napoleon's reforms led to an oppressive regime. Italian musicians sought a better life, and, usually at the suggestion of Domenico Barbaja (the impresario who first sent Rossini abroad), they found their way to Paris. The centralization of the French nation there, plus the traditional obligation of the government to support and encourage cultural activities made the trek westward seem exceptionally promising.

Jovial, genial Rossini was born under a lucky star. Both his parents were musicians, encouraging rather than frustrating him in his quest for upward mobility. Acclaimed rather slowly in his own country, Rossini quickly achieved fame once he came under the tutelage of Barbaja. No doubt Barbaja's appointment to the Kärntnerthortheater helped his younger compatriot on the road to success. (Barbaja resembles the French playwright Beaumarchais in the way he made his fortune. A waiter, he became a financial speculator, who first used whipped cream with coffee and chocolate, the *barbajatà* or *granità di caffè*.[13] He had a gambling concession from 1808 to 1821 in Naples, where he was introduced, by his Spanish mistress Isabella Colbran, to Manuel Garcia, who became one of the most famous Spanish tenors of the nineteenth century and the father of both Malibran and Viardot.[14]) As director of theaters in Naples, of La Scala in Milan, and of the Kärntnerthor in Vienna, Barbaja encouraged his most promising talents to go to Paris, presumably because he believed that once successful there, they would become greater attractions when they returned home. A number of these young people traveled from France to Italy, and then to Austria. The French, however, profited the most from this arrangement. They also paid the highest fees, and they had more theaters concentrated in a smaller area than any of the other large cities. Sooner or later, most musicians evaluated the conditions for survival and settled in the French capital which, already in 1788, had established a theater expressly for Italian operas.

Before he left his native land in 1822 at the age of thirty, Rossini had composed thirty-one operas, most of them superb examples of opera buffa. (In fact, he directed his talents to serious opera only after he married Isabella Colbran, who wanted works more suitable to her own voice and temperament.) In Vienna, reviewers spoke of his courteous and obliging personality and his agreeable manners. "He charms everyone with his unassuming style," reported the *Allgemeine musikalische Zeitung* of Leipzig on 8 May 1822. Extremely facile, he tossed off his music at a speed that made his achievements the object of suspicion by others who sketched and drafted and revised their pieces. The Viennese responded so enthusiastically to his work that Schubert immediately tried his hand at an Overture in the Italian Style. Commissioned to write for theaters in Vienna, London, and Paris even before his arrival in these cities, Rossini was always careful in the early years not to offend the native composers he met on his visits, while his imperturbable spirits prevented him from taking umbrage at the many unfavorable remarks jealous colleagues made about his music.

The peripatetic Rossini in Paris in 1860 described to Richard Wagner his meeting with Beethoven in Vienna in late March or early April 1822. He explained how he climbed the steps to the elder composer's apartment with trepidation and left later concerned about the disparity of their living arrangements. Why didn't the authorities undertake to provide Beethoven with better housing? The reigning German composer, renowned throughout Europe, should not be forced to live in such squalor. His Austrian associates assured him that the situation reflected Beethoven's personal choice. "No matter where you put him, within a month, he becomes listless and changes his lodgings," they told him.

Rossini, whose nationalism was never strong, became increasingly conservative in his political attitudes. The French press accorded him considerable space; various actresses and patronesses sponsored dinners and parties in his honor at which he met the leading singers of the day. He found the perfect place for himself in Paris. The banquet tendered him at the Restaurant du Veau qui Tette in the Place du Châtelet on 16 November 1823, when he was on his way to London, strengthened his resolve to return and settle there:

> More than 150 guests assembled in a room decorated with flower-encircled medallions bearing in golden letters the titles of Rossini's operas. As Gambaro led an orchestra in the overture to *La Gazza ladra*, the guest of honor was conducted to a seat above which his initials gleamed brightly. He was seated between [actress] Mlle Mars and [singer] Giuditta Pasta; opposite them, the composer Jean-François Lesueur [later Berlioz's mentor at the Conservatoire] was flanked by Mme Colbran-Rossini and the actress Mlle George. Many facets of artistic endeavor were represented: the composers present included [Daniel] Auber, [Adrien] Boieldieu, [Ferdinand] Hérold, and Auguste-Mathieu Panseron; the singers were headed by Pasta, Laure Cinti-Damoreau, Manuel Garcia, Jean-Blaise Martin, and Joseph de Lafont, and Talma; the painters by Horace Vernet. Piquancy is added to the meeting of Rossini and Vernet by the fact that at this time Vernet's mistress was Olympe Pélissier, who was later to become Rossini's second wife.[15]

The Death of Berlioz and the Birth of the Société Nationale

In London, where he arrived on 13 December 1823, Rossini also fared extremely well. He received high fees for his operas staged there; he was entertained regularly by royalty. Due to nervous exhaustion from the Channel crossing, he had to decline an invitation from King George IV, when he first arrived. The monarch himself sent an aide daily to inquire after the composer's health.

Rossini's own instrument was his voice; he was a tenor and evidently a passable pianist. (Amateurs called his mastery over the instrument miraculous.) At the request of his London hosts, he often accompanied many well-known singers in the homes of the nobility. For his services he received extravagant fees. He commented in passing—just as Clara Schumann did several decades later—that English musicians would do anything for money. Rossini had little difficulty adapting to the local custom.

Not wanting to be outdone, the French sent their own ambassador to England, the Prince de Polignac, directly to Rossini's rooms at 90 Regent Street and offered him a huge salary to become the director of the Théâtre-Italien. Rossini and his wife returned in glory to France at the end of July 1824. Diplomatically, he worked with Ferdinando Paër, another Italian who had preceded him as the French king's favorite. In two years he was appointed Premier Compositeur du Roi and Inspecteur Général du Chant, with an annual income of 20,000 francs to keep him permanently settled in Paris. For his first French opera, Rossini prepared *Le Siège de Corinth*, in part a remake of his earlier *Maometto II*. He also refashioned *Mosè in Egitto* into a French grand opera, *Moïse et Pharon, ou le Passage de la Mer Rouge*, given its premiere at the Opéra on 26 March 1827. He enticed Eugène Scribe, whose efforts eventually produced more than four hundred libretti for various composers, to work with him on his first Parisian comedy, *Le Comte d'Ory* (20 August 1828) which yielded a gold mine for both composer and librettist. At about this time, Rossini sensed a change in the political climate. Determined to make his position more secure, he asked Charles X to give him a contract with an assured annual salary. From 1829 he promised to give the government five operas in ten years, one every two years, and he would compose for no other stage but Paris. He wanted 15,000 francs per opera, a pension of 6,000 francs a year, and the profits of five benefit concerts at the Opéra.

By now, Rossini had become, in the words of critic Castil-Blaze, "the first musician of Europe." England, Germany, Russia, and Italy clamored for his works and his presence. In those days, an impresario or a manager customarily purchased an opera, and its composer usually lost all rights to the money that accrued in subsequent performances. Rossini determined not to let that happen. French theaters had done well with his operas and now, at the age of thirty-six, he wanted to assure himself a comfortable retirement. He first sent his request for a favorable financial agreement to La Rochefoucauld, Directeur des Beaux-Arts. When no reply was forthcoming, he prodded Emile-Timothée Lubbert, director of the Opéra, asking that he plead his case. *Guillaume Tell* was in rehearsal when the King hesitated to agree to Rossini's terms. Threatening to call off the entire production and hold back the last acts of the opera, Rossini finally got what he wanted. Evidently, he was not always the even-tempered, easy-going, obliging Italian.

In Bologna in 1830, visiting with his father after his mother's death, Rossini learned of the revolution in Paris and of the abdication of Charles X. The composer was convinced that his contract with the government was secure. It took a law suit extending over several years to prove his point; he won, but it was a Pyrrhic victory. Either in exasperation or in a fit of pique, the composer continued from that time to resist all efforts to woo him back to the business of music. He gave various excuses over the years to those who sought an explanation for his renunciation of the profession at the height of his career. He told Wagner he quit because there were no more good singers on the stage; the castrati had disappeared and nobody else at the Conservatoire could teach as they did. Later he told composer Giovanni Pacini, years after his retirement, that the climate of the times was not propitious; the public thought of nothing but politics. To the tenor Domenico Donzelli, one of his good friends, he admitted he was lazy. To Ferdinand Hiller he complained of chicanery in the Opéra administration. To this day, the mystery has not been solved. However, the career of Rossini, an Italian at the French court, offers such a contrast to the grievous series of events that characterize Berlioz's professional life that it bears retelling if only to confirm that Berlioz's paranoia was understandable.

In his music, Rossini built on the Italian operatic tradition of two and a half centuries. Sprightly tunes supported by innocuous accompaniments enlivened dozens of libretti whose plots and characters were already known to their audiences. Aware of the public's penchant for fioritura-style singing, Rossini wrote with specific singers in mind. He graciously supplied embellishments to show them off to advantage and was justifiably irritated at the practice many had of adding their own ornaments to his already decorated melodies. He set the stage for the *bel canto* operas of Vincenzo Bellini and Gaetano Donizetti. (Rossini invited Bellini to come to Paris in 1833 and encouraged the younger man to write *I Puritani* for the Théâtre-Italien in 1835.) Active in a place and at a time that produced some of the best voices in Europe, Rossini proved the adage that "the times make the man."[16]

Rossini habitually acted like a politician, befriending the right people. He did not particularly like Giacomo Meyerbeer, but he noticed that the German composer's star was in the ascendancy and watched curiously as the new favorite jockeyed for position. It is not inconceivable that Meyerbeer learned from Rossini how best to comport himself in Parisian society. Francis Toye relates an amusing story of Rossini and a friend who met Meyerbeer one day while out walking. Meyerbeer inquired about his health and Rossini replied with a long list of his ailments. After the German had left them, his friend suggested they return home since the composer obviously was ill. "Not at all," said Rossini, "I feel perfectly well, but dear Meyerbeer would be so delighted to hear of my death tomorrow that I hadn't the heart to deny him a little pleasure today."[17]

The fervor for Rossini was by no means restricted to the unsophisticated layman. Consider Schopenhauer, whose theories meant so much to Wagner, and who reserved his highest praise for music, ranking it above all the other arts. He stressed the significance of melody and insisted that language was inferior to music. Although he placed opera before all the other genres, he complained that the opera composer concerned with the details of plot and libretto has strayed from his obligation to maintain the balance between words and music. Unlike the operatic reformers who urged that music be the servant of poetry, Schopenhauer likened music to the fundamental source of emotion. Regarding Rossini, Schopenhauer said that "his music speaks its own language so distinctly and purely that it requires no words and produces its full effect when rendered by instruments alone."[18]

Stendhal evidently agreed with Schopenhauer. In 1824, when Rossini settled at last in Paris, Stendhal wrote his biography of the composer. He, too, questioned the necessity of reading a libretto. An inveterate operagoer in Milan, he went so far as to caution his readers to avoid studying the text of an opera and simply to prepare for the basic emotions each of the arias would express. He overwhelmed his readers with a list of the remarkable progress that had been made in operatic art, which he attributed exclusively to Rossini: he had rid the opera of dry, unnecessarily long recitatives; he had extended complicated ensembles where each character sings of his own problems and experiences, and yet instead of the expected cacophony created of them a totally homogenous sound; he had mastered the art of dramatic harmonization, using the instruments as an effective means of characterization. Stendhal compared Rossini to Sir Walter Scott, implying that they were equivalent masters of romantic aesthetics.

Further competition for Berlioz appeared in the person of Giacomo Meyerbeer, one year younger than Rossini, and the son of a German-Jewish banker. A student of the composer-pianist-businessman Muzio Clementi, he performed Mozart's d-minor piano concerto (K. 466) in public in Berlin at the age of seven. He studied theory with Mendelssohn's teacher Carl Friedrich Zelter, Goethe's favorite musician, and in 1810 moved to Darmstadt to work on composition with the celebrated Abbé Vogler. Not unexpectedly, because they were both pianists, Meyerbeer's closest friend in Darmstadt was Carl Maria von Weber, also a student of Vogler. True to the pattern followed by many aspiring young operatic composers, Meyerbeer traveled to Vienna where one of his comic operas was scheduled for production at the Kärntnerthortheater. He also intended to concertize in the Austrian capital, but a chance hearing of a recital by Johann Nepomuk Hummel made him reconsider his options. For advice, he sought out the reigning musicians—the pianist Ignaz Moscheles and the opera composer Antonio Salieri—and followed the latter's advice to study vocal writing in Italy.

Weber had urged Meyerbeer to concentrate on German opera and not to attempt to change his style. But *Il Crociato*, Meyerbeer's first great Italian success, led him to Paris, where Rossini staged the opera at the Théâtre-Italien in 1826. Meyerbeer and his family moved to Paris about 1831, and his first French opera, *Robert le diable*, brought him instant acclaim. His collaborator, the ubiquitous Scribe,[19] became his principal partner in his Parisian ventures.

Of all the prosperous composers in Paris in the first half of the nineteenth century, Meyerbeer was the most apprehensive. Given to regular fits of anxiety, he went to extremes to assure the success of his works. He regularly made changes in orchestration, in the music, in characterization. He wined and dined reviewers; some said he bribed them. In any event, he was determined to win them over to his side.

All the successful opera composers in Paris carefully studied their audiences and gave them what they wanted to hear. Therefore, to accuse Meyerbeer any more than Rossini or Auber or Offenbach of purchasing his good reviews shows a lack of understanding of the social situation. Berlioz and Wagner, both exceedingly innovative, swam against the current. Unfortunately, the Frenchman never made it to the shore. Wagner survived, but not through the efforts of the French.

It is not difficult to understand the taste of the citizens of the Second Empire. Theirs was a mercantile society. For many, it was the first experience with discretionary income.[20] The aristocracy had a traditional affinity for the theater, but for the bourgeoisie it was a novelty. It aided their understanding of upper-class life; it provided them an opportunity to display their new clothing; it offered a chance meeting with an appropriate family to arrange a marriage for their adolescent daughters; it afforded the head of the household a chance to survey the field and arrange for a choice assignation. But more important, the theater and the opera—provided the fare was not too heavy—allowed them to relax and enjoy themselves, offering amusement and all varieties of entertainment.

Artists, writers, painters, and poets went to cafés, particularly those that now boasted their own chanteuses. At the salons of the numerous patronesses of Parisian society, at the soirées hosted by Princess Mathilde, cousin of the Emperor, these creative artists met talented and interested members of the nobility. Workers sought relaxation in the newly opened bars and saloons. The middle classes went increasingly to the theater.

While Paris continued to be the mecca for foreign composers of operatic music, the capital was hardly hospitable to her native sons. The dismal statistics on the production of operas by Frenchmen discouraged all but the boldest among them to forgo that genre completely. Because of the restrictions placed on works considered for the Opéra, one would have imagined the French to have the advantage.[21] Yet they did not. With the possible exception of Auber, whose seventy-odd operas graced the stage for half a century, along with a few by Boieldieu, Adam, Halévy, and Hérold—and these mostly at the Opéra-Comique—foreigners Rossini, Donizetti, Bellini, Meyerbeer, and more recently Offenbach proudly saw their works become the principal attractions of the Opéra. Unbelievably, between 1852 and 1870, the period of the Second Empire, Félicien David's *Herculaneum*, Ambroise Thomas's *Hamlet*, and three operas by Charles Gounod—*Sapho*, *La Nonne sanglante*, and *La Reine de Saba*—were the only significant French works presented at the Opéra.[22] The directors agreed to produce Gounod's *Faust* only after it had had ten successful years at another theater, the Théâtre-Lyrique. They persistently rejected Berlioz's *Les Troyens*, though imperial intercession enabled one Mermet, a rank amateur, to achieve a production of his *Roland à Roncevaux* in 1864. The epic nature of its subject recommended it, but the music was reportedly miserable. The Opéra's repertory consisted mainly of Rossini's *Guillaume Tell*, Meyerbeer's *L'Africaine* and *L'Etoile du Nord*; Donizetti's *Lucia di Lammermoor* and *La Favorite*, Auber's *La Muette de Portici*, and Halévy's *La Juive*, mostly dating from the 1830s or 40s. The Opéra-Comique, slightly less rigid than the Opéra in its rules and regulations, nevertheless held to a policy of producing works with a successful past history. David's *Lalla Roukh* gained the administration's approval, as did Ambrose Thomas's *Mignon*. And of course Auber, who had been the mainstay of that house for some time, managed, even at ninety, to get his *Rêve d'amour* staged at the Opéra.

The Théâtre-Lyrique, far less well endowed than the two official houses, the Opéra and the Opéra-Comique, showed more consideration for French music than either of the other two. The Lyrique had presented the premiere of *Faust* in 1859; and it was so successful that conductor Léon Carvalho felt sufficiently bold to mount, in succeeding years, several other Gounod operas including *Philémon et Baucis* (1860), *Mireïlle* (1864), and *Roméo et Juliette* (1867). The Lyrique staged the first part of Berlioz's epic *Les Troyens à Carthage* in 1863; also two operas by Ernest Reyer, *Maître Wolfram* (1854) and *La Statue* (1861); Georges Bizet's *Les Pêcheurs de perles* (1863) and *La Jolie Fille de Perth* (1866); and Victorin de Joncière's *Sardanapale* (1867) and *Le Dernier Jour de Pompéi* (1869). They tried educating the public with contemporary works by French composers, but it was not enough.

The Concerts Populaires, organized and conducted by Pasdeloup[23] in 1860, enlightened the public about German instrumental music,[24] but only occasionally provided a boost to French music. (The low-priced tickets at these concerts attracted a new audience. And assembling and educating an audience was a prime function of all of these new concert series.) Once or twice in ten years, new names like Saint-Saëns, Bizet and Massenet appeared on their programs.[25]

By 1880, Félicien David, François Bazin, and Napoléon Reber, three composers who had achieved a degree of visibility with performances of their works, had died. With *Françoise de Rimini* Ambroise Thomas tried in vain to duplicate the success he had had with *Mignon*. The Franco-Prussian War found Gounod in London and though he continued to compose other operas and two sacred works, *Redemption* and *Mors et Vita*, before his death in 1893,[26] admirers awaiting another *Faust* or *Mireïlle* were doomed to disappointment. Artists and audiences alike finally voiced their impatience and a kind of nationalistic fervor gathered momentum.

On 28 January 1871, Paris capitulated and France signed an armistice with Germany, ending the Franco-Prussian War. Less than a month later, on 25 February, an incident occurred that changed the course of French musical history. Perhaps the defeat by the Germans served as a catalyst for this phenomenon: the formation of a totally new and bold organization. In any event, furious at their persistent rejection by the authorities, angry that German music had so long replaced their own homegrown compositions in concert halls and that Italian opera had usurped their position on the stage, the composer Saint-Saëns and the singer Romaine Bussine gathered around them a band of young French musicians and decided to avenge themselves and their colleagues. They formed the Société Nationale de Musique, specifically geared to the promotion and dissemination of French music, and they took as their motto *Ars gallica*. It is not surprising then that their efforts, coupled with the inauguration of Charles Garnier's magnificent new opera house in 1875, resulted in an organization that would ultimately be responsible for the revival and the efflorescence of French music.

The Société Nationale penetrated to the heart of musical productivity in France. Pledged to encourage all attempts at musical composition by artists with verifiably serious intentions, they gave their first concert on 25 November 1871. By 23 May 1914, they had held 411 concerts. Then, after an interruption for World War I, they started again on 10 November 1917; they resumed their momentum and continued to press forward with the same vigor they had had in the early years. That the Société began its work at the moment the French dedicated themselves to the renewal of their political and economic systems seems most appropriate.

Almost from its inception, the Société counted about one hundred and fifty members. Bizet, Ernest Guiraud, Saint-Saëns, César Franck, Massenet, Théodore Dubois, Alexis de Castillon, Edouard Lalo, Louis-Albert Bourgault-Ducoudray, Charles-Marie Widor, Charles Lenepveu, and many others of lesser fame joined in meetings that took place in the Salle Pleyel. Although the organizers would have liked to present their initial concerts with an orchestra, they made do with pianos. Composers arrived at meetings prepared to offer their own compositions or to accompany singers who performed their *mélodies*. Thus they provided an additional dimension to the interpretation of these new works, an indescribable flavor that differed enormously from the customary tensions accompanying professional virtuosi.[27]

Composers grasped at the opportunity the group offered them. For example, on the eve of a Sunday performance of his Orchestral Suite by Pasdeloup and his orchestra, Guiraud played a piano transcription of the piece for members, thus learning of their impressions of the work in advance. The ubiquitous Saint-Saëns, assisted by his student Gabriel Fauré, presented his *Marche héroïque* and *Rouet d'Omphale* on two pianos. Massenet accompanied his *Poème du Souvenir*; Madame Lalo sang several *mélodies* by her husband and did not hesitate to have him accompany her in songs by other composers. Bourgault-Ducoudray conducted several choral groups who sang selections from his sacred music. Although they faced a shortage of rehearsal time during their first season, the Société more than made up for it later on, with numerous rehearsals for new music. Sometimes, performers sight-read their parts in renditions of new chamber works. Lalo's cello and piano sonata, for example, was on the first program without any advance preparation; so too was one of Franck's early cyclical piano trios from 1841, along with fragments of his oratorio *Ruth*. In addition to Madame Lalo, the renowned singer Pauline Viardot participated in these performances. Musicians Jules Armingaud, Léon Jacquard, Jules Garcin, and Charles Lamoureux joined with several of the pianist composers to play chamber music.[28] In time, owing to the full cooperation of

18

numerous musicians, the Société Nationale was able to give a few orchestral concerts each year.

When the official government-sponsored organizations realized that this group of young French musicians presented a united front, their attitude toward them changed. Their hostility dissolved and they began slowly to cooperate, all except the Opéra personnel who insisted that theirs was not an experimental theater, but rather a "Musée de la musique," an epithet directed ironically at them for many years. Content to produce another *La Favorite*, *La Juive*, or *Robert le diable* interpreted by singers past their prime and surrounded by shabby sets, they had no intention of bowing before the demands of a group of *nouveaux jeunes*.

On the other hand, the Opéra-Comique, under the direction of Camille du Locle, recognized the need for renewal. In the half dozen years preceding 1870, the Opéra-Comique had staged a few works by Guiraud and Massenet, but its stock-in-trade were the operas of François-Adrien Boieldieu, Adolphe Adam, and Daniel-François Auber from the earlier years of the century. The start of the war on 19 July 1870 interrupted the director's efforts, but they resumed in 1872 with new works by three young musicians: Emile Paladilhe's *Le Passant* (24 April), Bizet's *Djamileh* (22 May), and Saint-Saëns's *La Princesse jaune* (12 June). For some reason, the public decided these were distinctly *wagnérienne*. Massenet's moment came shortly afterward, when the Opéra-Comique offered parts of his *Don César de Bazan* (29 December). Guiraud and Dubois both achieved performances at the Athenée, which tried to replace the former Théâtre-Lyrique. None of these operas, however, proved masterpieces worthy of retention.

Pasdeloup began to modify the profiles of his programs which, for ten years, had been almost exclusively devoted to pieces by German masters. Here and there the name of a young French musician began to appear among them. Pasdeloup conducted Massenet's second orchestral suite, *Les Scènes hongroises*, at the reopening concert in November 1871. Soon afterward, he followed with Saint-Saëns's *Marche héroïque*, Gounod's *Air de ballet*, and Charles Lenepveu's *Marche funèbre*. The next season Guiraud's orchestral suite had a resounding success. A youthful symphony of Saint-Saëns, along with his symphonic poem *Rouet d'Omphale* (conducted by the composer himself), de Castillon's piano concerto, and an Adagio by V. Joncières paved the way for Bizet's *L'Arlésienne Suite* and Lalo's *Divertissement*.

Another orchestral association, the Concert National, led by Edouard Colonne,[29] gave its first concerts at the Odéon, opening with two significant works: Franck's *Redemption* and Massenet's *Marie Magdeleine*. Eventually, Colonne's orchestra moved across the river to the right bank's Châtelet Theater, where it prospered for decades.

Soon even the venerable Société des Concerts du Conservatoire began to feel the pressure of the new movements. During the 1871–72 season, they performed Gounod's *Gallia*, fragments of Franck's *Ruth*, excerpts from Saint-Saëns's Second Symphony, several pieces from Dubois's *Sept Paroles de Christ*, and Lenepveu's *Requiem*. The next year, the "Andante" and "Scherzo" from Widor's Symphony in F and Massenet's *Scènes dramatiques* after Shakespeare had their turn.

Before Berlioz died, he was reported to have said with perfect assurance: "One day they are going to play my music." His day came, finally, too late to comfort him, but soon enough to vindicate his belief. The revival of a powerfully nationalistic French spirit inevitably carried with it an appreciation of Berlioz's special brand of French music. The expected did, indeed, happen. The French, who were searching constantly for a native master to match those of nineteenth-century Germany, rediscovered their long lost native son and paid him the homage that was his due.

2

Wagner in France and France in Wagner

An account of Richard Wagner's peregrinations, financial deals, friends, enemies, successes, and failures must, of necessity, assume the contours of a kaleidoscopic tableau. Delving into his activities during the thirty years of his relationship with the French, one finds a colossal amount of diversified materials. How to cope with them poses a serious problem. Separating the facets of his life into two main areas, Wagner in France and France in Wagner, offers a possible solution.

The highlights of Wagner's career in France encompass his three Parisian concerts of excerpts from *Der fliegende Holländer*, *Tannhäuser*, *Tristan*, and *Lohengrin* in 1860; the short-lived performances by Pierre Dietsch of the French version of *Tannhäuser* in 1861, Jules Pasdeloup's *Rienzi* in 1869, and Charles Lamoureux's *Lohengrin* in 1887. Besides these performances, the publication and distribution of the *Revue wagnérienne*, which included contributions from preeminent artists and writers of the period, the activities of "Le Petit Bayreuth" and "Bayreuth de poche," along with the surprisingly large number of articles—favorable or critical—devoted to him and/or his works that appeared in journals and newspapers point to French interest in Wagner. The literati responded to him first— without having heard a note of his music. It was Henri Gautier-Villar, Colette's husband, who said so succinctly, "A literary man can understand Wagner, a musician never." That he influenced French music as well as French literature can be observed in works like Vincent d'Indy's *Fervaal*, Alfred Bruneau's *Le Rêve*, Gustave Charpentier's *Louise*, Ernest Reyer's *Sigurd*, Ernest Chausson's *Roi Arthus*, and Emmanuel Chabrier's *Briséis*.

In the 1840s, the French regarded Wagner as a madman; by the 1880s they had placed him on a pedestal. During the first decade of the twentieth century, his influence began to wane, particularly after the premiere of Debussy's *Pelléas et Mélisande*, ironically a work more Wagnerian than either *Tristan* or *Parsifal*. Consider, for example, Debussy's careful mating of text and tone; his elimination of arias, duets, and chorus; his use of musical interludes to connect contiguous scenes; his preference for a fleeting and elusive melody that disappears before it achieves complete shape; his utilization of whole-tone scales, which, lacking a leading tone, blur the tonality in much the same way as Wagner's extensive use of chromaticism; and finally, the continuous music from the moment the curtain rises to the moment it falls, with no set numbers at all. (Three hundred years after Monteverdi, Debussy actually achieved the goal of the originators of opera—a goal that Wagner sought, but did not always achieve—a play set in music.)

What precisely attracted the French to Wagner? Initially, not his music. His writings on opera and drama, his belief that both should stem from the same source, his reliance on symbolism, and his burrowing in and borrowing from epic legends of his own people appealed to intellectuals. When they finally heard his music, the innate sensuality of the gorgeous sonorities overwhelmed them— even those who were not musicians. All this occurred despite Wagner's fall from grace during the Franco-Prussian War. At that time, some apologized for his behavior; others simply agreed that one must separate the man from his music. Then, too, memories fade. The establishment of Bayreuth in 1876 and the pilgrimages made by French Wagnerites (who subsequently wrote their impressions of operas heard there) whetted the appetites of French writers, artists, and musicians.

His partisans comprised two disparate groups: bohemians and avant-gardists, and members of the artistocracy. The two were at odds. Because of his activities during the 1848 Revolution in Dresden and because he was anti-establishment, Wagner consistently appealed to bohemians. At the same time, he needed the aristocrats both for their financial support and for the clout they wielded with administrators in government and the arts. (Liszt, whose connections with society became firmer as he grew older, helped Wagner enormously, though Wagner was not above poking fun at him.) Curiously, Wagner revealed no anxiety when he had to decide with whom to align himself, bohemians or aristocrats. At his moment of need, he simply moved in the direction of those who he believed could be of most help to him.

In 1915 Romain Rolland, writing in *Musicians of Today*, remarked that nothing for him was as thrilling as the fragments of Wagner's music he first heard at Pasdeloup's Sunday afternoon concerts at the Cirque d'Hiver:

> How mysterious it was, and what a strange agitation it filled me with! There were new effects of orchestration, new timbres, new rhythms, and new subjects; it held the wild poetry of the Middle Ages and old legends, it throbbed with the fever of hidden sorrows and desires. I did not understand it very well. How should I? The music was taken from works quite unknown to me. It was almost impossible to seize the connection of the ideas on account of the poor acoustics of the room, the bad arrangement of the orchestra, and the unskilled players—all of which served to break up the musical design and spoil the harmony of its coloring. Passages that should have been made prominent were slurred over, and others were distorted by faulty time or want of precision. Even today, when our orchestras are seasoned by years of study, I should often be unable to follow Wagner's thought throughout a whole scene, if I did not happen to know the score. . . .
>
> What a place in my life those Sunday concerts held! All the week I lived for those two hours; and when they were over, I thought about them until the following Sunday.[1]

Later he added:

> Wagner's influence considerably helped forward the progress of French art, and aroused a love for music in people other than musicians. And by his all-embracing personality and the vast domain of his work in art, [he] not only engaged the interest of the musical world, but that of the theatrical world and the world of poetry and the plastic arts. One may say that from 1885 Wagner's work acted directly or indirectly on the

whole of artistic thought, even on the religious and intellectual thought of the most distinguished people in Paris.[2]

Wagner's fascination with the French constitutes an enigma also not easily solved. As Robert Gutman has said, his hatred of France remained a life-long obsession.[3] Despite his involvement with French operas while serving as conductor in opera houses in the German provinces, and his continuing desire to succeed in what he regarded as the central musical metropolis of Europe, Wagner wrote to his sister Cäcilie in 1843: "Oh, how I hate Paris, vast, monstrous, alien to our German hearts."[4] No doubt his need for recognition in Paris stemmed from his conviction that once successful in France, the Germans would take him more seriously.

Despite his criticisms, living in Paris seems to have nourished Wagner's creative spirit. *Rienzi, Der fliegende Holländer*, the libretto of *Die Meistersinger*, and the revised French version of *Tannhäuser* all saw the light of day there. An Alsatian, Abraham Flaxland, published three of his scores, and Jacques Durand a fourth. Intent on seeing his works reach the Parisian stage, Wagner, when necessary, compromised both his attitude and his work to achieve the goal. With the passage of time, loathing as well as loving his experiences in Paris, he forgot some of the pleasures and focused only on his disappointments.

Wagner compartmentalized his feelings for the French. Only with reluctance did he accept French conductors or instrumentalists; he preferred Germans in these positions. As for his operas, particularly after his arrival in Paris, Gutman reports Wagner used a number of Parisian devices: "the rolling scenery of the Odéon, those ever-effective ecclesiastical processions of Scribe, the collapsing splendors of a magic palace . . . the tolling bells and [in *Parsifal*] unbelievable reminiscences of the Passover scene in Halévy's *La Juive*."[5]

Finally, his declaration that French and German mentalities could never be mated evaporates when one considers his marriage to a French woman, his adored second wife Cosima (Franz Liszt's daughter). Because of his obsession, Wagner did not allow her to speak her native language in his presence.[6] And because of his inability to readily participate in conversations she had with compatriots, he grew furious with her when she spoke French to them.

Between 1839 and 1867 Wagner made at least ten visits to Paris. Some were very short, either to look for an apartment, to speak to his publishers or to arrange for performances of his music. His two longest sojourns in the French capital, one in 1839 and one in 1859, represented watersheds in the saga of Wagner in France. He found lodging in more than fifteen different apartments or hotels. Sometimes he moved to save funds or flee creditors; at other times he changed his residence to make a better impression on the French. In Paris, he alternately rejoiced and despaired, he praised the French and damned them, and finally exulted in his Teutonic origins.

The French, even more than the Jews, became Wagner's *bête noire*. Dreaming of success in the French capital long before he arrived, Wagner sought the means to realize productions of his operas in Paris as the epitome of achievement. If he could only get to Paris, convince Scribe or Meyerbeer, both of whom he recognized as masters of their art, to mount one of his operas, the Germans in turn would recognize his great gifts and pay him homage. At the time Wagner began to indulge in fantasies about Paris and the Parisians, the twenty-year-old musician had barely begun his career as choirmaster and conductor in the German provinces.

Before Richard Wagner, his wife Minna, and his dog Robber first arrived in Paris in September 1839, he knew little of France, and less of the French language. He had tried to take a few lessons in Riga before his departure for the French capital. Soon recognizing the difficulties of learning a new language in the four weeks he had allotted for the project, and forever manipulative when it came to his own affairs, he persuaded his teacher instead to prepare a translation of his recently written *Rienzi* libretto.[7] When completed, *Rienzi* must be mounted at the Paris Opéra. With that goal in mind, in 1836 he had written to Scribe, the foremost dramatist and librettist at the Opéra, offering first to send him an early work, *Die hohe Braut*, on the condition that Scribe guarantee Wagner a performance at the Opéra.[8] Scribe never replied.

The following year he wrote again, asking permission to send Scribe *Das Liebesverbot*, another youthful work.[9] The dramatist should show the piece to Auber and Meyerbeer, then the leading composers at the Opéra; once he had obtained their approval, he could arrange a production of the work at the Opéra. Again his request fell on deaf ears.

Now, more than ever, Wagner was determined to get to Paris. He was disgusted with the provinciality of German theaters, which took their cues from France or Italy. The acting career of Minna, his wife, rested at the moment on a plateau. Most important, Wagner's many creditors made it imperative that he leave Latvia as soon as possible. Paris, the center of musical Europe, where the Opéra paid composers handsomely for their works, beckoned encouragingly. (In Germany the composer received a one-time fee and no royalties.)

Accordingly, Wagner had familiarized himself with French operatic works. At Würzburg, where he began as chorus master in 1833, he rehearsed Louis Hérold's *Zampa*, Cherubini's *Les Deux Journées*, *La Muette de Portici* and *Fra Diavolo* of Auber, and *Robert le diable* by Meyerbeer.[10] Auber's *La Muette*, which provoked a revolution in Brussels on the occasion of its second showing in 1830, entranced him.[11] It became the model for *Rienzi*, and he praised it even during his periods of Francophobia.

At Magdeburg in 1834, in his first post as conductor, Wagner presented both Cherubini's *Les Deux Journées* and Auber's *Fra Diavolo* along with two other Auber operas, *La Maçon* and *Lestocq*. (He reports in *Mein Leben*, years later, that in his midnight meetings with Auber at the Café Tortoni in Paris at the conclusion of a performance, Auber delighted in his stories of these productions in Germany.) Continuing his musical Francophilia, at Königsberg in 1836 and at Riga in 1837, Wagner cultivated French opera, much to the pleasure of the theater directors. They ordered (from Paris) full scores of the works of Adam and Auber, and Wagner studied them.[12] In two years he conducted sixteen performances of Adam's *Le Postillon de Longjumeau* just produced in 1836, as against ten of his adored Weber's *Der Freischütz*; eleven *Fra Diavolo*, eight each of *La Dame Blanche*, *La Muette* and Méhul's *Joseph*, two of *La Maçon* and *Les Deux Journées*, as against three of *Fidelio*. Méhul's *Joseph* was a revelation; it was also the last opera he conducted before he fled the country.[13]

After a rough sea voyage of three and a half weeks, during which Wagner conceived the scenario of *Der fliegende Holländer*, Richard and Minna arrived in London, where they stayed only a week, long enough for Wagner to try to locate Sir George Smart, conductor of the Philharmonic Society, and to give him his *Rule Brittania* Overture.[14] (Wagner would write occasional pieces when he thought they would be useful, although he always denied he had such intentions.) Smart was not in London, so Wagner decided to find the writer Bulwer-Lytton to discuss with him the possibilities of dramatizing his novel *Rienzi* as an opera. (Imagine the determination of this young German composer who spoke no English or French and yet hoped to communicate his ideas to a distinguished member of the British parliament.) It being August, Bulwer-Lytton, too, was out of town.[15] The week passed unfruitfully and the Wagners left for France.

On the Channel crossing they met two women, the Mansons, mother and daughter, who gave them a letter of introduction to Meyerbeer, then spending the summer at Boulogne-sur-mer. (Despite his prejudice, Wagner did not hesitate to accept help from Jews.) Undaunted by their rapidly diminishing funds, the Wagners rented a place in the country nearby. Shortly after his arrival, the young composer presented himself to Meyerbeer, read him the first three acts of the *Rienzi* libretto, and left him two acts of the music just completed. Meyerbeer introduced him to the celebrated Jewish pianist Ignaz Moscheles and the pianist Marie Blahetka, and Wagner, experiencing his first exposure to world-famous artists, believed he had arrived.[16]

Meyerbeer gave Wagner several letters of introduction:[17] to the Jewish publisher Schlesinger; to Habeneck, conductor of the Conservatoire concerts; to Anténor Joly, director of the Théâtre de la Renaissance; to Charles-Edmond Duponchel, director of the Opéra, and to the singer Pauline Viardot. In November 1839, Meyerbeer himself wrote Viardot to suggest she might want to perform some works of a warm admirer, a young German composer. Wagner shrewdly had composed several songs in French—one wonders how he did it—that he thought would appeal to Gallic singers. These songs included *Dors mon enfant*, a cradle song, *L'Attente* by Victor Hugo from his *Orientales*, and *Mignonne* by the Renaissance poet Pierre de Ronsard.[18] Wagner reports that Viardot went over the manuscripts with him and said she liked them, but immediately afterward told him she could not use them in concert.

Eking out a perilous existence in fashionable Paris, Wagner swallowed his pride and agreed to make piano and instrumental arrangements of celebrated operas for Schlesinger.[19] These included Donizetti's *La Favorite*, Jacques Halévy's *La Reine de Chypre*, and even *Allons à la Courtille* for a vaudeville by one Dumanoir. Duponchel read Meyerbeer's letter but dismissed Wagner peremptorily. Habeneck, the conductor, offered him a rehearsal at the Conservatoire of his Overture to *Christoph Columbus*—actually the first work by Wagner performed in France.[20] The musicians did not care for it, so it had no public performance. Joly agreed to present *Das Liebesverbot* at the Théâtre de la Renaissance, but the theater went bankrupt and with it went Wagner's hopes for a production.[21] (He insisted it was Meyerbeer's doing.)[22] His funds steadily diminished. He spent three weeks in October in debtors' prison, and ultimately was forced to appeal for funds to his brothers-in-law, Edward Avenarius, newly married to his half-sister Cäcilie Geyer, and Hermann Brockhaus, a philologist married to Ottilie Wagner.[23] Both sisters lived in Paris. (Luise Wagner, another sister, was married to Friedrich Brockhaus, the Leipzig publisher. Hermann acted as agent in France for Friedrich, his older brother.) It was at this time, too, that Wagner began writing articles for Schlesinger's journal *La Revue et Gazette musicale*. His honoraria rarely exceeded 60 francs. By comparison, George Sand, writing for the same publication, received 500 francs per article.

Wagner happened on his career as a journalist by chance. Still attempting to gain a foothold in Parisian musical quarters, he wrote *Les Deux Grenadiers*, to a French translation of Heinrich Heine's *Die beiden Grenadiere*, and dedicated it to the Jewish poet.[24] He contended that because Schlesinger would not accept his song, he published it at his own expense. The truth is that Schlesinger engraved it, but when no copies were sold, he suggested that Wagner pay off this debt with an article. Half of his fee went to a translator; Wagner had little left for himself and Minna.[25]

Despite the hardships of life in Paris, the German composer recognized that the French musical public was the best informed in the world. He admired the technical facility of members of the Conservatoire orchestra under Habeneck, whose performances of Beethoven's symphonies proved a revelation to him.[26] (Later he decided that their playing revealed only superficial virtuosity.) Before his arrival in Paris, Wagner had only praise for Meyerbeer. After his stay there, he vilified him, writing in an 1851 letter to von Bülow (18 April), "He's my opposite. The French can't comprehend me or other Germans. The forest of *Freischütz* is that of Novalis, Eichendorff, Hoffmann. It's not like the Parisian Bois. In Paris I realized my destiny and resolved to return to bring the essence of Germany into my music." The more he detested Paris, the more he sought refuge in things German.

Wagner met Berlioz for the first time at Schlesinger's and for a few years they maintained cordial relations. Wagner praised the originality of Berlioz's works. When they met again about fourteen years later, in 1855 in London, Wagner promptly wrote Liszt (5 July 1855) that a "profound friendship exists between us." Eventually, when the Opéra reached a decision to mount *Tannhäuser* at about the same time they rejected Berlioz's *Les Troyens*, the Frenchman could not hide his disappointment. His articles showed his bitterness. Not unnaturally, Wagner counterattacked.

The Société des Concerts du Conservatoire presented Wagner's newly composed *Faust* Overture at a rehearsal in March 1840 and the *Gazette* of 24 March carried a complimentary review of the piece, but it did not make it to the concert hall. During this year, Wagner wrote a number of articles for the *Gazette*, attended several concerts of works by Berlioz and others that appealed to him, accompanied Meyerbeer to a meeting with the new director of the Opéra, Léon Pillet, to whom he presented a resumé of *Der fliegende Holländer*, and met Liszt for the first time on 20 October, also at Schlesinger's. Besides writing prose, Wagner continued with the orchestration of *Rienzi* which, when completed, he sent to the Court Theater in Dresden. Again to show his sensitivity to the French mentality, he composed *Der Kaiser kommt zurück* on the occasion of the transfer of Napoleon's ashes to the Invalides.

Wagner's Overture to *Christoph Columbus* finally achieved a public performance at the ninth subscription concert of the *Revue et Gazette musicale* on 4 February 1841. He continued writing articles for the review, and he also busied himself composing sections of *Der fliegende Holländer*: Senta's "Ballade" (from which, he tells us, the entire opera originated) and the "Norwegian Sailors' Song," both translated by Emile Deschamps. (Again, Wagner intended this opera for Paris.) In March he joined the staff of Dresden's *Abendzeitung*,[27] submitting pieces on the theater, the actors, the concerts, the Opéra, *Freischütz*, Berlioz and Liszt in Paris, much like Heine had done for other journals. He completed the libretto of *Der fliegende Holländer* at just about the time Weber's *Der Freischütz* appeared at the Opéra with recitatives by Berlioz.[28] (It was not the Frenchman's idea to render this disservice to Weber. The Opéra, however, had a rule: no spoken dialogue. Weber's opera, a *Singspiel* with dialogue, not recitative, could not be performed without these alterations.)

During the spring of 1841, under the pseudonym W. Freudenfeuer, Wagner wrote two articles for the journal *Europa*: "Pariser Amüsements," and "Pariser Fatalitäten für Deutschen." In these he included some strong denunciations of Berlioz (for the latter's recitatives in *Robin des bois*, as *Der Freischütz* was called in Paris) and of the French in general.

"They think only of entertainment, of amusement, of reaching as many people as possible, despite their protests that they aim for ennoblement through art. Effects of the moment are most important for them." Of Berlioz he wrote that he knows of "no living musician who knows *Freischütz* so well but is as incapable of completing it." He continued: "Berlioz understands nothing of German music; the French are closed off from the German spirit. Meyerbeer is a counterfeit; France is rotten with Jews and the Latins are powerless to defend themselves."[29] Did he imagine that the French knew nothing about these articles? Wagner never displayed a modicum of tact or thoughtfulness, yet he expected boundless consideration from others.

In the summer of 1841 an incident occurred that confirmed for Wagner the duplicity of the French and, as he thought later, of Meyerbeer as well. Meyerbeer took him again to see the new director at the Opéra, Léon Pillet, with whom he had left his résumé of *Der fliegende Holländer*. Pillet explained that a performance of an opera by an unknown young German composer was unlikely and suggested he write a ballet instead. Wagner adamantly refused. Pillet then told him that Paul Foucher, Victor Hugo's brother-in-law, was already working on a libretto. After all, the story of the accursed seaman, sometimes described as the Wandering Jew, was anybody's property. Pillet offered to buy Wagner's scenario and reluctantly Wagner accepted his offer of 500 francs, a reasonable sum at the time.[30] Composer Pierre Dietsch set the work to music; his opera, performed the following year, failed, and Wagner had his revenge. Unfortunately, the very same Dietsch, an incompetent conductor as well as a bad composer, would lead the orchestra at the three performances of *Tannhäuser* in 1861. He had the last laugh on Wagner.

In December 1841, Wagner saw Halévy's *Reine de Chypre* and liked it. (Later he preferred *La Juive*.) Halévy was the only Jewish composer who did not suffer indignities from Wagner's pen. They remained on good terms. Wagner made other friends in Paris: Gottfried Engelbert Anders, librarian of the music section at the Bibliothèque Nationale, philologist Samuel Lehrs, and also the painter Ernst Kietz, all of whom could and would assist him when necessary. He continued to work on the score of *Der fliegende Holländer* and when finished immediately sent it on to the Court Theater in Berlin. Before

Wagner in France and France in Wagner

Wagner left Paris for Dresden in April 1842, Lehrs had obtained for him the stories about the Venusberg and the song contest along with the epic of Lohengrin. (The composer always nurtured several projects simultaneously.)

Dresden brought Wagner his first success. Between 1842 and 1845 *Rienzi* (1842), *Der fliegende Holländer* (1843), and *Tannhäuser* (1845) all received their first performances at Dresden's famous opera house. (The one in which Wagner's operas were performed burned to the ground in 1869. Its 1878 replacement was destroyed in the Second World War. The current house, on the same site, has just recently been restored.)

Berlioz, in Dresden to conduct his *Symphonie fantastique* and his *Requiem*, wrote in the *Journal des Débats* on 12 September 1843 that "any man who can twice be successful with words and music deserves to be noticed." From this time forward, Wagner, indeed, began to be noticed. After the success of the *Holländer*, he became Kapellmeister at the Saxon Court in Dresden.

After 1848, as the result of his participation in the insurrection in Dresden, a warrant was issued for his arrest. Wagner, forced to flee and forbidden to set foot in Germany (until 1860), thought of France as his place of exile. Liszt, too, encouraged him to go there, but his prospects for success seemed dim, so he repaired to Zürich instead. Liszt now financed Wagner's second visit to Paris, where he arrived in June 1849. Liszt's secretary Belloni guided him about the city. Liszt urged him to attempt to have *Rienzi* performed that winter at the Opéra, but Wagner did not want his first opera in Paris to be a work he already regarded as outmoded. Because of a cholera epidemic, Wagner curtailed his visit, and Liszt agreeably paid his return to Zürich.[31]

In 1849, Liszt wrote an article on *Tannhäuser* for the *Journal des Débats*, after having presented the work earlier at his theater in Weimar. The following year he gave the premiere of *Lohengrin*. (Wagner, in exile, could not attend.) Gérard de Nerval, the French translator of Goethe's *Faust*, spoke about the impression *Lohengrin* made on him at Weimar. His comments in *La Presse* (18–19 September 1850), where he states that "the opera displayed a bold and original talent . . . which has as yet uttered only its first words," are among the earliest compliments Wagner received from a Frenchman. The German composer, however, still remained far from winning approval by the French. (He had sent his essay *Die Kunst und die Revolution* to the *National*, but the French journal declined to publish it.) Liszt continued to promote Wagner's music. In the *Journal des Débats*, he published an essay on his Weimar performance of *Lohengrin*, including complimentary statements by the French literary critic Jules Janin.

From February to April 1850, Wagner again visited France. On the first of February he conducted his *Tannhäuser* Overture at the Concerts du Conservatoire. He saw his friends Gottfried Anders and Ernst Kietz; Samuel Lehrs, the German-Jewish philologist, had since died. Although in dire need of funds, he fumed at Liszt's suggestion that he produce a salable volume of songs and ballads. Instead, he sketched a new work, *Wieland der Schmied*, but soon abandoned it. He was living, he told Liszt, on the generosity of a Zürich friend, one Jacob Sulzer. He asked Liszt for help, but the latter was strapped for funds, contributing as he did to the support of his mother and three children in Paris. Wagner assumed he could depend on the fortune of the Princess Sayn-Wittgenstein, Liszt's current mistress. Owing to her indiscretions, however, her Russian estates had been impounded by order of the Czar.

New French friends beckoned Wagner to Bordeaux, where Eugène Laussot, a wine merchant, and his wife Jessie resided. Wagner's liaison with Jessie, a pianist, with whom he fantasized about going to Greece and Asia Minor, terminated when her husband got wind of the affair. The composer returned to Paris, but his wife Minna's unexpected arrival from Switzerland forced him first to conceal his address from her and then to return without her to Geneva. Foiled in her attempts to find him, a disappointed Minna returned to Zürich.[32]

A few weeks after his flight to Switzerland, Wagner went again to Bordeaux—ostensibly to clear himself with Laussot, more probably to persuade him to offer some financial support. The police learned of his arrival and, because of irregularities in his passport, forced him to leave Bordeaux without even seeing Jessie.

Back in Switzerland, in August he wrote *Das Judenthum in der Musik*, principally a diatribe against Meyerbeer, and published it in Leipzig under the pseudonym F. Freigedank ("Freethought"). He achieved another performance of the *Tannhäuser* Overture, again indirectly through Liszt. François Seghers, a Belgian violinist who instructed Liszt's children, conducted the work at the Société Sainte-Cécile. Henri Blanchard, in the *Gazette musicale* of 1 December 1850 commented that "this genre of romantic and metaphysical music has seen its day." More important, Léon Leroy, who, in the future, would prove a wonderful friend to Wagner, was in the audience.

Wagner continued to dream of presenting *Tannhäuser* and eventually *Lohengrin* in Paris. In his articles he also continued, rather foolishly in view of his desired goals, to attack the French. The Belgian musicologist François-Joseph Fétis, who resided in Paris and whose *Revue* had merged with the *Gazette musicale*, replied to Wagner in a series of seven articles published in the journal. Wagner had acquired, by this time (1852), a formidable opponent in Fétis. In Zürich, however, he had made the acquaintance of an unusual couple who would prove enormously supportive: Otto and Mathilde Wesendonk.

Accompanied by Liszt, Wagner arrived in Paris for his fifth visit in October 1853. He had read the text of *Der Ring des Nibelungen* in Basel to violinist Joseph Joachim, Liszt, and conductor-pianist Hans von Bülow, and, with their encouragement, had decided once again to try to mount *Tannhäuser* in Paris. He dined with Liszt and his children, meeting Cosima, age fifteen, for the first time. Berlioz joined them as he read the text of the last act of *Götterdämmerung*. At the end of the month, he left for Zürich.

Two years later, Wagner was in Paris en route to London, where he conducted eight concerts of the Old Philharmonic Society. He remained there four months, during which time he met Berlioz again. By 1857, Wagner had settled into the Asyl, the house in Zürich offered him by the Wesendonks. That year, Liszt married off both his daughters: Cosima to Hans von Bülow and Blandine to Emile Ollivier, a lawyer and a future prime minister of France. The von Bülows visited Wagner during their honeymoon; the Olliviers, in their salon on the Rue St. Guillaume in Paris, afforded Wagner the opportunity to meet *tout Paris* during his Parisian stay from 1858 to 1861. In the course of a short visit in January 1858 to settle copyrights, Wagner went with Ollivier to the Palais de Justice, where he felt sufficiently confident to discuss his scenario at greath length with the judges, Ollivier's friends. Idealistically, he expected that the French might welcome a season of German opera. He even met with Léon Carvalho, director of the Théâtre Lyrique, and considered giving him *Rienzi* instead of *Tannhäuser*. He visited Berlioz, who read him the libretto of *Les Troyens*. Thanks to the Olliviers, he received an invitation to the Erards, piano manufacturers, where Mme. Erard promised to send him a grand piano. It arrived in Zürich in May. Gratefully, Wagner offered her the French version of *Tannhäuser*, but in a letter to his friend Wilhelm Fischer, Wagner requested that he withhold the news about the possibility of a performance of *Tannhäuser* at the Opéra. Wagner anticipated trouble ahead. A performance of the Overture to *Tannhäuser* by the Concerts de Paris under J. B. Arban elicited the following remarks in the *Gazette musicale* of 7 February 1858: "The public listened to this strange work in a religious silence." Wagner left Zürich and spent from August 1858 to March 1859 in Venice, leaving there for his new abode, which he called "Tribschen," near Lucerne.

On his arrival in Paris in September 1859, for his seventh visit, the Wagnerites began to gather around him: Madame de Charnacé, daughter of the Countess d'Agoult by her first husband; the young pianist Léon Leroy, sent to Wagner by that extraordinary gentleman Auguste Gaspérini, a physician who cultivated literature and the arts; M. de Charnal, who had begun what Wagner regarded as an unacceptable translation of *Rienzi* and Carvalho, who invited Wagner to give him a reading of *Tannhäuser* at the piano. Wagner was his own accompanist. Carvalho, who came to Wagner's home for the event, reports that the composer sounded "diabolic" in his performance—shrieking, whispering, shouting, gesturing so vigorously that Carvalho could not leave fast enough.[33]

Wagner had completed *Tristan und Isolde* in August 1859 at Tribschen. When his anticipated production of the opera at Karlsruhe did not materialize, he decided that his hopes for the future lay in French acceptance of his works. The Germans would then surely follow suit. The composer therefore petitioned the Emperor for the use of the Opéra for three concerts, concerts he intended would prepare French audiences for his works. He suspected the critics (whom he was convinced Meyerbeer had by their pockets) would malign him, but was equally sure the French public would show enthusiasm. When the Emperor failed to reply (actually his consent arrived too late), Wagner turned to Calzado, the crafty director of the Théâtre-Italien, ironically the former Théâtre de la Renaissance that had failed earlier in 1840. The composer paid the princely sum of 8,000 francs for the hall. The fee did not even include the musicians.[34]

Eager to round up a group of zealous followers, Wagner organized Wednesday evening soirées at his home—despite his worsening financial crisis. Among those who came were the Olliviers; Frédéric Villot, curator of Imperial Museums; Jules Ferry, the celebrated French statesman; artist Gustave Doré, two writers, Jules Champfleury and Catulle Mendès, and Edmonde Roche, Auguste Gaspérini, and Léon Leroy, all three of whom participated in the preparation of *Tannhäuser* for its eventual production at the Opéra; Paul Challemel-Lacour, who had translated the texts of four of Wagner's works; Emile Perrin of the *Revue Européenne*, former Director of the Opéra-Comique and soon to become the Director of the Opéra; and the peripatetic Malwida von Meysenbug, later Romain Rolland's constant companion and mentor. Von Meysenbug's reminiscences of the *Tannhäuser* rehearsals and performances can be found in her two-volume *Memoiren einer Idealistin. Der Lebensabend einer Idealistin*, published in Berlin with no known date.[35] Musicians present included, at one time or another, Stephen Heller, Saint-Saëns, Berlioz, Ernest Reyer, and Charles Gounod.[36]

With an offer from one De Lucy to help finance a "Wagner experience," the composer planned three concerts comprised of excerpts from *Der fliegende Holländer, Tristan, Tannhäuser,* and *Lohengrin.* Ever practical when it came to performances of his music, Wagner wrote a concert ending for the *Tristan* Prelude and personally arranged excerpts from the *Ring* before Bayreuth opened its doors. This despite his oft-quoted remark that he wished his music never to be extracted from the original context. Anticipating sales, publisher Flaxland signed a contract to buy three Wagner scores: *Der fliegende Holländer, Tannhäuser,* and *Lohengrin.*

The concerts, scheduled for three Wednesdays—25 January, 1 and 8 February 1860—took place in a theater that accommodated 1,550 persons. Wagner, true to his custom, distributed no tickets to the press. But they came in droves, no doubt expecting to be amused. Wagner rehearsed the orchestra in the theater's Salle Herz. The sixty-four strings pleased him; the woodwinds and brass irritated him. He complained in a letter to Mathilde Wesendonk that the oboes played without any passion.[37] Von Bülow, in Paris to give some piano recitals, rehearsed the chorus (made up mostly of German amateurs resident in Paris) in the Salle Beethoven. German instrumentalists, to whom Wagner paid five francs per rehearsal, reinforced his orchestra. He also issued a flyer, at his own expense, to explain the context of his excerpts, inasmuch as most of the public had not yet heard any of his operas. Excerpts featured the Overture to *Der fliegende Holländer*; the Overture, March, and Chorus, the Introduction to Act III and the Pilgrims' Chorus from *Tannhäuser*, the Prelude to *Tristan*, the Prelude, Bridal Procession, Prelude to Act III and the Bridal Chorus from *Lohengrin*. In his determination to make these performances successful he worked so feverishly that his health began to deteriorate. His persistence, however, paid off. The three Parisian concerts proved a turning point in his reputation in France.

Composer Victorin de Joncières, an ardent Wagnerite, recalled the performances in his *Notes sans Portées* in *Revue Internationale de musique* of 1 March 1898.

Tout Paris was there: the world of arts, of literature, the aristocracy, the world of finance and the critics. Behind the scenes the Princess Metternich, declared protectrice of the novel composer, waited expectantly. In the first box sat Auber, wearing an indifferent air, and accompanied by his two inseparable female aide-de-camps, Edile Ricquier and Dameron; Berlioz sat laced tightly into his redingote, his neck imprisoned inside a tie of black silk, in the fashion of 1830, his head looking like a bird of prey, his huge forehead under a shock of gray hair, his eyes with their piercing gaze. Fiorentino, critic from the *Constitutionnel*, caressed, with a fat prelate's hand, the opulent beard that extended down to his white waistcoat. In the orchestra seats, Gounod, whose *Faust* had just created such a sensation, chatted with conductor Carvalho. Blond Reyer, who had [to date] produced but a short one-act opéra-comique, *Maître Wolfram* [notice the name of a character in *Tannhäuser*], and a ballet *Sacountala*, conversed with his friend and collaborator Théophile Gautier of the leonine mane and flowing beard. Azevedo, the intractable critic of *L'Opinion nationale*, less grimy than usual, alternately cleaned his nails and his teeth with a penknife. Deep in the pit stood Hans von Bülow, fervent apostle of the new Messiah; he had rehearsed the chorus for a month in the Salle Beethoven. [He was] accompanied by his young wife Cosima, Liszt's daughter, who ten years later would divorce Bülow to marry the author of *Tristan und Isolde*. With them [was] Emile Ollivier ... who married the sister of Madame von Bülow, a charming creature dead at 27, a few years later. And everywhere the Germans, who came to uphold the cause of their compatriot. Professors from the Conservatoire, Ambroise Thomas, Carafa and Elwart were also there ...

Suddenly conversation ceases and a short fiftyish man comes forward to the stage. [He has] a large head and long hair brushed proudly to the back, a bulging forehead above two flaming eyes, minced lips, and a prominent chin encased in brown whiskers. Rapidly and nervously he crosses the rows of musicians. Following him, a servant, dressed as for the second act of *La Traviata*, carries an ebony baton on a silver platter. He hands [the baton] to Wagner, causing a few murmurs in the audience. Wagner quiets them with a few raps on the podium and signals the orchestra to begin. The astonishing tempest from the *Dutchman* is unleashed in strident gusts on a totally bewildered audience.

Joncières neglected to mention as well the attendance of Rossini, François Auguste Gevaert, the Belgian musicologist, and the painter Henri Fantin-Latour. Receipts amounted to 6,000 francs, while expenses exceeded 11,000. At the second concert, receipts decreased to 2,000 francs, but much of the house had been papered. The press confirmed the success of the third concert, but the deficit exceeded 10,000 francs. Later that year, the very generous Madame Kalergis, a Russian-Polish pianist who had studied with Chopin and through her marriage had become exceedingly wealthy, wiped out Wagner's debt.[38]

Berlioz, in the *Journal des Débats* of 9 February 1860, described the composer's "music of the future." Listing his dislikes, Berlioz says: "If such be the religion, I raise my hand and swear non credo." Wagner replied to the French composer in the same journal on 22 February 1860. He explained that one Herr Bischoff of Cologne had invented the phrase "music of the future." "The occasion for the comment," he said, "derived from the publication ten years ago of my book entitled *Das Kunstwerk der Zukunft* in which I analyzed relationships among diverse branches of art, drama, sculpture, mime, poetry and music which, when combined, would produce the perfect work of art."

Wagner's diligence paid dividends. Four powerfully effective partisans emerged as the result of these concert performances: Emile Perrin, mentioned above; Jules Champfleury, who immediately after the concerts left his own work unfinished to write a sixteen-page brochure on Wagner and his music; Charles Baudelaire, so moved by the music that he wrote a letter of thanks to the composer (and after the fiasco of *Tannhäuser*, one year later, published an extended essay, "Richard Wagner et Tannhäuser à Paris"); and Catulle Mendès, who offered Wagner the pages of his journal in which to reply to the opposition.

With the three concerts behind him, Wagner could return to his primary objective: a performance of the complete *Tannhäuser* at the Opéra in Paris. Liszt continued to believe it inappropriate for the French. In January of 1858, Wagner had written him that one Léopold Amat, a Parisian, currently director of music festivals in Wiesbaden and Hamburg, had sent him an outline of his activities on behalf of *Tannhäuser*. Wagner contended that the opera must be given without cuts or revision and with a good translation. The two conditions became stumbling blocks. The Paris Opéra always presented a ballet at the top of the second act, thus enabling members of the Jockey Club, the jet set of the time, to dine leisurely and still arrive in time to admire the shapely limbs of their girlfriends in the troupe.[39] *Tannhäuser* provided no place for a ballet, unless, and as Wagner reluctantly agreed to do, he placed it in the first act as a bacchanale. (Later the placement of this ballet became his undoing; for the time, it satisfied the director.) Another problem was the conductor, Pierre Dietsch, the very same who had made an opera out of Wagner's scenario for the *Holländer* twenty years earlier. At the Opéra, a composer could not conduct his own work; Wagner, therefore, had to rely on Dietsch and French instrumentalists, whom he found decidedly lacking in ability. When he wanted to hire extras, the Minister of State wrote to the Opéra director that their staff, the best in Europe, had proved good enough for all other composers— Wagner would just have to make do with them.

The translation posed a much knottier problem. All operas had to be given in French, and Wagner, with his imperfect knowledge of the language, could not handle the translation alone. M. de Charnal, an unknown writer, approached the composer, but Wagner rejected the writer's proposed excerpts. He insisted the French were unable to do it properly. The pianist Léon Leroy wrote Gaspérini that Wagner believed it imperative for the translator to know French, German, and the score of *Tannhäuser*—and he doubted such a man existed. Leroy thought first of the tenor Gustave Roger, who had sung German opera, knew the score of *Tannhäuser* by heart, and had translated Haydn's *The Seasons*. Initially enthusiastic, both translator and composer soon lost interest in each other's efforts, Wagner maintaining that Roger was a singer, not a poet, rich and therefore lazy, and lacking innate culture.[40] According to Wagner, Charles Nuitter, another candidate, "only aspired to vulgar vaudeville." To Mathilde Wesendonk he wrote that despite all his efforts "not one act of my opera is translated and the little that is disgusts me."[41]

Wagner finally found somebody who appealed to him but he too proved unsatisfactory. The French dramatist Victorien Sardou, in his preface to the *Posthumous Poems* of Edmond Roche, a customs officer, tells the story. One day, a German, struggling to deal with the bureaucracy at French customs in an effort to get hold of his furniture, heard a man humming passages from *Lohengrin* and *Tannhäuser*. Wagner, the German in question, determined this man, Roche, must become his translator. Roche knew not one word of German. For the placement of syllables and words, he needed the assistance of a singer, Lindau. Wagner called them his translation company. Sardou described Roche's torment. The poor man worked all week at the customs office. Sundays he was free. On Sundays Wagner would arrive at 7:00 A.M., hounding him to get started. By 1:00 P.M. he was famished, but the composer could not comprehend his need to stop for food. Grudgingly Wagner agreed, but urged him to eat quickly so that they could continue. The composer stood around giving advice, remaining as fresh as he had appeared early in the morning. Roche, on the other hand, felt ready to expire by evening.

To Paul Challemel-Lacour, who translated four of his operas, he meted out the same criticism. Under the pretext of quoting Voltaire, he said, "The French are mimics, the Germans artists. The French imitate, the Germans create. The French are barren, the Germans profound; the French are superficial virtuosos, the Germans are poets; the French are realists, the Germans idealists. French taste [whose goal] basically is to entertain, has infected all Europe. The new French school suffers from this malaise and at its fore stands Victor Hugo."[42] (Nevertheless, experts feel that Wagner knowingly borrowed ideas from the fourth act of Verdi's *Ernani*, whose libretto is based on Victor Hugo's play *Hernani*, for the third act of *Lohengrin*.)

Wagner had difficulty acknowledging several of his partisans. He never sought out or met Gérard de Nerval. He did meet Baudelaire, but preferred Champfleury. Not unexpectedly, the only Frenchman to influence the composer was Joseph Arthur, Comte de Gobineau, in his theory of race. The latter nourished an inexplicable hatred of Jews and passed along these sentiments to Wagner, already confirmed in his own brand of anti-Semitism.

At this point in his life, Wagner, as Ernest Newman has said, "was considerably richer in hopes than in assets." Besides his acquaintance with Halévy and Auber, he had met the young Saint-Saëns, then twenty-five, who astonished him with his facility at score-reading. He knew *Tristan* by heart, which delighted Wagner. Gounod too admired the German composer but Wagner did not reciprocate. He liked the man, but disliked his music, and refused to listen to his *Faust*. Before Wagner left Paris in 1861, he gave Gounod one of the three copies of the full score of *Tristan* which the publishers Breitkopf & Härtel had sent him in the middle of January 1860. He gave another copy to Berlioz with the inscription: "Dear Berlioz, I am enchanted to be able to offer you the first copy of my *Tristan*. Accept it and keep it out of friendship for me." Three weeks elapsed before Berlioz even acknowledged receipt of the score, and Wagner felt deeply wounded.

On 12 February 1860 von Bülow performed a number of paraphrases by Liszt on themes from *Tannhäuser* at the Salle Pleyel. On the seventeenth, Wagner received the first of Baudelaire's letters in which the poet reported, "It seems as if that music were mine; I acknowledge it as all men do with things they are destined to love."[43] Wagner paid his famous visit to Rossini in March and a few days later, thanks to the prodding of Princess Metternich, the Emperor Napoleon III gave the order to Alphonse Royer, director of the Opéra, to mount *Tannhäuser*. Royer immediately asked Wagner to rework the second act in order to introduce a ballet at the beginning. Meanwhile, Wagner left for Brussels to conduct two concerts (24 and 28 March); he hoped their proceeds would compensate his Parisian deficit.

Uncharacteristically grateful to Madame Kalergis for extricating him from the losses incurred by the Parisian concerts, he gave a reading for her of excerpts from *Tristan* at Pauline Viardot's home. Viardot sang Isolde; Wagner, Tristan. They were accompanied by pianist Karl Klindworth and their sole auditors were Kalergis and Berlioz. A few months later, Wagner reported to Liszt that the three of them, "you, [Berlioz], and I comprise an exclusive triad." A second soirée for Madame Kalergis, this time chez Wagner, offered the first act of *Die Walküre* with the singer Albert Niemann in attendance.[44]

Royer, the director, judged the translation of *Tannhäuser* by Roche and Lindau, now completed, totally unacceptable, particularly the recitatives. He called in Charles Truinet, known as Nuitter, the future archivist at the Opéra, to make repairs. Wagner, financially embarrassed as usual, now found a new backer, Emile Erlanger, a young Parisian Jew who had become enamored of his music in Germany. Erlanger offered to back him, anticipating profits from the production of the opera.[45] Several of his friends contemplated establishing a Wagner Theater devoted exclusively to his works. When that scheme failed, Erlanger withdrew his support. He did not demand that Wagner repay him for previous loans, but he refused to supply further funds.

In the summer of 1860, the government of Saxony removed the ban on Wagner, except in their own province. Twelve years earlier he had been exiled from Saxony as the result of his participation on the barricades in Dresden during the 1848 Revolution. In Paris, *Tannhäuser*, receiving the full support of the Emperor, would ultimately have 164 rehearsals. Wagner wrote Liszt (on 13 September 1860) that he had never before witnessed an occasion where the total forces of an institution were placed at the services of a composer.[46] Later he said he was most distressed by Dietsch's inability to conduct. He alternated between calling the French or the Germans the better musicians. A month before the long-awaited performances of *Tannhäuser*, the first Wagnerian review appeared, in the *Revue fantaisiste*, for which Catulle Mendès acted as editor. At the same time, a biographical essay on Wagner, written by one Charles Lorbac, appeared in *Le Figaro*. Despite his recent favorable publicity—conductor Jules Pasdeloup had programmed a *Lohengrin* excerpt by the Société des Jeunes Artistes du Conservatoire—Wagner worried about the outcome of *Tannhäuser*. Fuming at Dietsch's inadequacies, Wagner pleaded with Royer to let him conduct, but the latter refused. The policy of the Opéra remained firm. The composer engaged Emile Ollivier to defend him in a suit brought by the unsuccessful translators of the opera. He also had to contend with caricatures and spoofs, *Tribulations de Tannhäuser*, by the famous cartoonist Cham in the daily satirical pamphlet *Charivari*. Finally, on 13 March 1861, the much-anticipated premiere was given in the Salle Peletier of the Opéra, with the court in attendance.

The ensuing fiasco caused Wagner to withdraw the piece on 24 March, after the third performance, which he, himself, did not attend. The opera might eventually have succeeded, if he had permitted its continued exposure to the public. But even his heterogeneous partisans, a mixture of liberals and rightists, posed problems for him. In the main, his supporters represented the avant-garde, bohemian in dress and lifestyle. However, Princess Metternich, who bore responsibility for the Emperor's orders to produce the opera, and, of course, the Emperor himself, belonged to the aristocracy. The bizarre juxtaposition of these two entirely different political groups, combined with their internal conflicts, left Wagner with an insufficient base of support. Each of the three performances cost the Opéra management 100,000 francs.[47]

After the second performance on 18 March 1861, Blandine Ollivier reported to her father, Franz Liszt:

> Everything went well until the middle of the second act. The Emperor and Empress arrived and the singers sensed their support. Mlle Sax, Elisabeth, sang her role well; they applauded her warmly. A hiss came from the back of the theater. Bravos followed by more hisses—the Jockey Club had supplied its members with tiny whistles. Somebody shouted "Get the Cabal out of here" and people rose to protest the hisses. A din ensued. The Emperor stroked his mustache, smiled and clapped his hands! The Empress looked startled. The second act ended and the audience applauded again. In the third act, Niemann, atrocious Niemann [who had irritated Wagner with some of his demands for changes in his part] received applause at each pause in his recitative. Somebody whistled; bravos followed. They whistled again, but the bravos redoubled and Niemann greeted the public and thanked them for their support. The brouhaha lasted to the very end.[48]

Besides Baudelaire and Champfleury, Wagner's defenders included Léon Leroy of *La Causerie*, Arthur Pougin of *Jeune France*, Giacomelli of *La Presse théâtrale et musicale*, and J. Weber of *Le Temps*. De Beaumont, director of the Opéra-Comique, approached Wagner for the rights to *Tannhäuser*, but was turned down. Several parodies of the piece continued to appear on Parisian stages. Meanwhile, Flaxland published the score.

Wagner had indeed become known to the French. He had achieved his long-sought goal of seeing one of his works mounted at the Opéra, but success still eluded him. Taking reluctant leave of his few French friends, he departed Paris in July for Weimar, Vienna, and Venice.

Wagner returned to Paris for his eighth visit in December 1861, at the invitation of Princess Metternich. She had initially offered to lodge him at her home, but the death of her mother forced a change of plans. Instead, Wagner stayed at the Hôtel du Quai Voltaire, where he proceeded to write the text of *Die Meistersinger*. By the end of January he presented a reading of the libretto to the Countess de Pourtalès. (One wonders whether he deleted the tirade against the French—disguised as "foreigners"—that appears in Sachs's final monologue in the opera.) In February he left for Germany where, in Wiesbaden, he finally attended a performance of Gounod's *Faust*, entitled *Margarethe* by the Germans. At Leipzig he conducted the premiere of the *Meistersinger* Overture, most exceptionally the first completed part of the opera, as he customarily wrote his overtures and preludes last.

After hearing the three concerts of 1860, the artist Henri Fantin-Latour produced his first lithograph inspired by *Tannhäuser*, entitled *Venusberg*. He showed a canvas on the same subject at the Salon of 1864. This was to be Wagner's lucky year. He had been to Russia earlier on a tour organized by Madame Kalergis, but soon after his return, he once again had to hide from creditors in Stuttgart, where a representative of the newly crowned Ludwig II of Bavaria found him and gave him some very good news: hereafter, the King would provide him with a home and funds. He also promised to support him faithfully in the future production of his operas.

During his penultimate (ninth) visit to France, Wagner searched for a home in the Midi: Toulon, Hyères, Lyons, and Marseilles. He sought, as he wrote to an unknown correspondent, "a quiet place removed from that of the fashionable world." Again France seemed preferable to Germany. In Marseilles, he learned that Minna had died; his return to Tribschen a few days later did not allow him time to attend her funeral.

In Paris meanwhile, Heugel published Gaspérini's study, *La Nouvelle Allemagne musicale, Richard Wagner*. The first issue of *Esprit nouveau* included a defense of Wagner's concepts, without specifically naming him. The editors were his friends Gaspérini and Leroy. Their views brought them the wrath of the Minister of the Interior whose typical antipathy toward Wagner made him order the withdrawal of that issue.[49]

Cosima gave birth to Isolde, their first daughter, on 10 April 1865; two years later, on 7 February 1867, she bore Eva. Still married to von Bülow, Cosima had come to Tribschen, at the suggestion of her husband, to help the Meister, who was struggling to adjust to his newly acquired bachelor status. (After the birth of Siegfried, Cosima and Richard finally married on 25 August 1870 in Lucerne, following her divorce.) Wagner returned for a last time to Paris in October 1867 to see the Exposition Universelle. With Carvalho of the Théâtre Lyrique he planned for the production of *Lohengrin* under the supervision of von Bülow. Flaxland published the score and when Pasdeloup succeeded Carvalho at the Théâtre-Lyrique, he proposed to mount all Wagner's operas beginning with *Rienzi*. He asked the composer to conduct rehearsals; Wagner declined, but gave him complete rights to the works.[50]

Judith Gautier, daughter of the writer and critic Théophile Gautier, commenced her articles on Wagner in the French press in 1868. She wrote on *Lohengrin* in *La Presse*, then produced a piece for the journal entitled "Richard Wagner et la critique." Ernest Reyer, composer and friend of Berlioz, discussed the same opera in the *Journal des Débats*. The Belgians published a French translation of Wagner's *Deutsche Kunst und deutsche Politik* in which he had again lambasted the French for their perversion of German taste. The Belgians also brought out a new edition of *Das Judenthum in der Musik* (originally issued in 1852), and Wagner wrote von Bülow that the celebrated singer Pauline Viardot now felt impelled to forsake him.[51]

Conductor Jules Pasdeloup continued with preparations for *Rienzi*, and Wagner's followers kept busy. The composer had preferred to write a new opera, but he acceded to the appeals of Judith Gautier who, although she had not yet met Wagner, wrote him asking that he grant permission for a production of *Rienzi* without further delay. Before the performance, Edouard Drumont issued the brochure *Richard Wagner, l'homme et le musicien. A propos de 'Rienzi.'* On 6 April 1869 the first performance of *Rienzi* took place. Reviews and articles by Judith Gautier, her father Théophile, and Théodore de Banville appeared in three different journals—*La Liberté*, *Le Journal Officiel*, and *Le National*—a few days after the premiere. Schuré wrote "Le Drame musical et l'oeuvre de M. Richard Wagner" for the *Revue des deux mondes*; Durand Schoenewerk published the score of *Rienzi* with a French translation also by Nuitter.

Many years later, writing of the premiere in *Le Figaro* of 19 December 1904, the critic Henry Roujon recalled the times when "Pasdeloup delivered this music to the beasts in his circus and became the butt of their hoots and howls at each performance of the Overture. Two thousand whistled furiously, while twenty pairs of hands applauded. To subdue them, Pasdeloup spoke quietly, but firmly." On the occasion of the final rehearsal, which in France is always most important, Bizet remarked, "A din the likes of which cannot be described; a mélange of Italian motives; bizarre and bad style; music of decadence rather than of the future. Some detestable pieces, some admirable. In sum, an astonishing work, exceedingly lively."[52] When the press continued their hostility to Wagner, Pasdeloup reminded them that if this attitude had prevailed earlier, they would have rejected the music of Haydn, Mozart, Beethoven, Gluck, Rossini, Meyerbeer, Bellini, Donizetti, and Verdi.[53]

To celebrate Wagner's birthday on 22 May 1869, Cosima, by now living openly with him in Tribschen, engaged the Maurin-Chevillard Quartet from Paris to play the late quartets of Beethoven. On 6 June of that year, when Siegfried was born, his parents prevailed on Judith Gautier to become his godmother. A few weeks later, Judith, her husband Catulle Mendès, and the writer Villiers de l'Isle-Adam made their famous visit to Tribschen, later narrating their experiences in a spate of articles devoted to the composer and his work.

Wagner wanted to wait for the completion of the entire *Ring*, but at the insistence of King Ludwig, *Die Walküre* had its premiere on 26 June 1870 at Munich's National Theater, which had produced *Das Rheingold* the previous September. His French followers in the audience included Gautier, Mendès, Villiers, Schuré, Joly, Saint-Saëns, and Duparc. On 18 July 1870, Cosima divorced von Bülow. The following day France declared war on Prussia; the news was announced by her brother-in-law Emile Ollivier, speaking for the government.

In letters to their French friends, Cosima and Richard revealed unconcealed hostility. The death knell, for many French, sounded with his writing *Eine Capitulation: Lustspiel in Antiker Manier*, a parody of the French besieged by the Germans and condemned later to suffer the Commune. Wagner even approached Hans Richter to set the piece to music in the manner of Offenbach. Richter had the decency to decline. Wagner also wrote an ode in 1871: *An das deutsche Heer vor Paris*. Then, after completing his very flattering *Souvenirs sur Auber*—one wonders how these two works could appear so close together—Wagner concentrated on his dream of a theater at Bayreuth, where he moved in April 1872.

After the Franco-Prussian War concluded with the German acquisition of Alsace-Lorraine, many Frenchmen felt a strong revulsion toward Wagner and all things German. Pasdeloup's enthusiasm for his works had cooled, but only slightly. Like a lapsed alcoholic returning to drink, he could not remain on the anti-Wagnerian wagon

45

for long. Saint-Saëns, formerly an ardent Wagnerite, accused Pasdeloup of being a German agent or—because he programmed Wagner's works—interested mainly in box office receipts. The Germans living in Paris attended his concerts en masse. Catulle Mendès announced that the hands that applauded the music would not shake those of the composer.[54]

For a few years, the French had regarded the Germans as the *bons sauvages* of Europe. These impressions originated with artists and with German émigré musicians in France. The obligatory visit to Germany by creative persons, particularly by French writers, stimulated by the romantic movement, revealed their admiration for German art. (Germany also appealed to those in opposition to Catholicism, the state religion; before 1870, the pro-Germans in France represented the army of opposition.) With difficulty, they had tried to differentiate between the real Germany and the German intellectuals. Sometimes they focused on Bismarck as the brutal opponent whom they abhorred. The more liberal among them still believed, however, that in the terrain of science and philosophy the Germans had captured the field—until the War. The French defeat created a lasting divide between the two nations. It stimulated a rash of articles and novels that erased immediately the memory of the prewar "good German" and replaced it with a picture of the cruel, hypocritical, evil German.

Understandably, this attitude affected the French view of Wagner. Now the fulminating, mad musician, whom some regarded as a megalomaniac, became the epitome of the nation's enemy, corrupting French culture with his unhealthy music.

In November 1870, during the siege of Paris, and several months before he wrote *An das deutsche Heer vor Paris*—five stanzas in which he glorified the Germans as a nation of born conquerors, insulted the French, and hailed the creation of a new German Empire—Wagner took another shot at his neighbors to the West. *Eine Capitulation*, in the words of Ernest Newman, is "a tasteless, witless farce, the loutish Teutonic humors of which are ungraced by a single touch of literary finesse."[55] This parody of the besieged and starving citizens of Paris first appeared in print in 1873. That Wagner still felt the need to bring it to public notice, after the terrible defeat of the French, astonished even his friends. His actions only served to highlight his total insensitivity. The publication of *Eine Capitulation* became, for the French, the last straw.

46

* * *

Within a few years, thanks mostly to the efforts of writers and dramatists, most of whom had not heard a single note of Wagner's music, the tide turned in his favor. Grandmougin published his *Esquisse sur Richard Wagner* (1873) and Edouard Schuré his *Le Drame musical* (1875), of which the second volume focused on Wagner. A small group of orthodox Wagnerians continued to listen to his music and to read his prose works. Charles Lamoureux, the second of three conductors (Pasdeloup and Colonne were the others) to take up the cudgels for Richard Wagner, restored order to his concerts. He ejected from his hall those who whistled or hissed, disrupting the performance. At the journal *Le Ménestrel* in 1875–76, the editors considered the question of Wagner a political matter, not a musical one. "It is no longer in the critic's domain," they said. "It has now become a matter for the police. They must interpose themselves in order to restore order."[56]

On 13 August 1876, Wagner's music theater in Bayreuth opened its gates to the crowd assembled for the first performance of the *Ring*. The French contingent in attendance included Judith Gautier, Alphonse Duvernoy, Ernest Guiraud, Saint-Saens, Gabriel Monod, Catulle Mendès, Antoine Lascoux, and Fantin-Latour. On his return to Paris, Fantin-Latour began work on Wagnerian lithographs meant to convey his impressions of the festival. Reviews of the performances appeared immediately after the series concluded. Saint-Saëns wrote five articles for *l'Estafette*, Mendès three for *Le Gaulois*, and Guiraud three for *Le Moniteur*. Wagner, meanwhile, was enjoying his last romantic fling, this time with Judith Gautier.

Pasdeloup's performance of the Funeral March from *Götter-dämmerung* at the Cirque d'Hiver provoked a violent anti-Wagner demonstration. The following day, the conductor felt obliged to publish a letter in the newspapers justifying his position. For a very short while, from 1876 to 1879, Pasdeloup refrained from playing Wagner's music. When the reappearance of the *Tannhäuser* Overture on 9 March 1879 passed without incident, he became emboldened and presented the first act of *Tannhäuser* along with Beethoven's Septet, Berlioz's Pilgrim's March from *Harold en Italie*, and Benjamin Godard's *Concerto romantique*. The Wagnerites attended in full force, and competition between conductors commenced. Lamoureux and another young conductor, Edouard Colonne, gave carefully prepared Wagner programs.

Le wagnérisme permeated the works of writers and painters starting in 1850 and continuing up to the First World War in 1914. From Baudelaire to Beardsley, Nerval to Nietszche, Stanislavsky to Sulzer, Zimmermann to Zumpe, those who had sympathy with only some of Wagner's ideals happily jumped on his bandwagon. When the Belgian violinist Seghers conducted the Overture to *Tannhäuser* on 25 November 1850, Gérard de Nerval was unable to attend, but the pianist Léon Leroy was there. He introduced himself to the composer and vociferously proceeded to defend him in *La Presse théâtrale, l'Europe artistique, La Nation, La Liberté, La Réforme, L'Etincelle, Le Ménestrel, Le Petit Echo de la Presse, Le Nain jaune, Le Figaro,* and *L'Echo de Soir.* Paris intellectuals, who read or subscribed to these journals, began to hear about Wagner. To justify their activity on his behalf, his French followers would select a theme, an idea, or some item of his theoretical and philosophical platform with which they could agree. For example, Eduard Schuré, philosopher and ex-pianist, assisted Wagner with the reprint of *Das Judenthum in der Musik.* (After the Franco-Prussian War, in December 1873, Wagner wrote Mendès that he loved the French but "I detest the Alsatians; yet I give absolution to Schuré.") Wagner stated he wanted help "to combat the ethnic element with whom I don't want to be confused." The fear of being taken for a Jew had always haunted him.[57] Caricatures of Wagner as the Rabbi of Bayreuth proliferated in France during his lifetime. Romain Rolland, writing in his journal at Bayreuth in August 1896, describes Isolde, the Wagners' daughter, as "Semitic-looking. Funny, how that happens in a Wagner family."

When Lamoureux played Wagner, a religious fervor took hold of his audience; many were afraid to cough or even breathe lest they interrupt the performance of the new grand priest of Wagnerism. Proust, Mallarmé, the painters Jacques-Emile Blanche and Félix Valloton, along with other celebrated artists and writers, flocked to the Eden Theater, where Lamoureux held court. According to the critics, it seemed as if they were waiting for M. Lamoureux to give them his blessing.[58] In the early years, as he wrested the torch from Pasdeloup, he had the cooperation of all Wagnerians, regardless of their origins. In his first Wagner programs, Lamoureux explained that inasmuch as the current state of the theater precluded appro-

Richard Wagner in 1865. Romain Rolland said of him, "Wagner's influence considerably helped forward the progress of French art, and aroused a love of music in people other than musicians. And by his all-embracing personality and the vast domain of his work in art, he not only engaged the interest of the musical world, but that of the theatrical world and the world of poetry and the plastic arts."

Conductor Charles Lamoureux played Wagner with a religious fervor and threatened to eject all those who disrupted his performances.

Another Wagnerite, conductor Jules Pasdeloup proposed to mount all of Wagner's operas at the Théâtre-Lyrique, beginning with Rienzi.

Henri Fantin-Latour's lithographs illustrating scenes from Parsifal.

Parodies of Wagner's works were mounted on stage and caricatures appeared frequently in the press. Here, Berlioz and Wagner battle to put each other to sleep, and while hundreds of singers and musicians are necessary for his operas, only Wagner is applauding.

On 13 August 1876, Wagner's music theater at Bayreuth opened its gates to the crowd assembled for the first performance of the Ring. *Beginning in 1888, many French composers made the pilgrimage to Bayreuth.*

priate performances of the complete operas, the next best thing was to risk giving them in concert. Many Wagnerians, led by Edouard Dujardin, who would soon found the *Revue wagnérienne*, applauded his actions. When several theater directors wanted to stage some of the operas, they objected that unless these works could be presented properly in the appropriate halls with the appropriate settings, they could not be entrusted to those theaters. As long as Lamoureux limited his operations to the concert stage, all remained peaceful. When, in 1887, he decided to mount a staged production of *Lohengrin*, the editors of *La Revue wagnérienne* opposed him, badgering him about his choice of a translator. Lamoureux had invited Victor Wilder to perform the task; the editors, curiously, wanted the Jewish Alfred Ernst. Lamoureux announced ten performances, but after two he had to withdraw the work, owing to the vigorous demonstrations in the streets. Because several groups of anarchists made known their intention to mount a counter-demonstration on the second night, few members of the Ligue de Patriotes, a chauvinistic French group, bothered to show up; and only a small number of persons attending the performance were insulted as they entered or left the theater. Interestingly enough, the government did not demand cancellation, but Lamoureux, who was held personally responsible for the financial loss incurred, felt he could not continue.

Anti-Wagner sentiment persisted. *La Question Wagner pour un Français*, a brochure of eleven pages, sold for ten centimes on the streets of Paris in 1886. The writer commented that the death of Wagner in 1883 did not put an end to the matter; that Wagner was really as much to blame as Ludwig of Bavaria; that public indignation must confront those who dared stage *Lohengrin* in a theater supported by government subventions; and that the *Revue wagnérienne* was backed and written by Germans. Despite the author's wish to remain anonymous, the printer inadvertently let slip her name: Juliette Adam, a former Wagnerian, whose mother had been the governess of the Comtesse d'Agoult.[59] Parodies and caricatures continued to appear in many of the French papers and journals that offered information on the arts.

Again, what seemed like a defeat only promoted interest in Wagnerism. Beginning in 1888, many French composers made the pilgrimage to Bayreuth. The composer Gustave Charpentier went there in 1888 with his musician friend Gaston Carraud; he returned again in 1891 with Anténor Joly, of the Théâtre-Italien. Debussy went in

1888. Emmanuel Chabrier, in Munich to hear *Tristan* in the company of composer Henri Duparc, as early as 1879, burst into tears at the sound of the "A" on the cello, a sound he said he had dreamed about for years.[60] When Lavignac published his *Le Voyage Artistique à Bayreuth* in 1897, he provided a list of all the French who had attended performances there. His opening lines offer a picture of the fervor with which the faithful made their visit. "They go to Bayreuth in any way they wish," he said, "on foot, or horseback, in carriages, by bicycle, railroad, etc., but the true pilgrim must go there on his knees." This from a Frenchman! Lavignac said he did not want to write the thousand-and-first book on Richard Wagner, but he did want to prepare a practical guide for the French going to Bayreuth. For the project, he used his own experiences, Judge Lascoux's archives, and Vincent d'Indy's letters. The Germans did not neglect the needs of their French visitors. In Leipzig in 1894 (and in a revised edition in 1897) a *Manuel pour les Visiteurs de Bayreuth* by Frédéric Wild appeared, a booklet to help the bewildered French as they arrived for the festival. André Messager published a *Souvenir de Bayreuth, Fantaisie en forme de quadrille sur les thèmes favoris de 'l'Anneau du Nibelung' de Richard Wagner*, with a small contribution as well from Gabriel Fauré. Chabrier later wrote a *Souvenirs de Munich, Quadrilles* for piano four-hands on favorite themes from *Tristan und Isolde.*

Joining the faithful Wagnerians imposed considerable hardships on many of his followers. In 1882 Lamoureux began his preparations for *Lohengrin.* He and the publisher Jacques Durand visited Wagner's favorite impresario, another Jewish Wagnerite, Angelo Neumann. A contract was signed, the press heard about it, and the violent opposition that ensued forced its nullification. Neumann was left with a bill of 15,000 francs to be paid to the theater manager. Lamoureux persisted. When Edouard Dujardin wrote Wagner a report of the Neumann incident, the composer replied: "Not only don't I want *Lohengrin* performed in Paris, but I fervently hope it will not be done there."[61] That same year, Renoir, in Palermo, painted his seemingly half-finished portrait of Wagner, mentioning later the composer's puzzling anti-Semitic comments in the course of the mere forty-five minutes he agreed to pose for him.[62] Judith Gautier, who had returned to Bayreuth in 1881, appeared there again for the premiere of *Parsifal* (1882), this time accompanied by Saint-Saëns, d'Indy, Léo Delibes, Lamoureux, and others. Shortly thereafter she published *Richard Wagner et son oeuvre poétique depuis 'Rienzi' jusqu'à 'Parsifal.'*

Wagner died in Venice on 13 February 1883. One year later, one Wagner Society brought out a commemorative album, *Bayreuth Festspiel Blätter*, with contributions from Nuitter, J. Gautier, Adolphe Jullien, Louis de Fourcaud, Charles Toché, and Fantin-Latour. Camille Benois translated the non-French articles for the publication of his *Souvenirs*; and Edmond Hippeau translated into French Wagner's recently published autobiography *Mein Leben*, written mostly by Cosima.

A grave political crisis shook the Third Republic in France in 1885. The populace believed the government incapable of assuring supremacy over the Germans or of forging a new nation. Chauvinism had already reared its ugly head with the founding of the Ligue des Patriotes in May 1882. Général Boulanger, named Minister of War, gathered together the opposition and intensified his campaign against the Germans. Anti-Wagnerism became part of their reform platform. Bismarck reacted by strengthening his government in Alsace-Lorraine.

On 21 April 1887, a French police commissioner was summoned by his German equivalent and arrested. The nationalists shouted for war against Germany. President Grévy refused to comply with their demands and eventually found a way to resolve the matter. Precisely at this moment Lamoureux was preparing the performance of *Lohengrin* at the Eden Theater. Placing appropriate announcements in their journal *La Revanche*, the nationalists sought to incite as many demonstrations as possible. Lamoureux brought suit on 16 April. Three days later the journal carried the following announcement:

> Since M. Lamoureux has decided to engage *La Revanche* in a personal struggle, by which he hopes to satisfy the rancor against his wounded beloved, we accept the challenge and the defender of Richard Wagner can count on our not neglecting any way to inform the public of his initiative.

With this goal in mind, they naturally published the story of *Eine Capitulation* on the front page.

In addition to public concerts of Wagner's music, it filled the salons of his admirers, who devoted entire evenings to him. The most celebrated were those of the "Petit Bayreuth," founded by the fervent

Wagnerian, Judge Antoine Lascoux, and by the painter Charles Toché. The concerts took place at their homes or at the homes of Marcel Gaupillat and Marguerite Pelouze. When the number of participants became too large, they rented the Salle de la Société d'Encouragement. Pelouze, daughter of the Scottish engineer Daniel Wilson, who amassed a fortune with the installation of gas lights in Paris, had been given the Chateau at Chenonceaux for a wedding present. (Her brother Daniel married the daughter of the French President Jules Grévy. Daniel's embezzlements and l'Affaire Wilson with its ensuing scandal provoked one of the significant crises of the Third Republic.) Pelouze made the pilgrimage to Bayreuth in 1876 and then returned every year from 1884 to 1891. She played an important role in the founding of the *Revue wagnérienne* and in the organization of the concerts of the "Petit Bayreuth."

Members of the "Petit Bayreuth" formed a chamber orchestra comprising amateurs and professionals. At their meetings, they sight-read excerpts from the *Ring* or *Parsifal* in Engelbert Humperdinck's arrangements. Henry Bauer, paying homage to Lamoureux in *Le Journal* of 23 November 1899, described the activities at one of these meetings: "Madame H[ellman] and two amateurs formed a group who sang in German. The orchestra (a chamber one) included several unusual performers: besides d'Indy, Fauré, Messager, Raoul Pugno and Taffanel, Lascoux played first violin." They first undertook these meetings in utter secrecy, owing to threats from anti-Wagnerians who resented even their singing in German. Eventually, they relaxed and published news of their proceedings.

In addition to the "Petit Bayreuth," Judith Gautier organized what Wagner called "Bayreuth de poche." Totally devoted to the master, Gautier gathered about her a group with similar sentiments. The war of 1870 had physically separated her from the Wagners, preventing her attendance at the baptism of Siegfried. But after her divorce from Mendès, she made the trip to Bayreuth in 1876 and later attended the first performance of *Parsifal* in 1882. Her Parisian apartment provided the background for a coterie of adherents who recited Wagnerian verse in front of a bust of the composer placed before several Japanese panels. Her butler regularly called guests to dinner by playing the "Ride of the Valkyries" on his cornet.[63]

With her current constant companion, the Dutch-Jewish composer Louis Bénédictus, in March 1880 Gautier organized evenings of Wagner's music at the Salle Nadar. At Wahnfried, Wagner's home

in Bayreuth, helped by the Wagner children, she produced performances of the *Ring* with marionettes, making the marionettes herself and sewing all their costumes. In May 1894, using the marionettes,
she presented two performances at her home to an invited audience
of twenty-five guests.[64] She performed *Die Walküre* on a miniature
stage with decor by the painter René Guérin. The wax figures were
molded by the hostess. Bénédictus handled the music and the singers included the cream of Parisian musicians. In June 1898, Judith
decided to produce *Parsifal*—she had made one of the original French
translations of the opera and had traveled in the French provinces
to promote the work—or at least the first and third acts. The French
pianist Alfred Cortot agreed to participate along with Bénédictus in
a two-piano version of the piece. Unfortunately, Cosima intervened
with a sheriff's notice prohibiting the performance. Cosima knew
of the affair between her husband and Gautier, but certainly during
his lifetime she preferred not to make a fuss about it. One cannot
help wondering if her actions at this date resulted from her pent-
up hostility toward the younger woman. Sâr Péladan, guru of the
Rosicrucian movement, wrote Judith that she had a gift from God;
she was unbelievably talented and he would never forget the puppets
of *Parsifal*.[65] Other "soirées wagnériennes" took place once weekly
from 1880 to 1890 at the home of Victor Wilder, the translator of
several Wagner texts, at Lamoureux's home, and at the residence of
the Jewish publisher Enoch.

First sold at the entrance to the Chateau d'Eau on 8 February 1885,
before a Lamoureux concert, the *Revue wagnérienne* originated the
summer before with the plans of Edouard Dujardin and Houston
Stuart Chamberlain. British by birth, French by upbringing, and
German by choice, Chamberlain married Wagner's daughter Eva,
whom he met in Munich's Cafe Roth. For the most part, the philosophical and prose writings of Wagner remained beyond the reach
of the French, who desperately required translations. Dujardin and
Chamberlain figured that their journal would answer a need. Sub-
scriptions would come in easily, provided the magazine carried good
translations. Together with the amiable Alfred Bovet, industrialist
from Doubs, the Geneva millionaire Agénor Boissier, the most pa-
ternalistic of the group, and Judge Lascoux, they collected members
and launched the *Revue wagnérienne*. First to join were the celebrated Wagnerians Léon Leroy, Mendès, Schuré (author of *Le Drame*

musical), and several journalists and writers beyond the pale, including Elémir Bourges, Edouard Rod, and Bergerat. Finally, Villiers de l'Isle-Adam, who had gone to Tribschen with the Mendès couple in 1869, offered his services as well. With this group, one could almost hear the rattling of swords!

The *Revue wagnérienne*, which appeared on the eighth of each month, soon became the principal instrument to promote the composer. The *Revue* also hoisted the banners of the new "Symbolist" movement. Many of Wagner's operas demand that listeners be familiar with the myths and symbols they contained. For Wagner, a recurring theme or symbol was the redemption of man through the love of a good woman. His leading motives—those "flexible moments of feeling" as he preferred to call them—represented different persons, objects, events, things, and emotions as they underwent thematic transformation throughout the operas. For the contributors to the *Revue wagnérienne*, Wagner became a symbolist par excellence. They affirmed that his conception of art, his philosophy, his formulas provided the basis of symbolism.

Initially the *Revue* pleased the Wagnerian public. Gradually, however, the stance of Dujardin and his Polish-French collaborator Théodor Wyzéwa began to irritate some responsible readers. In the *Revue musicale* of 1 October 1923, Dujardin recalls that the bad press began with J. K. Huysmans. On Good Friday, he had brought the Belgian symbolist writer Huysmans, together with Stéphane Mallarmé, to a Wagnerian soirée at Lamoureux's home. Mallarmé, moved by the music to the depths of his being, became a regular at the Sunday concerts. Huysmans, though, was seemingly more of a painter than a writer and did not know how to discuss the music. Fascinated by the new (Wagnerian) tubas that joined the orchestra for Siegfried's Funeral March, he reported that they reminded him of intestines ravaged by some exotic disease. On his program, he wrote:

> In a landscape nature would not know how to create, in a landscape where the sun dissolves sublimely in a golden yellow hue, under a morbidly luminous sky, [sit] opalescent mountains beyond the bluish valleys, with white crystals at their peaks! In a landscape accessible to painters because it was composed of visual fantasy. Of quiet shudders and simmering moisture, a song arises, a song singularly majestic, an august and peaceful canticle hurled from the souls of pilgrims who marched forward together.

54

It seems the Venus of the musician is the descendant of Luxuria of the poet, of the white Belluaire, steeped in perfume that crushes its victims with aggressive flowers in one swoop. It seems that the Wagnerian Venus attracts and collects the most dangerous deities of Prudence; those of which the religious writer wrote with trembling the name Sodomoita Libido.[66]

Nothing could have been farther from Wagner's intentions. A few days later, word came from Agénor Boissier, the Geneva millionaire, that he could not tolerate two things: insult to religion or to morals. The *Revue* pulled back, retrenched, and Villiers contributed a milder piece on Bayreuth. In August, Mallarmé's article appeared, confounding even the most rabid Wagnerites. (Later it was published in his *Divagations*. Apparently it was just as well that the Wagnerians had trouble understanding it because Mallarmé was not entirely complimentary.)

The supreme blow was struck the following month when the *Revue* carried eight sonnets honoring Wagner by Mallarmé, Verlaine, Rhené Ghil, Stuart Merrill, Charles Morice, Charles Vignier, Wyzéwa, and Dujardin. The last six passed unnoticed; they were reasonably accessible to the public. The two by Verlaine and Mallarmé created what the French like to call "un drame." The trio of Wagner patrons, Judge Antoine Lascoux, Alfred Bovet, and Agénor Boissier, notified Dujardin that their original intention centered on drawing attention to Wagner and his works, not to publishing the poems of symbolist poets. The brouhaha between Dujardin and Lamoureux, coming at the moment when the latter planned to produce *Lohengrin*, led to the demise of the *Revue*. In the last issue of 1888, Alfred Ernst announced that the publication would cease with that number.

Dujardin would not admit defeat. Thanks to his efforts and those of his colleagues, Wagner would now have numerous performances in France. "All singers dragged from the old world to the new by Jewish bankers and American colonels," Dujardin said, "would now alternate the roles of Elsa and Lakmé on their operatic posters."[67] The heroic period of the Wagnerites drew to a close and the practical, commercial era began. Devout Wagnerians remained impervious to this movement, believing it beneath their dignity to keep track of the number of new productions. In retrospect, Dujardin insisted his efforts had formed a link between Wagner and Mallarmé, Schopenhauer and symbolism. The list of Wagner works presented at the

Opéra increased dramatically after 1890 and Wagnerism no longer remained the exclusive domain of a cult group.

The saga of Lamoureux and *Lohengrin* paralleled and exceeded the life span of the *Revue wagnérienne*. First, in 1885, Lamoureux's counterpart at the Opéra-Comique, Léon Carvalho, a Sephardic Jew, attempted to stage *Lohengrin* there. He went to Vienna and Munich, immersing himself in the local Wagneriana, engaged the eminent Wagnerian conductor Hermann Levi, son of the Rabbi from Giessen, to conduct rehearsals, and instructed Charles Nuitter to redo the translation. Again the press intervened and the project failed. The following year Lamoureux signed another contract for the Eden Theater, engaging it from 15 April to 1 June 1887. In the interim a parody of *Lohengrin* entitled *Lohengrin à l'Alcazar* had made it to the stage and a new journal, the *Revue indépendante*, boasting the same contributors as the *Revue wagnérienne*, made its appearance. Adolphe Jullien published his magnificent book *Richard Wagner, sa vie et ses oeuvres*, with fourteen lithographs by Fantin-Latour, thus beginning the run of Wagner-inspired paintings by Jean Delville, Gaston Bussière, Jacques Wagrez, Henri de Groux, Odilon Redon, and others, and Catulle Mendès completed the first full-length biography (1886) of Wagner in France. A performance of *Die Walküre* in Victor Wilder's French translation took place in Brussels the following year, with Chabrier, Delibes, Massenet, Messager, Reyer, and others making the trip to hear it. Saint-Saëns continued his anti-Wagner campaign, but the German composer's staunch defenders included composers Edouard Lalo, Paladilhe, Delibes, d'Indy, and Gounod, who stated that "intelligence should not be equated with feelings of the heart, and the insults of our national enemy are as nothing compared to the homage his works deserve."

In 1891, Lamoureux finally gave the premiere of *Lohengrin* at the Opéra and then traveled to Russia, leaving his son-in-law, Camille Chevillard, to conduct the concerts. The latter remained at the helm until 1898, when the musicians reconstituted the group as a society with Lamoureux as their leader. Lamoureux conducted next in London and worked seriously on a project dear to his heart: the complete *Tristan und Isolde*. A performance of the opera took place on 28 October 1899 at the Nouveau Théâtre. Lamoureux died two months later, unable to realize his grand scheme of a theater in Paris devoted exclusively to Wagner's operas. A concert performance of this *Tristan*, on one of Lamoureux's Sunday concerts in 1896, made a tremendous impression on two young musicians, the French composer Maurice Ravel and the Catalan pianist Ricardo Viñes. Viñes wrote in his journal:

> Ravel came and picked me up to go with him to the afternoon Concerts Lamoureux. [We heard] a young woman, Alba Chrétien, whom we enjoyed very much. She sang an aria from *Oberon* [Weber's opera] and Isolde's *Liebestod*. Before that they played the Prelude to *Tristan*. Just at the moment that I felt terribly moved—nothing ever created is as sublime and divine as this superb Prelude—at that moment Ravel touched my hand, saying: "It's always this way, each time I hear it." . . . and actually, he who appears so cold and cynical, he, Ravel, the super eccentric decadent, Ravel trembled convulsively and cried like a baby, intensely, with sobs escaping from him. Until now, despite the high opinion I have had for Ravel's intelligence, constantly reaffirmed by everything he undertakes, I believed he had a slight prejudice [a feeling for what was] fashionable in his literary opinions and tastes. But since this afternoon, I see that this boy was born with [certain] inclinations, tastes, and opinions, and when he expresses them, he doesn't do it snobbishly, to follow fashion, but because he truly feels these things. I hereby take the opportunity to say that Ravel is [one of] the most unhappy human beings, misunderstood, because he appears [to be] ordinary, a failure, and in reality he is an intellectual, a superior artist, a poor soul, an outcast deserving of a marvelous fate. It is furthermore very complicated. There is in him a mélange of Catholicism of the Middle Ages along with an impious satanic quality, but also the love of art and of beauty that guides him and makes him feel very candidly, as he demonstrated this afternoon by crying while listening to the Prelude from *Tristan und Isolde*. Me, too, this Prelude produced the same effect on me; only I cry inside, which is perhaps even more intense than crying externally. But I'm so used to that already. And I declare that the Prelude to *Tristan* is the most splendid, superhuman, marvelous, colossal, tender, sumptuous, religious, ideal, sublime, ethereal, passionate, celestial, seraphic, immense [work], replete with God, with the heavens, with a spaciousness, a grandeur, eternity, and love that has ever existed since heaven is heaven, since the few choice planets have turned on their axes, and that ever existed into the eternity of coming centuries. I consider together the Prelude and the Liebestod that completes it and deifies it, as death deifies all, and love even more, and love beyond death, the union that compensates the sorrows suffered through love and the surrender of consent. O Wagner, O Leonardo da Vinci! O Edgar Poe! O Baudelaire! O Gustavo Adolfo Becquer! O . . . but Wagner contains them all and this endless, endless, endless death of Isolde with the infinity of the Prelude. O this Prelude, Ariel! Balaam! and all those who can't speak for a lack of adequate words![68]

The campaign against Wagner continued; but, at the same time, the number of his partisans increased. A practitioner of mysticism and the occult, Sâr Péladan, went to Bayreuth in 1888. In 1890 he published *Théâtre complète de Wagner*, an analysis of each scene of each opera. His lyric prose appeared with the title *La Queste du Graal*. In *Les Secrets du Troubadour de Parsifal à Don Quichotte* he claimed that Quixote was a resurrected Parsifal. The writers Marcel Proust, Gabriele D'Annunzio, George Moore, and Emile Baumann all seem to have succumbed to Wagner's influence. And historian Gabriel Monod was so impressed with Bayreuth that on his return he expressed regret that their knowledge of *Eine Capitulation* prevented the French public from full enjoyment of the Bayreuth experience.

During the First World War, the French banned German music, perhaps as a result of Saint-Saëns's series of articles entitled "Germanophilie" in *l'Echo de Paris*. He urged French musicians to seek a return to French music unadulterated by Wagnerism—echoing the *ars gallica* movement of 1870. Critic and composer Jean Poueigh posed the question in *La Renaissance*: "Must we play Wagner after the war?" Those who responded positively included Sâr Péladan, Vincent d'Indy, Adolph Jullien, and Jacques Rouche. During the war, Franz Stassen published an illustrated postcard with a picture of a militaristic Siegfried, hero of the *Ring*, instead of the customary romantic one. Many later stated that this view prefigured the Siegfried of the Nazis.

In the *Bayreuther Blätter* of 1886, Louis de Fourcaud reminded Frenchmen that Wagner told them not to imitate him, but to cultivate their own national genius.[69] Unfortunately, few followed Wagner's advice. By 1900, as more of his operas were performed—the complete works and not just fragments in concert—a strong anti-Wagner reaction set in. In 1902, the premiere of *Pelléas et Mélisande* marked the beginning of the liberation of French theater from *le wagnérisme*. Nevertheless, French writers kept him on a pedestal.

As late as 1923, forty years after his death, André Suarès wrote, "Wagner was the greatest artist of his time, the Titan of art, of music, in France as in Europe as a whole. And he is *responsible for the musical resurrection of France* (my italics). By marrying the symphony to drama, he gave music back to France. He made good music universal for the first time. There had been court music (Monteverdi, Lully, Rameau, Gluck, and even Mozart), church music, bourgeois music (created by the Revolution), and popular music. A common

58

thread existed only in church music. But that made good music synonymous with religion!"[70]

In France, as in Germany, Wagner's reputation underwent radical shifts. From 1850 to 1875 he was considered a charlatan, while from 1875 to 1900 he became a god. His failures in Paris were spectacular; and therefore his hostility, even his public hostility to the French, was understandable. Only after the First World War did the critics view his accomplishments in a more judicious manner. It was not Beethoven who made Wagner comprehensible to Paris, it was the comprehension of Wagner that opened France to Beethoven and to Bach. Because of Wagner, music took the place in the taste and minds of men that hitherto had been reserved exclusively for poetry.[71] Yet to Wagner himself, success in Paris represented his most cherished dream, despite his misgivings about the French. All the same, nobody would have been happier than the slight-figured German composer to learn of the enormous shadow he cast over French culture so soon after his death.

3

Le Japonisme et l'Orientalisme

When United States Commodore Matthew Perry sailed into Japanese waters in 1853, opening the country to trade with the West, Japanese art and artifacts were almost unknown in Europe and America. Within ten years, the situation had changed so radically that Japanese art had become one of the principal points of departure not only for the Impressionists, but also for several peripheral groups of artists as well. Japanese woodcuts inspired Monet, Whistler, Degas, Henri Fantin-Latour, Odilon Redon, Félix Valloton, James Tissot, Henri Rivière—and also Manet and Van Gogh, although these two did not themselves produce much in the way of woodcuts. The swift acceptance and popularity of this art of the East stemmed from the efforts of a small group of devotees, some of whom had read of the treasures of Japan while others had stumbled upon Japanese artifacts and become enamored of them.

Two specific circumstances lent support to the movement: the opening of several shops in Paris—particularly the Boutique de Soye

(La Porte Chinoise) at 220 Rue de Rivoli in 1862—devoted to artistic and commercial products from Japan,[1] and the series of Universal Expositions at which various countries displayed their wares in Paris from 1867 through 1900. Dealers offered Japanese prints, illustrated books, bronzes, lacquer goods, fans, vases and other porcelains. For the 1867 Exposition, although Japan had undergone a major political crisis that very year—the fall of the shogunate—the country rented a pavilion and gave Frenchmen an opportunity to see their first formal exhibition of oriental art. By this time, admirers of Japanese art constituted a sizeable population; the more knowledgeable among them considered themselves experts. When the Exposition closed, the hundred-odd prints that portrayed Japanese life to Parisians were quickly sold and the vogue for *le japonisme* commenced in earnest.

Today, historians lament that by the time woodcuts became popular in the West, they had suffered a decline in quality to the point where later prints could not hold their own with the earlier ones. The leading print designers of the 1860s, Kuniteru, Sadahide, Hiroshige III, and Kunisada II represented the last and weakest generation of printmakers. In 1856, the etcher Félix Bracquemond found a volume of Hokusai's *Manga* (sketches) at Delâtre, his printer, who refused to part with the copy.[2] Later, Bracquemond acquired another copy from his printmaker and shared his bounty with his friends, Philippe Burty, Zacharie Astruc, and Manet. The French edition (1860) of Laurence Oliphant's *Narrative of the Earl of Elgin's Mission to China and Japan* (London 1859) included reproductions of prints by Toyokuni, Hiroshige I, and Hiroshige II. The Baron de Chassiron's *Notes sur le Japon, la Chine et l'Inde* (1861) featured facsimile designs from Hokusai's *Manga*. The Goncourts mentioned Japanese prints in their journal on 8 June 1861 and Baudelaire wrote in a letter: "Quite a while ago I received a packet of *japoneries*. I've split them up among my friends."[3]

Edmond de Goncourt established Hokusai's reputation in France through *Hokusai*, his book on the artist, in 1896. Goncourt wrote intelligently about the prints and thus enhanced French understanding of these designs. For example, in his description of Hokusai's famous picture of *The Wave*, which Debussy would later use as the cover for his orchestral tone poem *La Mer*, Goncourt wrote that "it was made by a painter who lived in a religious terror of the overwhelming sea surrounding his country on all sides; it is a design which is impressive by the sudden anger of its leap into the sky, by the deep blue of the transparent inner side of its curve, by the splitting of its crest which is thus shattered into a shower of tiny drops having the shape of animals' claws."[4]

The entry made in Goncourt's famous journal on Monday, 28 December 1886, says, "At this evening's gathering of Japanese enthusiasts at Bing's, Hayashi shows us a series of fifty-seven compositions by Hokusai executed for his *One Hundred Poems*, fifty-seven sketches that have not been included in the well-known series. According to Hayashi, these drawings were bought by an Englishman for 25,000 francs."[5] Two years later, on Friday, 25 May, Goncourt mentions that he would like to write a book on Japanese art of the sort he had published on eighteenth-century art, "one which would be less documentary than the latter, one going further in a penetrating and revelatory description of things. This book would be made up of four studies: one on Hokusai, the modern renewer of ancient Japanese art; one on Utamaro, their Watteau; one on Korin and another on Ritsono, two celebrated painters and lacquerists."[6]

Ten years after his discovery of the *Manga*, Bracquemond designed a table service with motives from Hokusai and Hiroshige, probably used at dinner meetings of a group he had organized known as the Club Jinglar, where chopsticks appeared instead of Western cutlery.[7] As early as 1868, the Goncourts, always sure of their taste, could flaunt their superior knowledge of Japanese objects. After all, a year before, they had jointly published a novel, *Manette Salomon*, where a chapter offers a description of *le japonisme* surrounding the hero in his apartment. The year of the Exposition, 1867, found Zacharie Astruc writing a series, "L'Empire du Soleil Levant" for the newspaper *L'Etendard*; Manet painted Emile Zola's portrait (1868) in which a Japanese print appears beside a sketch for his painting *Olympia* and a year later Ernest Chesneau published the pamphlet *L'Art japonais*. In his book *L'Art français* (1872), Jules Claretie of the Comédie-Française became one of the first to describe the movement as *le japonisme*.

After a major exhibition of art from Japan, China, India, and Java at the Palais d'Industrie (1873) and another Exposition Universelle (1878), *le japonisme* became part of the French cultural milieu. In the 1880s, the movement peaked. Louis Gonse, director of the *Gazette des Beaux Arts*, published *L'Art japonais* (1883) in two lavish

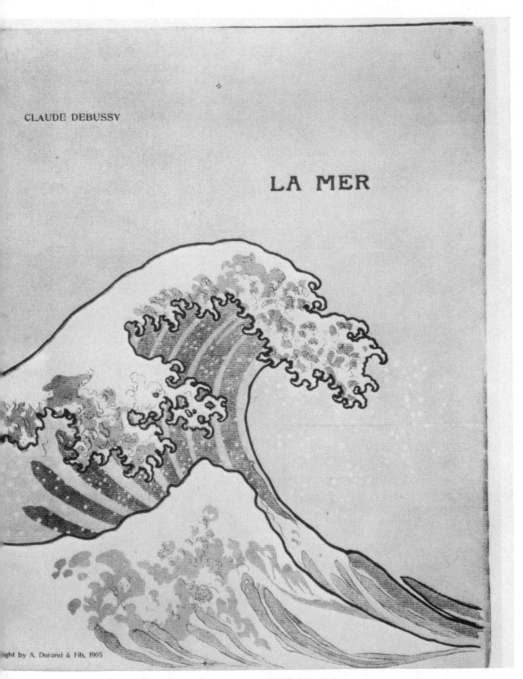

CLAUDE DEBUSSY

LA MER

Japanese art became one of the principal points of departure not only for the Impressionists, but for other artists as well. Edmond de Goncourt had established Hokusai's reputation in France. Debussy would later use The Wave *as the cover for his orchestral tone poem,* La Mer.

In addition to an interest in music from Japan itself, French composers found inspiration in subjects and themes popular in Japanese art and music. *Ravel's* Histoires Naturelles *was, like many Japanese works, influenced by the natural world.*

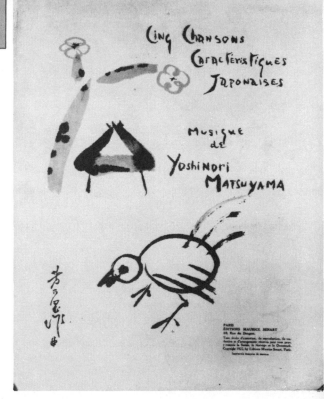

volumes and the Georges Petit Galleries exhibited three thousand pieces of Japanese art, including prints from private collections. Siegfried Bing, a German dealer, went to Japan in 1875, and returned to Paris, opening a shop in 1877 at 22 Rue de Provence, where he hosted monthly meetings of the *japonistes*.[8] Theo Van Gogh and his brother Vincent organized an exhibition of Japanese woodcuts at the Café Le Tambourin (1887). Referring to Japanese art, Vincent wrote his sister, "By strengthening all colors, one obtains ... something similar to Wagner's music. . . ."[9] Pierre Loti wrote a novel *Madame Chrysanthème* (1888), an account of a sailor's stay in Japan and in 1891 Edmond de Goncourt completed *Outamaro, Le Peintre des Maisons Vertes*, the first volume in his intended series on Japanese art history. (That same year the American Mary Cassatt prepared a set of ten color aquatints in imitation of Japanese woodcuts.)

At this point, with French interest in Japanese objects at its height, the Japanese expert in Paris, Tadamassa Hayashi, and S. Bing were selling fans, parasols, combs, and textiles. Their objets d'art triggered a new movement: *art nouveau*, similar in its way to William Morris's craft movement in Britain. Jewelry, glass, and ceramics of Lalique, Gallé, and Chapelet owed their inspiration to *le japonisme*. *Ukiyo-e*, a term often used to describe the floating world of Japanese art, led to Toulouse-Lautrec's illustrations of the world of entertainment: theaters and cafés, picnics and boating parties, busy street scenes. Curiously, Baudelaire and another literary figure, Champfleury, along with painters Fantin-Latour and Valloton—all four eminent Wagnerites—became promoters of Japanese art in France.[10]

Much has been written about the impact of *le japonisme* on fine art, even on literature, but few have commented on its influence on music and musicians. The 1889 Exposition stimulated Debussy's interest in the decorative arts of the Orient. Indeed, his preoccupation with the covers of his musical publications also reflect his affinity with the *art nouveau* movement. For example, his cantata *La Damoiselle élue* (1887–88) features a typical *art nouveau* illustration by Maurice Denis; the score itself connotes a visual perception of the music. For the *Cinq Poèmes de Baudelaire* (1887–89), from the poet's *Fleurs du mal* (1857), Debussy used different types of oriental art papers. (His friends Ernest Chausson and Etienne Dupin underwrote the expensive publication.) Debussy seems to have appreciated Swinburne, whose poem *Nocturne* described the sea. Indeed, many artists at the end of the century conceived of the sea as a mother figure.

At the first concert devoted entirely to Debussy's compositions, given at Brussels's Libre Esthétique, the main center of the avant-garde movement at the time, the gallery displayed paintings, buckles, and bracelets designed by artists of the group. Debussy's preference for the term "arabesque" for one of his early works and the floral imagery (*De Fleurs*) in his *Proses Lyriques* (1892–93) demonstrate again his connection to *art nouveau*, a derivative of *le japonisme*.

Edward Lockspeiser, speaking of the Japanese artists Hokusai and Hiroshige, mentions that their interest in landscapes, seascapes, and the effects of light appealed to French painters. Hiroshige, for example, depicted falling rain in a manner that influenced French artists, among them Pissarro.[11] Debussy learned of Hokusai's art through his friendship with the sculptress Camille Claudel, who apparently owned a number of Japanese objects. Léon Vallas says that all fellow students at the Villa Medici—which Debussy attended after he had won the Prix de Rome—remembered his love for Japanese objets d'art. "He couldn't refrain from buying more than his resources permitted." In later compositions, he transposed into music impressions produced on him by some Japanese works. *Poissons d'or* of 1907 was inspired by contemplation of a piece of lacquer in his possession. In Debussy's correspondence with Pierre Louÿs the subject of *le japonisme* occurs frequently.[12]

Debussy's close friend Pierre Loti included in his trilogy, not only *Madame Chrysanthème*, a forerunner of Belasco's *Madame Butterfly*, but also *Japoneries d'Automne* (1889) and *La Troisième Jeunesse de Madame Prune* (1905). Later, Stravinsky, a composer whose music reveals a distinct affinity to Debussy's, wrote *Three Japanese Lyrics* (1913): "Akahito," dedicated to Maurice Delage; "Mazatsumi," dedicated to Florent Schmitt; and "Tsaraiuki," dedicated to Maurice Ravel. All three dedicatees themselves composed music that demonstrated an interest in *l'orientalisme*. Delage composed seven Haiku based on Japanese lyrics; Schmitt wrote a film score for Flaubert's *Salammbô* as well as three songs, *Kerob-Shal*, for voice and orchestra, and a symphonic poem from the *Ramayana* entitled *Combat des Raksasas et délivrance de Sîta*. Ravel's beautiful *Shéhérazade* and his *Chansons madécasses* are but two of his "oriental" works.

The taste for orientalia emerged early in France with Molière, who included a ballet of Egyptians in the second act of his *Le Malade imaginaire* (1673). A scene from *Le Bourgeois gentilhomme* (1670) calls for turbaned gentlemen, Moors, and dervishes, and the chorus repeats a Moslem refrain, "Allahou akbar," two Arab words that signify "Allah is the greatest." Félicien David's *Le Désert* and Henri Rabaud's *Marouf*, two centuries later, both borrowed the same refrain. Grétry's *Caravan du Caire*, too, owed much of its success to its oriental costumes and sets. Does any of this music represent the genuine article? Absolutely not. At the time these works were written, composers knew nothing of authentic oriental music; not one work had appeared in France pertaining to this kind of music. Musicians provided Eastern color with sets and costumes, but the music itself remained Western.

In the summer of 1912, Stravinsky read an anthology of Japanese lyrics, some of them Haiku. He wrote: "The impression they made on me was exactly that made by Japanese paintings and engravings. The graphic solution of problems of perspective and space shown by their art incited me to find something analogous in music. . . ."[13] For these pieces he chose three short Japanese lyrics about the arrival of spring. (A fourth *mélodie japonaise* is mentioned by Ravel in a letter written on 2 April 1913 to Madame Hélène Casella, but nothing is known about it.)

Japanese artists' favorite subjects included animals, fish, birds, insects, seascapes, and weather changes. These subjects often influenced Debussy in his choice of titles: the tone poem *Nuages*, the collection *Estampes* that includes *Pagodes* and *Jardins sous la pluie*, the aforementioned *Poissons d'or* and *En bateau*. Ravel's *Oiseaux tristes*, *Une Barque sur l'océan* and his song cycle *Histoires naturelles* (with a cover designed by Toulouse-Lautrec) derive their titles or subject matter from the stimulus of Japanese art.

In 1871, Saint-Saëns found his ideal librettist, Louis Gallet, who had already collaborated on operas with Bizet, Massenet, and Gounod. They were both thirty-six and practically neighbors in the Faubourg St. Honoré. Because of the vogue for Japanese art, they decided on a Japanese topic for their first work together, *La Princesse jaune* (from Maeterlinck's play), which predates *The Mikado* by thirteen years. In his biography of Saint-Saëns, James Harding describes the work as an amusing brand of Parisian exoticism. "*La Princesse jaune*," he says, "tells how the hero Kornélis comes under the influence of a drug and imagines himself in the land of 'silver dragons, walls of lapis lazuli, jade goblets and scented wines.' He falls in love with a

Japanese figurine and has visions of his yellow princess, only to awaken from his hallucination and find himself at the feet of the girl whom he loves in real life." Harding concludes, "If one can visualize Sullivan rewritten by a Frenchman endowed with an equally light touch, then he has some idea of the effect which is created."[14] (Saint-Saëns rarely missed an opportunity when in London to visit the current Savoy opera.) The premiere of *La Princesse jaune* at the Opéra-Comique in 1872 was not successful; twenty years later Messager's operetta based on Loti's novel *Madame Chrysanthème* fared much better.

There is a long history of European fascination with the Orient. Professor Edward Said, the orientalist, regards the East as almost a European invention. Since antiquity it had been perceived as a place of romance, exotic beings, haunting memories and landscapes, and remarkable experiences. For Americans, China and Japan represent the Orient; among Europeans, the French and the British have the longest tradition of orientalism. From 1800 until the end of World War II, these two nations dominated the East; and since the War, Americans have appropriated their attitude toward the Orient. Early in the nineteenth century, Paris became the preeminent center of Sanskrit studies; a Frenchman first deciphered the Persian *Zend Avesta* (c. 500 B.C.), scripture of Zoroastrianism.

Understandably, the British and French pioneered in oriental studies; these nations ruled over the greatest colonial empires in pre-twentieth century history.[15] Germans showed an interest in orientalism in the eighteenth century, but no colonial settlements of the Germans corresponded to the Anglo-French presence in India, the Levant or North Africa. In Germany, the Orient became the subject of fantasy; in France, it gave rise to a series of travel books whose authors evinced a genuine involvement in the country. Friedrich Schlegel, for example, went to libraries for his information, while Chateaubriand, Lamartine, Nerval, Flaubert, and later Loti and Barrès actually traveled themselves to the Orient. The painter Delacroix, too, felt drawn to Africa, the source of many of his works. Flaubert equated the Orient with fecundity and sexual promise; other French authors also describe a sensuality they experienced while in the Orient. For the British, the Orient meant India; for the French it had a much wider range.

Unfortunately, some of the studies in the field of orientalism focused on race. (One can understand Gobineau's interest in the field,[16] but philologist Ernest Renan, too, worked in this area.) Chateaubriand's *Itinéraire de Paris à Jérusalem* (3 volumes, 1811), Hugo's *Orientales* (1829), Lamartine's *Souvenirs, Impressions, Pensées et Paysages pendant un voyage en Orient* (1835) and Nerval's seven-hundred-page *Voyage en Orient* (1851) contributed to the exposure of French intellectuals to Orientalism. Musicians responded to the movement in a variety of ways. From Massenet and Debussy to Darius Milhaud and Albert Roussel and Léo Delibes and Verdi, composers borrowed oriental themes and titles for their pieces. Less evident is their use of actual non-Western melodies, for a number of reasons. First, many of them—those who wrote orientally-inspired music—only fantasized about the East; they did not go there, and even if they did, they did not notate the music they heard. One of the difficulties of Western musical notation with regard to Eastern melody concerns the use in the East of quarter tones and other notes of differing pitches—those which fall between the cracks on the piano keyboard. Rhythmic patterns, even exceedingly complex ones, lent themselves more readily to notation and thus to imitation. Harmony does not play a role in the East; melody and rhythm became their most important musical elements.

Debussy's magnificent *Chansons de Bilitis* (1897), to a text by Pierre Louÿs, his "Canope" from the *Préludes I* (1910–13), and "Pour l'Egyptienne" from *Six Epigraphes* (1915) bear the imprint of the Orient. Canope or Canopus, a city of ancient Egypt on the Nile river, provided the name given to earthen urns, four of which, containing the principal digestive organs of a deceased person, were buried with the mummy. A model of the head of Osiris, Egyptian lord of the Underworld and symbol of resurrection, one of the foremost Egyptian deities, formed the cover of each of the jars.[17] While Debussy does not expect his music to describe the urns, he does evoke a special mood in this Prelude. He writes parallel chords and succeeds in suggesting a modal rather than a tonal sonority. A unison statement of the melody sounds almost like a recitative. Dukas, too, succumbed to orientalism; he left incomplete a Hindu drama, *L'Arbre de Science* (c. 1905). After the arrival in Paris of the Ballets Russes, in 1909, orientalism became the rage. Ravel paid his respects to the movement early, with his *Shéhérazade* Overture (unpublished) from 1898, his *Shéhérazade* song cycle (1903) and his sensuous *Chansons madécasses* (1925–26). Roussel's opera-ballet *Padmâvatî* (1914–18) and his six *Poèmes chinois*, written between 1907 and 1932 (Opp. 12, 35 and 47), demonstrate this composer's involvement with orientalism. Florent Schmitt's *Salammbô* (1925) and Roland-Manuel's symphonic poem *Le Harem de vice-roi* (1919) reveal the continuation of the trend into the 1920s. The poems of Rabindranath Tagore inspired songs by Henri Sauguet and Milhaud. Fauré set an oriental poem, *Les Roses d'Ispahan* (1884), of another French Wagnerite, Leconte de Lisle; Saint-Saëns's *Orient et Occidente Marche* (1869), his *Mélodies persanes* (1870), his *Suite algérienne* (1879), and his *Africa Fantasy for Piano and Orchestra* (1891) fall into the category of Orient-inspired pieces. (For the French, the Near East and North Africa as well as the Far East, Russia and Spain, implied the Orient.) Massenet's opera *Cléopâtre* (1915) and d'Indy's *Istar Variations*, along with numerous ballets of Diaghilev's Ballets Russes sought their effects through orientalism.

In 1905–06, the *Revue musicale* carried two articles entitled "Notes sur la danse et la musique orientale;" in 1912, Robert Chauvelot's "Choses d'Asie: De quelques musiques et danses de l'extrême-orient" appeared in the same journal. In 1915, in a book of twelve *causeries*, Victor Loret accounted for "L'Orientalisme dans la musique française." (Much of the material included in this chapter derives from his commentary.)[18] In 1926 Mohammed Hajjage wrote "Sur la musique orientale," also for the *Revue musicale*. These articles indicate that at least some music historians recognized the importance of the oriental influence.

Except for the appearance of whole-tone and pentatonic scales, the music itself remained anchored in the West. The whole-tone scale was first heard in Western music in pieces by the Russians, Borodin, Dargomizhsky, and Mussorgsky. They had sought fresh melodic inspiration in folk music and also in the chants of the Russian Orthodox Church. It is important to remember that unlike the other fine arts, music cannot overtly interpret or explain the titles or extra-musical meanings that composers attach to their pieces. The best a composer can do is affix his title and try through his music to evoke the sensations he implies. The listener must also use his imagination to conjure up some of the images suggested.

If the music is not genuine Eastern music and the title requires the contributions of the listeners, what exactly prompted the trend towards orientalism in music? And what precisely did this movement produce?

Genuine oriental music rarely penetrated the music of Western composers. Musicians did, however, use descriptive titles and occasionally rhythmic and melodic figures suggestive of the East in both instrumental and operatic works. A real feeling for Orientalism began in France in 1829 and coincides with the advent of the romantic movement. The publication of Hugo's *Orientales*, a collection of lyrics based on Oriental themes, conveyed his conception of the East: its heat, its languor, and its underlying savagery. These lyrics incorporated bold imagery, striking rhythmic effects achieved through sound and coloring new to French verse. In his Preface to *Orientales*, Hugo wrote:

> In the time of Louis XIV, we were Hellenistic; today we're Orientalists. We're now in a position to know the entire Orient, from China to Egypt. The result is that the Orient, its thought and image, have become sort of a preoccupation to which I unconsciously submitted. Oriental colors are imprinted in our dreams. Hebrew, Turkish, Greek, Persian, Arabic, Spanish—for Spain is still the Orient, it's half African and Africa is half-asiatic—inhabit our thoughts.

Bizet set the *Adieux de l'hôtesse arabe* (1828) from Hugo's *Orientales*, and in 1832, Alfred de Musset published *Namouna*, which later provided the libretto for Bizet's *Djamileh* (1872).[19] The same year Lamartine visited the Orient, acquiring material for his books; and the next year, 1833, Félicien David, the first of the musician/orientalists, undertook voyages that led him to Egypt and across to the Red Sea.[20]

Most of those who borrowed themes from the Orient never explained why they did so. Hugo simply called it "fashionable in our time," but Loret cited specific reasons for the phenomenon. He said that it began in the years 1821 to 1830 when many Frenchmen sided with the Greeks in their struggle against the Turks. In 1830, with their conquest of Algiers, the French began their occupation of Algeria, and Egypt, too, stood revealed to French intellectuals, particularly after Champollion had deciphered the hieroglyphics of the Rosetta Stone. Interest in the East magnified after Napoleon's African campaign. Several intellectuals who accompanied him prepared a *Description de l'Egypte* which appeared in two publications, one in 1821–28 and the other in 1821–29. These papers offered a rich source of documents relating not only to ancient and modern Egypt, but also to a large part of the Far East.

The most passionate scholar was Villoteau, an Arabist and musician.[21] Intrigued not only by the Arabian music of Egypt but also by the Egyptian music of ancient times, he spent several years traveling along the banks of the Nile assembling his materials. Whenever he heard vocalists or ensembles he notated both words and music. He spoke fluent Arabic, and would question the singers and interrogate the musicians about how they tuned and played their instruments. In addition, he unearthed and translated Arabic manuscripts, consulting native musicians when he encountered problems.

A number of musicians in nineteenth-century France studied the *Description*; Félicien David, it was said, was carried away by his reading of it. There were special reasons, however, for his response. Attracted from his youth to the doctrines of Saint-Simon, the socialist philosopher—who incidentally came to America and fought against the British during the Revolutionary War—David followed Père Enfantin, one of the founders of the movement in France, when the latter left to preach in Egypt. David should have absorbed something from Egyptian melodies, but his so-called *Mélodies orientales* reveal few genuine oriental strains. If not for his masterpiece in this genre, *Le Désert*, a symphonic ode he wrote in three months, one might suspect that he spent his time in Egypt preaching or practicing Saint-Simonism rather than investigating the local music.

Le Désert received its first performance in 1844 and was a tremendous success. It describes a caravan that calmly crosses the desert until a scorching wind bursts furiously from the Midi. Men and camels take cover and call on the mercy of Allah. The danger passes, the cortege continues and toward evening its members stop and set up tents. Enchanted by the beauty of the city, an Arab sings a hymn to the night. Dancing girls perform. A young woman remains apart, dreaming of her beloved. At dawn the caravan continues. Of the various numbers of the score, the most oriental is the "Hymn to the Night." (Composer Charles Bordes thought it the most exquisite "inspiration" of French music.) The chants of the muezzin also merit attention. Unlike in the West, where bells call the faithful to prayers, in the Orient the muezzins ascend the minarets and chant the time for prayers, filling the air with their song, particularly at evening. In 1862 David wrote another opera seemingly based on oriental themes, *Lalla Roukh*, but it did not offer as close an approximation of Arab music as did *Le Désert*. Whereas nothing in the music contains specifically Egyptian melodies, *Le Désert* seems to evoke musical impressions heard on the Nile.

The French continued to use the term *orientale* to apply not only to the music of the Far East, but also to the music of India, the Near East, Persia, Turkey, Arabia, Libya, Tunisia, Algeria and Morocco. The seven-hundred-year stay of the Arabs in Spain and the proximity of Russia to Turkey and Persia help to explain the various "oriental" pieces that originated wtih composers in both of these countries.

Because the Arabs had been among the earliest mathematicians and acousticians, they studied music from the point of view of acoustics. Many of their early treatises demonstrate their sophistication. Their use of quarter and third tones makes their scale comprise more than our twelve-tones, and the *ud*, or lute, is the instrument they have selected for precise tunings. While they do not use harmony, their incredibly varied rhythmic patterns and their richly ornamented melodies, many of which utilize the notes between the white notes on our keyboards, enrich their music considerably. Most oriental music seems to contain a mélange of joy and sadness. Victor Loret recalled a story from his years spent in Egypt. "At dinners" he said, "in ancient times Egyptians placed a mummy in the middle of the table after a delightful repast to remind guests that joy is not eternal. In the middle of love songs, one hears funeral laments on the sad life one leads in the netherworld." Frenchmen commented on the resigned smiles on the face of the Sphinx. "Even in their beautiful country," Loret continued, "Egyptians don't stop thinking of death. The fragility of happiness is always present."

Charles Bordes insisted that the music of César Franck, Ernest Reyer, and Georges Bizet revealed the influence of David. Reyer had lived in Algeria for eight years (1839–47), from the age of sixteen to twenty-four. In 1850 he composed an oriental symphony in four parts that included a song entitled "Selam." Théophile Gautier wrote the poem; the piece includes a "Chant du soir" (as in *Le Désert*), a "Marche des derviches," an incantation of *djinns* (spirits), a scene with a raid, and other items that gave the composer justification for using Arabic music. He even has the customary "March of the Caravan." His own experiences in North Africa seem not to have left their mark on his music, except for the evocative titles he chose. (Another opera, *La Statue* (1861), has an oriental theme, but no authentic music.)

Bizet, on the other hand, never visited the Orient, but had a natural instinct for the character, particularly the rhythms, of Arabic music. While in Rome on a scholarship in 1860, at twenty-two, he composed an opera, *Guzla de l'Emir*, an unpublished piece which shows his early predilection for the Orient. His opera *Djamileh* (1872), based on Musset's *Namouna*, probably represents the best of the works inspired by David's *Le Désert*. Bizet's love of the Orient moved him to write *L'Arlésienne Suite* (1872) and *Carmen* (1873–74). (As Hugo stated so definitively: Spain is still the Orient.)

Berlioz in *L'Enfance du Christ* (1850–54) wrote a trio, an oriental dance played by a harp and two flutes, the instruments he believed best conjured up the East; Massenet's *Hérodiade* (1881) includes a "Danse galliléenne" with an oriental flavor in its accompaniment; Saint-Saëns evoked the ancient Orient in his "Bacchanale" in *Samson et Dalila* (1877). At first, he composed as an instinctive orientalist, but Saint-Saëns later traveled to the Orient, the Canaries, Algiers, Tunis, and Egypt, notating the melodies he heard. (His *Mélodies persanes* [1870], composed before his voyages, shows his natural instinct for this style of music.) The *Africa Fantasy* and the *Suite algérienne*, particularly the "Rêverie du soir" from the last piece, resulted from his exposure to the East. Saint-Saëns was one of the first of a group of French musicians to write documented oriental music.

The Orient has been the source of countless ballets and operas as well as a considerable number of instrumental works in the genre the French call *la musique pure*. While Verdi's *Aida* is probably the most popular opera based on an exotic, Eastern subject, compositions by the French constitute a vast corpus that reflects the spirit of *l'exotisme*. To a libretto by L. de Pesquidoux, Paul Vidal, for example, wrote *Ramsès*, which had its premiere at the Théâtre Egyptien de l'Exposition Universelle on 27 June 1900. In Jean Nouguès's *Narkiss* (Paris 1914)[22], Pharaoh Narkiss, who is doomed if he sees his face, unfortunately looks in a pool and sees his reflection. He disappears under the water, then surfaces transformed into a lotus. His flower head is cut from its stalk by a mysterious woman sent by the Egyptian priests who want to do away with him.[23] In Debussy's pantomime ballet *Khamma*, which he wrote for Maud Allan, the lovely dancer Khamma touches the heart of the god Amon-Ra, who agrees finally to aid the people of war-threatened Egypt. The priests and the Egyptian people had not been successful in their appeals to the god; Khamma succeeded where they had failed. Cleopatra stars in Leroux's opera of that name in Paris in 1890. The composer based his work on the play by Victorien Sardou, author of the drama *Tosca*. Massenet, too, composed a *Cléopâtre* (Monte Carlo 1914), but it does not rate with his other oriental pieces, such as the opera *Hérodiade*. Victor Massé left an opera, *Une Nuit de Cléopâtre*, posthumously performed in Paris in 1885. And Ida Rubinstein made her dramatic Parisian debut with the Ballets Russes in Diaghilev's ballet of that name. Vincent d'Indy explores a Chaldean legend in his orchestral piece, *Istar* (Paris 1912), in which Dumuzu, the young sun god killed in the holy forest of Eridhu, goes to the Chaldean Hades, from which there is no return. His beloved, the goddess Istar, follows him there. At each of the seven gates of this Chaldean hell, the gate keeper relieves Istar of one of her veils. D'Indy begins these symphonic variations with the most complex, thickly textured of all the variations, but they grow simpler as they proceed. Finally, only the bare theme is left; it represents the nude goddess, deprived not only of her jewels, but also of her vestments.

Operas with biblical subjects from both the Old and the New Testament may properly be classified as oriental. Gounod's *La Reine de Saba* (Paris 1862), for example, preceded Saint-Saëns's celebrated *Samson et Dalila* (Weimar 1877). Other Eastern religions provided the source for musical compositions. Dukas decorated his lyrical poem, *La Péri* (Paris 1912) with an oriental leading motive that helps unify this ballet score. In this piece, Iskender, the king of Iran, feels his youth ebbing away, and searches his kingdom for the flower of immortality. At the border of his land, he finds an imposing stairway that leads to the home of Ormuzd, the source of all good things. Here he sees the sleeping Péri, dressed in her jeweled robes, with the lotus of immortality clasped in her hand. As he seizes it from her, it bursts into flames. Péri, awakening, cries out in despair for she has thus lost her godliness (echoes of Brunnhilde in *Die Walküre*!). Iskender desires her for himself; she tries to escape. He is torn between his physical need for her and his equally pressing desire to extend his life. Finally, as she desperately dances the "Dance of the Winged Ones," coming ever closer to the king until their faces practically meet, he yields the lotus to her. She disappears and all that is left of her is her hand, holding the lotus. Iskender, seeing her vanish, realizes that he, too, has come to the end of his life.

Hindu India inspired several French musicians. Bizet's *Les Pêcheurs de perles* (Paris 1863) relates a tale of Ceylonese passion in prehistoric times. The priestess Leila prays to Brahma that the divers will return with lustrous pearls, and tells Nadir that she loves him, not his comrade Zurga, the captain of the pearl fishers. The high priest Nourabad, however, explains to Leila that earthly love is not for her. He has hardly departed, when Nadir enters and the two sing of their mutual passion. Nourabad has overheard their declaration and returns to tear Leila's priestly veil from her head. Zurga realizes that this is the woman he and Nadir had agreed never to meet—in order to remain friends. Zurga condemns her to death, then has a change of heart. He sets their camp on fire and substitutes himself on the pyre for the guilty couple, thus allowing them to escape together, as the people prepare to honor the god Brahma.

From the Sanskrit epic poem the *Mahabharata*, the Hindu poet Kalidsa fashioned his story of Sakuntala. (Several German and Italian composers—Felix Weingartner, Wilhelm Kienzl, and Franco Alfano among them—set the tale in operas.) The French composer Ernest Reyer, however, based his ballet *Sacountala* on the story. The celebrated librettist Louis Gallet supplied the text of Massenet's opera *Le Roi de Lahore*. This tragic tale, too, derives from the *Mahabharata*.

To a libretto by Debussy's friend, Louis Laloy, Albert Roussel set his opera *Padmâvatî* (Paris 1923). This touching story of a wife's fidelity in thirteenth-century India has wonderfully full choruses, much lyricism, and certain resemblances to Berlioz's music. One of the highlights of the piece is the "Sacrifice Pantomime" in which the gods of the nether world mingle with humans who officiate at the ceremony. Alaouddin, Sultan of the Moguls, is a guest in the home of the Hindu King Ratan-Sen. He enjoys the dancing girls, but he covets Padmâvatî, Ratan-Sen's wife. If he cannot have her, his Moguls will destroy the city. His demand is not met, but Ratan-Sen, concerned for his people, bids his wife sacrifice herself for them. She refuses and kills her husband, preferring his death to her dishonor. Later she joins the king on his funeral pyre. Alaouddin enters the city but finds it in ashes.

Several other operas reveal evidence of oriental influence. Reynaldo Hahn's *Le Dieu bleu*, with a book by Cocteau and Madrazzo (Paris

1912), tells a story inspired by the temple ruins of Angkor in Cambodia. Krishna's "Scene with the Monsters" is exceptional in this piece. Léo Delibes's *Lakmé*, from which the "Bell Song" has become so popular, is still another sensuous "oriental" work. And even Stravinsky's *Le Rossignol* (Paris 1914) to a tale by Hans Christian Andersen exhibits pseudo-Mongolian traits. The list is legion.

Salvador Daniel, born around 1830, studied music at an Arab school in Algiers.[24] He learned Arabic and in 1863 compiled a volume entitled *Musique arabe*. This collection of local songs soon went out of print. Although not well known today, Daniel became the director of the Conservatoire after Auber's death in 1871, appointed by the Commune. He immediately proposed reforms, but his tenure lasted only two weeks—he was accidentally killed on the barricades. The Englishman Henry George Farmer translated Daniel's *Musique arabe* as *Music and Musical Instruments of the Arab with an Introduction on How to Appreciate Arab Music*, edited with notes, memoirs, a bibliography, and thirty examples. (Costallat then republished the work in Paris as *Chansons arabes, mauresques et kabyles*.)

Curiously, most musicians did not avail themselves of the opportunity to use the materials of those who had notated Arab music. The first to recall the Arabist Villoteau was Alfred Bruneau in a two-act opera *Kérim* (1887). He borrowed two airs of Villoteau that fitted beautifully into his work. Henri Rabaud's *Marouf, Savetier du Caire*, a five-act opera, premiered with much success in 1914, but its performances ceased when the war began. Rabaud drew the subject from the *Thousand and One Nights*.

The story of Marouf is so delightful that one wonders why it has not returned to the opera repertory in recent years. (The Metropolitan programmed it first in 1917 in an English translation.) Marouf is a poor cobbler, but a *bon vivant* who, because he's a Moslem, doesn't drink. He makes up for that, however, by eating for six. The most extraordinary things happen to him. He leaves his wife, an abominable shrew who makes his life intolerable, and sets sail for Damiette. Shipwrecked on an unknown island, he follows the advice of a friend he happens to meet there and announces that he is a rich merchant awaiting his caravan of goodies. He greatly impresses the local ruler, who offers him his daughter in marriage. She has fallen in love with Marouf and he, naturally, is delighted. But the Sultan grows impatient waiting for the caravan and decides to cut off the head of his son-in-law. The execution block is prepared, the crowd has gathered, when suddenly they hear an approaching caravan. It arrives sumptuously loaded. It seems that Marouf had once rendered a service to a genie, who now has decided to repay him. Raboud may not have visited Egypt, but his g sharp-minor ballet music sounds very oriental. The marching scene recalls the "voix de Paris" of Charpentier's *Louise* (1900); and the song of the mule driver, the cries of hawkers in the streets, and even the calls of the muezzin seem absolutely authentic, as if recorded from real life.

Oriental music produced by French musicians falls into two categories: some was composed with documentary evidence of Eastern music at hand (David's *Le Désert*, Saint-Saëns's *Suite algérienne*, Bruneau's *Kérim*, and Rabaud's *Marouf* fall into this category), and other music, like Bizet's *Djamileh*, where the oriental element seems to arise instinctually with the composer. Many Frenchmen know that had it not been for the victory of Charles Martel at Poitier over Abd-er-Rahman, France, like Spain might have been occupied by Arabs. In any event, Arabs remained in the Pyrenees for about twenty years, not long enough to have left an impact, but certainly long enough to have penetrated the consciousness of interested parties. Loret heard a local song in Perpignan that seemed (in Catalan dialect) oriental in origin; another source exists in a collection of songs of the Pyrenees by Pascal Lamazou entitled *Cinquante Chants pyrénéens*.

Russia also had orientalists in the nineteenth century: Mussorgsky, Tchaikovsky, and Borodin all wrote Spanish-flavored pieces. Debussy, Ravel, and Albéniz (whose name is Arabic) succumbed to Iberian influences: Debussy in several of his *Préludes* for piano and in his suite *Iberia*; Ravel in his *Rapsodie espagnole* and in his opera *L'Heure espagnole*. Lalo's *Symphonie espagnole*, a violin concerto, and Chabrier's *España* complete the list. Some people believe that the best Spanish music has been written by French composers.[25]

4

Music at the Great Expositions

Any number of reasons have been offered for the proliferation of universal expositions during the second half of the nineteenth century. President William McKinley suggested several of the best of them in his introduction to the official picture book of the Lewis and Clark Exposition in Portland, Oregon, in 1905. "Expositions are timekeepers of progress," he wrote. "They record the world's advancement; they stimulate the energy, enterprise and intellect of the people and [they] quicken human genius. They go into the home and broaden and brighten the lives of the people."[1] Each country had its own reasons for organizing these universal exhibitions, most of which lost money for the host country, despite acting as a magnet to tourists and natives who feasted on the displays for the months or weeks that the fair was in progress. Initially concerned with industrial trade and technological progress, these exhibitions, at least in the hands of the French, soon fostered the wares, the arts and crafts of the host country as well. Once fine arts began to play a role, entertainments, too, became a feature. The British, under the sponsorship of Victoria and Albert, presented the first large-scale exhibition in London's Crystal Palace in 1851. Flaubert described it as "a very fine thing, despite being admired by everyone."[2] Principally dealing with industry, the exhibits of manufactured products enabled viewers to compare the quality of goods issued by various nations.

Whereas no specific theme necessarily dominated the exhibitions, sometimes a behind-the-scenes rationale was a country's determination to prove its revitalization after a particular catastrophe. In 1878, for example, what better way than a fair for France to boast of her complete recovery from defeat in the Franco-Prussian War and the disasters of the Commune? An eyewitness description of Paris by an Italian writer, Edmondo de Amicis, who visited the city for the 1878 Exhibition captures the spectators' amazement. Entering the city from the Gare de Lyons in the East, he writes, "The first impression is an agreeable one. It is the large irregular square of the Bastille, noisy and crowded, into which open four boulevards and ten streets, and from which one hears the deafening clamor of the immense suburb of St. Antoine. . . . It is the first quick, deep whiff of Paris life."[3] Amicis proceeds along the Boulevard Beaumarchais and admires the wide streets, the double row of trees. He comments on the "passing and repassing of carriages, great carts and wagons drawn by engines and high omnibuses laden with people." He enters the Boulevard du Temple and notices that the street "grows broader and the side ones lengthen, and the houses rise higher. . . . The grandeur of Paris begins to appear: the theaters, the Cirque and Olympique, the Lyrique, the Gaîté and the Folies, the elegant cafés, the great shops, the fine restaurants and the crowd assumes a more thoroughly Parisian aspect."[4]

He continues along the Boulevard St. Martin and then the Boulevard St. Denis, and enters the Boulevard Poissonière. He finally reaches the heart of Paris as we know it today. "The Boulevard Montmartre," he writes, "is followed by those of Italiens, Capucines and Madeleine." He proceeds to elaborate further on details of the buildings, the foliage, the vistas, the people, the crush, indeed the pulse of Paris, and concludes with a plaintive recollection. "How absurd our miserable valises look in the midst of all this elegance!"[5]

* * *

Fast on the heels of the British exhibition of 1851 came the French fair of 1855. Delacroix reports on it in his journal, not too favorably, but with a degree of respect. A permanent exhibition hall, the Palais de l'Industrie, was constructed beside the Champs Elysées, and a Palais des Beaux-Arts to display fine arts—Sèvres porcelain, Gobelin tapestries, Savonneries carpets—was built on the Avenue Montaigne.[6] For the first time, the French charged admission: one franc every day except Sunday, when it cost five francs. The price was later reduced to two. (Fees, of course, were arranged to discourage the mobs on the days that the upper classes would want to attend.)[7] Considering that the British exhibits were all privately financed, while the French government paid for all of *their* exhibits, it is surprising that the French affixed prices on all the wares displayed, making some regard the whole exhibition as one grand bazaar. Then again, the mentality of the French, often described as "a nation of shopkeepers," prevailed even at the top. (After the Battle of Trafalgar, Napoleon derisively referred to the English with these words, but they seem more appropriate to the French.) The exhibition lost over 8 million francs.

The first exhibition with a theme was that of the international French Exposition Universelle of 1867. It also represented the first time that participating countries themselves paid for the buildings in which they displayed their products. Representatives of nearly all the royal families of Europe attended the opening, for which Rossini composed a *Hymn to the Emperor*. The focus of this world's fair was work, perhaps a better word is labor—*le travail*—the different kinds of work produced in countries throughout the world.[8] Each country's exhibit was intended to show its progress as it advanced through various stages of civilization until it had reached its current level. Because "work" could also refer to artistic production, the official committee agreed to accept paintings completed in the twelve years since the 1855 exhibit. Some were immediately rejected, including those by Pissarro, Cézanne, and Monet, who quietly accepted the verdict of the jury. Manet and Courbet, however, insisted on showing in their own galleries outside the fairgrounds.[9] The grounds themselves were a work of art.

Following the design of the central building, they were elliptical in shape, carefully planned by engineer/economist Frédéric le Play and his associate Jules Simon, both Saint-Simonians. Hydraulic lifts carried visitors from the ground floor to the roof, several floors above, from which they could enter the *promenoirs*, or platforms, that gave them optimum views of their surroundings. All manner of items went on display: workers' tools, surgical instruments (and artificial limbs from the United States!), textiles, furniture, military materials such as cannons and shells, petroleum, aluminum (for the first time anywhere), clothing and even some exotic musical instruments. On the periphery, exhibits of fresh and preserved foods of great ethnic variety tempted restaurateurs, and their customers in turn. While people ate, they were often serenaded or entertained by native Asiatic or Indian musicians. The Bateaux Mouches commenced their popular sightseeing trips along the riverside and Nadar, the famous Parisian photographer, took twelve tourists at a time up in his double-decker balloon to see the sights from the air.[10] To assist as well as to impress the expected multitude of visitors, the government engaged Victor Hugo to write the introduction to Lacroix's *Paris-Guide* to the fair.[11]

One of the most popular exhibits in 1867 was a large-scale model of the Suez Canal, complete with ships passing through it. Other exhibits that particularly fascinated the French were those from what they regarded as the exotic lands of the Near and Far East. The official government guidebooks highlighted materials and displays from India, China, Turkey, Persia, Russia, New Zealand, Australia, Egypt, Algeria, Tunisia, and Morocco. Western Europeans suddenly became aware of the cultures of other non-Western peoples. Closer to home, the exhibits of Spain and Portugal attracted the French who, at the time, regarded these neighbors to the West as "oriental," too.

Another surprising discovery was the enthusiasm of the Japanese. Their country had only recently been opened to the West, and they sought to promote their own products. When they returned to Japan, sixty-six technical engineers from their official delegation prepared a ninety-six-volume report on the fair. Orientalism, more specifically *le japonisme*, and exoticism moved into the foreground by the time of the 1867 Exposition Universelle. The government-sponsored *L'Exposition Universelle de 1867 illustrée*, in two volumes, yields some interesting information.[12]

Space in many of the government's monthly publications was given to Russian, Japanese, Turkish, and Egyptian exhibits. An article in Issue 17 (the monthly publication of the government) listed several musical instruments on display and described the details of their manufacture.

Issue 33 focused on Arab performances in the Théâtre International and offered illustrations of Arabian dances, while Issue 35 featured the Shah of Persia with exhibits of his nation. Pages 78–79 of the same issue described French industrial methods of manufacturing woodwind instruments. Evidently, a few military band performances included a new instrument, the saxophone, and its inventor, the Belgian Adolphe Sax, was on the scene.

The French were among the first to charge admission to their exhibits; in Issue 40, reported that a decrease to fifty centimes in the price of admission to the Exposition during the evening led to an increase in the number of visitors. The same issue carried an article on Russian luxuries such as caviar and sturgeon. Articles on Spain and Portugal citing a Moorish influence confirm again that the countries of the Iberian peninsula were regarded, certainly by the French, as exotic.

The government reports do not contain much information on music, aside from the description of instrument manufacture, but one self-appointed archivist at the Exposition Universelle of 1867 had a different story to tell. Oscar Comettant's remarkably detailed and copiously illustrated *La Musique, les Musiciens et les Instruments de Musique chez les différents peuples du monde* reveals that perhaps only a musician could fully appreciate the diversity of the musical scene. Comettant argues that the "considerable role music has played in the International Exposition of 1867 is without precedent in the history of the art." For too long, he complains, music was regarded as a charming recreational art, not serious enough to rank with painting, sculpture, literature, or architecture. The manufacture of instruments and the printing, engraving, publishing, and distribution of musical materials were commercial ventures of relative significance; but music *per se* did not count. Comettant maintains that the imperial commission for this 1867 Exposition took a different stance, and he determined that one observer, at least, should give a full account of the place of music at this exposition. Recognizing his own limitations, he nevertheless attempted the task himself.

Comettant's book is divided into four parts. In the first, he discusses the history of recent industrial expositions and the organization, particularly with reference to music, of the 1867 exhibition.[13]

He continues with a review of military music and fanfares, both foreign and native. The second part is devoted to musical performance: the activities of the newly organized *orphéons* or choral societies; the number of orchestral concerts given right on the premises of the fair; music in the parks, and music at the various pavilions—Hungarian, Chinese, Tunisian, and others.[14] In the third section he treats the pedagogical methods and notation of the different musical systems, the teaching tools, the printing and engraving of musical literature and, finally, the dissemination of music.

In the last part of the book he examines the various types of musical instruments—string, wind, brass, percussion, and keyboard.[15] He notes that he saw a wind instrument in New Caledonia that reminded him of one he had heard played in an amusing concert in New York. For those who like the sound of rattles, he recommended the *matacra* of the Mexicans. He mentions that the Japanese and the Siamese play several bizarre instruments, but that more unusual ones are in the possession of the redskins, for instance, the *raquette*, which produces a rhythm rather than a pitch. From reading *Voyages pittoresques dans les déserts du Nouveau-Monde*, he learned about the kinds of instruments favored by doctors, medicine men, and priests. The Indians prefer percussion instruments, especially effective on occasions when the group surrounded a palefaced prisoner.

Clarinets, guitars, and marimbas punctuate the music of Brazil. "Don't judge them," warned Comettant, "by what they showed in the 1867 Exhibition. Rio has four theaters, one for opera and another, a kind of café, where drinks are served during performances of Offenbach's operettas. Even Theresa Stolz [a prominent Verdi soprano] has sung in this city." More than 150,000 citizens of Buenos Aires made the city, after Rio, one of the best to visit in South America. They have excellent schools, museums, libraries, and theaters, including one that gave performances exclusively in French. In Paraguay, the tambourine and the whistle flute were played. In Hawaii, which Cook discovered in July 1774, the natives performed on skinless drums. A society of music lovers, founded in 1853 by resident foreigners, also promoted interest in "serious" music there.

Comettant continues his account by looking to the East. One Francis Magnin had the good fortune to visit Japan and hear its music played on Japanese instruments by Japanese performers. (Magnin reported that their music consisted of three notes—*do, la,* and *si*—

repeated endlessly in different dynamic patterns.) The author touches on the music of Siam, Cambodia, and of the Turks and their whirling dervishes. Beethoven's *Ruins of Athens*, he says, sounded nothing like what could actually be heard there! In Greece, large guitars and lutes were popular, while in Egypt he finds several of the instruments Villoteau mentioned. Turning to the Spanish, he agrees that Spanish music has always sounded ravishingly beautiful, but, he says, "music, as such, really does not exist in Spain. What we hear as Spanish music is only a certain rhythm placed in the service of poetic sentiment borrowed from Arabic poetry. But this rhythm does excite the senses."[16] Comettant writes about the place of music in each of the principal cities of the world.

Speaking of the United States, Comettant could not praise their pianos, their Steinways, highly enough. Of course, he is also astonished at the number produced, at their price, and at the way they seem to sell as fast as they come off the factory receiving line. He includes a letter that Hector Berlioz wrote to the Steinways:

Sir,

I have just heard the magnificent instruments that you have brought from America, which come from your workshop. Allow me to compliment you on the beautiful and rare qualities that these pianos possess. Their sonority is splendid and essentially noble and, besides, you have found the way to weaken, almost to the point of rendering it imperceptible, the terrible resonance of the minor seventh that was still heard on the eighth or ninth low-pitched strings to the point of rendering cacophonic the most simple and most beautiful harmonies. It is a great improvement, among others, that you have brought to the manufacture of the piano, an improvement for which all artists and amateurs gifted with a delicate ear will be infinitely grateful to you.

Accept, I beg you, with my compliments, my warm and kind regards.

Your devoted
Hector Berlioz[17]

Evidently Steinway had just begun to use cross stringing and the sonority thus produced offered a welcome change to those blessed with musical sensitivity. Astonishingly, Comettant also prints a chart listing sales and receipts for fifteen different brands of pianos sold in New York, Boston, and Baltimore. Presumably this information originated with the members of the American delegation.[18] Comettant was apparently fascinated by Americana and he goes on at great length about the way everything American is superior. The largest or highest falls in the world are at Niagara, the largest caverns, Mammoth Cave in Kentucky, the largest river, the Mississippi, the largest lake, Superior. America had the largest hotels, the largest steamers, the largest fortunes, the largest jewelry store (Tiffany).

Although France could ill afford the cost of mounting a large-scale exhibition in 1878, the need to show the world that Paris remained a dominant cultural center forced the government to embark on yet another world's fair, only a few years after the enormous financial losses of 1870–71. And though the country would again ultimately lose 32 million francs on the project, the government did not regret its decision to proceed.

The most spectacular structure was the main exhibition hall surrounded by a number of kiosks and smaller buildings. The organizers under J. B. Krantz, the Commissaire-général who had been the chief designer of the 1867 building, abandoned the idea of decentralization and returned to the idea of housing the entire exhibition in a central building. Individual nations erected facades representative of their countries, making an extended "Rue des nations" overlooking a common courtyard. Gustave Eiffel, who had participated in the construction of one of the main buildings of the 1867 fair, now designed the curved sheet-metal roof of the main entrance, along with the side pavilions. More than any of the earlier fairs, however, the Exposition of 1878 was dominated by large manufacturers. There was so much to see that the average visitor could easily get lost as well as exhausted. One of the best ways to view the exhibits was in one of the *fauteuils roulants*, those self-propelled chairs that were available for hire. The crowds made it hard to get a good meal. The Pavilion of Mineral Waters offered the best restorative in the form of six different types of natural French mineral waters.[19]

Information about the place of music in this 1878 Exposition is not readily available. The *Rapport administratif sur l'exposition universelle de 1878 à Paris* includes a list of the exhibits that explain the technique involved in manufacturing instruments and a mention of the various musical instruments on display. Evidently, the authorities expected that music would play a role in their exhibition because they do mention the rules and regulations for musical presentations.[20] Their view of music, however, was limited to its anthropological significance, particularly with regard to the non-Western nations represented.[21]

Government statistics list a total of 108 official "concerts." Forty-three were foreign. Scandinavia, for example, presented two choral recitals and one chamber music concert; Russia offered four grand concerts—that is with orchestra, chorus and soloists—and one concert of "musique pittoresque."[22] "Exotic" recitals were not counted; they did not bring in any revenue, probably because they required no admission fee.[23] Government figures also include a listing of income from musical recitals, a record of dates of "paying" concerts for which an admission fee was demanded. This curious list cites official concerts from 6 June to 10 October; chamber music from 7 June to 20 September, three "solennités orphéoniques" from 21 to 23 July and three fanfares from 25 to 27 August. Understandably, the recitals were costly, with payments made to the orchestra conductor, the chorus master, and the musicians. The official government report compares concerts given by the French to those given by foreigners. Most of the pieces for orchestra and soloists, choral recitals, and nearly all the "musique pittoresque" were composed by foreigners; chamber music seems largely to have been the work of the French, if the names of the performers are any indication.[24]

The Exposition of 1878 added displays on medicine, hygiene, and public assistance, the last two housed in the newly built Trocadero Palace (razed for the French exposition of 1937). A primitive phonograph, rubber tires, and some typewriters made their early appearances here; another section was devoted to photography.[25] Total attendance reached 16 million, more than twice the number that visited the Exposition of 1867.

The Exposition Universelle of 1889 coincided with the centenary of the French Revolution. The commemoration of an event that marked the overthrow of an established monarchy disturbed many foreign—particularly European—governments, some of whom decided against participating officially, fearing a rash of violent demonstrations and civil disorder which never occurred.[26] Yet the 1889 exposition was so successful it actually made a small profit, despite a cost of 27.5 million francs.

The exhibits again took over the site of the Champs de Mars and the most famous monument of the fair was the tower of M. Gustave Eiffel. Selected through a competition, his project was not completed without a struggle. A month after Eiffel had signed a contract to proceed with the construction of the tower, a petition from the foremost writers, artists, musicians, painters, and sculptors appeared in *Le Temps* on 14 February 1887 and demanded, in the name of good taste, that Eiffel cease and desist with this "menace to French history."[27] Among the artists who signed the protest were Gounod, Charles Garnier, the architect, Alexandre Dumas, Victorien Sardou, Guy de Maupassant, Leconte de Lisle, Sully Prudhomme, and François Coppée.[28] Totally unruffled and certainly not intending to stop what was already well under way, Eiffel declared, "When it's finished, they will love it."[29] And they did. Crowds waited for hours to ascend by elevator to the second floor for a price of three francs; another elevator took the more adventurous to the top for an additional two francs.[30] Three and a half million people paid 6 million francs to see Paris from one or another of its platforms.[31]

The other engineering masterpiece at this Exposition was the Galerie des Machines—housing 16,000 machines—where Edison's phonograph was displayed. Inside this building—the largest iron-framed building ever constructed[32]—visitors viewed huge industrial machines by means of a kind of traveling platform, *les ponts roulants*. This exhibit also boasted the first extensive use of electricity, and the twinkling lights of the fair as night fell over Paris left an indelible impression on tourists and natives alike.[33] A Liberal Arts Palace in front of the Galerie des Machines contained examples of art nouveau, among them Emile Gallé's glassware from Nice.

The official report, *L'Exposition de Paris (1889) publiée avec la collaboration d'écrivains spéciaux*, consisted of four volumes, again divided into issues. It lists all of the previous exhibitions—fourteen, to be exact—starting in 1798. Rumania, Greece, Serbia, Turkey, Montenegro, Japan, Siam, Persia, Mexico, Egypt, and the Transvaal appear as "exotic" countries which had participated. (Officially the Chinese did not send any exhibit, but private entrepreneurs from that nation did.) A "Street of Cairo" was the scene of a number of more titillating activities, among them the belly dancers who captivated visitors.[34]

Issue 15 of the report contained an article, "La Musique à l'Exposition," by Charles Darcours. He explained that although the previous fairs incorporated music in their activities, such music was mainly that of military bands and fancy balls. The current Exposition, he wrote, had four sections devoted to music. The first, for

Composition, would present five great concerts in the Trocadero. Those in charge were Ambroise Thomas, president, Léo Delibes, vice-president, and pianist André Wurmser, secretary. Members included some of the most important musicians of the day,[35] who gave a series of Thursday concerts. A synopsis of the programs looks like this:

> 23 May: Concert Lamoureux, featuring music by Bizet, Félicien David (*Le Désert*), Berlioz, Fauré, Massenet, d'Indy, Joncières, Lenepveu and Chabrier (*España*);
> 6 June: Colonne's Association Artistique, offering music of Berlioz, Bizet, Dubois, Franck, Godard, Guiraud's *Dance persane*, Augusta Holmès, Lalo, Pierné, Widor, and others, including David's *Le Désert*, which indicates a continued French interest in orientalism;
> 20 June: Société des Concerts, under Garcin, playing music by Cherubini, Auber, Thomas, Saint-Saëns, Reyer (*La Madeleine au désert*), Delibes, and Gounod;
> 5 September: M. Danbe conducting the Opéra-Comique with excerpts from works by Hérold, Reyer, Delibes, Boieldieu, Saint-Saëns, Auber, Méhul, Adam, Massé, and Bizet;
> 19 September: the Opéra orchestra, under M. Vianesi, playing excerpts from operas by Adam, Auber, David, Halévy, Massenet (*Roi de Lahore*), Paladilhe, Spontini, and Ambroise Thomas.

Unlike 1878, when all official concerts were given by a single orchestra, the five major musical organizations in Paris now went on display. Their offerings, though almost exclusively French, were more varied than before. This held true also for the other musical entertainments. The Orphéons et Sociétés Chorales had a two-day recital (11–12 June) and a two-day competition (25–26 June). Their program included music by Thomas, Delibes, Massenet, Gounod, Saint-Saëns, Rameau and Rossini. Fanfares et Musiques d'Harmonie featured two competitions (18–19 August and 1–2 September). This program, too, included music by Berlioz, David, Thomas, Gounod, Reyer, Massenet, Saint-Saëns, Bizet, and Delibes. And the fourth segment of music at the Exposition, Musiques militaires, included Beethoven's *Egmont* Overture and Gluck's "Marche religieuse" from *Alceste*, as well as music by Auber, Meyerbeer, Joncières, and Delibes.

At this time French organists were at the top of their profession. Widor, Guilmant, and Dubois, among others, gave fifteen organ recitals. On 22 and 29 June, Rimsky-Korsakov conducted two concerts of Russian music, and a Russian choral group directed by one Slavianski d'Agreneff performed on 4, 8, 10, and 15 August. Norwegian choral recitals took place on 27 and 29 July; two Spanish concerts of the Orphéon No. 4 de la Coruña (20 and 23 August) and four symphonic concerts of the Société des Concerts de Madrid, conducted by M. Breton, played all Spanish music with Spanish performers on 10, 13, 17, and 20 September. All concerts took place in the Trocadero.

La Société de Musique de Chambre pour instruments à vent ("wind instruments"), under Taffanel's direction, gave concerts on 18, 25 June, and 2 July; La Société des Compositeurs gave two concerts, and M. Delsart organized two concerts of old and new chamber music including some performances by Diémer at a harpsichord.[36] For the July 4th celebration, there was an international competition of "pittoresque" or exotic music.[37] Open air recitals of national music took place along the Champs de Mars.[38]

The allure of the mysterious East was intensified by the swarms of colonials mixing with the native Parisians at the Exposition. Among French colonial soldiers were Annamites (Vietnamese), Senegalese, and Madagascans. Still other Eastern music is highlighted in Issue 26 of the official report. Its author wonders why all oriental melodies are sad.

The Javanese musical exhibit captured the attention of many, including Debussy. Issue 27 reports on its extensive popular success. The fourth volume of the government's official report features an article, "La Musique à l'Exposition," by Adolphe Aderer.[39] He discusses the Serbs, Russians, Rumanians, and the Gypsies of Hungary and recounts a story about Liszt. On visiting Rumania, it seems that the composer heard a Rumanian gypsy king, a *Lautar*, and his musical band. On the spot Liszt improvised a piano composition, which inspired the *Lautar* who, with his entire band, joined in to repeat and ornament Liszt's already elaborate composition. Apparently, critics showed more interest in music as an anthropological phenomenon than as an aesthetic experience. Nevertheless Aderer distinguishes *"la musique sérieuse"*—as heard at the Trocadero, Champs de Mars, and l'Esplanade des Invalides—from *"la musique gai, dans des costumes et avec des instruments pittoresques."*

The prolific writer Julien Tiersot (1857–1936) surveyed the 1889 Exposition in a slender volume entitled *Musiques Pittoresques: Promenades musicales à l'Exposition de 1889.* "Rome is no longer in

Rome," he wrote, "nor Cairo in Egypt, nor the island of Java in the East Indies." All had taken up residence in the Champs de Mars, the Esplanade des Invalides, and the Trocadero. He did not want to speak about the serious music of which he had often written. Instead his essay comments on the use of "exotic" music to highlight the ancient origins of our own Western music. Gypsy music, although exotic in 1878, now seemed commonplace. Even Arab music, though not heard as often, offered less than "oriental" music. In his first "Promenade" of 23 May 1889, Tiersot supplied an overview of the industrial exhibit that portrayed the construction and mechanism of musical instruments. He wrote an interesting essay about Edison's phonograph. "How unfortunate," says he, "that Liszt did not live long enough to record on this machine for posterity."[40]

The collection of ancient instruments at the Musée de la Couture-Boussey, a town in Eure, engaged Tiersot next on 8 June. He was fascinated by lutes, flutes, trumpets, strings, certain medieval instruments reconstructed from drawings and sculptures in books and cathedrals, and a most unusual specimen, an Egyptian harp that was five thousand years old. In their own way, these instruments prepared him for the concerts on original instruments that pianist Louis Diémer and cellist Jules Delsart would give in the Trocadero.

On 15 June, Tiersot devoted his Promenade to the Annamite theater. The dominant people among the Vietnamese at that time, the Annamites resided in the eastern part of Indochina. A reconstruction of an Annamite village at the fairgrounds provided the writer with some insight into living conditions in the East and also, after he questioned some of the natives, with astonishment at the depth of oriental culture and psychology. Most importantly, he listened to four or five of their musicians playing native instruments of the theater, and he attempted to analyze some of their melodies.

Leaving aside the "musique pittoresque," Tiersot next offered an account of the founding of the Russian Five, the "Mighty Handful." Excluding what he describes as the three "cosmopolites," Tchaikovsky, Anatoly Liadov, and Anton Rubinstein, he focuses on the careers and the music of the nationalist composers: Rimsky-Korsakov, Glazunov, Borodin, Balakirev, Mussorgsky, Glinka, and César Cui. He then returns to the exotic or picturesque music, describing in detail the musical contests held for peasants and unsophisticated amateurs. "And they don't even read music!" he exclaims.[41]

Finally on 11 July, he reached the Javanese dancers, the real hit of the fair, at least for many classical musicians, particularly Debussy. He devoted fourteen pages to a technical description of the Javanese instruments and the music played on them, and explained the sonorities obtained by the gamelan orchestra. (The gamelan is an ensemble of percussion instruments—gongs, gong-chimes, metallophones used in Indonesia, Malaysia and Surinam, as well as in Java. Traditionally, the instruments of the gamelan, handed down from one generation to the next, are more important and are held in higher regard than the players.) Tiersot's may be one of the earliest European descriptions of this unusual group of instruments. After carefully speculating about the qualities of their vocal music, Tiersot compared European and Javanese taste in music.

In his essay of 16 July, Tiersot reported on the military music and parades in celebration of the centenary of Bastille Day. The rather droll article, maliciously satirical, contrasts the martial spirit of the day with the popular spirit of the Revolution. He slyly comments that the reactionary army is thinking of one thing but honoring another. He also says that it is inevitable that official musical commissions eschew music with "advanced" tendencies. Even in 1878, when Colonne expressed the desire to conduct Berlioz's *Symphonie funèbre et triomphale*, the committee had refused permission.[42]

In his next chapter, Tiersot comments on the musical programs offered by the Finns, the Americans, the Norwegians, and the Belgians, and devotes a portion of this section to what he calls the music of "popular tradition." Under this rubric he mentions the collections of folk songs compiled by Bourgault-Ducoudray and Weckerlin in France and the Russian songs of Rimsky-Korsakov. The young Americans he cites were associated with van der Stucken's concert at the Trocadero. "The young American school," he says, "gets its inspiration from the German 'neo-classic' composers: Mendelssohn, Brahms, and Raff. One can also pick out a certain Wagnerian influence, if only a superficial one, in certain [sic] harmonic formations. Then, too, occasionally one is reminded of the music of our best-known French masters, Massenet, Gounod and even Ambroise Thomas. Except for the lack of originality, the workmanship is serious, correct, solid, and always practical. And these young Americans appear blessed with much energy; their school has scarcely been formed and already they have a significant repertoire." Tiersot limits his discussion to those composers whose works were performed at the Trocadero: Arthur Foote, E. A. MacDowell, G. W.

Chadwick, Dudley Buck, H. Huss, John K. Paine, A. Bird, Mlle [*sic*] Margaret Ruthwen Lang and, above all, Frank van der Stucken, who "conducted the performances with the same sure hand that he displays when he conducts the works of our French composers in America."

Tiersot proceeds to a comparison of the Hungarian gypsies and the Rumanian *Lautars* or gypsy musicians. The author warns against false "exoticism," Parisians masquerading as foreigners and playing "composed" romantic versions of folk airs. In his Promenade of 12 August, he takes the Spaniards to task for their "overkill" at the exposition. "Spain is just too much in fashion these days," he says, "what with innumerable bullfights, Spanish choruses, Spanish soirées, Spanish fiestas, all crowding the exposition calendar." The Union Artistico Musical de Madrid, directed by one Perez, played Spanish music and he dismisses their performance as mediocre romanticized efforts. He has better words for the Gitanas of Granada. After a technical analysis—with musical examples—of Spanish dances, he insists that the loveliest and most characteristic piece of Spanish music at the exposition was one by Rimsky-Korsakov, the *Fantaisie espagnole*.[43] The composer wrote that "the Spanish themes, of dance character, furnished me with rich material for multiform orchestra effects. All in all, the *Capriccio* is undoubtedly a purely external piece, but vividly brilliant for all that. I was a little less successful in its third section ("Alborada," in B-flat major), where the brasses somewhat drown the melodic designs of the woodwinds; but this is very easy to remedy, if the conductor will pay attention to it and moderate the indications of the shades of force in the brass instruments by replacing the *fortissimo* with a simple *forte*."[44]

Nobody at the exposition played as much music, so constantly, as the Arabs, Tiersot observes. Entering the Esplanade des Invalides on the quai side, one was overwhelmed by the sounds of wind instruments along with some instrumental squealing emitted from the first Algerian buildings. It was the *nouba*, a kind of processional band, of the Turks in concert. This *nouba*, Tiersot explains, is an assemblage of various Arabic percussion instruments, accompanied or joined by a singer. Evening festivities of the exposition featured parades of musicians including the *nouba*, Senegalese, Congolese performers, and the Canaques of New Caledonia, along with the Javanese and Annamite musicians. In one of his most extensive chapters, Tiersot offers a technical analysis of several Arabic melodies, a few tunes of the *nouba*, a description of the Egyptian café, belly dancers and whirling dervishes, a Moroccan café-concert, Tunisian and Algerian cafés, and Egyptian court music. These native musicians and their music made a rather good impression on this writer.

In his penultimate Promenade, Tiersot discusses the music of "Les Nègres." His comments about the Congolese, Senegalese, and Pacific Islanders and their "primitive" music are typical of the sort of pseudo-scientific racialism prevalent in the nineteenth century. "Lazy races of low intellect," he decides, "love music." He speaks of the rhythmic accompaniment to so many dances of black people and remarks that he has noticed the same kind of percussive beats with the "redskins" of North America. Apparently he had seen Buffalo Bill's Wild West show in Neuilly.[45] Tiersot even ventures to discuss the Tahitian villagers and their music. On 2 November, taking one last glance at the fair, he concludes that "in the face of truly mediocre serious music today, modern music has much to learn from 'exotic' music and musicians of non-Western nations."[46]

Peasants and small town provincials made their first trip to the city to see the fair. To lure them, government and fair organizers kept admission prices low. In 1900, the one-franc admission price was the same as in 1889; there were also bargain train fares. Instead of catering to monarchs, the mayors, in 1889—representing citizens from all corners of France—were feted with gargantuan meals. Thomas Edison, whose outdoor electric exhibit was among the most notable of the American displays, described these feasts: "I could never get used to so many dinners. At noon I would sit down to what they called *déjeuner*. That would last until nearly three o'clock, and a few hours later would come a big dinner. It was terrible. I looked down from the Eiffel Tower on the biggest dinner I ever saw, given to the Mayors of France by the Municipality of Paris. I saw 8,900 people eating at one time."[47] Most kinds of entertainments—racetracks, circuses, cabarets, music halls—also kept prices low so that the masses could enjoy their offerings. At a café-concert like Alcazar d'été in the 1890s, one could enter and drink a "bock" for fifty centimes. One could go to the Cirque d'hiver for half a franc or pay two francs for the best seat. Even the chic Nouveau Cirque cost only two to five francs in 1900. The cheapest form of entertainment were dance halls. Admission to the Moulin de la Galette

A month after Gustave Eiffel had signed a contract for his tower, a group of writers, artists, and musicians petitioned him to cease and desist with this "menace to French history." Eiffel countered, "When it's finished, they will love it."

LES MUSIQUES BIZARRES À L'EXPOSITION

G. HARTMANN & Cⁱᵉ EDITEURS

An introduction to "exotic" music was one of the highlights of the Expositions Universelles from 1867 to 1900.

The Exposition of 1900 was the most magnificent of all. Luminous fountains sprayed lighted water to dazzle the visitors, and a Palace of Electricity became one of the favorite exhibition halls, heralding in the new century.

in 1898 was twenty-five centimes for women and fifty for men. Yet the lowest-priced seat at the Opéra, although it was substantially government subsidized, was four francs.[48] The fair sold booklets of prepaid tickets of admission called *bons*; and serial numbering of booklets had provision for lotteries to be held until 1964!

The exposition grounds covered 237 acres, 53 more than 1878; exhibits totaled over sixty thousand; visitors could manage to "see" the exhibition in ten to twenty days. Musical entertainment included gypsy orchestras, Spanish mandolins, military bands, Arab tambourines, etc.[49] To commemorate the centenary of Bastille Day, 2,000 musicians went to the Champs de Mars with banners of districts of 1790 to give a "concert gigantesque." On 4 August, after releasing thirty thousand pigeons in the Tuileries Gardens, 1200 musicians played for an audience of twenty thousand. "Colossal" is the only word to describe these events.[50]

The Exposition Universelle of 1900 outdid all its predecessors. The grounds remained mostly the same, except for being enlarged to more than 277 acres, not counting the Vincennes annex. Nothing could really replace the Eiffel Tower, but a ferris wheel—the Grande Roue de Paris that could carry 1,600 passengers at once—offered competition. The three entertainments that brought in the most revenue were the Swiss Village, the Palais du Costume and "Old Paris."[51] Moving pictures and panoramas still enticed the public, but they looked for more than just novelties from the cinema. Moving sidewalks and an elevated railroad helped them get around, but the crowds were still absolutely overwhelming, particularly to those who came in from the provinces. Paris was full of fountains and there were *bains chauds* along the Seine. Magic shows, clown routines, the Cakewalk done by black dancers at the Nouveau Cirque, Loïe Fuller, the American dancer who created a sensation with her billowing scarves, all these eye-catching events drew thousands of visitors. Many Parisian intellectuals voiced concern that once workers were exposed to this gigantic hedonistic experience, they would have a difficult time returning to their mundane tasks—they had been exposed to a fairyland. Indeed a surfeit had probably been reached.

The expositions show a steady progress. In 1867, there were fewer plans for music to play a substantial role in the entertainment scene, despite Comettant's comments to the contrary. Concerts and performances were in the nature of light entertainment to soothe frazzled visitors. The dominant mentality revealed a peculiarly parochial kind of industrial world view. Thus, the expositions of foreign and exotic musical instruments were concerned with every material aspect, but with no human or musical ones. Each instrument was carefully labeled with its name and place of origin, and the materials out of which it had been made. Many even had extensive notes describing in detail the techniques used in making the instrument and finishing it. But nowhere were there explanations about how and where such instruments might be played, in what combinations or by whom. No visitor could guess what sound these bizarre instruments might make. Even at the time, this omission was widely noted. Nonetheless, curiosity was aroused in the wide variety of instruments shown.

By 1878, the public was ready for a glimpse of the human side of alien or foreign music. Music played a role from the start of the plans for the exposition of that year. The committees made elaborate arrangements for new composers and new pieces; they held competitions and presented many concerts—not merely to entertain the public, but to engage their interest. Among the performances, there were many recitals on "exotic" instruments by foreign musicians. But this public did not listen to the "exotic" music as they would to their own. The interest they demonstrated in these events was chiefly anthropological and sociological. Their attitude probably partakes of the revived imperialism of the later 1870s. The pains taken by authorities to explain the nature of each performance and when and how it would be given set it rigidly in the framework of an alien culture and discouraged speculation about the music being in any way comparable to Western music. Nonetheless, it was performed and people showed an interest in it.

The two exhibitions of 1867 and 1878 prepared the way for the great impact of exotic music in 1889. The committee in 1889 envisaged music as one of the principal attractions of the exposition. They conducted performances all over the fairgrounds, often holding several events at once. Curiosity with regard to alien cultures by now had become intense. Indeed, the full heat of the imperial rivalries for Asia, Africa, and the Pacific Islands was being felt, so the exhibitors continued to take a didactic and anthropological approach. For the first time at this exhibition, there were performances of "exotic" music which were perceived as "musical" performances.

Music at the Great Expositions

The public listened to oriental music and it made a profound impression. The immense variety of musical sonorities proffered, from Java to Japan to Mexico to Spain to Turkey to Russia dazzled the public's imagination. Like a breath of fresh air, it opened people's ears and eyes to new possibilities. Great excitement hovered around all of the "exotic" musical performances.

The three expositions—1867, 1878, and 1889—appear as symptoms of deeper cultural values, values that shifted rapidly in this epoch. The general cultural horizons had expanded, and this extension led, in turn, to greater and also to more subtle appreciation of all aspects of human culture. By 1889, many Europeans showed a readiness to listen to music as a cultural universal, even if its origins were Cambodian or Sioux. A clear forerunner of twentieth-century tastes, this perspective stemmed from tolerance and from openness to new influences. The various fairs had whetted the appetite of the public for non-Western music; without them audiences would not have understood the sincerity and meaning behind these new sonorities. As Louis Pasteur, a contemporary, said, "Chance favors the prepared mind."

The Exposition of 1900 was the most magnificent of all. Luminous fountains sprayed lighted water to dazzle the visitors, and a Palace of Electricity became one of the favorite exhibition halls, heralding in the new century. An escalator, invented in the United States, was installed. The *trottoir roulant*, a moving sidewalk consisting of three concentric platforms—one stationary, one traveling at a speed of 2.25 mph and another at 4.5 mph—enabled visitors to move along a circular route connecting the Champ de Mars with the Esplanade des Invalides. The fare was fifty centimes. During the approximately five months it was open nearly 51 million visitors—fewer than anticipated but more than the total population of France—bought tickets to the Exposition.

Nevertheless, the Exposition Universelle of 1900 held the seeds of its own destruction. The public had already been satiated by world's fairs and at this one the authorities seemed determined to exceed even the colossal achievements of its predecessors. Not even counting the Vincennes annex, it boasted forty more acres of sights. The Galerie des Machines this time offered the first moving pictures on a huge screen viewed by audiences of up to 25,000. In retrospect, except for the cost, despite the lack of financial gains, from every other point of view—for international public relations, the promotion of Western as well as non-Western culture, the focus on technological advances, the introduction of new foods and new products to the European public, and even the emphasis on historical themes—the Exposition of 1900 was a great success, one that could not be duplicated.

5

Café-Concerts, Cabarets, and Music Halls

At the same time that serious composers, seething from neglect at the hands of their very own countrymen, demanded the right to be heard, and during the years that *le wagnérisme* had cast its somber shadow over French operatic music, a particularly French brand of lighter music was slowly establishing its roots in Paris. First the café-concert, then the cabaret, and finally the music hall emerged as institutions to be reckoned with. The origins of these quintessentially French entertainments reached back to the eighteenth century, and the source of even the grand revues was none other than the French chanson.

All kinds of events—public and private, sad and gay—found expression in chansons. Whether sung at the table, in the theater, in the ateliers and studios of artists and musicians, or in the streets of Paris, these songs reflected the thoughts and feelings of the populace. We could almost trace the history of the French through the texts of their chansons, whose lyrics are permeated with spontaneity, common horse sense spiced with a touch of malice, camaraderie, tenderness, delicate grace, and a taste for the *mot juste*.

Over the centuries, the chansons took on different forms, but their basic elements did not change greatly.[1] Several French savants recognized the unique qualities of the French chanson. In the eighteenth century, Voltaire said, "There is no people with as many lovely chansons as the French people." And La Harpe, a dramatist and journalist disciple of Voltaire, added "because there is none more lively!" In his time Heinrich Heine commented, "The French are as merry as a guzzler of wine." And Pierre-Jean Béranger, himself the author of chansons, insisted that "in France, the chanson is an indigenous plant."[2]

Thérésa (stage name of Emma Valadon), a top entertainer at the Alcazar, one of the foremost café-concerts in Paris in 1870, earned from five to six thousand francs a month. Her audience was not restricted to the lower classes. The Comtesse Tascher de la Pagerie went to hear her and was astounded to see that Thérésa was dressed as a respectable woman, not at all *décolleté*. The Comtesse offered a vivid account of her performance: "Her speciality is little songs, which are broad, with the most scurrilous double meanings; she sings them with the most perfect diction you can imagine, and a full voice, with attitudes and gestures which are rather *canaille* [risqué], if you like, but generally graceful. She surprises you, she makes you laugh, she charms (that is the word), she carries you with her, and you have to applaud her like everyone else."[3]

During the Franco-Prussian War and also during the terrible year of the Commune, entertainers in the café-concerts helped maintain popular morale. The *Marseillaise* was sung regularly, along with other amusing chansons.

A contemporary journalist, Adolphe Brisson, describes the café-concert as a place for the relaxation of those who are exhausted from their daily activities and don't feel like doing anything that requires thinking—in other words the great majority.[4]

The boîtes and clubs, where chansons became the principal modes of expression, in time began to compete with the theaters. Actors, theater managers, and drama critics soon demonstrated a concern with the competition, deploring and at the same time deriding the presentations at the cafés and cabarets, for the most part unaware that the songs presented by performers in these nightspots featured numerous extraordinary artists who chose their lyrics with an eye and ear for timely topics. Then, too, the locations in which they performed, offered additional freedom to their clients: to drink and smoke and enter into these often hilarious entertainments at relatively modest cost.[5]

A uniquely French institution, the café-concert made its appearance as early as 1731, when the Café des Aveugles set up shop in the basement of the Palais Royal, where about half a dozen entertainers plied their trade until one o'clock in the morning.[6] Benefitting from the radical tendencies of the last years of the eighteenth century, the political freedom gained after the Revolution, the cafés continued to flourish until Napoleon banned those of a blatantly political nature, on the grounds that they provided encouragement to potential insurgents. Forbidden under dictatorships, the cafés surfaced intermittently whenever restrictions were lifted.

With the liberalization of theatrical censorship for about five months in 1848, an unemployed comedian and musician by the name of Darcier scored a hit with L'Estaminet lyrique, a café he established in the new Passage Joffroy.[7] Outlawed in March 1852, the café-concerts did not flourish again until the relaxation of rules under the Empire during the years 1861–67. As part of an effort to rehabilitate the Champs Elysées in 1861, several cafés that featured concerts were permitted to open outdoors in the shade of the illustrious avenue, offering patrons an alternative to the sweltering heat of the traditional theaters. The middle class sought relaxation in these smoke-filled arenas where they ate, drank, and roared with laughter at the jibes directed at local politicos, at the boredom of traditional family life, and the frustrations of their work. Entertaining in these cafés required extraordinary stamina, of course, exceeding the demands placed on players in traditional theaters. Harried waiters took orders, dodged each other and their customers, refilled glasses, cleared ashtrays and tables, and offered their own comments on the entertainers as well as on the proprietor, thereby contributing to the general mêlée.

Artistic personnel in the best places usually consisted of a tenor, a baritone, three comics, one singer who would belt out his lyrics, another with a more mellifluous voice, a contralto, two singers who specialized in lighter music, and two female comediennes. The musicians were stationed at first on the same level as the patrons; eventually they moved to a raised platform, where fourteen to twenty of them regularly held forth. Singers earned between 150 and 700 francs a month; musicians only 70 to 150, but conductors managed to command between 300 and 400. All the entertainers, male and female, wore evening clothes, which they purchased themselves. (Lest they compete with actors on the legitimate stage, costumes were prohibited until after 1867.) Entertainment began at 7:00 P.M. and lasted usually until 11:00 P.M.; on Sundays and holidays the show started between 2:00 and 3:00 in the afternoon. Patrons had to continue to order drinks and the waiters urged them to do so. The few cautious or penurious individuals who held back were reported to the management. Waiters earned tips of about 5 percent, and they could accumulate as much as 300–400 francs a month. Receipts each evening ranged from 500 to 1,000 francs, but on a good Sunday, 2,500 to 3,000 was not unusual.[8]

The first directors of these café-concerts were musicians, but their entrepreneurial talents were soon needed to balance assets and liabilities. Before paying their singers, musicians or waiters, impresarios were obliged to contribute a portion of their receipts to the Société de Bienfaisance and the Société des Auteurs. In 1863, two hundred café-concerts raised 100,000 francs for each of these social welfare organizations.

In the early years of the café-concerts, authors and lyricists had not yet made a claim for royalties. Then in 1850, Paul Henrion, a watchmaker turned comedian, refused to pay for his drinks on the ground that he should at least be entitled to a drink on the house for his efforts. Together with the publisher Jules Colombier, he sued the café owner; the performers won their case. That year they established the Syndicat des Auteurs, Compositeurs, et Editeurs de Musique (S.A.C.E.M.). In 1866, S.A.C.E.M. distributed close to 380,000 francs among 160 members. (Twenty years later, in 1886, Eugène Baillet reported that 4,000 authors, publishers, and composers divided royalties of about 1,050,000 francs among them.) About 50 members earned between 2,000 and 2,500. Two of the most successful, Lucien Delormel and Villemer (pseudonym of German Girard), each pocketed about 10,000 a year. On the fifth of January, April, July, and October, receipts were tabulated and distributed to members at meetings at S.A.C.E.M.'s headquarters on the third floor of the building at 17 Rue de Faubourg Montmartre.[9]

Café-Concerts, Cabarets, and Music Halls

* * *

The lyrics of the chanson reflected various aspects of life: the family, the workplace, the politics and preferences of those who frequented the cafés, largely the new bourgeoisie. The texts appropriated by the most successful entertainers included not only those of the dozens of lesser lights in the business, but also the efforts of such illustrious poets as Victor Hugo, Alfred de Musset, and Hippolyte Monpou. Recognizing the increasing popularity of these chansons, publishers engaged artists to provide attractive designs for the covers of the sheet music—several reveal the impact of the vogue for orientalism—and then rushed to bring the chansons out individually.[10] By and large the texts had alternately rhyming lines and many included refrains in which the patrons could join. In a witty article of 1 October 1885 in the *Revue des deux mondes*, Ferdinand Brunetière described the inexhaustible vein of couplets of a historical or political nature and of popular chansons that could be traced back to the eighteenth century or earlier. His article was an attempt to quell the criticisms of those who decried the popularity of chansons. According to Brunetière, they were an art form not only eminently French, but with a long history in the French capital, preceding their appearance in the café-concerts. The melodies and even the accompaniments of the chansons owe much to their composers' familiarity with several of the operetta numbers of Offenbach and Hervé among others.

After the War of 1870, patriotic songs surpassed all others in popularity; sentimental romances, too, were sung by vaudevillians Madame Judic and Théo,[11] both adored by the public. Many of the presentations concluded with a kind of ensemble piece using all the entertainers who had appeared earlier in the evening. The performers were not necessarily the polished artists who graced the stages of the Opéra or the Opéra-Comique, but they possessed charisma and a talent for communicating with their audiences that often surpassed that of the luminaries of the musical world.

The best-known establishments that catered to the Parisian public in the 1870s were the Eldorado, founded in 1858 on the Boulevard de Strasbourg, and the Alcazar, built in 1859 on the Rue de Faubourg Montmartre; admission cost between 70 centimes and 3 francs. Also famous were the Folies-Bergère, where Olivier Métra conducted the orchestra; the Ba-Ta-Clan, with Chinese decor, erected on the Boulevard Voltaire; the Folies Montholon on the Rue Rochechouart; and the Tivoli on the Boulevard de Clichy.[12]

Fast on the heels of the café-concert came the cabaret, where again chansons emerged as the principal form of entertainment, though the subject matter differed somewhat from that at the more boisterous café-concerts. The cabaret was a meeting place for artists and writers, where quasi-improvisational performances took place among peers; thus the ambience was more intimate and the material more ambitious. Patrons enjoyed love lyrics and mood pieces, but chansons here also functioned as alternatives to newspapers—generally controlled by the ruling classes—and as a medium for commentary on and response to daily events. Satires of the authorities caught on quickly, particularly among the intelligentsia.

> *Moi, j'vas vous dire la vérité,*
> *Les princ' il est capitalisse,*
> *Et l'travailleur est exploité,*
> *C'est ça la mort du socialisse.*
>
> *Les princ' c'est pas tout. Plus d'aurés,*
> *Plus d'gendarmes, plus d'militaires,*
> *Plus d'richards à lambris dorés,*
> *Qui boit la sueur de prolétaire.*
>
> *Enfin qu'tout l'mond' soye expulsé,*
> *Il rest'ra plus qu' les anarchisses.*
>
> Me, I'm going to give you the truth,
> The princes, they are capitalist,
> And the worker is exploited,
> And that's the death of the socialist.
>
> Besides princes, no more lordly ones,
> No more cops, no more military men,
> No more filthy rich in the mansions,
> Who drink the sweat of the proletarian.
>
> Finally when everyone's been thrown out,
> There'll be only anarchists about.

The song above typically voices the people's protest against the government.[13]

While the café-concert had a larger audience, the cabaret had a higher quality audience. The latter, more of a laboratory or testing ground for the young avant-garde, continuously mirrored contem-

The café-concert, cabaret, and music hall of the late nineteenth century became frequent meeting places for musicians, artists, and writers. Paul Verlaine (above) en café. One of the most popular cabarets is depicted (below) in Edouard Manet's A Bar at the Folies-Bergère.

Toulouse-Lautrec's lithograph of La Goulue, who held forth at the Moulin Rouge.

porary, topical events. Theirs was a flexible medium with an impromptu stage and program that might include as many as fifteen acts: songs, monologues, sketches, poetry, and dance. Just as often, however, the entire program might be improvised.

One of the earliest of the cabarets grew out of a literary society known as the Hydropathes. Its members—writers and poets—met weekly to perform their works for one another.[14] Some of their more improvisational pieces were first tested here in semi-private performances among friends.

Rudolphe Salis, amateur painter and poet and son of a rich brewer and member of the Hydropathes, possessed the talents of an impresario and businessman.[15] In 1881 he founded the Chat Noir, initially for his friends, poets, composers, writers and painters who gathered at his place in Montmartre to perform their works for one another. News of his "club" spread and before long strangers demanded admission, particularly after Salis began serving drinks. With Salis's flair for decoration, the club soon drew a fairly large constituency. At first, the programs were unstructured, performers improvising on each occasion. Satire, irony, and expletives of the kind that upper-class ladies and gentlemen were not even supposed to understand characterized the entertainment. Indeed, many entered the Chat Noir knowing they would be insulted, but looking forward to the experience.[16]

Jules Jouy, a contributor to two revolutionary papers, often treated the audience in the Chat Noir to his own political commentary:

Ouvriers et rustres	Workers and peasants!
Assez de pasteurs!	Enough of priests!
Plus de chefs illustres!	No more illustrious leaders!
De triomphateurs!	And conquerors!
La levée en masse	A nation in arms
Forge des héros.	forges heroes of its own.
En France, on se passe	In France, we can well
Bien des généraux!	do without generals![17]

For this latter, General Boulanger might well have been a member of the audience. (Georges Boulanger, 1837–91, was Minister of War 1886–87, and leader of a nationalist reactionary movement which anticipated fascism. He won an overwhelming victory at the polls in 1889.)

In 1882, Salis launched a magazine, also called *Le Chat Noir*.[18]

To promote the attractions of his cabaret, he hired some of the finest graphic artists of the day, among them Théophile-Alexandre Steinlen and Adolphe Willette, along with the poster artists Caran d'Arche and Jean-Louis Forain.[19] As his establishment grew more popular, it began to attract a more monied clientele. Occasionally, the more prosperous guests were physically attacked and robbed by some of the less well-heeled.

The police, many of whom were on Salis's payroll, could not always maintain order. Undaunted, he decided to move to a new and more elegant neighborhood, forgetting that he might have other problems there—noise restrictions and confrontations with snobbish residents, who disapproved of his type of establishment. Nevertheless, shortly after Victor Hugo's death in 1885, Salis and company put on a rather remarkable spectacle: accompanied by a band and singers and carrying furniture and memorabilia, they moved from the old house to new headquarters on the Rue Victor Massé.[20] Until about 1897, the Chat Noir enjoyed unsurpassed popularity with the upper crust of Parisian society and also with famous writers such as Guy de Maupassant, J. K. Huysmans, Villiers de l'Isle-Adam, and Théodore de Banville.

A novelty, produced at the Chat Noir and seen for the first time in Paris, was the Théâtre d'Ombres or the Shadow Theater.[21] A creation of the symbolist and landscape painter Henri Rivières, it emanated, once again, from the Orient. With decor painted or superimposed on glass and paper, with cut-outs and Japanese style puppets, Rivière produced a forerunner of the moving picture. Sometimes these scenes included musical accompaniments, either instrumental or vocal; often narrators supplied the necessary commentary to provide more cohesiveness to the presentation. At one time or another, Debussy and later Satie participated in the musical portions of these entertainments. (Satie, after a disagreement with the proprietor, moved on to the Auberge du Clou, where he assumed the role of resident pianist and eventually met and became friends with Debussy.)

Rudolphe Salis was not the only one to mine the riches of café life. His enterprise encouraged new talent. The parents of Aristide Bruant, too poor to provide for their son at home, sent him to Paris at the age of fifteen to fend for himself. The ambience in many of the lower-class bistros where he ate, shocked him at first because of the language used there by his coworkers and peers. Determined to acquire the argot of the inhabitants of the streets—the prostitutes, vagabonds, ruffians, and dispossessed who were his associates in the big city—Bruant soon learned to swear with the best of them. He started to perform, singing and reciting in several of the café-concerts, and caught the attention of Jules Jouy, who invited him to the Chat Noir. Dressed in a flamboyant black velvet jacket, red shirt, yellow waistband, scarf, and high boots, Bruant became a familiar sight in Montmartre. (Toulouse-Lautrec did so many lithographs of him that his black cape and bright red scarf are known even to those who cannot place him in the context of his club and Parisian nightlife of the time.)[22]

In 1885, Bruant opened his own cabaret, on the premises of the first Chat Noir, and called it Le Mirliton.[23] (The word literally refers to a reed pipe, but it also means "doggerel.") Bruant decorated the walls of his club with the works of Steinlen, Lautrec, and others, and created an ambience that epitomized low life, spoofing the sort of atmosphere that characterized *The Beggars' Opera.* His guests and clientele seemed to thrive on insults, and so did his business. He never hesitated to poke fun at his audience, to demolish with a snide comment even the most respected among them, but they returned for more.

Bruant himself was the principal entertainer. Accompanying himself on the guitar, he would sing in his abrasive voice, of the people of the streets—the homeless, the unwed mothers, the prostitutes, the victims of social injustice—whose existence might otherwise have gone unrecognized by the people who frequented his club. Whether or not this kind of entertainment eventually effected social change cannot be documented. Suffice it to say that talented impresarios and performers of the calibre of Bruant believed they made a difference and hoped they were a force for reform. A splendid example of one of Bruant's songs appears below.

A's sont des tas	They are those
Qu'ont pus d'appas	With no more charm
Et qui n'ont pas	Not a penny
L'sou dans leur bas.	In their hose.
Pierreuses,	Street-walkers,
Trotteuses,	Sidewalk-stompers,
A's marchent l'soir,	They walk at night,
Quand il fait noir,	When there's no more light,
Sur le trottoir.	On the sidewalks.

Les ch'veux frisés,	Hair frizzé
Les seins blasés,	Breasts blasé,
Les pieds usés	Feet worn away.
Christ aux yeux doux,	Christ with mild eyes,
Qu'es mort pour nous,	Who died for our lives,
Chauff' la terre oùs-	Warm the earth where
qu'on fait leurs trous.	Holes are dug for them.[24]

The café-concert and the cabaret led eventually to the music hall. Indeed, some of the veteran performers of the cabarets, Yvette Guilbert, for example, went on to appear in the new music halls after several successful years at Bruant's Mirliton.[25] The French appropriated the English name, and it would seem that they borrowed the concept from their rivals across the channel as well. But in fact the French preceded the English in this enterprise. The British music hall, supposedly born in 1848 at Canterbury Hall on the day women were first admitted to the London pubs, actually began *after* the establishment of similar places of entertainment in the Palais Royal in Paris.[26]

The man who might rightfully be called the "founder of the music hall" was Joseph Oller, born in 1839 near Barcelona. An inventive spirit, he established the Pari Mutuel in Paris and ran it until 1875, when the courts deemed the enterprise illegal. Undaunted, he closed his ticket windows and on the premises opened the Fantasies Oller, the first music hall on the Boulevards.[27] Once Oller mounted a successful show he lost interest. Nurturing and maintaining it did not appeal to him. In the end, however, he founded two enduring establishments: the Grande Piscine Rochechouart and the Nouveau Cirque. The latter remained in operation until 1960.

After the Revolution, with the relaxation of mores and morals during the Directoire, numerous cafés—the Café du Sauvage and the Café Borel, among others—came into existence. Some featured ventriloquists, either alone or *à la* Edgar Bergen and Charlie McCarthy;[28] some offered an orchestra and talented instrumentalists; others celebrated the evening with fireworks. A few like the Café d'Apollon on the Boulevard du Temple presented short plays or sketches; many, like the Tivoli at 78 Rue Saint Lazare, offered the talents of chanteuses of the caliber of Madame Tallien. Occasionally a menagerie of circus performers entertained in one of these boîtes.

At first most of the spectacles ended with chansons; by the time the music hall had become entrenched on the entertainment scene, everything *began* with chansons. Coffee, beer, and brandy cost the same price as routine drinks in ordinary cafés—two sous for a *café simple* and five for one with alcohol and as much sugar as desired. How could one do better than that?

At first, accompanied by a pianist at a simple upright piano, artists sang right in the midst of all the diners. Later, a raised platform brought the entertainer more clearly into view; finally, three or four instrumentalists joined the lone piano. The violinist generally kept time and functioned as the leader of the group. Béranger, Nadaud, Thérésa, and Paulus[29] are among the best known of the regular performers in the early days, and their appearances at the Eldorado, the Alcazar d'été, and the Café aux Ambassadeurs represented the best of Parisian entertainment. The incredible facility of the composer Hervé, who was known mostly for his successful operettas, extended as well to the Eldorado, where he conducted the orchestra. One of Hervé's favorite artists, Blanche d'Antigny, later starred in *Chilpéric*, a revue that attracted Toulouse-Lautrec for at least twenty visits in the last year of his life. So many of the stars of these spectacles, like the very beautiful young Théo (who used no last name), burst forth on the entertainment scene at the tender age of sixteen or seventeen and burned out within a few years. A male star, Max Bouvet, debuted at the Eldorado in 1875 simply under the name of Max. The creator of the popular *François les bas bleus*, he became one of the delights of the Opéra-Comique and, at his death, was a professor at the Conservatoire.

In 1900, Dranem (stage name of Armand Ménard) was the man of the hour, and chic Parisians discovered him at the Eldorado.[30] In order to entice some of the regulars from that nightspot, the proprietors of La Scala, situated across the way, were obliged to feature a number of other stars: Polin, Fragson, Max Dearly, Polaire, and Paulette Darty. (The competition didn't hurt the proprietors of the Eldorado, Monsieur and Madame Marchand; they were also the owners of La Scala and of the Folies-Bergère.[31]) Mayol, another star of the time, suffered as a result of his frank homosexuality. He might have reached the heights of Darly or later Maurice Chevalier but for his sexual preferences. Many of those who held the stage at the turn of the century still revealed characteristics of the lively band of bohemians that Henri Murger described in *Scènes de la vie de Bohème*. Their life was far from luxurious; only later, when the music hall came of age, could superstars indulge in the kind of hedonistic living that today we regularly associate with celebrated movie stars.

The center for Parisian nightlife became Montmartre, the Butte.[32] Its most popular clubs were the Olympia, the Bobino, and particularly the Cigale with its mobile ceiling painted by Willette. Among those who sang there were Mistinguett, Irene Bordoni, Yvonne Printemps—who was either fourteen or fifteen years old when she began her career there—and even Marguérite Carré, the celebrated opera singer. The neighborhood also boasted, at 17 Rue des Martyrs, Le Divan Japonais, famous as the home of Yvette Guilbert.[33]

One of the principal chanteuses and diseuses of the Belle Epoque, and certainly the most successful over the longest period of time, Yvette Guilbert performed on two continents. Born Emma Laure Esther to Hippolyte and Albine Guilbert on 20 January 1865, she started singing as a youngster of five or six and soon began to imitate the café-concert favorites, Thérésa and Judic. At sixteen, she took a job as a model; later she became a salesgirl. At twenty, she met Edmond Stoullig, the drama critic, who suggested she go on the stage. Guy de Maupassant, when asked by a friend to suggest a stage name, came up with "Yvette," and thereafter she was known by that name.

Evincing an unusual interest in art and literature, she began to visit the museums and to read Balzac, Stendhal, Chateaubriand, Voltaire, and Molière. She attended performances at Antoine's Théâtre-Libre, thus getting acquainted with the plays of Ibsen, Tolstoy, and Zola. She watched carefully the gestures, the turn of phrase, and the manner in which the best actresses projected the characters they portrayed. She made a brief appearance at the Chat Noir, but after receiving a good review in the *Gil blas*, she opened at Jehan Sarrazin's Le Divan Japonais, where she came to the attention of Toulouse-Lautrec, who commemorated her appearances with one of his celebrated posters.

While Yvette was singing at Le Divan, Aristide Bruant was entertaining at Le Mirliton. But she also worked the Moulin Rouge, thus gaining two publics and two salaries. She turned every song into a miniature drama.[34] She used a technique of half-spoken recitative and was therefore sometimes called a *diseuse*. Francisque Sarcey, for thirty years drama critic of *Le Temps*, reviewed Guilbert's performance on 22 December 1890. "Mademoiselle Yvette Guilbert," he said, "is a young woman who debuted recently at the Eden-Concert, where she learned her metier as a chanteuse. Her face is not exactly pretty, rather comical; [she has] a fair voice, and unusually clear diction. Vivacious and graceful, she has presence. I experienced extreme pleasure listening to her. I would have enjoyed her more if she hadn't—several journalists being in attendance—forced her voice for effect. She sang Xaurof's *Le petit serpent*. One could die of laughter! I won't be surprised if one day she will be very much in demand."

Jean Lorrain, poet, novelist, playwright, and critic, devoted a number of columns to her in *L'Echo*. He offered her material that she was quick to use. Tremendously ambitious, she was never content with her status and reputation. In the early 1890s, the Nouveau Cirque on the Rue Saint-Honoré was a favorite of high society. Yvette made her debut there on 16 January 1891. In the avant-garde city of Brussels, when Hugues Le Roux gave a series of lectures on French song, Yvette was there to illustrate them. When Yvette and Le Roux appeared for the first time on 5 February 1891 at Paris's Théâtre d'Application, the resulting traffic congestion in the Rue Saint Lazare was formidable. By this time she was singing evenings at the Parisien and the Nouveau Cirque and matinees at the Théâtre d'Application. (Sardou, author of *Tosca*, told Yvette she was not so much a chanteuse as a comedienne.)

Continuing to conquer audiences at one theater after another, providing the subject matter for any number of journalists and reviewers in the local press and media, Yvette Guilbert soon acquired English and American fans. On 10 February 1893, a New York newspaper described her tremendous success for American readers; and the English essayist and critic Arthur Symons gave her a favorable review in the *St. James Gazette*.

After the turn of the century, when she wanted to refresh her repertoire, Yvette turned to the chansons of old France and the ballads of the Middle Ages, searching for these treasures in old bookstores and libraries. She never thought she would perform in Germany, because of her memories of the Franco-Prussian War, but when she arrived, she was warmly welcomed there. In 1906, she was back in New York, singing in Carnegie Hall. On her return to

Paris, she co-starred with the comedian Max Dearly. During World War I she was always willing to participate in benefit performances, and afterward was again enthusiastically received in Germany.

Born in the time of the café-concert, nurtured in the era of the cabaret, Yvette Guilbert performed as well in the later music halls. As a singer whose professional career extended over four decades, she epitomized the combination of intelligent actress and singer who lifted the native folksy chanson to unexpected heights.[35]

Still another of the places celebrated by Lautrec and several of the post-Impressionists in their paintings was the Moulin Rouge, where La Goulue held forth. Much of the success of these nightspots stemmed from their style of construction. The best of them gave the audience unobstructed views while they dined, and even patrons who had to wait their turns for the next revue could observe the gambols of the show girls awaiting *their* turns.

Following the success of the Moulin Rouge, where the can-can regularly brought down the house, Auguste Bosc founded the Bal Tabarin in February 1904 and determined to borrow some of the novelties that had tipped the scales in favor of the older spot.[36] Despite considerable changes that the dance had undergone since its heyday in the 1880s, Bosc transported the can-can to his new boîte with its interior decorated in the current *art nouveau* style. One year the girls arrived on stage in an arch of balloons; another time they looked like modern Valkyries on a merry-go-round. Suitable girls—suitable, that is, for performing the can-can—were difficult to find. They had to have long legs and be able to lift them high, seemingly without effort. They had to be nimble enough to leap into the air, do a split, and land squarely on the ground—all with a smile. Few "cancaneuses" practiced their trade for very long. Indeed its demands caused many of them to die rather young, worn out after several years on the stage. A less flamboyant attraction at the Tabarin was Bosc, the proprietor, an eminent conductor and composer in his own right who led the orchestra. In later years, the Tabarin sheltered couples doing the "boogie-woogie," the mambo, and even, on occasion, the waltz.

The basement of the Tabarin housed a cabaret called *Le Paradis* and here the management catered to a lower-class clientele. The Tabarin prospered under Bosc's direction, for more than twenty years, until 1921. In that year, a tavern opened by the Moulin Rouge in *its* basement with Pierre Sandrini as the manager, captured the fickle hearts of the Parisians. Bosc, recognizing his competition was too much, sold out to Sandrini.

The Folies-Bergère, the Olympia, and the Casino de Paris ultimately became three of the most outstanding music halls of Paris where native stars like Edith Piaf and Maurice Chevalier and foreigners like Josephine Baker would later achieve fantastic success.

6

Music and Art

In the incredible cultural kaleidoscope that was fin-de-siècle Paris, musicians and artists were in constant touch; they socialized frequently, and on occasion made forays into the fields of their counterparts in the sister arts. Saint-Saëns and Fauré both sketched their contemporaries; so did Debussy. Satie's calligraphy alone would have assured him a place among the artists of his time, but he also made numerous drawings on letters to friends and on musical manuscripts. Manet and Degas made music as young men. And Jacques-Emile Blanche studied piano in London, played passable Bach, and as a child was called "the little Mozart" by none other than opera composer Charles Gounod. Furthermore, Manet, Toulouse-Lautrec, and Pierre Bonnard decorated sheet music covers for several of their musician friends, and Debussy, in letters to Durand, his publisher, often made specific requests about the artistic format of these covers.

One letter reads as follows:

Bichain, Thursday (August 1903)

Dear Friend,

No. 8 [a reference to a typeface] is perfect . . . only it seems to me now that the shade chosen originally for the letters is a bit harsh? I suggest something that would be really admirable, the following combination:

(pale gold)
    Estampes

   (blue)   (blue)
Pagodes–La Soirée dans Grenade
     (blue)
  Jardins sous la pluie
     (pale gold)

The blue would be the color of the address printed above [on his stationery], and the gold would be pale yellow.

The printing in gold will not present any difficulties nor be too costly, since certain books by Ollendorf are finished that way.

Please believe that I will be infinitely grateful to you for giving in to my mania with printing. Like all maniacs, that's the way [through printing] to my heart.

My affectionate friendship.

C.D.

(I'm not saying I'm working, because I'm too superstitious for that.)[1]

The Austrian composer Arnold Schoenberg, ranked his own paintings in 1910–11 with the best Expressionist works in Berlin; he firmly believed he had a contribution to make. Numerous artists were inspired by Wagner's music dramas; Henri Fantin-Latour, Odilon Redon, and Jean Delville are but a few of the better-known artists who either painted large canvases depicting characters or scenes from the operas or prepared lithographs for inclusion in several exceptionally well-illustrated books of the period (Adolphe Jullien's *Hector Berlioz* and *Richard Wagner*, for example) or for publication in the short-lived *Revue wagnérienne*. When Romain Rolland said that "Wagner's genius dominated nearly the whole of French art for ten or twelve years,"[2] he meant music, art, and literature, the entire cultural spectrum. "The whole universe was seen and judged by the thought of Bayreuth."[3]

Yet not only Bayreuth. Schopenhauer, Nietzsche, Baudelaire, Verlaine, and, later, Mallarmé also stressed the supremacy of music over the other arts.[4] All art must aspire to the expressiveness of music, which meant that of necessity, writers, poets, dramatists, artists should all know something about music. The more the better. Poets, writers, and playwrights had just deserted Realism for Symbolism and they sought to imbue their creations with the kind of symbolism they associated with music. After all, what art could better reflect Symbolism than music? Perhaps for this reason the

113

interrelationships that existed between artists, writers, and musicians have not been duplicated since.

Several common themes and variations attracted painters as well as musicians: scenes of nature and the seasons; children and their games; the café, the cabaret, the circus, and the music hall; Iberia; orientalism; Wagnerism; and the *hommage* or *tombeau* (painting or composing in the style of an earlier master). Many painters did portraits of musicians, some of whom they knew well, and others through commissions. Finally, there were musicians and painters who married into families where one or more members of the group practiced a sister art. In such instances a kind of cross-fertilization took place naturally.

The number of artists who responded to music or musical theater was far greater than the number of musicians who were inspired by the fine arts. Several of the better-known artists either had studied music in their youth or had gone regularly to the opera or concerts. Some, like Degas and Manet, consciously sought their subject matter at the opera or in the wings of the theaters; Toulouse-Lautrec haunted the cabarets and cafés for scenes and people to paint. Seurat, too, was attracted to these places.

Historically speaking, as early as the Renaissance *painters* had revealed an interest in musical subjects, often including musicians or musical instruments in their works. But until the nineteenth century, most musicians showed little interest in the pictorial arts. One of those who responded was Liszt, who in the middle of the nineteenth century, after viewing works by Raphael and Michelangelo, composed "Sposalizio" and "Il Penseroso," both fine examples of artistic inspiration. From one of Moritz von Schwind's paintings, the composer derived the subject for his oratorio *Die Legende von der heiligen Elisabeth*. Later, inspired by *Der Triumph des Todes*, a fresco he viewed at Pisa, Liszt wrote the *Totentanz* for piano and orchestra. Modest Mussorgsky, deeply moved by the death of his close friend, the painter Victor Hartmann, composed his celebrated *Pictures at an Exhibition*. Later in the century, the Spanish musician Enrique Granados said of himself, "I am not a musician, but an artist." An excellent painter, he made some sketches on the subjects of the *Goyescas*—his pieces inspired by Goya's drawings—and he did a self-portrait as a Goyaesque young man. These musical works reflect their composers' response to specific artists or works of

art, but the process does not occur often. The unusually rich confluence of the arts in fin-de-siècle Paris therefore suggests totally different circumstances.

Unlike Germany and Italy, both of which had remained a collection of city-states or dukedoms throughout most of the century,
France was a unified country with a centralized government located
in Paris from the time of the Revolution. The French had always
prided themselves on the glory of their arts and the government
regularly provided support for art and artists and also for certain
privileged musicians. Unfortunately, the artists and musicians whom
they supported were not those posterity remembers today. Academic
artists, Thomas Couture, Alexandre Cabanel, William-Adolphe Bou-
guereau, the "establishment" of the time, received the funding and
the protection offered by the government. Often patrons, mainly
women, hosted salons at which the artists met not only musicians
and writers, but also wealthy aristocrats—Maecenas, as the French
call them—who became their sponsors. Princess Mathilde (1820–
1904), daughter of Jerome Bonaparte and niece of Napoleon I, hosted
a splendid salon in Paris and in her country house during the Second
Empire, when her cousin Napoleon III was head of state. She had
a fairly influential position and enjoyed collecting writers, including
Théophile Gautier, Gustave Flaubert, Edmond de Goncourt, Charles-
Augustin Sainte-Beuve in her coterie.[5] She also revealed a penchant
for composers. Royal orchestras played music by Queen Hortense
and operas by Prince Poniatowski. Léon Carvalho is the best remembered conductor. Marie Miolan-Carvalho, his wife, created
Marguerite in the operas *Faust* and *Mireille* (both by Gounod) as
well. Composer Reynaldo Hahn said she "possessed a talent which
was indeed miraculous, with ineffable bad taste, an immense arrogance concealed under bourgeois charm and an implacable will,
to which her husband lent the support of his effective directorial
powers."[6]

But those musicians who could find no wealthy patrons had to
fend for themselves. Newly independent, they also acquired new
responsibilities: they had to anticipate the taste of the public (or
else cultivate it) and they had to learn to merchandise their wares.
Often they thrived or perished according to their success as busi-
nessmen. And many lacked the necessary acumen. As a result, an
impoverished group of artists, musicians, and writers, finding solace
in numbers, began to populate the fringe areas of urban centers,

where they could afford housing, food, and entertainment. In France, wanting to be near Paris, from which all bounties came, they settled in Montparnasse or Montmartre, the Greenwich Village of the day. Living there as outsiders, they formed friendships with other creative persons with similar tastes and social aspirations, and in similar financial situations.[7] As outsiders they began to revere the name of Richard Wagner, whose aesthetic tenets exercised an extended influence on many of them. Some remembered his fiasco at the Opéra; others had only heard about it.

Tannhäuser, after inordinate delays and unbelievable obstacles, finally arrived at the Opéra in March of 1861. In each of its three performances it was jeered off the stage by members of the Jockey Club. These dandies had mistresses in the corps de ballet and they expected to see them perform at the top of the second act. (During the first act, the young men were busy eating their dinner.) Owing to the exigencies of the drama, Wagner had placed the Bacchanale and orgy at the opening of the first act. Furious that their demands had gone unheeded, the Jockey Club contingent determined to destroy the perpetrator of the crime. Destroy him they did, but only temporarily. Wagner's own memory of this catastrophe naturally colored his response to the French and theirs to him.

Yet this humiliation caused Wagner's followers to close ranks and the rising tide of *le wagnérisme*, which reached its apogee in the 1880s and 90s, did not recede completely until the First World War. Astonishingly, in 1870, only nine years after the *Tannhäuser* debacle, when the French were embroiled in a bitter war with Germany, and Wagner was penning his infamous parody of the French, *Eine Capitulation*, the composer and his music continued to attract the French.

Writers and artists succumbed first, without having heard a note of his music. The literati read his prose works and discussed his aesthetic theories; for them, he set the stage for Symbolism. His minute instructions for stage design, costumes, and settings, when they were finally realized at Bayreuth, attracted legions of French artists who returned home transformed, as if having undergone a religious experience.

On 8 June 1885 at the entrance to the Concerts Lamoureux, the first issue of the *Revue wagnérienne* went on sale.[8] Edward Dujardin, one of the founders of the journal, insisted in 1923 that the review was organized not to promote the works of Richard Wagner, but to penetrate them.[9] This despite the fact that the French avant-garde had long looked to Wagner as the creator of a new art form. Gérard de Nerval, translater of Goethe's *Faust*, on 18–19 September 1850 wrote for *La Presse* his impressions of the *Lohengrin* he had heard in Weimar on 28 August under Liszt. Nerval was convinced that Wagner's theories corresponded to his own with regard to music and poetry. Seven years later, in 1857, Théophile Gautier lauded *Tannhäuser* in the *Moniteur universel*. Wagner's visit to Paris in 1859, the excerpts from his works programmed by the Concerts Lamoureux in January and February 1860, and Baudelaire's famous letter to the German composer all kept Wagnerism percolating in Paris.[10] Joining mysticism to sensuality, the composer prepared the way for Symbolism. With *Lohengrin* and *Tannhäuser*, he introduced the French to German literature and philosophy.[11]

Artists and writers vied to prove the seriousness of their empathy with Wagner's theories. Théodore de Wyzewa, in the *Revue wagnérienne* announced that Villiers de l'Isle-Adam was the perfect artist,[12] probably after the poet had dedicated his poem *Azraël* to Wagner "the profound Prince of Music" in 1869.[13] *Axël*, first written in 1872, appeared in print in its final form in 1890, absolutely impregnated with the ideals of Schopenhauer; it was regarded as the closest literary realization of Wagner's music dramas.

Painter Odilon Redon followed closely the evolution of Wagnerism in France. Always passionately in love with music, he contributed his "Brünnhilde" as the frontispiece for the seventh issue of the *Revue wagnérienne* in August 1885. Redon was unwilling to restrict himself to painting, and yielded to the attractions of other arts. He was exposed early to music, thanks to his brother Ernest. Sacred melodies that he heard in his adolescence inspired him with a sense of the beyond. In his journal, *A Soi-même*, he not only comments sensitively about Berlioz and Schumann, but frequently states that he owed the most lively emotions of his youth to music. "It fashions the soul," he wrote in 1876, "and one remains faithful longest to these early emotions."[14] Redon calls his brother, born in Orléans five years before him, a musical prodigy. "At my birth, he was already playing. In the cradle, I heard Beethoven and Bach. I was born on a sonorous wave."[15] As he matured, Mozart, Beethoven, and Schumann became his favorites, particularly Schumann. He was also among the first to defend the music of Berlioz, Franck, and Debussy. Nothing new in music left him indifferent. And he was a good enough pianist to play Beethoven for company.

In 1904 Redon followed the avant-garde to Brussels for a performance of Chausson's *Roi Arthus*, a Wagnerian work.[16] Because of his affinity for music, he frequently used musical terms to describe works of sculpture, assigning to his own work the same goals he saw in music. He wanted his painting to suggest rather than depict precisely, to set thoughts in motion. His paintings, certainly those inspired by Wagnerian works, occupy the symbolist, hazy, ambiguous world of the indeterminate. Yet he recognized differences between music and painting: music he called an "interior" art, painting demanded a focus on the "exterior."

After *Tannhäuser* failed in 1861, Henri Fantin-Latour created a lithograph of *Der fliegende Holländer*. Later he executed a series of prints on musical themes starting in 1873 with the Schumann celebration in Bonn. He first heard Schumann's music in London in 1861 and loved it. After Schumann, his chief musical gods were Berlioz and Wagner, but Brahms, Rossini, and Weber all appealed to him. A regular at the Pasdeloup, Colonne, and Lamoureux concerts, he went so far as to postpone his marriage after he got a ticket for the third *Ring* cycle at Bayreuth. The performance left him absolutely ecstatic. It stimulated him to do four lithographs of "Evocation of Erda" from Act III of *Siegfried* and three of Klingsor's "Evocation of Kundry" from *Parsifal*. These represent moments of the deepest and most solemn music of the operas. The love music of Dido and Aeneas, their "Nuit d'Extase" from Hector Berlioz's opera *Les Troyens*, inspired seven separate works and the capture of Troy brought forth a Fuseli-type of painting. Latour also did two paintings of Berlioz's *Harold en Italie*. The French composer's setting of "Sara la baigneuse," the nineteenth of Hugo's *Orientales*, inspired a beautiful painting and revealed his continuous interest in vocal music. As he watched the Wagner cult take increasing hold of French art in the last three decades of the century, Latour, like Redon, began contributing to the *Revue wagnérienne*.

In one of his best-known group portraits, Fantin-Latour has Chabrier seated at the piano, surrounded by critic and Wagnerite Edmond Maître, music journalist Adolphe Jullien, art critic Camille Benoît, violinist Boisseau, and composer Vincent d'Indy.[17] The celebrated Belgian symbolist painter Jean Delville also succumbed to

As the two groups
frequently
associated, portraits
of musicians and
musical subjects
are common in the
art of the period.
Fantin-Latour
portrays Chabrier at
the piano, with the
composer Vincent
d'Indy at his right.

Madame Manet at the Piano, *by Edouard Manet*

Erik Satie, *by Pablo Picasso*

Wagner with two paintings, one of Parsifal and one of Tristan and Isolde's night of love.[18]

Jacques-Emile Blanche wrote to André Gide in August 1892 about Bayreuth and the music dramas.[19] From the time of his youthful piano studies in London and throughout Blanche's life, music played a significant role. Together with his friends, Félicien Rops, Auguste Rodin, Alphonse Legros, Albert Besnard, and Paul Helleu, he attended Sarasate's concerts. He wrote his mother from Bayreuth, saying that Cosima, Wagner's widow, treated him as an adopted son.[20] Blanche, a fine pianist, became the preeminent portrait painter of contemporary musicians.

Gustave Moreau, who regularly went to the opera and to vocal recitals, was initially attracted to the music of Mozart, Gluck, and Rossini. When Bizet was spending his Prix de Rome year at the Villa Medici, he grew very close to Moreau. This friendship led Moreau to Wagner's music. On his return to Paris, Moreau, too, became a Wagnerite. His fascinating Salome paintings come to mind as musical illustrations, and his designs could well have been used by Debussy, had the latter's planned production of *Orphée-roi* in collaboration with Victor Segalen ever taken place. Gauguin was trapped in the whirlwind of Wagnerism and used musical terms—harmonics, symphonies—to describe his paintings. Often he used a mandolin motive, anticipating abstract artists such as Picasso and Braque. He said that he wanted his art to force people to think, just as music does. (Paul Serusier did a tiny drawing of Gauguin playing the accordion. Although it is doubtful that he actually played the instrument, the drawing does exist.)[21]

Heinrich Morstatt, a German musician, served a commercial apprenticeship from 1864 to 1866 at Marseille, in order to satisfy his father's wish that he learn a trade. In Marseille, Antoine Fortune Marion, a childhood friend of both Cézanne and Zola, introduced Morstatt to Cézanne, who continually urged him to come and play Wagner for them.[22] Entranced with the German composer's music, Cézanne did several paintings entitled "Overture de *Tannhäuser*", each showing a young woman at the piano. To the uninitiated, the titles make no sense. They have nothing to do with *Tannhäuser*. Knowing that so much of Wagner's music was heard in those days in piano arrangements helps make those paintings understandable: the young woman was simply playing a piano transcription of the Overture.

When the Nouvelle Athènes succeeded the Café Guerbois as a meeting place for artists, writers, and musicians, Mallarmé, Zola, Villiers de l'Isle-Adam, Phillipe Burty (of the Japanese prints), and Maître met there fairly regularly. Maître, a most intelligent critic and patron, with the help of the wealthy painter Frédéric Bazille, initiated Renoir into the music of Wagner, but Renoir finally got fed up with Bazille's intense infatuation. Another fervent Wagnerite, Judge Lascoux, tried in vain to convert Renoir to the cult.

Auguste Renoir had a fine singing voice. He would repeat passages from *Orphée aux enfers* to his children and sometimes asked his friend Abel Faivre, a cartoonist, to sit at the piano and play him some of the other Offenbach airs he liked. Because of his good voice, when he was a child, his teachers wanted him taken into the choir of Saint-Eustache. The choirmaster then was an unknown young man by the name of Charles Gounod, who liked the youngster and gave him private lessons. Gounod also gave Renoir a ticket to a performance of *Lucia di Lammermoor* one evening and Renoir loved it. Always optimistic, Gounod sent his friend, a priest, to Renoir's parents' home to propose a musical education for the young man, promising to get him into the Opéra chorus. Renoir himself felt he "was not made for that sort of thing." Instead, a M. Lévy took him into his porcelain works as an apprentice in porcelain Limoges. Gounod reminded him that the tenor in *Lucia* earned 10,000 francs a year, but Renoir still refused to change his decision. Even then, money meant little to him.

Renoir showed enough patriotic fervor to hesitate about giving a full endorsement to Wagner. According to his son Jean, he recalled a performance of Berlioz's *Les Troyens* before an almost empty house and a very hostile audience; and Renoir empathized with the French musician.[23] When Hugo's literary romanticism was already *démodé*, Berlioz's musical romanticism finally began to take hold. Renoir was not averse, however, to doing a portrait of Richard Wagner, when both painter and musician were in Italy. The Frenchman describes the sitting as an unpleasant experience, Wagner claiming that the French only liked "German-Jew music." Renoir countered with very laudatory remarks about Offenbach, a friend and neighbor on the Butte. Wagner replied that it was true "if he were not a Jew, he'd be a Mozart. I meant Meyerbeer." Renoir insisted that Wagner hated the French because of their hostility to his music. And when Renoir went to Bayreuth, he remarked after hearing *Die Walküre*,

"They've no right to shut people up in the dark for three solid hours. It's taking mean advantage of you."[24] (It was lucky he saw *Walküre*, the most popular opera of the *Ring* and not one of the real blockbusters.) Renoir was opposed to darkening the theater. His complaint, typical of a Frenchman, was that "you are forced to look at the only place where there is any light, the stage. I might want to look at a pretty woman sitting in a box. We might as well be frank about it: Wagner's music is boring." Renoir, irritated by the Nibelungen, continued to object: "No one has the right to bore people to that extent. I felt like shouting 'Enough of genius.' " Yet he continued to see Judge Lascoux and remark on his musical activities with astonishment. "Think of it," he commented, "a magistrate of the criminal court who travels all over Europe with his own piano in the luggage van the way other people take their trunks."[25]

On the other hand, Renoir never missed an operetta by Offenbach, although nowhere does he mention his feelings about *Les Contes d'Hoffmann*, Offenbach's masterpiece. He was also a devoté of Hervé (Florimond Ronger), another composer of operettas. What delighted Renoir was his heightened awareness the minute he entered a theater. The festive side of the theater attracted him. Offenbach lived in a handsome residence at the lower end of Rue La Rochefoucauld. After work, Renoir often strolled down Butte Montmartre to drop in for a cigarette with the composer. It was late afternoon, but the household was not yet awake. The Offenbachs rose late; evening was their early morning hour, with the composer just taking his cup of coffee and croissant. His first regular meal was supper at midnight. Renoir sometimes accompanied him to the Variétés. "It was the most beautiful theater in Paris," he said. "You felt the excitement even before the curtain rose. Besides, a theater is not a theater unless it is all red, white and gold."[26]

Seurat, who exhibited with Alfred Sisley and Camille Pissarro at the Vingtistes Salon in Bruxelles, also contributed to the *Revue indépendante*, along with James McNeill Whistler, another of his collaborators in Belgium. Huysmans singled him out for praise, admiring how such works as *Le Chahut* and *Le Cirque* captured the marvelous abandon displayed by turn-of-the-century dancers at the numerous boîtes in Paris. Like Lautrec, Seurat lived in the Parisian night world. Several of his paintings, for example *Au Concert Européen* and *High C*, bear musical titles. Though he does not seem at all an intellectual painter, Seurat sought a relationship between the laws of optics and the laws of music.[27] He even asked a friend if he thought that the innovations in painting had a technical similarity or a kinship with the new music of Richard Wagner. He concluded that the laws of aesthetic harmony of colors can be taught as the rules of musical harmony are taught.[28]

The painter Henri Lerolle and the composer Ernest Chausson were married to sisters. As they mixed and matched their friends, cross-fertilization among the arts proved inevitable. For example, in 1891 Lerolle began to notice the works of Maurice Denis and Bonnard. Lerolle introduced Denis to music about this time; Pierre Bonnard, through his own brother-in-law, composer Claude Terrasse, was already at home with music and musicians.[29] Chausson, the husband of Madame Lerolle's sister, recognized the impact of painting on his work. "I am astonished to see the ideas that pictures evoke in me," he wrote. "There are some that give me the whole form of a symphonic poem." Some of Denis's paintings reveal an exquisite relationship to Chausson's music, particularly to his tone poems.[30] Chausson spent summers working in Tuscany and apparently so did Denis. There they became close friends. For his magnificent home on the Boulevard de Courcelles in Paris, Chausson commissioned a ceiling painting from Denis, who proceeded to duplicate some of the beautiful Tuscan views on their ceiling. Chausson introduced Denis to the group around Franck: Henri Duparc, Charles Bordes, Pierre de Bréville, and Vincent d'Indy. Denis soon painted d'Indy's daughter, the Countess de la Laurencie; and when the Opéra mounted d'Indy's *La Légende de Saint Christophe*, Denis did the decor, having heard the work first on a piano chez Lerolle.

In 1894, also on Lerolle's piano, Denis heard Claude Debussy's first version of the death of Pelléas from his opera *Pelléas et Mélisande*. Denis later watched as it grew, scene by scene, at Arthur Fontaine's. It was Denis who eventually illustrated Debussy's *La Damoiselle élue*, after Dante Gabriel Rossetti's poem. Denis continued meeting musicians at the Lerolles. There he encountered composers Paul Dukas, Albéniz; pianists Alfred Cortot and Blanche Selva; violinist Eugene Ysaÿe, the singer Blanche Croiza, and attorney Paul Poujaud, whom Denis regarded as the best critic of his time. Catholic in his musical preferences, Maurice Denis took an interest in Charles Bordes's performances of the masses of Schumann, Schubert, and Franck at Saint-Gervais; he regularly attended concerts of Gregorian chants and the music of Palestrina. Indeed, his second wife was a singer at the Schola, the organization founded in Franck's memory by his students. Maurice Denis wrote often about music. In a letter from Rome to Madame Chausson in February 1898, he excitedly spoke of having discovered a Bach Society, where he and his friends heard the *Magnificat* and also a short motet by Palestrina. He speaks of "indescribable pleasure from the concert."[31] He also states that Redon had spoken to him of one Janmot with whom he had played Beethoven trios. Leaving the church of Sainte-Clothilde after a concert featuring music by Franck and Franck's pupil Vincent d'Indy in October 1904, Denis noted that "more and more, music has great effect on my sensitivities."[32] His account of all the pieces he heard gave detailed descriptions of a Moscow recital on piano and harpsichord by Wanda Landowska, and of the wonderful *Stimmung*—he uses the German word—achieved by Schumann and Wagner in their music.[33]

Pianist Blanche Selva, another Franck student, played her teacher's *Variations symphoniques* and transcriptions of several orchestral pieces and won Denis's approval in 1910. Shortly afterward, Denis had a conversation at the Café Weber with Selva's colleague, Vincent d'Indy, in which d'Indy tried to give him a short course in music history. (Always the pedagogue, d'Indy had difficulty restraining himself when an opportunity arose to instruct or proselytize.) D'Indy continually overemphasized the importance of Wagner, while Denis insisted that Berlioz or Schumann must come before Wagner, and that the Russians, Debussy, and perhaps Strauss should follow him.

Although he was a close friend of many contributors to the *Revue wagnérienne*, Denis had apparently seen only *Götterdämmerung* by May 1911. Later, after having heard the complete *Ring*, he was totally overwhelmed.

The critic Roger Marx remarked that attendance at theater or at concerts sparked a profusion of notes and sketches from Auguste Rodin. He noticed this phenomenon one day after the sculptor had heard Berlioz's *Danse des Sylphes*.[34] Judith Cladel, one of Rodin's biographers, writes most sensitively in 1936 about his preoccupation with music:

> It had not struck me until now how music and art are related in Rodin's work. I had not discerned the gift he possessed—one imparted to only a few sculptors—to create a correlation between the art of forms and that

of sounds, between the most defined and the most ephemeral. This parallelism, which Rodin noted subconsciously but very definitely, results in part from his sense of harmony. The rest is due to his prejudice, his need to maintain an intermediate zone between his sculptures and their ambiance, a sort of aura that subtly joins them . . . and that inscribes them with the imprecision of musical expression. The particular rhythm, the very personal rhythm according to which he arranges the texture of his sculpture, as well as that of his drawings and watercolors, accentuates this relationship. Not surprisingly, the fundamental laws of all arts reconcile the ideal constructions of a Bach, a Mozart, a Gluck, and a Beethoven. Rodin's dramatic romanticism, the inexhaustible flow of his imagination, disposed him to express a fraternal tenderness towards the master of the symphonies [Beethoven]. Hardly familiar with this very complex art, he found the Wagnerian forest impenetrable and, dragged to Bayreuth by a friend, he declared ingenuously that *Parsifal* was a nasty Mass. While he was delighted to hear Wanda Landowska as she picked out fugues and sonatas on the clavichord specially transported to her home, Rodin did not respond to Debussy's music when the composer came to Meudon to play him several of his pieces.[35]

Cladel is not alone in her recognition of the significance of music in Rodin's oeuvre. Oddly enough, according to de Caso and Sanders, he called one of the studies he made of Hanako, the Japanese actress Ohta Hisa, "Beethoven."[36] In a later book translated by these same authors, Rodin is quoted as saying, "If by methods of his art, a sculptor succeeded in suggesting impressions that literature or music ordinarily provide, why pick a quarrel with him? Lately a writer criticized my [sculpture] *Victor Hugo* at the Palais Royal, declaring that it was not a sculpture but music, and that this work brings to mind a symphony by Beethoven. If this were only true!"[37]

Gustav Mahler, the Austrian-Jewish composer and conductor, had already acquired an international reputation when Rodin carved his bust in 1909. Mahler had arrived in Paris in 1900, where he conducted concerts with the Vienna Philharmonic at the Théâtre du Châtelet and at the Trocadero. Three of his *Lieder eines fahrenden Gesellen*, sung by Madame Faliero-Dalcroze, appeared on the Lamoureux Concerts in 1905, and a visiting orchestra from Munich performed his First Symphony at the Salle Gaveau in 1909.[38]

Victor Frisch claimed he had introduced Rodin to Mahler during the intermission, when the composer's *Das Lied von der Erde* was first performed.[39] It seems, however, that it was in 1909, on the occasion of the premiere of the First Symphony.

Rodin told Alma Mahler that he was most touched by the appearance of her dying husband. He saw "Mahler's head [as] a mixture of Frederick the Great's, Franklin's, and Mozart's."[40] And later, "I find his features remarkable. There is a suggestion not only of the Eastern origin, but of something even more remote, of a race now lost to us—the Egyptians in the days of Ramses."[41] Doubtless, Mahler's music would not have appealed to Rodin, who preferred the eighteenth-century masters. Yet something of the dichotomy in Mahler's personality moved him to produce one of his finest late works.

Many artists focused on musical themes. Félix Vallotton, for example, planned a series of forty-five woodcuts, called "Satirical Portraits," and intended for them to portray "immortals of the past, present and future," including Berlioz, Gounod, Schumann, and Wagner. When he proceeded to illustrate musical instruments, he portrayed Joseph Holman at the cello, Ysaÿe with his violin, Raoul Pugno at the piano, and Louis Schopfer with his guitar. He also did a woodcut of the Ysaÿe Trio.

Other nineteenth-century artists painted canvases depicting scenes from musical compositions. Several went so far as to title their compositions after a scene in an opera or a musical genre such as a nocturne, etude, or concerto. Those who deliberately set out to illustrate musical works, Odilon Redon with his illustrations for Wagner's operas, for example, or Maurice Denis with his drawing for the cover of Debussy's *La Damoiselle élue*, demonstrated more readily the impact of music on fine artists.

Among paintings with musical subjects, Degas's oil of the Opéra orchestra remains a favorite of viewers. Early in his life, Degas's sketchbook revealed his interest in the orchestra as possible subject matter. Both he and Manet were regular subscribers to the Opéra, perhaps because of—though maybe in spite of—the fact that both their parents were avid music lovers. The Degases and the Manets (seniors) mingled frequently with musicians, and had musical evenings at their homes, where they often played alongside professionals (their friends) in chamber music performances.

Degas's painting shows the bassoonist Désiré Dihau, in midperformance, surrounded by other members of the orchestra and also by some of Degas's own friends. The composer Emmanuel Chabrier is on the left in the background next to the stage; the cellist Pillet is in the left foreground. There is an unidentifiable figure, perhaps the Spanish guitarist Pagans, and seated before him the dance master of the Opéra. Degas also includes the two first violinists Lancien and Gout and on the extreme right Gouffe, the double bassist.

Interestingly when artists included musical instruments in their compositions, they almost invariably selected those with rounded shapes, usually string instruments such as violins, cellos, guitars, or banjos. All these instruments follow the curves of the female figure. The woodwinds, conceivably phallic symbols, did not attract their attention—except for the bassoon, particularly as it appeared in Degas's oil of the Paris orchestra. Then again, the bassoon's curves markedly differentiate it from the other woodwinds, the oboe, flute, or clarinet.

Another favorite instrument of many painters was the piano, again probably because of its curving outlines, but also because in the nineteenth century the piano was one of the most popular home instruments, something like the lute or virginal in the sixteenth century. James Tissot, Mary Cassatt, Gustave Caillebotte, Degas, and Cézanne were among the artists who used the piano as a prop. Renoir painted the daughters of the writer and dramatist Catulle Mendès seated at the piano. These youngsters were also the daughters of Augusta Holmès, the Irish-French composer (a Wagnerite) with whom Mendès lived after his divorce from Judith Gautier, Théophile's daughter. The girls might well have inspired Debussy's *La Fille aux cheveux de lin*.

An astonishingly large number of artists painted pictures of women at the piano: Toulouse-Lautrec, James Tissot, Whistler, Vuillard, Bonnard, Cézanne, Caillebotte, Fantin-Latour, and Renoir are but a few. Cassatt, Renoir, Degas, and Toulouse-Lautrec captured the sense of expectancy of members of the audience seated in a box at the Opéra or the theater. Cassatt restricted her "operatic" settings to views of those seated in a loge; the others painted stage scenes. Seurat and Toulouse-Lautrec, along with Jules Cheret, the fine poster artist, documented Paris at nighttime. The circus and music hall also inspired them as they later attracted Debussy, Chabrier, and Milhaud.

Two American artists, John Singer Sargent and James McNeill Whistler, both received their education in Europe, mostly in France, although Whistler spent long stretches of time in England. Sargent traveled a good deal and, like many painters, was impressed with

Andalusia and things Spanish. He also warmed to the music of the Hungarian czardas.[42] When he left Boston for his studio in France, his New England piano teacher warned his parents that they were robbing the world of a great pianist. Music was the key to Sargent's friendships. He relaxed his subjects by playing as they sat for portraits. Sargent became close friends with composer Charles Martin Loeffler, pianist Heinrich Gebhard, and singer Povla Frijsh. He adored the music of Gabriel Fauré, and remained intimate with the composer for almost thirty years. He might almost be said to have handled public relations for the composer in England in 1898, when Fauré traveled there to conduct his incidental music to *Pélleas et Mélisande*.[43] In his late years, when the French composer needed money, Sargent discreetly purchased a manuscript from him. The transaction profited Fauré and ultimately the Harvard Library, which now owns the manuscript of Fauré's Second Quintet.[44] A passionate music lover, Sargent faithfully attended concerts at the Cirque d'Hiver, Pasdeloup's regular Sunday concerts. He painted many "musical" portraits, among them one of conductor Sir George Henschel in 1889.[45]

James Whistler, though not particularly musical, recognized that the other art offered an aesthetic principle which accorded with and suited his own aims.[46] He was enough of a Francophile to know that a character in a Murger novel had composed a *Symphonie sur l'influence du bleu dans les arts*; that Gautier had written a poem entitled *Symphonie en blanc majeur*; he knew, too, that his compatriot, Edgar Allan Poe, had stated that "in music perhaps the soul most nearly attains the great end for which, when inspired by the Poetic Sentiment, it struggles—the creation of a supernal Beauty."[47] He was one of several artists who used musical terms to describe his work. He titled his paintings *nocturne* or *symphony*, as he sought a variety of tones or colors. "Among my works are some night pieces," he said. "I have chosen the word *nocturne* because it generalizes and simplifies the whole set of them."[48] Analogies between painting and music enabled Whistler to provide an easily-grasped definition of his goals. The art of painting consisted of the blending into harmony of the disparate colors available to the painter, either in nature or on the palette. For Whistler, "Music is the poetry of sound, [as] painting is the poetry of sight, and subject matter has nothing to do with the harmony of sound or of color."[49]

In the face of all of this involvement with music by painters, it is interesting to compare and contrast these visual artists with musicians who painted or cared about art. Both expressed a commonality of interest in nature. Some musicians responded more readily to a scene from nature than to a painting that spurred their imagination. In the early nineteenth century, Schubert's Lieder illustrated many scenes from nature. Indeed, both of his principal song cycles, *Die schöne Müllerin* and *Die Winterreise*, are rife with examples of pianistic figurations meant to resemble flowing water in streams and brooks—and sometimes even tears. The last, while hardly a nature scene, reflects a universal emotion and often elicits in a listener, particularly one who also understands the accompanying text, a stronger response than a picture of a man or woman in tears will provoke from a viewer. Music, with its ephemeral sonorities, intangible and elusive as they always appear, has the power to move men's souls—despite a lack of representational qualities. Its potency poses a question that many have tried to explain, but few have succeeded.

Rainwater does not inspire German musicians. French composers, on the other hand, have risen to the occasion and created several splendid pieces that illustrate falling rain. Chopin's delightful "Raindrop" Prelude (No. 15 in D-flat)—the title may have been coined by George Sand—supposedly alludes to the rain on the roof of their home in Majorca. Jacques-Emile Blanche tells us that Debussy, taken with the view of Blanche's lovely garden during a thunder storm, wrote his "Jardins sous la pluie," one of a group of three pieces entitled *Estampes*, dedicated to Blanche. Even the word *estampe* is an artist's term. Debussy responded to nature scenes but was equally enamored of paintings and objets d'art. His "Poissons d'or" reflects the Japanese lacquered screen he kept in his studio; his "Puerto del vino" was composed after receipt of a picture postcard from Spain sent him by the Catalan pianist Ricardo Viñes.

Many French keyboard works and chamber compositions of the fin-de-siècle bear titles that reveal their composer's interest in or focus on water.[50] The seasons, *printemps* (spring), and the weather —in particular, wind and fog and snow and moonlight—captured their musical imaginations and resulted in wonderfully illustrative piano compositions.[51] Only a few French composers indulge in musical illustrations of their countryside. Déodat de Séverac (1872–1921), a lesser-known contemporary of Debussy and Ravel, composed in this style.[52] On the other hand, several of the Spanish composers resident in Paris in the late nineteenth century, Albéniz and de Falla, for example, demonstrated a kind of regionalism, depicting scenes from their particular town or village, much in the manner of the Russians Mussorgsky and Borodin.

That many musical subjects show similarities with those chosen by painters of the period bears repetition: animals, children and children's games, the music hall and circus, Spain and other exotic or oriental countries, and pieces written in the style of earlier composers as a sort of tribute or homage. Ravel's *Histoires naturelles* (1906), based on a selection of Jules Renard's prose poems of the same name, include musical descriptions of a peacock, a swan, a kingfisher, and a cricket. The sheet music features a cover illustration by Toulouse-Lautrec with a fox, instead of Renard's name. (Renard means fox in French.) In Ravel's *L'Enfant et les sortilèges*, the delightful opera on which he collaborated with Colette, cats and other animals also take on anthropomorphic characteristics. Children and children's games inspired compositions from Debussy, Fauré, de Séverac, and also Ravel; but each composer responds slightly differently to this common stimulus.[53] Similar to Toulouse-Lautrec and Seurat, Debussy found the circus and music hall very attractive, and several of his best-known piano pieces stem from those sources.[54]

Spain beckoned many French composers, beginning with Bizet and his celebrated opera *Carmen*, written at about the same time that Spain was exercising her fascination over Manet. He, too, did scenes of the bullring that readily call to mind the locale of *Carmen*. Chabrier's *España* and the many Spanish-flavored pieces by Debussy and Ravel highlight the importance of this country in the scheme of musical compositions of the period.[55] Albéniz, de Falla, and Granados, along with the Catalan pianist Ricardo Viñes, lived for long periods in the French capital and acquired technical training at the Conservatoire, where they surely played some of their native music for their French colleagues. The French found Spanish rhythms and melodies, with their Moorish accents, particularly enchanting. (As far away as Russia, Rimsky-Korsakov, too, succumbed to Spanish influences with his delightful *Capriccio espagnol*.)

The customs and inhabitants, also the music, the instruments, and even the art of oriental lands, of exotic Eastern countries fascinated Debussy, just as they attracted visual artists. The list of Debussy's pieces that reflect this interest include the beautiful *Chan-*

sons de Bilitis, *Syrinx* for solo flute, the ballet *Khamma*, the two piano preludes "Danseuses de Delphe" and "Canope," and "Pour l'Egyptienne."[56] Maurice Delage and Albert Roussel are two other composers who delighted in the oriental influence; Roussel's opera *Padmâvatî* reveals his obsession with the East.

In the same way that many fine artists prepared canvases "after" an earlier artist (Manet, for example, after Velasquez or Goya), composers often wrote pieces "A la manière de . . ." or, as de Séverac did in *Sous les lauriers-roses*, imitated the textures, piano figurations, rhythms, and melodies of honored teachers, in this instance Albéniz, Chabrier, and Bordes.

One enterprise which, by its very nature, had to utilize the talents of both artists and musicians was the Ballets Russes, when they arrived in Paris about 1909. Musicians who participated in Diaghilev's fantasies included Debussy, Ravel, Satie, Stravinsky, de Séverac, d'Indy, Florent Schmitt, Proust's friend Reynaldo Hahn, Georges Auric, Milhaud, Poulenc, and Honegger—the last four were members of "Les Six"—and the Spanish composer Manuel de Falla. Cocteau, Gide, Valéry, Verhaeren, and, later, Claudel are only a few of the writers who contributed their efforts to the project. Later, Picasso, Bakst, Benois, Gris, and others created a fusion of the arts such as even Wagner had never dreamed possible.

Many musicians socialized with painters; some fraternized regularly with writers and artists, either at cafés (the Café Guerbois or the Nouvelle Athènes, or Procope) or at salons hosted by women like Misia Natanson (then Edwards and finally Sert) and the Comtesse de Polignac, who was actually the American Willametta Singer, heiress to the sewing machine fortune. Then too, musicians like Debussy, Dukas, or Reyer, who contributed articles to the many small reviews that appeared at this time, inevitably got to know some of the artists who provided the drawings or the caricatures that decorated their pages.

Several painters had relationships with musicians, performers, or composers whose names have not been recorded by posterity. For example, the Dihau family, originally from Lille, included three musicians who were prominent at the time. Désiré Dihau is the bassoonist in Degas's painting of the Paris Opéra orchestra. He happens also to have been a fairly prolific composer whose sheet music covers were illustrated by both Manet and Toulouse-Lautrec. His sister, a

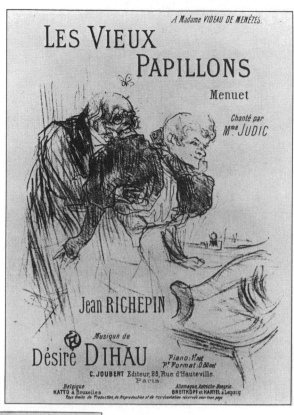

Contemporary painters frequently illustrated sheet music. Toulouse-Lautrec illustrated both Les Vieux Papillons, *with music by Desiré Dihau, and* Le Paon, *from* Histoires naturelles *by Maurice Ravel.*

An illustration by Raoul Dufy from Le Boeuf sur le toit *by Darius Milhaud.*

In the works by both painters and musicians can be found some prevalent themes: animals and the natural world, childhood, the circus and music hall, and the exotic. In Ravel's L'Enfant et les sortilèges, *his delightful collaboration with Colette, cats and other animals take on anthropomorphic characteristics.*

piano teacher, was intimate with Manet, who painted her on several occasions. It seems that the Dihaus were distantly related cousins of Toulouse-Lautrec. Désiré's brother Henri played the violin in the Paris Opéra orchestra.

With the new popularity of the photograph, painters began to imitate the kind of groups that posed for photographs. The painter's atelier, the composer's studio with, in each instance, the prominent artist surrounded by his friends and/or disciples frequently became the subject of paintings. Fantin-Latour's *Autour du piano* and Georges Espagnat's *Réunion de musiciens* are two well-known favorites.

Painters, particularly Impressionists and Post-Impressionists, took to the outdoors for many of their works at the end of the century. And composers continued to use titles that mirrored an interest in nature and the outdoors. The tendency became so prevalent that the critic Vuillermoz actually described several of Debussy's works with words that seem more suitable to painting, words like "shimmering iridescences, glimmerings, ripplings, and shudderings."[57]

Just as musicians in the nineteenth century sought fresh sources of melody in the Near East, Asia, India, and Africa, painters searched for exotic influences and inspirations outside Europe. In about 1888, Bonnard, Vuillard, Denis, the writer Pecheron, the musician Pierre Hermant, and the actor Lugné-Poë began meeting on Saturday afternoons at the home of Paul Serusier, an artist and friend of Gauguin. Serusier rarely left his home except to attend performances at the Opéra or the Opéra-Comique in the company of his parents or musician friends: Saint-Saëns, Delibes, Verdi, Chabrier, or Gounod. Serusier became a fervent Wagnerite after his initial exposure to *Lohengrin*. Sunday afternoons, won over by the enthusiasm of the crowds he surrendered to the Pasdeloup concerts at the Cirque d'Hiver. Often he contemplated the *Gesamtkunstwerk*, the "total art work," which was only possible, he decided, with music. Several years later, Gauguin spoke of Bonnard, Vuillard, and Serusier as artists whose painting had entered a musical phase.

The group of painters around Serusier viewed themselves as forerunners of the future, and borrowing a Near Eastern word, called themselves *Nabis*, Hebrew for prophets. Within a few years, artists, writers, and musicians had seized upon one or more of several mystical religious movements that apparently characterized the epoch. Wagner, too, toyed with a scenario about Buddha and Siddhartha at the end of his life. The Rosicrucian movement under its guru Sâr Joseph Péladan captivated Erik Satie for a short time. (Ironically, Péladan was a French Wagnerite, and nobody could have been less of a Wagnerite than Satie. It may have been one of the reasons why he eventually broke with the Rosicrucians.) The other quasi-mystical movement, the Symbolist movement in literature, found its artistic counterpart in the works of the Belgian painter Jean Delville. But Fantin-Latour, too, had bowed to their otherworldliness in several of his Wagnerian lithographs, along with Jacques-Emile Blanche, particularly in his "Parsifal."

After Pierre Bonnard's sister Andrée married the musician Claude Terrasse, Bonnard produced the lithographic covers of Terrasse's *Petites scènes familières: Solfèges*, a rather boring adaptation of Czerny. In 1894 Bonnard did a portrait of his brother-in-law and also a poster for the *Revue blanche*. Through his work on this journal, he met a host of creative people: Proust, Verlaine, Mallarmé, Maeterlinck, Lautrec's close friend Romain Coolus, Jules Renard, André Gide, Alfred Jarry, and composer Claude Debussy. Jarry and Terrasse collaborated on the former's *Ubu Roi*, while Bonnard provided the designs for their costumes.

While many painters studied music and a number of them claimed musicians among their friends and acquaintances, others definitely received their inspiration from musical compositions. A few just enjoyed listening to music as they painted. Maillol, for example. Almost Germanic in his attention to details of recordings and soloists of the music he listened to as he worked, Aristide Maillol insisted it was the only remedy for the occasional "artist's block" with which he was afflicted.[58]

Maillol instantly comes to life in a book of conversations with Henri Frère, in which he described his inspirations:[59] Bach, Mozart, particularly Mozart, and Beethoven transport him. Like Denis, he, too, was impressed with Wanda Landowska. He tried unsuccessfully to draw her hands as she played; her fingers moved too rapidly. He could not catch them. He became familiar with musical styles, the Classical style and the Baroque style and the differences between them. And he was pleased as a child when he recognized on the radio—before the announcer gave away the title—a baroque piece: Handel's *Alexander's Feast*.[60]

Maillol enjoyed the artistry of Wilhelm Kempf in the Salle Pleyel in Paris. "There is such silence," he wrote. "One is suspended in mid-air by this music. Thousands of people there, hearts beating— all because of a man who's playing some notes."[61] Here this artist reveals a fantastic sensitivity to the extraordinary power, almost a hypnotic power that only a few performing musicians manage to acquire over their audiences.

Picasso, according to intimates, knew little serious music and understood it even less. This despite the seeming significance of musical instruments in many Cubist pictures. When Picasso and his Spanish friends first met Max Jacob, they had no common language. As they sat around for a while, unable to communicate, somebody suggested that they sing the symphonies of Beethoven, and they all joined in with great enthusiasm—all except Picasso, who didn't know them. "He could not understand symphonic music," says Fernande Olivier. "He preferred to deny himself an emotion that was only instinctive. He never went to a concert."[62]

Picasso's 1920 portraits of De Falla, Satie, and Stravinsky look like three variations on a single theme. Stravinsky's ugliness fascinated him. But his portrait caused problems with the Swiss customs agents. Examining the rolled-up canvas as the composer prepared to enter the country from Italy, the customs inspectors insisted the portrait was a secret map and refused him permission to bring it in. Stravinsky promptly mailed it to Lord Berners in England who then sent it by diplomatic pouch to Paris.[63]

Between 1917 and 1924, Picasso designed at least five curtains for ballets: *Le Tricorne* (1917), *Parade* (1919), *Pulcinella* (1920), *Cuadro flamenco* (1921), and *Le Train bleu* (1924). Here work drew him into contact with musicians. Evidently, Picasso enjoyed working with musicians, contributing suitable backdrops for their projects, but he was not really sensitive to nor knowledgeable about music.

Braque, on the other hand, had some musical education. He studied flute with Gaston Dufy, Raoul's brother, a musician who was also the editor for the *Courrier musical*. Like Picasso and Juan Gris, he incorporated musical instruments in his canvases, particularly the mandolin and the guitar, and also introduced the names of Bach and Debussy into his paintings. Speculation on why these three artists utilized musical instruments as frequently as they did has remained just that. Some theorize that Braque, in particular, felt that paintings evolved much as musical compositions do; others that in a world of changing artistic values the shape of these instruments had remained constant and it was their constancy that these painters sought.

A list of *peintres mélomanes* (painters enamored of music) has no counterpart among musicians. Only rarely do multiple artistic talents appear among the composers. Could it be that it is easier to be an amateur musician than an amateur painter? Few would agree with that suggestion. Yet Bazille played piano arrangements for four hands with his friend Edmond Maître, the obsessed Wagnerite; together they attended Pasdeloup's weekly concerts. (Many artists were subscribers to the Lamoureux and Pasdeloup concerts. Some of them first heard Wagner's music during these series.) Bazille attended Berlioz's funeral in March of 1869, and adored Gluck, Mozart, and Wagner. Renoir, as mentioned earlier, had sung in the choir of Saint-Eustache under Gounod, who tried to persuade him to become a professional singer instead of a painter. Degas, too, had a pleasant singing voice, a good musical memory, and a knack for picking out tunes on the piano. His musical tastes crystallized early and remained rather constant. He liked the music of Gluck, Cimarosa, Weber, Meyerbeer, Verdi, Gounod, Chabrier, along with café-concert songs, ballads with guitar accompaniment, and the ballets of Delibes, Minkus, and Adam. He found Beethoven depressing and resisted Wagnerian religiosity. He enjoyed theatrical elements, as did many painters. If Degas had made a trip to Bayreuth, like many of his colleagues, he would have disapproved of the covered orchestra pit. Typically French, he preferred intelligibility and sensuality over German symbolism and idealism. According to Saint-Saëns, Degas might be regarded as a Second Empire middlebrow who worshiped melody. Wagnerian converts like Fantin-Latour, Bazille, and Cézanne described Degas as a reactionary, a precursor of the 1920s tastemakers who liked music-hall jazz, praised Stravinsky's return to the eighteenth century, and detested Teutonic fog.

Finally, personal relationships emerge as the strongest inducement to move visual artists toward the musical experience. Caillebotte's brother was an excellent pianist who also composed piano pieces and works for organ and orchestra; Manet's wife Suzanne Leenhoff was an accomplished Dutch pianist; Dufy's father, an amateur musician, made music an integral part of his family's life; one son, Léon, became an organist at Le Havre; another, Gaston, a flutist, edited the *Courrier musical* and regularly obtained tickets to the best concerts in Paris for his brothers; Moreau's mother, Pauline Desmoutriers, was a fine musician; Bonnard's sister Andrée married composer Claude Terrasse; Suzanne Valadon, Satie's only lover, was intimate as well with Degas and Renoir; Lerolle and Chausson married two sisters; the musical Dihaus were cousins of Toulouse-Lautrec; and Henri Rousseau enjoyed playing a violin which he kept handy in his atelier.

As for musical portraits, most artists in the late nineteenth century continued to paint portraits of musicians in the tradition of Ingres, Delacroix, and Courbet: Carrière, Redon, Whistler, Sargent, Boldini, Blanche, Manet, and Rodin are but a few of the better-known artists who painted musicians. Sargent, a passionate music lover, was a fine pianist. Rodin, although impressed by the Austrian composer Gustav Mahler, disliked Debussy's music.[64] Leger, Picasso, Picabia, and Brancusi were all close friends of Satie. Brancusi helped design his tomb.

French artists continued to exercise an influence on French music, first through their early interest in Wagner, his theories, his prose works, and his music; then through the Ballets Russes and several of its principal composers like the émigré Russians, Stravinsky and Prokofiev; and finally because the very nature of French music was programmatic, requiring extra-musical material for realization of its potential. The cultural melting pot that was Paris in the twenties offered an ambience and an atmosphere in which musicians, artists, and writers flourished in symbiotic relationships—all to the benefit of listeners, viewers, and readers.

7

Music and Literature

On 17 February 1860 Charles Baudelaire wrote Richard Wagner a long and exceedingly complimentary letter. He had heard the three concerts at the Théâtre-Italien—on 25 January, and 1 and 8 February—of excerpts from Wagner's operas and he was overwhelmed by the music.[1] He felt that this music represented the closest thing to his own sense of correspondence among the arts. Because he did not want the composer to think he was looking for favors from him, he did not even include his address. Wagner had no difficulty finding him, however, and Baudelaire soon became a regular visitor to his Wednesday evening receptions.[2] Incredibly, because he says in his letter that he was "born in a country where poetry and painting are hardly better understood than music," Baudelaire showed more insight and understanding in his comments on Wagner's music than even some of the bona fide critics of the time.[3] He had also read Liszt's brochure on *Lohengrin et Tannhäuser* and the English translation of *Oper und Drama*. He could not read

Das Kunstwerk der Zukunft or *Die Kunst und die Revolution* because he knew no German.[4]

The following year, several days after the *Tannhäuser* fiasco on 13 March 1861, the writer Catulle Mendès, just twenty at the time, invited Wagner to reply to his critics in *La Revue fantaisiste*, the Parnassian journal he edited. Wagner wrote Victor Cochinat, editor of *La Causerie*, that a young man of sixteen or seventeen had invited him to rebut his critics and he was delighted with the opportunity to do so. Unfortunately, the collaboration came to naught, because the *Revue fantaisiste* closed its doors a mere nine months after they opened. But a small group of literary activists had, however, already taken notice of Wagner and his ideas. Three weeks after the *Tannhäuser* performances—there were three before Wagner withdrew it—on April 1st Baudelaire published his famous essay "Richard Wagner et *Tannhäuser* à Paris" in the *Revue européenne*. Here a prominent writer took his countrymen to task for their treatment of a man he regarded as an extraordinary artist.[5]

Baudelaire wrote: "Thirteen months ago ... there was a great uproar in Paris. A German composer who had lived long among us [1839–42] without our knowledge, poor, unknown, existing by means of wretched tasks, but a man whom for fifteen years now the German public had been acclaiming as a genius—this man was returning to the city which had witnessed his youthful struggles, to submit his works to our judgment." It was known that "on the far side of the Rhine the question of reform in opera was being hotly debated and that Liszt had espoused the reformer's opinions with enthusiasm." Baudelaire mentions Fétis's indictment against Wagner, but calls the Belgian musicologist's articles "hardly more than a depressing diatribe."

It seems that as soon as word spread that excerpts from Wagner's music would be offered to the public at the Salle des Italiens, the French proceeded to debate the matter, though few of them had ever heard any of his compositions. "Wagner's concerts [became] ... one of those solemn crises of art, one of those free-for-alls into which critics, artists and the public are in the habit of hurling indiscriminately all their passions."

Then Baudelaire quoted Berlioz, from the composer's article in the *Journal des Débats* on 9 February 1860. " 'The vestibule of the Théâtre-Italien was a strange sight on the evening of the first concert, a mêlée of passions, shouts, and arguments which seemed always on the point of degenerating into acts of physical violence.'

"Wagner had shown great daring," Baudelaire continued, "the program of his concert contained neither instrumental solos, nor songs, nor any of those exhibitions so dear to a public which dotes on virtuosos and their tours de force." [This selection was made expressly to prepare the public for the elimination of the operatic numbers—solos, duets, or trios—in his operas and the use, instead, of continuous music.]

"I have often heard it said that music cannot pride itself on being able to translate all or anything with precision, as can painting or writing. This is true up to a point, but it is not entirely so. Music translates in its own way and using means which are proper to it. In music, just as in painting and even in the written word, which is nevertheless the most positive of the arts, there is always a lacuna which is filled in by the listener's imagination."

Baudelaire continued offering explications of *Lohengrin* and *Tannhäuser* from Liszt and Berlioz and explained that while he could not read *Die Kunst und die Revolution* or *Das Kunstwerk der Zukunft* because they had not been translated, he finally got hold of Wagner's *Oper und Drama* in an English translation that he could understand. He quotes Wagner:

"I decided to seek my point of departure in ancient Greece . . . thirty thousand Greeks were capable of following performances of the tragedies of Aeschylus with unflagging interest. [This was possible because of] an alliance of all the arts uniting in a common object, which was the creation of the most perfect, the only true artwork [a reference to Wagner's *Gesamtkunstwerk*]."

Baudelaire grasped the concept of the leading motives—the thematic transformation of melodies that referred to persons, things, sentiments, or events—incorporated by Wagner into his operas. "I have already spoken of certain melodic phrases whose relentless reappearances in different passages from the same work had keenly intrigued my ear at the first concert given by Wagner. . . . In *Tannhäuser*, at each recurrence of the two principal themes, the religious motive and the hymn of the flesh, the audience's attention was quickened and its state of mind transformed into one in keeping with the new situation. . . . Using a method which he applies in an entirely original manner, Wagner succeeds in extending the empire and the territorial rights of music."

138

Portrait of Emile Zola by Manet, which also illustrates the current vogue of le japonisme. Writers like Zola, Valéry, Gide, Verlaine, Cocteau, and many others had personal relationships with musicians and their work was often set to music.

STRAWINSKY DIAGHILEV COCTEAU SATIE

Cocteau was the writer with whom Satie collaborated most successfully. Cocteau had brought Diaghilev into the group and along with Picasso, who designed the sets, they fashioned a masterpiece of twentieth-century ballet, Parade.

Jules Massenet (right) knew his audiences and gave them regularly what they wanted.

The precursor of the Parnassians was Théophile Gautier (far right), the apostle of l'art pour l'art.

"... the success or failure of *Tannhäuser* can prove absolutely nothing; ... in the not so far distant future we may well expect to see not only new composers, but even some for long accredited, taking more or less profit from the ideas put forth by Wagner. ... What history book has ever shown us a great cause lost in a single round?"

18 March 1861

A continuation of the article on 8 April of the same year concludes with several questions. "What is Europe going to think of us? What will they say of Paris in Germany? A handful of rowdies [referring to members of the Jockey Club] is disgracing us collectively!"

Unquestionably Baudelaire evaluated Wagner and his music much as we do today. The poet understood the composer's aesthetic and how he went about achieving his goals. Baudelaire was just angry and embarrassed that he could not convince his countrymen to accept and esteem Wagner as he did.[6]

After receiving Baudelaire's letter, Wagner asked writer Jules Champfleury to thank him. He couldn't understand how a French literary man could comprehend so easily so many things that seemed foreign to him. Champfleury, Baudelaire's friend, had written a short piece on Wagner in 1860, even before the first concert at the Théâtre-Italien. "If you're successful immediately," he had said to Wagner, "I'll keep quiet. You won't need me. If you're attacked, however, I place my pen at your service."[7] Needless to say, Champfleury's essay was reprinted the following year, after the *Tannhäuser* debacle, in his volume of essays entitled *Grandes Figures d'hier et d'aujourd'hui: Balzac, Gérard de Nerval, Wagner et Courbet*. Théophile Gautier's daughter Judith, who later would introduce *le japonisme* into French culture, was also affected by the failure of *Tannhäuser*. She described it in three separate works: *Richard Wagner et son oeuvre poétique depuis Rienzi jusqu'à Parsifal* (1882), *Le Second Rang du collier* (1903), and *Le Troisième Rang du collier* (1909). Shortly after her marriage to Catulle Mendès, the young couple, accompanied by writer Villiers de l'Isle-Adam, visited Wagner and Cosima at Tribschen in July 1869. There they enjoyed the antics of Wagner, who was showing off his youthfulness with arduous activities on his lawn. (Years later, after her divorce from Mendès, Judith and Wagner became lovers. Perhaps he was already attracted to her at this time.)

Undoubtedly, Richard Wagner's theories and writings would have the most powerful impact on nineteenth-century French writers, particularly those struggling to free their verse from the constraints of classicism, but many other musicians also worked closely with writers and poets as they sought fresh inspiration for their pieces with texts. Franz Liszt, for example, composed about ninety-three sacred and secular choral/vocal works and almost a hundred songs and recitations. For these he had to choose his texts carefully. Also, his many sojourns in Paris brought him into close touch with the foremost writers, dramatists, and artists of his time. Even his thirteen symphonic poems show the influence of literary works.

Many composers also wrote prose, most often music criticism. Starting with Carl Maria von Weber in the early nineteenth century, Schumann, Berlioz, Liszt, Saint-Saëns, Debussy, Dukas, Satie, and others proved themselves gifted writers. Yet with very few exceptions—Ezra Pound and perhaps Cocteau and Tristan Klingsor come to mind—writers did not compose music. But they had definite ideas about the powers of music, and for many, particularly the Symbolists, all art aspired to the level of music, which they considered a universal language.

Maurice Barrès insisted that "music alone can intervene at the time when literature and painting have for long confessed their failure. Music can suggest visions of human sensibility."[8] "I know nothing about music," he said, "but my thoughts can be translated into music.[9] . . . I sense a powerful force capable of lifting crowds, a religious force. Through music one can reach the soul of a nation.[10] . . . After theology, music is the most beautiful thing in the world."[11] Barrès speculated often about music. For him, the analogical use of musical terms described not only what is most mysterious in the human condition, but also staked a claim for words in the poetic border zone that Paul Valéry speaks about, where discourse merges with music in an effort to communicate this mystery.[12] Barrès believed that rhythm was at the base of all art and that art was only significant when it comprised dance and music. "The artist is not a contemplator, but a dancer," he wrote.[13] As a confirmed nationalist, Barrès also invoked regular comparisons between German and French musicality. His preoccupation with music, even in his novels, is not unusual at this time because the musicalization of the novel came into fashion in both France and England after the First World War. (Romain Rolland's *Jean Christophe* is a good example of the genre.)[14]

Eight years after the appearance of Baudelaire's piece in the *Revue européenne*, on 15 April 1869, critic Edouard Schuré contributed a long analytical article entitled "Le Drame musical et l'oeuvre de M. Richard Wagner" to the *Revue des deux mondes*. In this article, which appeared six years before Schuré's principal work, *Le Drame musical*, the author made some of the same points as Baudelaire in his "Richard Wagner et *Tannhäuser* à Paris." (Schuré did not know Baudelaire personally; he frequented the society of Charles-Augustin Sainte-Beuve, Ernest Renan, and Jules Michelet.) It was startling that Schuré could publish his article in the *Revue des deux mondes*, where Pierre Scudo, the reigning critic, maintained a decidedly anti-Wagnerian stance. Apparently, his article, although accepted for publication, underwent considerable censorship and he protested, but he never was given the opportunity to rebut.[15]

Pierre Louÿs, the very close friend of Debussy—who had set to music selections from his *Chansons de Bilitis* and also his *La Joueuse de flûte*—had attended Wagner's second Bayreuth festival in 1892. He had seen *Parsifal* seven times and wrote Debussy that "Richard Wagner is the greatest man who ever existed."[16] Louÿs recorded the names of pieces he had heard at the various concerts he attended. He was a regular at the Lamoureux and Colonne concerts, and the Overture to *Tannhäuser* was his favorite orchestral piece, so much so that in 1896 he wrote a short story entitled "Une Ascension au Venusberg." Another of his favorites was Reyer's opera *Sigurd*, based on a story similar to that which inspired Wagner's *Ring*.

Young Jules Laforgue liked the "Ride of the Valkyries," which he complained was hissed at a Colonne concert. He enjoyed concerts of the music of Liszt, the opera *Carmen*, a recital of Essipova (a pianist who was the second wife of the celebrated teacher and pianist Theodor Leschetizky), and the piano quintets of Schumann and Brahms. Laforgue saw *Tristan und Isolde* three times in one year, and he adored the piano. "It's a full orchestra," he wrote in one of his letters, which were replete with mention of musical compositions.[17] Laforgue even used Lohengrin, the son of Parsifal, as the basis for a morality tale in his *Moralités légendaires*.[18]

Leconte de Lisle, another French Wagnerite, wrote "La Légende des Nornes," wherein each of three Norns weaves the threads of life, as in Wagner's *Ring*. He also wrote *La Mort de Sigurd*, another offshoot of the *Ring*. De Lisle, a leader of the Parnassian poets, used his home as a meeting place for his disciples, *Le Parnasse contem-*

porain, in 1866. "La Légende des Nornes," part of his *Poèmes barbares* or non-Greek poems, was inspired by Nordic mythology. Similar to Wagner, who at the end of his life revealed an interest in Eastern religions, de Lisle was taken with Buddhist thought and religion.

Emile Zola did not demonstrate any particular interest in music. Yet in a letter of 26 December 1878 to Henry Céard, Zola accepts Céard's suggestion that he write an article based on Berlioz's correspondence. The piece appeared in the issue of *Le Voltaire* of 14 January 1879. Also, collaborating with Alfred Bruneau, he provided the libretti for Bruneau's operas *La Rêve* (1900) and *L'Ouragon* (1901).

Tristan Klingsor, pseudonym of Léon Leclerc, was an art critic and poet whose *vers libre* was often very musical. His very name was a combination of two of Wagner's operatic characters—Tristan and Klingsor, the latter appears in *Parsifal*—and some of his poems (like *Filles Fleurs*) reveal the Wagnerian source of inspiration.[19] Klingsor also wrote musical compositions.

François Coppée, poet and dramatist, was an early Parnassian. During the Dreyfus case he was active in the anti-Semitic *Ligue de la patrie française*. Like many of his colleagues who showed a preference for musical terms, he divided his *Symphonie de l'attente* into four movements: allegro agitato, adagio, scherzo, and finale.[20]

J. K. Huysmans, the Belgian Symbolist writer, used musical references in many of his novels.[21] And Alfred Jarry, who selected Claude Terrasse to do the score and incidental music for his satirical farce *Ubu Roi* (1896), wanted an orchestra of sixteen musicians, timpani, and trombones, to drown out catcalls for his play. Owing to a lack of funds, at the premiere the piano was played by Terrasse and his wife. Occasionally Terrasse would leave the keyboard to bang on the cymbals.

Roland-Manuel, Ravel's student, was supposed to have provided the music for Max Jacob's comic opera *Isabelle et Pantalon* (1922).[22] Colette was one of the few writers who could play the piano, and she appears to have preferred the music of Schumann.[23] She wrote often of her musical friends, and her first husband Willy (Henri Gauthier-Villars) penned music reviews fairly regularly. She also collaborated with Ravel on his opera *L'Enfant et les sortilèges*, but their discussions and negotiations were all undertaken through correspondence, similar in a way to those of Strauss and von Hofmannsthal.

Often composers revealed their special doubts and concerns, particularly about the selection of a text, in letters to friends. In February 1907, in an unpublished letter from his home in Saint Félix, Déodat de Séverac questioned Charles Bordes about a libretto he was considering.[24] Should the story be condensed and how should he do it? Was there enough dramatic action to sustain interest on the part of an audience? His poet friend Lafargue [not Jules Laforgue] had agreed to help him with the libretto. Was he a good choice? He concluded that only a discussion of these problems in person would lead to a solution.

Occasionally, collaborations produced unexpected problems. Five days after the first Paris performance of *Die Walküre*, Maeterlinck's play *Pelléas et Mélisande* was staged on 17 May 1893 at a single performance at the Théâtre des Bouffes-Parisiens. Aurélien-François Lugné-Poë, director of the Théâtre de l'Oeuvre, and Camille Mauclair produced the work and Lugné-Poë himself played Golaud. Henri de Regnier, Whistler, Mallarmé, and Debussy were all in the audience. Mallarmé and Debussy were entranced by the play, and Debussy decided it was the perfect vehicle for an opera, but first he had to get the playwright's permission to proceed. Debussy then met Maeterlinck through the efforts of Camille Mauclair and Henri de Regnier. Together with his close friend Pierre Louÿs—who later married Louise de Heredia, daughter of another literary man, the poet José-Maria de Heredia—Debussy visited Maeterlinck at Ghent.[25] In an undated letter of 1893 to Chausson, Debussy reports that Maeterlinck was friendly, authorizing him to make any cuts he liked in the play, even suggesting some himself. "He says he knows nothing about music and when it comes to a Beethoven symphony, he is like a blind man in a museum. . . . When I thanked him for entrusting me with *Pelléas*, he insisted that it was he who should be grateful to me for setting it to music."[26]

Louÿs had a different memory of the meeting. In a letter to his brother Georges he insisted that Debussy was too shy to speak and Maeterlinck was even more shy, and that he was obliged to speak for Debussy and reply for Maeterlinck. At any rate, when Debussy chose the Scottish soprano Mary Garden for the role of Mélisande —a role Maeterlinck expected would be sung by his mistress Georgette Leblanc—trouble began. Maeterlinck may have been timid at their first meeting, but he now exploded. He challenged Debussy to a duel and threatened to beat him with his walking stick.[27] Fortunately, friends intervened. (Maeterlinck was an accomplished swordsman and Debussy would not have survived.) Two weeks before the premiere of the opera, however, the playwright wrote a letter to *Le Figaro* indicating that he hoped the opera would be a resounding failure. Not until many years later, after Debussy's death, when Maeterlinck heard the opera on a visit to America, did he acknowledge that without Debussy's setting *Pelléas et Mélisande* would have fallen into oblivion.

In February 1893 Debussy met Oscar Wilde at a banquet at the home of Georges Louis, Pierre Louÿs's brother. Writers among the guests included Valéry, Gide, Regnier, and Heredia; the painters Antoine de Rochefoucauld, Jacques-Emile Blanche, and Albert Besnard, and sculptor Pierre de Coutouly were also present. Several diplomatic figures rounded out a list that featured "pas un juif," as Pierre Louÿs noted with satisfaction.[28]

Unless the author of the text they determined to set was already dead, many composers felt obliged out of courtesy to meet or to write to the author before embarking on their composition. Some writers' responses were rather astonishing.

Thadée Natanson, Misia Sert's first husband and a good friend of Ravel, visited the contemporary French novelist and man of letters Jules Renard to tell him of Ravel's interest in his *Histoires naturelles*.[29] "He is an avant-garde musician who is highly thought of. . . . Surely you must be pleased." "Not at all," was the reply. "Wouldn't you like him to let you hear his music?" "No, certainly not." And to his journal, on 12 January 1907, Renard confided: "I told him I knew nothing about music, and asked him what he had been able to add to the *Histoires naturelles*. He replied: 'I did not intend to add anything, only to interpret them.'" Not unlike many of his contemporaries, Renard not only knew nothing about music, he was wholly disinterested. Ravel was far more precise about his decision to set the *Histoires naturelles*. In his biographical sketch for the Aeolian Company[30] he said: "For a long time, I had been attracted by the clear, direct language and deep hidden poetry of these sketches by Jules Renard. The text itself demanded a particular kind of declamation, closely bound to the inflexions of the French language." And he used a typically French declamatory, arioso style, but added his own personal touches.

Ravel's songs, *Histoires naturelles*, had their premiere at a Société Nationale concert at the Salle Erard on 12 January 1907. Singer

Jane Bathori[31] was the featured soloist with the composer at the piano. The audience was downright hostile and critic Pierre Lalo in *Le Temps* of 19 March 1907 wrote that "the idea of setting to music the *Histoires naturelles* is in itself surprising. Nothing could be more foreign to music than these little fragments of arid and precious prose . . . M. Ravel has discovered something lyrical in M. Renard's *Guinea-fowl* and *Peacock*; in my opinion this subtle musician has never been so completely mistaken." Ravel also set poems by Ronsard and Clément Marot, and he wrote the piano pieces of *Gaspard de la nuit* after the poems of Aloysius Bertrand. For these he needed no permissions or authorizations. On the other hand, for works of contemporaries like Mallarmé, the Belgian Symbolist writer Emile Verhaeren, Tristan Klingsor, and certainly Franc-Nohain, he was in touch with the authors. Mallarmé was his favorite poet and Baudelaire and Poe were close seconds. Ravel also admired Villiers de L'Isle-Adam's *L'Eve future* and Huysmans's *A Rebours*.

Ravel's acquaintance with prominent writers and artists was extensive. He was very friendly with Cipa Godebski, Misia's half-brother; and he benefited from his frequent visits to the Godebski apartment on the Rue d'Athènes, where the elite of writers, artists, and musicians would meet.[32] Regular visitors to their Sunday evening soirees included writers André Gide and Jean Cocteau, Ravel's closest friend Léon-Paul Fargue, Paul Valéry and Valéry Larbaud, Jean-Aubry, Arnold Bennett and Ambroise Vollard, painters La Fresnaye and d'Espagnat, Valentine Gross (who later married Jean Hugo, Victor Hugo's grandson), musicians Albert Roussel, Florent Schmitt, Déodat de Séverac, Darius Milhaud, Georges Auric, Maurice Delage, Roland-Manuel, Ricardo Viñes, Alfredo Casella, Manuel de Falla, Igor Stravinsky, Erik Satie, and occasionally Diaghilev and Nijinsky. It was quite a line-up of luminaries who surrounded him there.

Another circle of even more intimate friends met at the home of painter Paul Sordes and later at Maurice Delage's studio in Auteuil. They called themselves the "Apaches" and included (in addition to several mentioned above) poet Tristan Klingsor, composers André Caplet, Paul Ladmirault, and D. E. Inghelbrecht, critics Emile Vuillermoz and M. D. Calvocoressi, Lucien Garban of publishers Durand et fils, a very close friend of long standing, Abbé Léonce Petit, Charles Sordes (Paul's brother), and another painter Edouard Bénédictus.

Ravel met Franc-Nohain through Claude Terrasse. The composer had seen Franc-Nohain's comedy *L'Heure espagnole* at the Odéon theater and considered setting it as an opera-bouffe. His father was not well and Ravel hoped a successful theater piece would convince the older man that his son was a successful composer. Albert Carré, director of the Opéra-Comique, found the opera too licentious, but after four years made up his mind to stage it. By the time of the premiere Ravel's father had already died. It is an oft-told tale that when Ravel played over the score for the author, Franc-Nohain's only comment at the conclusion was to remark, after glancing at his watch, "Fifty-six minutes."[33]

Early in his career, Saint-Saëns met the librettist Louis Gallet, who had already provided libretti for Bizet, Massenet, and Gounod. In fact, he produced well over fifty libretti, twenty plays, and many volumes of poetry.[34] Gallet knew little about music, but he showed sensitivity to its powers. Saint-Saëns wrote: "We shared the same tastes in literature and art." Because things Japanese were popular at the time, they both decided to give their first venture a Japanese setting. *La Princesse jaune* was the result.

As a very young man, Saint-Saëns made the acquaintance of several prominent authors at the salon of Princess Mathilde, Napoleon's niece and the cousin of Emperor Napoleon III. At her home in the Rue de Courcelles and at her chateau in St. Gratien, he spent time with Flaubert, the Goncourt brothers, Sainte-Beuve, and Dumas père et fils. When the composer felt sufficiently at ease in this company, he hinted to the Princess that she might help him to obtain a production of one of his operas. Her reply was transmitted by a mutual friend: "What! Isn't he satisfied with his position? He plays the organ at the Madeleine and the piano at my house. Isn't that enough for him?"[35]

In addition to the occult writer Sâr Péladan, whose work he adorned with music, Erik Satie befriended and wrote music for Jules Bois, author of a book on Satanism and magic that included a preface by Huysmans. Debussy himself speculated about writing music for his play, *Les Noces de Satan*, but ultimately he rejected the project, possibly owing to the rather sordid atmosphere in which Bois moved. Not Satie, who also wrote the *Sonneries de la Rose-Croix* for a series of art exhibitions that Péladan organized each year from 1892 to 1897.[36]

An international movement of short duration (1916–21), born in Zurich and founded principally by Tristan Tzara, a native of Rumania, Dadaism attracted many refugee artists and writers. Members of the group emphasized the importance of instinctive expression, independent of control by the intelligence. Among Tzara's colleagues were the French sculptor and painter Hans (Jean) Arp and the German Hugo Ball. A similar group from New York—including the Frenchman Marcel Duchamp and Francis Picabia, a Spaniard— joined the Zurich Dadaists and by 1920 made their joint home in Paris, where they published their review *Littérature*. While its name means "nothing at all," Dadaism's significance seems to be its preparation for the Surrealist movement.[37]

The credo of the movement appealed to Satie, who apparently rated high marks from two luminaries of Dada: André Breton and Louis Aragon. For their part, they enjoyed the unusual titles Satie bestowed on his works. Their review, *Littérature*, published pieces by Paul Valéry, Gide, Fargue, and Stravinsky, poetry by Raymond Radiguet and music criticism by Georges Auric, and their three editors included, besides Breton and Aragon, another poet, Philippe Soupault. With the assistance of Tristan Tzara, in January 1920, the magazine staged a *Premier Vendredi Littérature* at the Palais des Fêtes. The music they presented featured works by Satie and "Les Six," along with pieces by some of the younger school of Arcueil. Recitations of poems by Max Jacob and Apollinaire completed the bill. When Breton began to denounce some of the pictures by Gris, Léger, and de Chirico that were on display, a riot ensued and the first Friday became the last offered by *Littérature*.

Satie, like Ravel, was very close to Léon-Paul Fargue, whose parents did not marry until he was close to thirty. (His paternal grandmother would not accept his mother as her daughter-in-law, so there was nothing to do but wait for her demise before legalizing the union.) As a result of this peculiar familial situation, Fargue always felt himself an outsider and according to the writer and critic M. D. Calvocoressi, Satie and Fargue had much in common.

Also like Ravel, Satie was friends with the Godebskis. Cipa's sixteen-year-old daughter Mimi, one of the children for whom Ravel had earlier written his *Ma Mère l'Oye*, composed the text of his song "Daphenéo." "Le Chapelier," in the same group of *Trois mélodies*, derived from the work of the critic and poet, René Chalupt. Satie dedicated it to Stravinsky, whom he called "one of the most outstanding geniuses music has ever known."

Cocteau was the writer with whom Satie collaborated most successfully. Cocteau had brought Diaghilev into the group and along with Picasso, who designed the sets, they fashioned that masterpiece of twentieth-century ballet, *Parade*. Cocteau knew everyone—from Proust to Gide, and Péguy to Mauriac—and guaranteed Satie an audience for his works. In the spring of 1916, in the middle of the war, Cocteau provided the composer with a scenario. Satie insisted that he could not be rushed and that the music would not be ready before October. Meanwhile, Satie approached Misia (now married to Alfred Edwards) to sponsor a concert of his music. He hinted that he would dedicate *Parade* to her. When she discovered that Cocteau had written the scenario she was furious, believing that the poet had tried to lure her protégé Satie away from her and Diaghilev. When the four-hand piano version appeared with her name as the dedicatee, she relented. By January 1917 the collaborators gave several private performances at Ricardo Viñes's home. After rehearsals in Rome, the work had its premiere at the Théâtre du Châtelet in Paris on 18 May. A celebrated audience, the funds from whose ticket purchases were destined for war relief, turned hostile as the work unfolded. Guillaume Apollinaire, in his program booklet, anticipated this reaction, but assured everyone that in time they would come to like it.

Saint-Saëns introduced Fauré to Parisian society in 1872 via the Viardot family. The celebrated Spanish contralto Pauline Viardot and her husband Louis Viardot hosted weekly soirees to which the cream of the intelligentsia were invited. Fauré recalled that Turgenev—Viardot's lover for forty years during her ménage à trois—and Flaubert performed charades while George Sand, Ernest Renan, and the left wing politician and historian Louis Blanc were spectators.[38] Although fairly reticent as a young man, Fauré nevertheless frequented many salons, particularly those of Madeleine Lemaire and the Comtesse Greffulhe as well as those of the Princesse de Polignac at the Rue Cortambert in Paris. The latter's home was a gathering place for the avant-garde. Despite mingling freely with many writers, poets, and dramatists, Fauré was not as literary-minded as many of his musical colleagues.[39] As Edward Lockspeiser noted, "Fauré was less concerned with the ultimate union of words and music than with an opportunity for displaying his lyrical gifts, for endowing the singer with a grateful line regardless of the details of inflection and emphasis demanded by the prosody."[40] Because of this tendency, Fauré occasionally misplaced accents or emphases in some of his lyrical settings. "Incidental music is the only genre which suits my limited abilities," Fauré is supposed to have told Saint-Saëns.[41] The younger man was hesitant about composing theatrical music and large-scale works.

After Fauré's Venetian holiday, late in 1891, the Princesse de Scey-Montbéliard (who later became the Princesse de Polignac) suggested a project on *La Tentation de Bouddha*, a collaboration between the composer and Verlaine, whom he knew well. Fauré considered it out of deference to her, but he eventually rejected the idea. Verlaine, who desperately wanted the money promised him for this project, offered another idea, from the Commedia dell'arte, a scene in a hospital ward (where Verlaine was lately spending his time), with Pierrot, Columbine, and Harlequin discussing aspects of life and love. This, too, had no appeal for Fauré, who had had his fill of Verlaine stalling on submitting poetry that Fauré was to set. Many are the letters that Fauré wrote his patroness complaining of Verlaine's constant procrastination.

Always careful to request permission of poets whose work he set to music, Fauré was also concerned that they listen to his setting of their poetry whenever possible.[42] He set several of Victor Hugo's poems as a young man, but admitted that he never quite succeeded with Hugo.[43] Hugo himself was musically insensitive. Verlaine's sensitivity, on the other hand, made his work appear as excellent material for Fauré. And in the song cycle *La Bonne Chanson*, in which Fauré set nine of Verlaine's twenty-one poems, he proved his point. The cycle was inspired by Fauré's love for Emma Bardac, who became Debussy's second wife. Bardac sang through each of the songs as they were written, suggesting changes.

After 1860, a group of poets known as the Parnassians represented a reaction against romanticism. Many were associated with the *Revue fantaisiste*, the journal founded by Catulle Mendès. The precursor of the Parnassians was Théophile Gautier, supposedly the apostle of *l'art pour l'art*. Actually the group, which included de Banville, Sully-Prudhomme, and even Baudelaire, took their motto from a theme propounded earlier by Victor Cousin in his *Cours de Philosophie* at the Sorbonne in 1818. For them, art assumed the role of religion with the poet as high priest. "Art for art's sake" stemmed from Cousin via the writings of Théophile Gautier. Fauré set the work of many of these poets, but his best "collaborations" after Verlaine and the Dutch writer Van Lerberghe were with Leconte de

Lisle. A Parnassian, Théodore de Banville insisted that "a poem cannot be altered without reducing it," but Fauré did not agree and even in *La Bonne Chanson* split stanzas at incorrect places. Surprisingly, this foremost composer of French *mélodies* was not above using the texts to suit his music rather than the other way around. Fauré was extremely forthright about his difficulty in setting the works of many of the Parnassian poets. "I have never been able to set the pure Parnassians to music," he admitted, "because their form, so elegant, pretty, and sonorous, resides entirely in the word—and because the word does not hide a single true thought." Of the poems of Leconte de Lisle, he confessed that "his verse is too full, too rich, too complete for music to be effectively adapted to it. Attributive adjectives take on enormous importance. Thus 'Helen with the white feet' is charming to say; it provides an image. If one adds notes to it and tries to sing it, those feet become gigantic, entirely disproportionate. It would be absurd and ridiculous, impossible not to smile at."[44]

Chabrier regularly associated with theater people. He also won the respect of men of letters and painters.[45] Mendès and Verlaine provided him with libretti for his operas, the latter supplying him with two opera-bouffes, *Fisch-Ton-Kan* and *Vaucochard et fils Ier*, neither of which was produced. Chabrier, a Wagnerite, gave composition lessons to the writer Villiers de l'Isle-Adam, another passionate Wagnerian. He set verses by Rostand (of *Cyrano* fame) and Richepin and often frequented literary salons, particularly that of Nina de Callias, where in 1880 he hobnobbed with the Goncourt brothers, Huysmans, Zola, Alphonse Daudet, and Mallarmé. Painters James Tissot and Marcellin Desboutin (Manet painted him as the male figure in *L'Absinthe*) both did crayon sketches of Chabrier, and Manet painted an oil portrait of the composer. At his death, Chabrier was the proud possessor of a remarkable collection of paintings by the foremost artists of the era. Chabrier was closest to Verlaine, whom he probably met at the salon of the Marquise de Ricard, headquarters of the Parnassians. The Marquise's son Xavier de Ricard, along with Mendès, often led the group, and Sully-Prudhomme, Mallarmé, Jean Moréas (who introduced the term "symbolist"), Verlaine, and Coppée appeared at their meetings as well. Chabrier was also intimate with Verlaine's brother-in-law, Charles de Sivry, who played piano at the Chat Noir. He first met and became friends with Cabaner, the bizarre musician friend of Renoir, at La Nouvelle Athènes. Impressionists, Symbolists, Parnassians, and French Wagnerites all provided Chabrier with inspiration for his work. He read widely and his tastes were so eclectic that at one point he even considered setting Pushkin's *The Captain's Daughter*.

The French critic Pierre Lalo, son of the composer of the same name, said of Chausson in 1947 that he was "one of the best French musicians and he is nearly forgotten."[46] Chausson had a solid knowledge of literature and chose his texts from the romantics, the Parnassians, and the Symbolists. He selected poems expressing elegiac sentiments, particularly those by Gautier, Verlaine, Villiers de l'Isle-Adam, Leconte de Lisle, Banville, Moréas, and Richepin.[47] He revealed a preference for song cycles, somewhat like the German composer Hugo Wolf. Chausson set cycles of poems by Shakespeare, Maeterlinck—his *Serres chaudes* is particularly well-known—Verlaine, Leconte de Lisle, Gautier, Mauclair, and his close friend Maurice Bouchor, whose name does not merit being included among these others because his work is inferior to theirs.

Chausson labored over his work. When Debussy wrote him about his own difficulties with Act IV, scene iv of *Pelléas*, Chausson reassured him, but complained about his own musico-textual problems. Around 7 September 1893 Chausson wrote "Le Roi Arthus . . . is causing me distress. . . . I notice after a few months of rest, that there are many things in the words that do not fit. It always has to be done over again."[48]

Literature dominated the arts during the time that Chausson wrote his compositions, but many literati looked to music for inspiration. While Verlaine and the Symbolists had broken down barriers separating text and tone, in Mallarmé's circle poets and musicians established a very close union of the two art forms. Indeed, the French art song, the *mélodie*, reached its apogee during this period. Richard Wagner's concept of a *Gesamtkunstwerk*, a total art work and the fusion of the arts, left a deep impression among artists in France.[49] The Dutch musicologist Frits Noske, in his book *French Song From Berlioz to Duparc*, quotes Becq de Fouquières's opinion that "a verse is a sonorous conception, representative of a mental conception . . . the word that generates the idea becomes the generator of the sound of the verse." This concept reflects Wagner's thinking on the matter, although several French music historians disagreed with de

Fouquières. Nevertheless, the texts of any number of French poets, including Hugo, Gautier, de Banville, Leconte de Lisle, Villiers de l'Isle-Adam, Lamartine, de Musset, and Silvestre, continued to inspire and stimulate the musical imagination of French composers of *mélodies*, and poets, for their part, showed no reluctance to review music.[50]

Chausson recognized the positive as well as the negative aspects of *le wagnérisme* in France, particularly with regard to his own work. To the lawyer and critic Paul Poujaud, a friend to many of the musicians of the time, he wrote about his opera *Le Roi Arthus*: "The greatest defect of my drama is without doubt the analogy of the subject with that of Tristan. That would still not matter, if only I could successfully de-Wagnerize myself. Wagnerian in subject and Wagnerian in music, is that not too much altogether?"[51] As he struggled to loosen the hold of Wagnerism on his own creations, Chausson spoke of "the red specter of Wagner" or "that frightful Wagner who is blocking all my paths."[52]

Ernest Chausson was born into a wealthy Parisian family. His father was a building contractor who participated in Haussmann's extensive renovations of the city. He came to music late, having studied law first, and was repeatedly discouraged from pursuing music as a career. A student of both Massenet and Franck, he switched to the latter exclusively, after recognizing the differences in their approach to music. His wife Jeanne, a pianist, and their five children made his home on the Boulevard de Courcelles a very happy one. When the painter Henri Lerolle married Jeanne's sister, the soirees chez Chausson made for extensive cross-fertilization among artists and musicians along with many writers as well. The list of their friends who participated in these evening receptions and private recitals is exceptionally long.[53] After Chausson's fatal bicycle accident on 10 June 1899, most of the "regulars" attended his funeral along with Pierre Louÿs, critic Pierre Lalo, pianist Raoul Pugno, and Octave Maus of Brussels.

Jules Massenet is the French counterpart of Puccini. Indeed, like Puccini and Strauss, he knew his audiences and gave them regularly what they wanted. Pandering to their taste was natural for Massenet. Recognizing the appeal to the public of the reformed courtesan, he selected this subject rather often. Even in his sacred dramas, *Marie-Magdeleine*, *Eve*, and *La Vierge*, which feature three heroines from his extensive feminine gallery, he emphasized the sexual sides of their natures. And when d'Indy, who intensely disliked this pseudo-religious eroticism, criticized it, Massenet replied, "I don't believe in all that creeping-Jesus stuff, but the public likes it and we must always agree with the public."[54] Mostly he focused on women—although he did write *Le Jongleur de Notre Dame* for an all-male cast. His women, whose feminine psychology he explored so thoroughly, included Hérodiade, Thérèse, Manon, Thaïs, La Navarraise, Sapho, Cendrillon, Ariane, and Cléopâtre. He was very fortunate in his publishers, first Georges Hartmann, the remarkable philanthropist and publisher who gave Debussy an annual stipend of 6,000 francs from about 1894. Hartmann published one of Massenet's first works, the song cycle *Poème d'avril* (1866) to a text by A. Silvestre and even after his bankruptcy in June 1891 still helped him in his career. Hartmann's office at the Boulevard de la Madeleine was a rendezvous for Bizet, Saint-Saëns, Lalo, Franck, and Augusta Holmès. With Edouard Colonne as conductor, Hartmann created the Concert national in 1873. He introduced Massenet to Colonne, who shortly afterward performed his *Les Erinnyes*, one of Massenet's first sacred dramas. Before Hartmann closed his doors, he permitted Massenet to rescue some of his manuscripts and scores that had remained there. Other autographed scores went to Heugel, who took over Hartmann's plates. With Heugel in France and Sonzogno and Ricordi in Rome, Massenet was practically guaranteed publication of each of his operas as rapidly as he composed them. And he did work fast. As prolific a composer as Charles Gounod wrote him: "You go at such a pace one can scarcely keep up with you."[55]

Because he was such a productive composer, Massenet had the opportunity of working with a number of librettists. Among them were Catulle Mendès, whom he called a "superb, inspired collaborator, a poet of ethereal hopes and dreams . . . a great scholar."[56] Massenet wrote that although "severe on me in his criticisms in the press, [Mendès] had become my ardent collaborator . . . he appreciated joyfully the reverence I had brought to the delivery of his verses." He worked with Gallet, that veteran librettist, and with Jules Claretie of the Comédie-Française. (When they collaborated on *Thérèse*, Massenet insisted that a telephone be installed in his home. He was delighted that his number would not be in the *annuaire*, so he would not be disturbed by phone calls, but he could phone out.)

Henri Cain, a "busy man of the theater" as James Harding calls him,[57] usually collaborated with another writer for his innumerable theatrical texts. Very close to Massenet, he even accompanied the Massenets to London once where, as the composer writes "we remained in conference for several hours reviewing different subjects which were suitable for works to occupy me in the future.[58] Finally we agreed on the fairy story of Cinderella: *Cendrillon.*" *Sapho,* for example, was the creation of Cain and Arthur Bernède. The day after its premiere on 27 November 1897, Alphonse Daudet, from whose novel it was derived, sent Massenet warm congratulations. And the morning of the premiere of *Le Roi de Lahore* at the Opera on 27 April 1877, Flaubert left a card for Massenet with the following note: "This morning I pity you; tonight I shall envy you."[59]

Massenet, who said "I have never been able to let my mind lie idle,"[60] was constantly percolating with ideas. One day he saw a play that he enjoyed very much at the Théâtre-Français. He immediately went to the home of the author François de Croisset and asked him if he could set his *Le Cherubin.* Cain collaborated with de Croisset on the opera and Mary Garden sang the principal role. Although Cain was essentially a writer, his wife, the singer Julia Guiraudon, who sang the title role in both *La Navarraise* and *Cendrillon,* continued to initiate him into the musical requirements of a libretto.

The day after the first performance of *Thaïs* at the Opéra, Massenet received the following note from Anatole France.

> Dear Master,
>   You have lifted my poor *Thaïs* to the first rank of operatic heroines. You are my sweetest glory. I am delighted. "Assieds-toi près de nous," the aria to Love, the final duet, is charmingly beautiful.
>   I am happy and proud at having furnished you with the theme on which you have developed the most inspiring phrases. I grasp your hand with joy.[61]

By and large, this is the kind of reaction Massenet usually encountered after he had set the work of a contemporary author. Occasionally, he had to request permission of a family or the executor of an estate before he could embark on a project. But even then, he usually met with success. Several of his operas had runs of between sixty and one hundred performances, extraordinary for those years. Some even reached America. Massenet also can be credited with having a significant influence on several of his prominent students, who also wrote operas that achieved the stage in their day: Charpentier, Pierné, Rabaud, and Reynaldo Hahn.[62]

* * *

On 16 January 1920, in an article in *Comoedia*, the critic Henri Collet described *"les cinq russes, les six français et M. Satie,"* thus grouping "Les Six," the six French composers—Georges Auric, Darius Milhaud, Arthur Honegger, Germaine Tailleferre, Francis Poulenc, and Louis Durey—in a cluster similar to that formed by the five Russian composers—Mily Balakirev, Alexander Borodin, Nicolas Rimsky-Korsakov, César Cui, and Modest Mussorgsky—known as "The Mighty Handful." Most of the French "Six" had given concerts as "les nouveaux jeunes" since 1917. The first time that the names of all six appeared on a program together was at Jane Bathori's song recital in November of that year. The first three, Auric, Milhaud, and Honegger (he was born in Le Havre to Swiss parents), were students at the Conservatoire of French theorist André Gédalge. With Satie and later Cocteau, whose 1918 book *Le Coq et l'arlequin* helped promote them, they entered the limelight. Cocteau, as Catulle Mendès had done earlier, urged these French musicians to discard German influences and proceed on their own indigenous musical paths. Three of them did: Milhaud, Honegger, and Poulenc. The others eventually ceased their participation.

Of the group of composers known as "Les Six," Darius Milhaud was by far the most prolific. He composed hundreds of pieces, even going so far as to set to music a seed catalogue. Over a third of his compositions feature a soloist or chorus, reflecting the importance texts had for him. Jammes, Claudel, Gide, Tagore, Chateaubriand, René Chalupt, Mallarmé, Rimbaud, Cocteau, Blaise Cendrars, Goethe, Ronsard, Desnos, Laforgue, Rilke, and Mistral were among the poets whose words he used. Sometimes, as with the *Love Poems* of Tagore, he set the same texts in two languages, first in English and then in a French translation by Elisabeth Sainte-Marie-Perrin. For a biblical work, *Le Cycle de la création*, with a text by Don Luigi Sturzo, an Italian priest who had been a leader of the Christian Democratic Party, Milhaud noted on the manuscript the prosody of the Italian language in order to facilitate his work and avoid unnecessary errors.[63]

Speaking of a translation of *Romeo and Juliet* by Jouve and Pitoëff, Milhaud wrote: "With the manuscript open before us, we would pick out the passages in which music was required and work out the timing together. Then I composed my music, which corresponded exactly to the spoken text."[64]

Milhaud found a remarkable collaborator in Paul Claudel and

together they forged a close friendship. Claudel, diplomat, poet, and dramatist, frequented Symbolist circles. Before the turn of the century he could be seen regularly at Mallarmé's Tuesday evening soirees in the Rue de Rome. A writer with an intensely lyrical gift, Claudel translated much of Aeschylus's works, and his plays and poems reveal the influence of the Greek dramatist as well as that of Rimbaud, particularly the latter's *Illuminations*. His own verse has neither rhyme nor meter and is halfway between verse and prose. Claudel was very aware of how he thought music ought to accompany his works. For example, when Milhaud started to write music for *Agamemnon*, the first part of the *Oresteia* trilogy, Claudel indicated precisely where he thought music should figure in the play. Milhaud wrote that Claudel "had observed that in Aeschylus's style, especially in certain choruses or dialogues, there were sudden transitions to a lyrical utterance of such a pitch that it absolutely demanded the support of chorus and orchestra. He would not have any music until Clytemnestra came out of the palace with her bloodstained ax in her hand and encountered the Chorus of Old Men. It was from their violent altercation that the music sprang."[65]

Milhaud continued:

> I tried to avoid the usual type of incidental music, a form of expression I detested at that time. There is nothing more false than the intrusion of a musical phrase while the actors go on speaking their lines without a pause, for melody and speech exist on absolutely incompatible planes. To bring out this lyrical content, what is wanted is a transition from speech to song. In my score, the strophes sung by Clytemnestra (dramatic soprano) alternate with the antistrophes sung by the Chorus of Old Men (male choir) against the background of a normal symphony orchestra.[66]

In 1916 Claudel was appointed French Minister to Brazil and invited Milhaud to accompany him to Rio as his secretary. During the two years they spent in South America, Milhaud absorbed much of the atmosphere and native music that he heard. He also grew even closer to Claudel. Their collaboration continued after their return to Paris in 1918, although Milhaud entered Cocteau's circle and became one of "Les Six." Milhaud, the scion of an old Jewish family of Provence, set a number of Hebrew texts, as well as a Sabbath service. His awareness of his Jewish heritage and the number of his compositions that reflect this concern caused Blaise Cendrars to comment "on the Jews' almost masochistic passion for lamen-

The Symbolist movement began in the 1870s with the work of Stephane Mallarmé and became one of the most significant in French poetry of the late nineteenth century. This portrait of the poet was painted by Manet.

(Right) In his work, Apollinaire sought to wed poetry and music.

(Below) Poulenc wrote 137 mélodies, of which only twenty are not based on texts by contemporary poets.

LIPNITZKI
PARIS

tation. Perhaps this may be related to Milhaud's predilection for librettos based on Greek tragedy: the *Oresteia*, *Les Malheurs d'Orphée*, *Médée*, etc." His work also shows the influence of jazz, the invention of another dispossessed and persecuted race.[67]

Francis Poulenc, in recent years one of the most visible members of "Les Six," gave the best of himself to his vocal works. He spent considerable time and thought selecting texts and he apparently had a fine sense of what kind of verses worked best with music. Pierre Bernac noted that "it is astonishing to realize to how great a degree the words, their colors, their accents, the rhythm of a phrase or of a line as well as its sense, the general movement, the pulsation, the form of the poem or literary text in addition to its meaning, all combined to awaken in Poulenc the musical inspiration."[68] He served poets well, and they were among the first to recognize his talents.

Besides his three well-known operas, *La Voix humaine* to a text of Cocteau, *Les Mamelles de Tirésias* derived from Apollinaire, and *Dialogues des Carmélites* of Bernanos, Poulenc wrote 137 *mélodies* of which only twenty are not based on texts by contemporary poets. From childhood, he adored poetry and attempted to set his favorite poems to music. Writer Claude Rostand was certainly correct when he wrote, "It is Poulenc who should be consulted by those who do not entirely understand the meaning of the poetry of Max Jacob, of Jean Cocteau, of Louise de Vilmorin, and above all of Guillaume Apollinaire."[69]

Poulenc once explained how he decides on the type of setting he believes appropriate.

> When I have chosen a poem of which the musical setting at times may not come to mind until months later, I examine it in all its aspects. When it is a question of Apollinaire or Eluard, I attach the greatest importance to the way in which the poem is placed on the page, to the spaces, to the margins. I recite the poem to myself many times. I listen, I search for traps, at times I underline the text in red at the difficult spots. I note the breathing places, I try to discover the inner rhythm from a line which is not necessarily the first. Next I try to set it to music, bearing in mind the different densities of the piano accompaniment. When I am held up over a detail of prosody, I do not persist. Sometimes I wait for days, I try to forget the word until I see it as a new word. . . . I rarely begin a song at the beginning. One or two lines chosen at random, take hold of me and very often give me the tone, the hidden rhythm, the key to the work. . . . It is not only the lines of the poem that must be set to music, but all that lies between the lines and in the margins.[70]

He selects those poems that can best tolerate the presence of music.

The perennial dialogue concerning the rivalry between words and music has been solved best by Debussy and Maeterlinck, Strauss and Hofmannsthal, Berg and Büchner, and certainly in the *Dialogues des Carmélites*, by Poulenc and Bernanos. There Poulenc, too, uses Bernanos's original text as his libretto with only a few minor cuts.[71]

Any discussion of literature of this period must highlight the movement known as Symbolism.[72] It began in the 1870s with the work of Stephane Mallarmé and became one of the most significant in French poetry of the late nineteenth century. The seeds of the movement were sown already by Baudelaire, whose sonnet "Correspondances" sought to demonstrate the relationships among scent, sound, and color. The Symbolists intended to liberate the technique of versification in a way that would make for greater fluidity. Poetry was to evoke, not to describe. The poet should offer impressions, intuitions, sensations, not precise details or description. Maeterlinck's play *Pelléas et Mélisande* is a fine example of a Symbolist drama, where nothing really happens and "men and women are helpless corks on the sea of fate," as Ernest Newman once put it. Symbolism permeates Wagner's operas, where people, objects, sentiments, and specific acts are brought to the attention of the audience through the use of recurrent leading motives that evoke these items. Furthermore, Wagner's preference for myths and his preoccupation with the theme of death all linked him to the Symbolists. Symbolism coupled with the cult of Wagnerism in France produced the conception of the essential musicality of poetry. The theme of a poem could be orchestrated and expanded by the choice of words having color, harmony, and an evocative power of their own.

Rimbaud, Verlaine, and Mallarmé are three poets whose names are generally associated with Symbolism. And although it was Verlaine in *Art poétique*, who stated "La musique avant toute chose," it was Mallarmé who had the greatest impact.[73] Mallarmé regarded poetry as incantation.[74] He insisted that a crisis existed in literature and that the hard and fast rules of official prosody had dried up creators. Language, individual languages were imperfect; there were too many of them. What was needed was a universal language and that language was music. Mallarmé envied its power. He determined that there was music within words and that it was the obligation of the poet to bring it out. If Richard Wagner could combine music and verse to produce poetry, why could not the poets do the same? Mallarmé sought the musicalization of poetry. Through music, he believed, poets would liberate their forms, rid themselves of the yoke of versification, and acquire more supple fluidity.

Indeed, the new *vers libre* came from a desire to separate free rhythms from rigorous meters. Since 1874 and Verlaine's *Romances sans paroles*, there was a tendency to treat words as musical notes, to have a more sinuous melody and rhythm. From 1880 to 1886, many young poets made multiple attempts to do this as they wrote prose poems and experimented with new kinds of punctuation. Laforgue and de Regnier, for example, attempted to endow poetry with musical powers formerly unknown. Like Wagner, they tried to create a *Gesamtkunstwerk*, a total artwork. In line with this fusion of the arts, René Ghil expounded his *Traité du verbe*. Each instrument, he says, has its own harmony and timbre. And so have vowels:

    A = organ = black = glory and tumult
    E = harp = white = serenity
    I = violin = blue = passion, prayer
    O = brass = red = sovereignty, glory, triumph
    U = flute = yellow = ingenuity[75]

A poem is a piece of music, suggestive of colored images. As a matter of fact, while Ghil saw "I" as blue, Rimbaud saw it as red. The basic aesthetic principle held that a letter or color could express a sentiment. Rimbaud had earlier invented colors of vowels and produced images associated with them.[76] Suggestive writing instead of description appealed to Verlaine. He thought that words which imply emotion are more powerful than words which designate it.[77] Verlaine sets a mood as a musician chooses a key with words like skies, clouds, the moon, the wind, the snow, the rain, the plain—all to become meaningful to the Symbolists.

Anna Balakian, the eminent scholar of comparative literature, finds three different concepts of music in nineteenth-century poetry. Baudelaire, she says, perceives in words the same suggestive properties inherent in musical notes, which evoke moods without communicating specific meanings. Verlaine's poetry is concerned not with single words but with combinations. He looks to the sound of a phrase rather than to its meaning. Mallarmé, on the other hand, simulated the composition of a musical work and inquires into musical forms rather than sounds: theme and variations, symphonic orchestration, pauses between images as between notes with verbal images replacing musical phrases. Memory and dreams were more sensual for him than experience. He felt there should always be an enigma to poetry. In an encounter between Mallarmé and Debussy, the composer supposedly told the poet that he had set *L'Après-midi* to music and Mallarmé replied, "Oh, I thought that I had done that myself."[78]

For many, Mallarmé's works represent the summit of the Symbolist movement. He belonged to the same generation as Mendès, Verlaine, de Banville, and Villiers de l'Isle-Adam—and Manet, whom he saw every day for ten years and who illustrated *L'Après-midi d'un faune*. But the poets who attended his Tuesday evenings in the Rue de Rome were, for the most part, twenty years younger, and looked to Mallarmé for leadership. The most frequent subject of these soirees was Richard Wagner, though Mallarmé had not seen a Wagner opera performed. Yet in his 1894 significant Oxford lecture about Symbolist theory, he called music and poetry two forms of the "Idea." "Music joins Verse," he said, "starting with Wagner, to form poetry."

Curiously, in 1926, Geneviève Mallarmé, the poet's daughter, said that her father never wanted her to take piano lessons.[79] Not until 1885 did music begin to appeal to her father. She may have been exaggerating; in 1869, it seems, he wanted to study music to learn its vocabulary. He constantly noted a rivalry between music and poetry and often evinced skepticism about the "pretended supremacy" of music. As an adult, however, he eagerly awaited the fall-to-spring concerts given every Sunday afternoon by the Lamoureux orchestra at the Cirque d'Eté. He often left the concerts feeling that music had robbed his art of some of its powers, that it was more evocative than poetry. Debussy noticed him there and so did Paul Valéry, who, in 1934, wrote a wonderful memoir, "Au Concert Lamoureux en 1893" in his *Pièces sur l'art*.[80]

Guillaume Apollinaire used no punctuation in his verse and at times experimented with pictorial typography. His poem "Il pleut," from *Calligrammes* (1918), is printed with the letters trickling down the page. Erik Satie's drawings illustrate the same tendency; the composer also occasionally eliminates bar lines in his musical notation. Madame Faure-Favier says Apollinaire "appears to have had very little musical sensitivity." She also described his lack of enthusiasm for concerts. And the composer Georges Auric says that music was "un art . . . auquel il [Apollinaire] était insensible."[81]

On the other hand, critic James R. Lawler believes that "music had a central relevance to the creative process in Apollinaire. . . . For him the creative process originates in song. Poetry becomes the verbal echo of a rhythm, a melody, a musical pattern as it was for folk-poets or lyric writers in general before the seventeenth century."[82]

In 1913, Apollinaire wrote to Henri Martineau, one of his friends, that he composes "generally while walking and singing two or three tunes that come to me quite naturally and that one of my friends [it was Max Jacob] has jotted down."[83] The poet made a recording at the Archives de la Parole in May 1914 and, in his recitation, the first line of the poem contains the highest pitch, while the last line has the lowest. At the beginning of each stanza there is a slight rise in pitch, but within the stanzas the movement consists of a descent by steps or half steps.[84]

The Symbolists, instead of making each detail of their poetry precise and distinct, blurred their details and merged them in fleeting images. This "musicalization" of his poetry suited Apollinaire, who conceived of it as a fleeting, flexible element, which he described in musical terms. He speaks of the "chant des moissonneuses" (the Song of the Harvesters); the machine gun on the battlefield "joue un air de triples croches" (plays a tune in three-quarter time); the noise of cannon is like "lourdes cymbales" (heavy cymbals) and "la terre tremble comme une mandoline" (the earth trembles like a mandolin).[85] Apollinaire constantly links his poetic creations with music; like the Symbolists, he sought to wed poetry and music.

André Gide had a special affinity for music. His early work reveals the influence of the Symbolists; his middle works, written between 1896 and 1914, show the non-Western elements acquired during his three years in Algeria; and in his later works, between the wars, he became the true leader of the literary avant-garde. In 1908 he founded the *Nouvelle Revue Française*, through which he eventually surrounded himself with the foremost new young writers of France.

Gide lost his original love for Schumann, but maintained an interest in Chopin all his life. G. Jean-Aubry calls him "the most music-loving writer who ever existed."[86] Musical allusions abound in his work. Jean-Aubry found about a hundred. Symphonies and operas held little attraction for Gide; but he was absolutely seduced by piano music. In 1891 he first mentions music in his work. Between 1896 and 1902, when he wrote his first literary essays, he began to discuss music, especially oriental and black music. Early in the century he became involved with Les Vingt and the Libre-Esthétique and started to practice some Debussy pieces on the piano, along with those by Fauré and Albéniz. As for Wagner: "Germany," he said, "has perhaps never produced anything at once so great and so barbarous."[87] Gide detested Wagner's personality. He studied the piano for forty years and practiced two to six hours daily. If he missed a day, he found he had no desire to play even "the finest page of music." He could negotiate the first and third Chopin Ballades and the Barcarolle. But "if I leave it [the piano] for a while, I am more handicapped than a beginner, and that more severely year by year. . . . To master a piece with transient perfection (which I never do without learning it by heart), I return to piano practice as to an opiate."[88] "For my health," he would say, in 1906. And in 1931, "As an opiate." Despite his steady practice, he was most uncomfortable playing publicly and rarely did so. Bach, Beethoven, Albéniz, and Chopin appealed to him most, though as he grew older, he grew more fond of the works of Bach. He also enjoyed playing Beethoven's symphonies in Liszt's piano arrangements—which indicates his high level of pianistic ability.

Curiously, Gide's participation in the works of composers was limited to the words he supplied for Stravinsky's *Perséphone* in another collaboration dreamed up by the unflagging, enthusiastic Ida Rubinstein.

Marcel Proust wrote that during his lifetime, when he was inconsolable, music always soothed his soul. Displaying a most sophisticated taste, he adored Beethoven's c-sharp minor quartet and continued to believe Germany unsurpassed in the domain of music. "[The composition of] music reveals to the listener the unknown, invisible soul of its creator," he wrote.[89]

Music plays a significant role in Proust's oeuvre; in *A la recherche du temps perdu* the sound of a familiar piece recalls certain events associated with its performance. Most readers believed that Proust's interest in music began with his friendship with composer Reynaldo Hahn, but this is not true according to Denise Mayer, who edited the excellent special number of the *Revue musicale, Proust et la musique d'après sa correspondance*. He certainly had what the French call a *formation musicale*—a musical background; he understood and enjoyed music many years before his first meeting with Hahn. As a matter of record, in the period of their friendship, from 1894 to 1915, they frequently disagreed on musical matters.

Proust learned to play the piano as a child, just as he learned to read and write. It was part and parcel of the educational training of all bourgeois families, particularly his, where his mother was an excellent musician and a fine pianist. In 1885, at the age of fourteen, in a letter to his grandmother he described what music meant to him. He wrote that it would be great to live near to all those he loved, to enjoy the charms of nature, and to be surrounded by a quantity of books and scores [*partitions*] and not to be too far away from the French theater. Later, when he could sight-read well, Proust performed opera transcriptions at the piano and four-hand versions of symphonic and chamber works.

While still in school, Proust met Pierre Lavallée, whose family was involved with music. Each member played an instrument and along with their friends comprised an active group of amateurs and connoisseurs. Pierre's brother married a *marseillaise*, whose sister Germaine was close to composer Augusta Holmès. Although Proust was exposed to much of Holmès's work, he refrained from praising it, recognizing that its quality did not measure up to some of the other pieces he enjoyed. He loved the songs of Schumann and Fauré. Particular favorites were the German composer's *Dichterliebe* to poems by Heine and Fauré's exquisite "Le Parfum impérissable." He adored the operas of Wagner—particularly *Walküre* and *Parsifal*—although his ardor cooled somewhat in later years.[90]

In his first book *Les Plaisirs et les Jours*, Proust wrote an elegy to what he called *La mauvaise musique*, perhaps thinking he could convince Hahn to reconsider some of his pet peeves regarding Debussy and his music. Hahn favored Massenet; he disliked Debussy's music, particularly *Pelléas et Mélisande*, although he definitely rated vocal music above instrumental music, what the French call *la musique pure*. Proust, on the other hand, regularly preferred instrumental music. A story concerning his love of chamber music is told by Proust's friend, the younger writer Louis Gautier-Vignal, in *Proust connu et inconnu*.[91]

Gaston Poulet, a very fine violinist and conductor, who was for a long while first violinist of the quartet that bore his name, reported to Gautier-Vignal that one night somebody rang the bell of his apartment on the Rue Herran. He awoke and opened the door and discovered that his nocturnal visitor was none other than Proust, whom he did not know, but who expressed a desire to hear the César Franck quartet. [All of this occurred after Proust had already confined himself to his quarters to write his great novel, rarely venturing forth from his house.] "When would you like to hear it?" Poulet inquired. "Would it be possible to hear it tonight?" Proust replied. Gaston Poulet accepted the challenge. He dressed, got into a taxi that Proust had waiting at the door, and gave the address of his cellist. They awoke him and waited until he was ready. Then they proceeded to the Rue Jacob to pick up the second violinist and went together to Proust's place on the Boulevard Haussmann. [Presumably they fetched the violist as well.] The performers set up their music stands in the salon while Proust lay down on the bed in his room, leaving the door open. The musicians played the Franck quartet and after the concert they had an excellent supper, for Proust always fed his guests well. Several days later, Proust appeared again at Poulet's apartment and presented him with some beautiful roses along with a "very important" check. Poulet apparently returned again to play at Proust's and when Vignal asked how often, he was told "about ten times."[92]

The following year Gautier Vignal invited Proust to his home to hear the Liszt Sonata played by the Roumanian pianist Georges Boskoff. Proust had another engagement for that Sunday, 15 December 1917. He replied in a note to his host, regretting his inability to come and adding, "I think, however, that I would rather go to your place (not for the attraction of Liszt, great genius and supporter of so much for the glory of others, but at this moment, it is Franck and Debussy I prefer to hear—and late Beethoven)."[93]

Apollinaire, Gide, Proust, and many other writers owe much of their musical education and inspiration to the Lamoureux concerts. Valéry spoke of the enormous debt of literature to Charles Lamoureux, and claimed that all literary history written at the end of the nineteenth century which does not mention music is totally valueless. "Worse than incomplete; inexact, worse than inexact, unintelligible. . . . Any literary history that speaks only of literature is as weak as political history that does not mention economic events."[94] The movement in poetry that began around 1840 or 1850 cannot be understood if the role that music played would not be considered along with it. For this reeducation of poets from 1880 to 1900, Lamoureux and his concerts are of prime importance. Like Baudelaire with the Pasdeloup Orchestra, Mallarmé and his followers have the Concerts Lamoureux. Enthusiastic critic and apostle, connoisseur and enchanter, captain and virtuoso, Lamoureux was a guardian of the Beautiful, communicating emotion through musical works.

Among the six hundred souls in rapt attention each Sunday for the Concerts Lamoureux as the conductor raised his baton were the most elegant and *cultivé* of the Parisian public. Valéry singled out a very particular group of *mélomanes* [music lovers] who, while sharing in the general enthusiasm, participated as well in the performance in a manner not dissimilar to the conductor's. This group of "littérateurs" promoted the musical education of a growing French public which had undergone a remarkable transformation. An unusually close relationship of music and poetry, marked on occasion by symbiosis and at other times by malaise, encouraged a climate of reciprocal elucidation. Writers and composers collaborated or inspired one another, maintained close personal relations, involved themselves in each other's polemics, aspired toward a convergence of their arts, or worked toward their essential demarcation, reeducating each other and prodding each other into the avant-garde. During this era, French literature underwent a stylistic purification, discovered the ideal of art for art's sake, ventured into the forest of symbols, and opened new paths into imaginary space. Poetry discovered within language the possible concordance of meaning, rhythm, and sonority, discarded the ballast of objective description, and took flight toward newly accessible, crystalline worlds. Composers, in turn, found literary experiments analogous to their own musical creations.

From the crescendo of calls for total art (*Gesamtkunstwerk*) to the musicalization of a poetry bereft of Teutonic metaphysics, from Verlaine's insistence on "music before everything" (*La musique avant toute chose*)[95] to Jarry's intention of drowning out with music the expected catcalls of his unsophisticated audience,[96] two phases delineate themselves in the history of this creative entanglement. Merging into one another rather than remaining distinct and discrete, they nevertheless highlight a perceptible shift in the temper and scope of artistic cross-fertilization increasingly evident around the first decade of the twentieth century. In tracing these changes, one becomes increasingly aware that they parallel the changing fortunes of *le wagnérisme* in France.

The romantics prepared the advent of music on the literary scene, where it became the basis of the interaction between poetry and music. It entered into the subject matter of the literati, their themes and, with the Symbolists, into their ideas about literature itself. Poets greeted music with open arms as a liberator from old forms and as a catalyst for experimentation. Under Mallarmé's direction, music erupted into the more fluid rhythms of free verse and the poem in prose and penetrated the words of the Symbolists, modulating them into poetic incantations. Whatever the degree of involvement, of individual approach, from facile borrowings to total immersion into the musical experience, few French poets or writers escaped the enchantment or denied the preeminence of all-powerful music (*la puissante Musique*). It was the period of obligatory attendance at concerts or the opera, of the regular ritual of the public cult of music by poets, writers, and literary critic alike, of competing schools and raging disputations within and outside the pages of the *Revue wagnérienne*. In this period the most persistent literary calls for a fusion of the arts came under the aegis of Music. The era witnessed Mallarmé's heroic struggle with the gods of Music to wrest back from them what they had taken away in marvelousness and importance.[97] The symphony must be transformed into a book, and to do so one must locate the true source of music by looking beyond the sounds of brasses, strings, and woodwinds.[98] A fervent Wagnerian, yet more subtle than the Master, Mallarmé sought to make of *La Poésie* the supreme instrument through which the superior music of the spheres could be heard.[99]

Toward the end of the nineteenth century, amid intimate collaboration and close cooperation, a disentanglement of the two arts began to occur. The phenomenon of *le wagnérisme*, with its hordes of admirers and detractors, both musical and literary, ceased to be the center of controversy. As the musicalization of poetry became a permanent acquisition, music itself becomes less and less the quintessential art. The two arts, having benefited from their association, exhibit a clearer and more overt awareness of the irreducible specificity of their means and preoccupations. Initially merged, they now separated.

Debussy, inspired by Verlaine, Mallarmé, and Maeterlinck, disdained the *trop littéraire* and Wagnerian expectations.[100] Poet and composer worked with one another, but not toward the *Gesamt-kunstwerk*. A stricter scrutiny controlled their exchanges, a more rigorous discernment transformed them beyond recognition.[101] Proust captured the fleeting yet grandiose sweep of *temps perdu* in a synthesis as close in range as it is removed in spirit from the musical pronouncements of the prophet of Bayreuth. Wagner's work is "beau," but "plus il est légendaire, plus je le trouve humaine."[102] Still a Wagnerian, Proust was uncomfortable with the ponderous structure, the imperfections of detail.[103] Like Debussy, he disliked the pretentious passage that resists dissolving into the poetic flicker of original sensation. Like Mallarmé, he searched instead for the "relationships and intervals, however few or multiple, to bring to the novel the poet's exigency to conceive an object in its fleeting moment, in its absence, faithful to some special vision deep within."[104] But the enchantment breaks easily, the landscape darkens for long stretches. With Proust, Wagnerism enters its age of prose and the novelist, ready to pay homage to music, worries that literature is incapable of speaking as music.[105] His masterpiece dissolves into the evanescent glow of *la belle époque*, leaving in its wake the few lingering moments of *le temps* found. "The more a poem conforms to poetry," Valéry said, "the less it can regard itself, without peril, as prose."[106]

The public cult of music subsided into solitary enjoyment. Gide kept his predilection for music separate and private, the stuff for diaries and outside interest.[107] Max Jacob and friends improvised scenes from various operas in irreverent *mélanges* as the poet, at the piano, "parodied, without transitions, Donizetti, Wagner, Verdi, Massenet, Debussy."[108] Literature and music learned independence from one another. Wagner no longer exalted "so much as he crushed."[109] In the silence of the spheres, the avant-garde erupted separately, if simultaneously, in music and in literature with the anti-Wagnerian abruptness of Stravinsky and the enigmatic surrealism of Apollinaire, lighting up the crepuscule of earlier gods. The final, harsh words belong to Gide. "Wagner," he wrote, "permitted a large number of snobs, of literary people, and of fools to think that they love music, and a few artists to think that genius can be acquired."[110]

8

The Spaniards in Paris: From the Unpublished Journal of Ricardo Viñes

Unlike the Russians who arrived in Paris in a blaze of glory or the Americans who came as heroes in the aftermath of the First World War, the Spaniards who entered France at the turn of the century came as impoverished immigrants, artists, and musicians who trickled into the country after they had saved sufficient funds to reach the French capital. There they hoped to refine their craft, make contact with native artists, enhance their professional prospects, and generally better their financial and social situations. Most expected to return home when the political and social climate in Spain improved. They sought out the traditional arrondissements for newcomers, and clustered together for companionship and mutual assistance. Many of the Spaniards came from Catalonia, the Spanish province closest to France.[1] Some stayed almost an entire lifetime, making Paris a second home; others went on to capitals and cultural centers in Europe and North and South America. A few returned to Spain having failed to adjust to émigré life, but most benefited from their stay in Paris. One of these young Spaniards kept a diary, as yet unpublished, which he began writing when he left Barcelona with his mother for Paris in 1887. His story adds a touching element to the saga of the immigrant artist in the cultural capital of Europe.

Ricardo Viñes (1875–1943) was the foremost champion of the new French, Spanish, and Russian piano music that emerged in the first decades of the twentieth century. He introduced and repeatedly performed almost the entire piano repertory of Debussy and Ravel, innumerable pieces by de Séverac, Fauré, and Satie, many compositions by his countrymen Granados, de Falla, and Albéniz, along with the works of the Russians—Mussorgsky, Borodin, Balakirev, Glazunov, Rimsky-Korsakov, and Prokofiev — all little known at that time outside their native lands. In later years, particularly while living in South America in the thirties, he offered the first performances of piano pieces by dozens of aspiring young Latin American composers. His repertory, as Jean-Aubry once said, was "prodigious. Perhaps no pianist ever had one like it. One wondered how he even had time to *read* all the music he actually played from memory!"[2]

Viñes was born in Lérida, near Barcelona, and took his first piano lessons with the local organist and teacher Joaquín Terraza. At ten, he enrolled at the Barcelona Conservatory and after two years of study with Juan Battista Pujol won first prize in piano in 1887. At that time, his mother, who regularly made the family's decisions, determined to seek professional advice. She approached Isaac Albéniz, who, at twenty-seven, was already a veteran of concert stages around the world. (He had been a runaway teenager who, when his ship stopped in Havana harbor, was reclaimed by his father who had been sent to Cuba as the Spanish consul.) Señora Viñes asked this seasoned musician for an opinion of her son's playing. Could Ricardo achieve the success she envisioned for him? Albéniz conceded the boy had talent, but cautioned against concertizing too early and suggested a stay in Paris where young Viñes could study at the Conservatoire. Enrique Granados and Joaquín Malats were already there, both studying with Charles de Bériot—himself part Spanish. Furthermore, the thriving Spanish "colony" could help make the adjustment to life in a foreign city more comfortable. Mother and Ricardo would go first. If things worked out well, Papa and brothers Pepe and Eugenio would follow.

From the moment of his family's departure for France, Ricardo Viñes kept a journal. The twelve-year-old was quite precise in his entries.

October 1887:
On the 12th, a Wednesday, at eight o'clock in the morning, we left Barcelona for Paris. We arrived in the French capital at 4:30 in the afternoon of the next day. We went first to the Hotel du Calvaire on the Boulevard des Filles du Calvaire (18th).

[Viñes was carried away by numbers. Indeed his fascination with them, which led to his penchant for gambling, hastened his demise.]

Friday: I showed up at M. Fissot's at 4 rue de la Tour Auvergne. I played for him the f-minor sonata by Schulhoff[3] which he seemed to like a lot. He then gave us a letter for M. de Bériot which we took to him immediately.
Monday: We moved from our hotel to the Hotel de Cologne, 10–12 rue de Trevise (9).[4]
Tuesday: I rented a Pleyel piano at 15 francs a month.[5]

November:
Monday at 4 PM, I took the test for admission to the Conservatoire and I was accepted as an auditor because there was no more room for foreigners. But I was only accepted on condition that I do the work along with the other students so that I can officially enter the class as soon as there *is* an opening.
Saturday: Papa [who had since arrived on the scene] and Mama and I went to the Opéra to see the 500th performance of *Faust* conducted by its composer Gounod, an admirable conductor. The singers were:

Jean de Reszke	Faust
Edouard de Reszke	Mephistopheles
Escalais	Marguérite

Today I took my first lesson at M. de Bériot's.

Viñes continued to write in his journal almost every day for close to thirty years, from 1887 to 1916, and intermittently thereafter. Because of his keen eyes and sensitive ears, his diary represents a remarkable source of information on the life of a young expatriate artist in fin-de-siècle Paris.

In his journal, young Viñes writes that he is short and weighs about 36 kilos, approximately seventy-eight pounds. Despite his size, he seems to have comported himself with a maturity and self-reliance often observed in sensitive children who adapt to new surroundings and learn new languages easily.

The Spanish émigré community had settled into the eastern end of the 9th arrondissement, the portion that borders closely on the 10th; some also lived in the 18th. Those who became successful moved to the 8th and the 16th on the right bank and the 6th and 7th on the other side of the Seine. Pauline Viardot lived at 243 Boulevard St. Germain (6); Albéniz at 7 Chaussée de la Muette (16), although later he moved to Auteuil. Charles de Bériot, Viardot's nephew—he was the son of her sister, soprano Maria Malibran, and the Belgian violinist Charles de Bériot—was a "natural" as a teacher for young Spanish musicians. Granados and Malats, a few years older than Viñes, were already his pupils; Maurice Ravel would soon become one. De Bériot empathized more with the Spanish students than did Louis Diémer, the other prominent piano pedagogue at the Conservatoire. Diémer had studied with Antoine-François Marmontel, whose students included Albéniz, Bizet, d'Indy, Guiraud,[6] and Dubois. Diémer's star pupils were pianists Edouard Risler and Alfred Cortot. Interested in early music on original instruments, Diémer presented some of the first such concerts in Paris in the closing years of the century.

When Viñes enrolled at the Conservatoire, Ambroise Thomas[7] was at the helm. Thomas, who held himself accountable—through his charges—for the future of French music, ruled with an iron hand. Students did as they were told with no questions allowed. Repertory at the school consisted of Bach, Cramer, Beethoven, Chopin, Liszt, and Schumann, but also the newly composed works of Dubois, de Bériot, Diémer, and frequently, for political reasons, Saint-Saëns, who was the senior statesman of French composers of instrumental music. He did not appear often at the Conservatoire, but when he did, each of the instructors vied with the others to show off his progeny. After Saint-Saëns came Gounod, but in view of the many operas he had composed, he showed more interest in vocal students. Widor trained the organists;[8] when he made suggestions to piano students, they ignored them completely, at least when out of his presence. Godard, too, had difficulties with many of the advanced pupils, who were convinced they knew more than he did.[9] Godard's ensemble classes, which lasted anywhere from two and a half to four and a half hours weekly, were long neglected by the virtuoso-minded piano students. Finally the administration made these classes compulsory. Lavignac conducted harmony courses for the advanced students, and Viñes was not permitted to enter until he had been at the Conservatoire for several years.[10] When Lavignac finally considered him for admission, he extracted a promise from the young man that he would attend classes regularly. Pianists generally had a reputation for spotty attendance.

Viñes arrived in Paris with a small scholarship—150 pesetas a month—from the city of Barcelona. After some lobbying on the part of friends back in Spain and his own plea to the exiled Queen Isabella (she had been deposed in 1868 and fled to Paris), the stipend was raised. But it was never enough and he was forced to earn his keep at the same time as he learned his trade.

Earlier émigrés had organized a Société Nationale d'Acclimation expressly to help newcomers adjust. Viñes attended their scheduled events, but he would also drop in at odd times—sometimes with his mother, sometimes with friends like "Mauricio" [Viñes's name for Ravel]—to satisfy a nostalgia for his homeland. (Viñes had met Ravel through his mother in 1888; both mothers spoke Spanish.) At the Society's headquarters he mingled with other Spaniards: pianists Mario Calado, Jaime Riera, Joaquín Malats, Carmen Matas; composer Gaspar Villate; painters Ulpiano Checa, Edouard Dreyfus-Gonzalès, Ricardo Canals, Isidro Nonells, Santiago Rusiñol, Enrique Serra, and José Sert; actress Maria Guerrero; politicians like Zorillam, former Minister of Public Works, now in exile, and anarchist Guardia Ferrer. For the older folks, this organization was essential, more comfortable than socializing in a French milieu. For the younger émigrés, the established Spaniards acted as conduits, forming a network through which Viñes and later his two brothers would find work.

At the age of thirteen, Viñes began to play at soirees for about twenty francs a night. Sometimes his host threw in an extra franc for Ricardo to take a carriage home, but when he found himself

Young Ricardo Viñes (standing) soon after his arrival in Paris. He became the foremost champion of the new French, Spanish, and Russian music that emerged in the first decades of the twentieth century.

Enrique Granados, who formed part of the Spanish émigré community in Paris.

The score of Maurice Ravel's Pavane, *autographed for Ricardo Viñes.*

short of funds, he walked. A small but steady increase in the number of families who required his services led to higher fees. (When he was too timid to ask, his mother negotiated for him.) Expenses increased as well. Unable any longer to appear in proper company without a suit, Viñes needed to order one. Olde England, the department store regularly patronized by Señora Viñes when she was able to stretch her meager income, did not have a suit to fit Ricardo. A tailor, appropriately named M. Schneider, was found, and his first custom suit cost twenty-three francs.

The family moved often. Rooms were not hard to come by; and when the Viñeses fell into arrears for a couple of months, there was no alternative but to find new lodgings. (Shrewd landlords began demanding four months' security.) Papa Viñes tried valiantly to land a steady job, but without success, and money problems haunted each member of the family. The diary records every instance in which Mama or Ricardo or Pepe found a purse or a pair of glasses or a few coins on the street, as if such items were manna from heaven. Rent cost the family about six hundred francs a year. Private lessons with de Bériot, who lowered his fees for young Viñes, were thirty francs a month. Upright pianos rented at Pleyel's and Erard's (the foremost French manufacturers of pianos) for about fifteen francs a month; a tuning cost three francs. The Colonne and Lamoureux orchestras usually performed on Sundays, and occasionally students received free tickets. More often they had to buy their own, the cheapest in the house. At the Opéra, a good seat cost sixteen and a half francs, but Viñes soon learned to volunteer for the claque and get that same *fauteuil* for three and a half.

Ricardo did an inordinate amount of reading. In addition to his music, reading was his only escape from the mundane cares of existence. He found a spot on the concrete ledge surrounding the Tuileries at the Place de la Concorde where he would hide himself whenever he could and spend hours transported by the excitement of James Fenimore Cooper, Walter Scott, or Rider Haggard. He had taught himself English and German and worked constantly on his French. Sometimes he even considered translating into French some of his favorite Spanish authors, like Gustavo Adolfo Becquer. He negotiated the price of books with the *bouquinistes* on the quais. Sometimes he traded books, upward—he did have a collector's instinct—as he could afford better editions. The *bibliothécaires* got to know him rather well.

The curriculum at the Conservatoire was geared to performance contests scheduled for each July. A preliminary recital was held for those whose teachers thought they might qualify. Based on applause—and enthusiastic supporters had no hesitation about breaking into applause after a *perlé* scale passage or a double-thirds run—and on the way the musicians comported themselves on stage, finalists were chosen. About the middle of May, teachers would try second-guessing the jury in order to prepare their most promising students for the *morceau de concours*, the single piece that was compulsory for all contestants. One year the requirement was Saint-Saëns's *Theme and Variations*, a fiendishly difficult virtuoso piece; another, it was the f-minor Chopin *Fantaisie*. (De Bériot even suggested cuts for this piece.) There was no way to prepare for the sight-reading selection, except through rigorous and continued exposure to the process. (The French have traditionally concentrated on this procedure in training young musicians.) Most of the experienced students regularly performed the chamber works of Schumann, Beethoven, Saint-Saëns, Franck, and Godard. They also accompanied singers privately in coaching sessions and at rehearsals, as well as at soirées given by the reigning social divas of Paris. Other opportunities to flex their sight-reading muscles arose on the occasions when Massenet or Chabrier wanted to hear their new operas for which they could not arrange an orchestral rehearsal, or when de Bériot needed some perspective on his newest piano concerto. Then the composer and a music student would run through a four-hand transcription of the work.

The diary notes occasional respites from this heavy-duty schedule, particularly during the summer. Viñes had come to Paris in October of 1887. A year and a half later, the great Exposition Universelle of 1889 opened and remained for him a perpetual attraction. He had read about the last fair in 1878, and he eagerly anticipated the new sights. Less than a decade after one of the more disastrous wars in nineteenth-century European history, a conflagration exacerbated by the terrible year of the Commune that followed, the French government determined to show that Paris was still a vital cultural and political center, one that even the Germans had better reckon with, despite their superior military might.

In the extraordinary Exposition of 1889 the arts and crafts of non-Western nations were on display for the first time: Javanese dancers and a gamelan orchestra; Japanese Noh dramas, Indian dancers, and Chinese crafts and craftsmen; lavish offerings of the pavilion of Czarist Russia—in addition to the construction of the most daring and memorable of all exposition structures, the Eiffel Tower.

When the Fair opened on 6 May 1889 the government declared a holiday for all school children, including students at the Conservatoire. At the opening day ceremonies, cellist Jules Delsart, Auguste-Joseph Franchomme's pupil,[11] and Louis Diémer were scheduled to play, and they presented their students with tickets of admission at sixty-five centimes each. Once inside, Viñes visited other booths and pavilions as he records in his journal. For twenty centimes he purchased a guide to the Fair; for seventy-five centimes he bought himself a beret emblazoned with its logo, the Eiffel Tower. Buffalo Bill and his Indians, horses and buffalos direct from America drew enormous crowds. The hippodrome featured pantomime shows; the Théâtre du Vaudeville, cabaret numbers. The Galerie des Machines was a favorite of little boys as well as big ones. Edison's early phonograph was unveiled at this Exposition. Although intrigued by its possibilities, Viñes himself never warmed to the machine.

Wherever he went and whomever he saw, Viñes kept alert and observant—what he needed were contacts, introductions, opportunities. When Grieg arrived from Norway, Hubay from Hungary, Paderewski from Poland, the young musician would arrange to meet them and, if possible, play for them. Most introductions came through the efforts of women: patrons or wives of famous conductors. Mesdames Colonne and Carvalho were particularly helpful. His teachers and mentors, de Bériot and Albéniz[12] (when he was in town), also saw to it that Viñes met people who might engage him. Despite his obvious handicaps—a stranger in a strange land, impoverished, sensitive, and desperate to succeed—he refused to curry favor, although his family repeatedly pressured him to cultivate members of the establishment who could do the most for him. To his journal he confided his disgust with the politics and manipulations that characterized the administration at the Conservatoire, the negotiations and machinations that brought success to several inferior performers while those with more talent struggled for recognition.

One day at Hartmann's, on the Rue Daunou, Viñes was about to buy some of Massenet's music, when the composer entered the store. [Massenet, after Gounod the preeminent composer of French operas, was exceedingly productive in the 1890s. Not only did he churn out operas in rapid succession—*Esclarmonde* (1889), *Werther* (1892), *Thaïs* (1894), *Sapho* (1897), and *Cendrillon* (1899)—but he also molded and prodded a string of younger French composers. He taught Gustave Charpentier, Charles Koechlin, Florent Schmitt, Gabriel Pierné, Henri Rabaud, and Reynaldo Hahn.] Explaining that he had had a letter of introduction, but was unable to find Massenet at home when he called on him,[13] Viñes introduced himself. Massenet acknowledged the introduction and offered Viñes and Ravel, who was with him, tickets to the opening performance of *Esclarmonde* that evening at the Opéra-Comique (14 May 1889). The boys loved it, but they dismissed with a shrug Meyerbeer's *L'Africaine*, featured later the same week at the Opéra.

The summer of 1889 found Viñes, Ravel, and family and friends at the Exposition, the Jardin des plantes, the Châtelet, the Pantheon, the Musée Grévin, the famous wax museum, and the Musée de Cluny. By 1890, Viñes had his first private pupil at twenty francs a month—only ten less than what he paid de Bériot for his own lessons. He performed during the entr'actes of comedies at the Salle Duprez, earning forty francs before an audience of five hundred. Performances of Albéniz pieces at a soiree on the Rue de Seine netted him an additional fifty francs. His pockets overflowing, he bought himself a hat for twelve francs at Olde England and took out a three-month subscription for music rental from the publishers of the music journal *Ménestrel* for another twelve francs.

In this same year, 1890, Berlioz finally came into his own on the French concert scene. The Colonne Sunday concert on 13 April featured his *La Damnation de Faust*. On 10 June the Lamoureux offered *Béatrice et Bénédict* at the Odéon with Viñes and Ravel in rapt attention in the balcony. When he heard something he liked, Viñes would try to buy the score. Because he was an excellent sight-reader, he could familiarize himself with the operatic and solo vocal repertory and was thus able to augment his income through accompanying singers. Pol Plançon and Félicia Mallet are but two performers who engaged him frequently. Whenever he sang, Plançon arranged for Viñes and Ravel to have tickets. On 26 August 1890 Plançon performed Friar Lawrence with Emma Eames as Juliet (she had made her debut in March in that role) in Gounod's setting of the Shakespeare play. They thought the opera sublime.[14] (Free tickets provided the opportunity to hear a wide variety of music.)

Viñes broadened his repertory rapidly. In addition to more pieces by Mendelssohn, several Weber sonatas, the Grieg concerto, and the Schumann piano quartet, he began to grapple with the works of Liszt. Recognizing the tremendous facility of his young pupil, de Bériot fed him a diet of virtuoso piano music. Liszt, Paganini, Anton Rubinstein études, studies by Isidor Philipp, and salon pieces such as *La Triomphale* by Wolff (Pleyel's son-in-law, soon his successor as Pleyel-Wolff), along with others by Godard, Duvernoy, and Chevillard, Lamoureux's son-in-law and soon *his* successor as conductor of the orchestra.

Viñes rented an Erard grand in June 1893 for forty francs a month and five francs cartage and began practicing for the July competition whose *morceau de concours* was Weber's A-flat Sonata. The jury consisted of Thomas, Guiraud, Pierné, Delahaye, Widor, Mangin, Lack, and Nollet who, in their decision, ignored him completely. This disappointment led to a month during which he went without practicing. Instead, he took in the Gran Guignol in the Tuileries, the Galerie de Machines at the Champs de Mars, Hugo's *Hernani* on the stage, and the Nouveau Théâtre on the Rue Blanche, where he enjoyed the French Quadrille and the high-kicking chorus girls. His reading included Jules Verne's *Vingt mille lieves sous les mers*, Hector Malot's *Sans Famille*, Walter Scott, Rider Haggard, George Sand, Henri Murger, Alphonse Daudet, and Prosper Mérimée. Goethe's *Werther* (Massenet's in 1892) and *Hermann und Dorothea* and Théophile Gautier's works became new favorites. He also attended the opera. One evening, Viñes had dinner at the Opéra Passage and heard his first performance of *Lohengrin*—the first since the French language performance of 1887. After his brief hiatus from the piano, he resumed his salon performances, which now included the flutist, Taffanel, and the harpist, Hasselmans. He was doing well, but not well enough, and the family had to move again.[15]

Massenet headed the jury in 1892, but again Viñes was passed over. In the fall, Viñes's time was preempted by Chabrier, rehearsing *Gwendoline* at the Maison Musicale. Chabrier had agreed to coach Viñes and Ravel for their performance of his Waltzes (1883) on two pianos. He promised to attend their 9 February performance at the Salle Erard, but never appeared and the boys were very disappointed. (Chabrier was slowly dying of syphilis.) Viñes learned from friends that Granados had just married the daughter of a wealthy Spanish industrialist. To his delight, Viardot, whom he had met at de Bériot's, immediately sat herself down near the piano the next time the two were together to watch him play. (Viardot had studied the piano with Liszt and had made piano transcriptions of some of Chopin's songs. She had also composed several pieces for the piano.) Actor Mounet-Sully, writers Heredia, Leconte de Lisle, and Catulle Mendès joined his circle of acquaintances. Chevillard, who lived in a deluxe apartment at 61 Avenue de Wagram, coached Viñes in his transcription of Chabrier's *España* as well as his own variations. (Chevillard had rehearsed the chorus for the Lamoureux *Lohengrin* of 1887, and he could talk to Viñes about their idol, Richard Wagner.)

In July Viñes again entered the annual Concours and de Bériot pinned his hopes on him. His journal reveals his own expectations:

Saturday the 21st at 1:00 PM the Concours started. There were 21 contestants, but one didn't show. We drew lots. I got no. 15 and I went on stage at 3:55. I was immediately applauded. I played the contest piece, the f-minor Chopin Fantaisie marvelously. I received applause and bravos after the first half. [This practice seems unbelievable, but was customary at the time.] When I finished, I had the most frenetic ovation—and it was merited because I could not have played better—from the point of cleanliness, security of technique, style, sentiment, warmth. In sum, the public was so enthusiastic about me that I had to get up and bow three or four times. Then I sight-read a piece by Théodore Dubois to perfection, in great style and with much taste. My success was electric. Again I had to return and bow. Afterward I put on my coat to leave. With that I committed an unpardonable error and everyone later reported to me how terrible it seemed. Nobody had ever done that, committed such a gaffe. They all kept repeating that. During the deliberations, around 5:30, after the conclusion, everyone congratulated me for having the first prize already in my pocket. Then Ambroise Thomas announced the first prizes: he called out Malats, Wurmser, and Niederholm, but not me. The second prizes: Mopain and Auber—and again nothing for me. The public thought Thomas had made an error. Pepe ran for Mama to take her home. He returned to find me surrounded by people of all ages and sexes, congratulating me. "Your defeat," they said, "is a victory for you." Cries of indignation against the jury were sounded all about me. I shook hands with at least 200 people. De Bériot left quickly, pale and unwilling to see any of us.

Le Petit Journal, *Le Figaro*, *Le Matin* and *Le National* all reported the injustice, praising me and condemning the jury for their total indifference to my abilities. Mama spoke to Dubois, Widor and Mathias [the last a pupil of Chopin]. None could understand the decision and all urged me not to resign. Next year I would surely win.

The year 1894 opened with a disastrous fire at the Opéra warehouse but it had no effect whatsoever on the record number of Wagner performances presented. (The Colonne offered the Prelude to *Parsifal* on 30 January, and on 25 February it was the Lamoureux's turn. On 23 March nine Wagner excerpts appeared on a Lamoureux program.) Is it a coincidence that the Dreyfus Affair, which divided families and friends, also began this year? [Viñes was an anti-Dreyfusard; Albéniz and de Bériot were convinced of the man's innocence. In the violent discussions that ensued, one senses the beginning of the deterioration of their relationships.]

Viñes passed the winter with the usual round of concerts, visiting performers and exhibitions alternating with his own engagements at soirees and rehearsals. Pablo Sarasate, the celebrated Spanish violin virtuoso, played a concert with the Colonne, and although the seats were terribly expensive, the concert was sold out. Grieg was in town and Raoul Pugno played his concerto. (Madame Colonne introduced Viñes to the Norwegian composer.) On 25 June President Carnot was assassinated by an Italian anarchist and the country was stunned. Viñes mentioned it only *en passant*, because he was concentrating intensively on preparation for the Concours. In early May, de Bériot confided to Viñes that he suspected that the Saint-Saëns *Theme and Variations* would be the *morceau de concours*. Before the month's end, his suspicions were confirmed. The big day dawned on 21 July 1894:

Our neighbor arrived this morning to say she had come over only because she always brought good luck. I crossed my fingers and noticed they were indeed supple. We ate at 11:00 AM, Mama, Eugenio (who hadn't gone to school) and I. Pepe, despite the contest, went to his office this morning. As we were about to eat dessert, we heard from outside the sounds of the Chopin Funeral March and when we looked out the window, we saw an impressive funeral procession passing in the rue Lafayette. Coming up the stairs, Eugenio, who had gone to buy some cookies, told us it was the Belgian Ambassador to France, whose coffin had just gone by. Because Pepe was late, I had no dessert. I didn't want to rush digestion. I also had no wine, coffee, or liquor so as to be more alert. Slightly before 12:30, Eugenio and I went to the Conservatoire. In the courtyard I met Pepe. Mama arrived a few minutes later to help bring in those of our friends who had no tickets. [She got them in] thanks to the assistance of the concierge at the Conservatoire whom we know well. Then when we were already grouped in the foyer, Mama left for St. Eugène [the church] and home. I was to go seventh, but since Roussel, the third, had withdrawn, I became sixth.

I played the first page of the Saint-Saëns' *Theme and Variations* divinely; on the second page I hit a wrong note in a R.H. [*sic*] arpeggio and I continued to play with a bit of nervousness and some hesitation until the finale of the theme (1st line of 4th page). I recovered my assurance and my mastery and I stacked marvels over marvels. Faced with thunderous applause from the entire room—although it was still before the sight-reading section of the exam—I nevertheless had to rise three times to acknowledge the applause.

Furthermore, I had been interrupted by applause that exploded before the start of the theme at the organ point on the second page, at the modulation on the seventh page, and after the big ascending scale in 6ths at the entrance of the grand finale before the last page.[16] In sum, I had an overwhelming ovation. And really, only afterward did I triumph in the piece to be sight-read which was by Widor, who was on the jury. There I accomplished what might be called surpassing oneself. Without even stopping to look at the piece and get a sense of the difficulties it represented—two large ms pages—I put them on the music rack, practically under my nose, and deciphered it all in one fell swoop from beginning to end without a single mistake. It was there I gave my all. The most finely shaded coloring and rubato, the kind one could usually give only to a piece studied in advance—and doing all this with taste and with a facility that mesmerized the audience. Even before I had finished, the public acclaimed me with bravos and applause. [This time there was no question of the outcome.]

Afterward, I took a walk in the courtyard of the Conservatoire. I returned to listen to Cortot who played and sight-read to perfection, but without charm, like the good pupil he always is. The critics mentioned him, too, as a possible winner, but he got nothing. That's the Conservatoire. There's always injustice here, every year. This time everybody was excellent. De Bériot and Diémer spoke with SS [Saint-Saëns] who must have been there—but none of us saw him. As usual, he remained out of view.

Of de Bériot's 10 contestants, 5 were winners; while only 3 of Diémer's 11 captured prizes. Thomas, Lenepveu, Mathias, Widor, Thome, Nolet, Ravina, Fauré and Philipp comprised the jury.

On Sunday, Viñes took the *bateau mouche* to Auteuil to thank the composer Bourgault-Ducoudray for his help and to report that he had won. When he played him the Saint-Saëns piece, the older man couldn't help remarking he didn't think Saint-Saëns had been *trop inspiré* when he wrote it. And, Viñes adds, on Bourgault-Ducoudray's face one could see inscribed some of the disappointments of his life. The following day they went to the Conservatoire to tip the help.[17]

* * *

Emmanuel Chabrier passed away in the fall of 1894. Before attending the funeral at Nôtre Dame de Lorette—for which the high-spirited composer had oddly requested only plainchant—Ravel and Viñes passed the time sight-reading *Gwendoline*, Chabrier's Wagnerian opera. Anton Rubinstein died in November 1894, and Viñes bemoaned the fact that he had not heard him, nor Liszt nor Tausig nor Thalberg nor [Theodore] Ritter, a Liszt pupil, all among the most prominent pianists of the nineteenth century.

On 1 November the Opéra-Comique presented Verdi's *Falstaff*, about a year and a half after its premiere, with Delmas in the title role. Viñes was enthralled. On the fourth, he heard the "Liebestod" in the evening and saw Sarah Bernhardt in *Gismonde* (much publicized by the Mucha poster) in the afternoon. Colonne programmed Berlioz again that fall: the *Requiem* was tremendous, but *L'Enfance du Christ* left him unmoved.

Right after New Year's in January 1895, Pleyel delivered the five-thousand-franc grand piano, Viñes's first prize trophy from the July contest. It had a singing tone, wonderful action, and a third pedal —Viñes called it an invention of Pleyel; at least it was touted as such. (It actually originated with Steinway.) Recommended by de Bériot for a six-thousand-franc-a-year position at the Budapest Conservatory, Viñes declined, preferring to remain in Paris.

Viñes began arranging his first public concert for 21 February at the Salle Pleyel, where M. Chevrier, the manager, asked three hundred francs for rental of the hall. Inasmuch as he was now earning two hundred francs for a soiree, the price did not seem too steep. Even so, Mr. Butterfield, the Englishman who had footed Viñes's bills for the past year (2,500 francs to the family and 1,000 to him) gave him an additional five hundred francs to defray the costs. Viñes picked up the tickets at Pleyel's, distributed them to members of the Spanish colony, and also disposed of some among his new acquaintances: proprietors of Le Nouveau Cirque, Olympia, Moulin Rouge, and ladies at whose salons he had performed. He planned a monstrously long concert, determined to prove his mettle. Unfortunately, a week before the event, de Bériot fell ill, and another student had to substitute for him at the second piano when Viñes performed his teacher's Second Piano Concerto. (Viñes announced the substitution midway into the program and was delighted when told he had hardly any accent.)

The program, which began slightly after 9:00 PM and concluded two and a half hours later, included Beethoven's *Appassionata Sonata*, the Schumann *Carnaval*, the *Berceuse*, Etude in f-minor (Op. 25, No. 2), and the c-minor Nocturne of Chopin, *Les Myrtilles* of Dubois, *Valse Chromatique* by Godard, *Sérénité* by de Bériot, Moszkowski's *Tarantelle*, a Schubert Minuet, Mendelssohn's Scherzo from the *Midsummer Night's Dream* music, *Un Sospiro* by Liszt, and the Paganini-Liszt *La Campanella* to close—all of these as well as the Second Piano Concerto, indicated on the program as *"accompagné par l'auteur,"* for which reason an explanation about de Bériot's absence was imperative. Tickets were available in advance at Salle Pleyel (Rocheouart) and at Durand's on the Madeleine. "I played by heart and had no memory lapses," he told his diary—which leads one to believe that some performers probably still used music in recital. "There were only 14 pieces, but with the first two and the concerto, it was more like 30!"

The crush of men and women in evening clothes and the lines of coaches at the entrance made for a resplendence that frightened away many of the performer's impecunious friends. At the conclusion of the concert, Viñes looked in vain for several who were too timid to mingle with the aristocratic audience. Several hundred people attended the recital and after deducting royalties of 50 francs and paying 315 to the house, Viñes made a profit of 2005.

The threat of military service for her son forced Señora Viñes to make frequent trips to the Spanish Embassy in Paris. Papa, back in Spain, finally had to make arrangements in Madrid to get him a deferment. Fortunately he was successful and Viñes, who had joined the French Wagnerites, was able to enjoy the Lamoureux orchestra's increasing number of Wagner concerts that season. To educate the public, Catulle Mendès was engaged to supply commentary between numbers. The "Prelude," "Liebesnacht," and "Liebestod" from *Tristan* and, before the year's end, the final act of *Götterdämmerung* were performed, as well as Chabrier's *España*. (The Colonne featured more Franck and Saint-Saëns.) In April, Viñes saw Bernhardt in Rostand's *La Princesse lointaine* and marveled that the author was only twenty-six.

How wonderful for Viñes this July! He didn't have to compete. He bought a Rachmaninoff Prelude and Balakirev's *Islamey*, one of the most difficult of all piano pieces. He sold his prize Pleyel, and made the decision to affiliate instead with Erard, the other piano manufacturer who not only gave him a piano but also put their hall at his disposal free of charge.

On Sunday, 1 November 1896, Viñes took Ravel to a Lamoureux Wagner concert where Ravel heard Wagner's "Prelude" and "Liebestod" from *Tristan und Isolde* for the first time. (Alba Chrétien sang Isolde.) Overwhelmed by the music, Ravel began to sob uncontrollably, leaving Viñes, who had always considered his friend cold and restrained, utterly astonished. How little we know, he thought to himself, even about those who are close to us.

Viñes contemplated hiring the Lamoureux orchestra for his next recital: the fee was 1,150 francs with one rehearsal and 1,450 with two. But he had to whittle down the price. Conductor Gabriel Marie had just been robbed of 23,000 francs and it would be awkward to try to negotiate the price at this time. The recital proceeded successfully—*sans orchestre*. De Bériot introduced Viñes to the works of Fauré (who was more modest than his contemporaries and would not promote his own pieces), and on his own, Viñes picked up Debussy's *Rêverie*, which he passed along to Ravel, to whom he had also loaned his copy of Bertrand's *Gaspard de la nuit*.[18]

Viñes's friends had continued to promote him. Madame Albéniz promised to speak to Madame Chausson, whose husband was a Franck pupil, about possible engagements, but unfortunately Chausson died in a bicycle accident on his estate before the conversation could take place. De Bériot arranged for Saint-Saëns to come to his home and listen privately to Viñes. Teacher and pupil awaited the visit of the great man impatiently. When he finally arrived, they had tea, and Saint-Saëns proceeded to engage de Bériot in a discussion about Chinese cooking. Finally de Bériot arose and announced that they would now perform his Third Piano Concerto. He took the second piano part, while Saint-Saëns remained seated at the table in the dining room, score in hand. When they had finished, Saint-Saëns commented: "He plays better than Saint-Saëns. Such strength, such brio and yet so much delicacy."

The Colonne played more Franck—*Le Chausseur maudit* and *Psyché*—and Viñes vigorously applauded their *L'Après-midi d'un faune*. Paderewski gave a recital to raise funds for the monument to French pianist-composer Henry Litolff, and conductor Nikisch brought the Berlin Orchestra to the Cirque d'Hiver. Singer Victor Maurel,[19] now retired in Paris, entertained one evening and Viñes met Odilon Redon, whose works he had admired from afar. Redon owned original Goyas; he knew Debussy, Mallarmé, Huysmans. Friendship with Redon finally brought Viñes into the appropriate milieu.

In the fall of 1897, Viñes and Ravel took an interest in the Russians — Balakirev, Glazunov, and Rimsky-Korsakov. Together they embarked on a sight-reading binge. But the French were not forgotten. Viñes read Franck's *Variations symphoniques*, purchased Chabrier's *Dix pièces pittoresques* and loaned Ravel a Maeterlinck work in exchange for some Borodin. The boys planned to visit Redon's show at the Jeffroy Passage, but Fauré's class ended too late. Viñes's reading this year included Verhaeren, Barbey d'Aurevilly, de Banville, Villiers de l'Isle-Adam (whom he was warned to avoid because of his profligacy), Léon Bloy, Albert Samain, Swinburne, Alphonse Daudet, and Adolphe Jullien. He was drawn increasingly to the occult, mysticism, and numerology. Poe, Huysmans, and the other Belgian symbolist Georges Rodenbach had become his idols.

The new year—1898—arrived and with it a new passion: the paintings of Manet and Monet, particularly the Rouen cathedral series, which fascinated Viñes. Ambroise Vollard had a Redon show and at Durand-Ruel the Pissarros and Renoirs captivated him. Gustave Moreau was another new favorite. In musical matters, the English pianist Leonard Borwick, Clara Schumann's pupil, and pianist-composer Ferruccio Busoni did not appeal to him. Chevillard—who had taken over the Lamoureux from his father-in-law—and increasing numbers of French composers, de Bréville, Ducasse, and others asked Viñes to play their works. Ravel gave him the *Menuet antique*, dedicated to him, and Viñes promised to play it at his next concert, only a few weeks away. At the Société Nationale, he and Marthe Dron had a near disaster with Ravel's *Sites auriculaires* for two pianos, when they finished two quarter notes apart. At the same time, Viñes was distracted for another reason. The 125-day Spanish-American War had ended in disaster for Spain, which lost Cuba, Puerto Rico, and the Philippines. Viñes's diary reveals an extreme animosity toward the United States.

More French music began to reach the concert stage, not only instrumental compositions but operas and vocal pieces as well. The Paris Conservatoire and its rival the Schola Cantorum took their places as prominent centers for training young musicians. In 1900, when Viñes, at the age of twenty-five, deliberated about going to Berlin, Albéniz asked him, "Why leave now? Paris is the center of music today."[20] Viñes went anyway, to concertize and to meet some of the Russians visiting the German capital at that time. Back in Paris, the Exposition of 1900 boasted moving sidewalks, and the Palais d'Electricité glittered in a sparkling show of lights. The swirling designs of art nouveau permeated the entire fairgrounds and filtered into the production of household goods, some of which Viñes, himself, could finally afford to purchase.

Viñes's reading now included Sâr Péladan, Camille Mauclair, Pierre Loti, Longfellow, Emerson, Walter Pater, Carlyle, and George Grove (*Beethoven's Nine Symphonies*). He became close to Maurice Denis and the Spanish artist Fabre and, curiously enough, to that French odd couple Colette and Willy whom he saw often. Musical colleagues now included Hortense Parent, Henri Duparc, Dandelot, Pablo Casals, Debussy, and Fauré.

President Felix Faure was brutally killed in 1899 and the new president Loubet (1899-1906) was a Dreyfusard, which distressed Viñes. This president obtained a complete pardon for Dreyfus. A flu epidemic hit Paris in 1900, along with an orientalist exhibit at the gallery of Durand-Ruel. One evening at the Gauthier-Villars's (Colette and Willy), Viñes met artist José Sert and composer René de Castéra. Debussy was there, but they had not really been introduced as yet. De Castéra brought Viñes to the attention of Bordes who, with d'Indy, was associated with the newly established Schola. Albéniz had already been teaching there and his recommendation helped bring about an invitation to Viñes. More secure now of his position, Viñes held out until he was promised the same kind of superior students as Albéniz, and a once-a-week schedule for classes. It was at the Schola that he met de Séverac and was finally launched on his remarkable career.

One of the most extraordinary descriptions of Viñes as a teacher comes from composer-pianist Joaquín Nin-Culmell of Berkeley, California. In a letter to the author of 15 July 1971, he wrote:

What makes his performances different from other performances? . . . They weren't performances. . . . They were the inner sharing of a discovery he had made on his own, but in which nothing of his own self remained. He *was* the *Pictures*, he *was* the *Nights in the Gardens of Spain*, he *was* the *Gallo Mañanero* of Joaquín Rodrigo. Viñes never played Viñes the way Segovia plays Segovia. It was almost a mystical approach to the art of interpretation. Disappear and the composition will come to life. Forget about yourself and Debussy or Ravel or Poulenc [another of his pupils] will speak out. He was self-effacing to the point of obliteration, but never quite. Viñes was always there, but always in good company. Chatterbox as he was, he never interrupted the music with personal gestures, or professional tics, or technical excesses, or limitation. His technique was there but only to be hidden. It was perfect in that it was never brought up.[21]

Albéniz, Granados, de Falla, Casals, and Turina are a few of the other Spanish musicians who made Paris their home and their training ground for many years. Albéniz was a regionalist, a musical landscape painter, and a free thinker who never belonged in the structured, academic atmosphere of the Schola. Debussy, whom Albéniz never liked, wrote a most complimentary article about Albéniz's *Iberia*, particularly praising the "Albaicín" and "Eritania."[22] Paul Dukas, too, called him an "impressionist . . . a landscape painter with a rich palette."[23] Vladimir Jankélévitch understood him best and wrote movingly about him in *La Rhapsodie*. "Albéniz," he said, "[is] more naive than Ravel, and more sentimental, willingly lets himself go."[24] Even as a youngster, Albéniz was a maverick. At the age of six (in 1866), he was ready to study with Marmontel in Paris. The attempt to enter him at the Conservatoire failed, however, because although he played the piano admirably, when he finished, in his excitement, he heaved a ball through the window. His entrance was thus deferred for two years on the basis of immaturity.[25]

Pablo Casals, who met Picasso in the late 1890s in Barcelona, says their paths never crossed in Paris.[26] Casals, when he moved to Paris at the beginning of the new century, lived in the Auteuil district, close to Albéniz, in one of a cluster of houses for rent on a small estate called Villa Molitor.[27] He enjoyed many wonderfully informal music sessions at violinist Jacques Thibaud's house, where their group included Ysaÿe, Thibaud, Kreisler, Monteux, Cortot, Harold Bauer, and Enesco. The Count de Morphy had introduced Casals to Queen Maria Christina and had obtained a stipend for the cellist which enabled him to continue his studies in Paris. This same financial aid had made it possible for Albéniz to enroll in a piano class at the Brussels Conservatory.[28]

Initially, with a letter from the Count de Morphy, Casals went to Brussels to see François-Auguste Gevaert, the baker's son who became one of Belgium's foremost musical scholars. In no uncertain terms, Gevaert told him he belonged in Paris, "the center of music today . . . with four wonderful orchestras, the Lamoureux, Colonne, Pasdeloup and the orchestra of the Conservatory." He also recommended that Casals play for the reigning master cello teacher at their Conservatory. Because he was a newcomer, the professor made fun of him in front of the students—before he played. The experience was so humiliating that Casals refused even to consider the scholarship he was offered there. When Casals returned to Paris to report to the Count de Morphy what had transpired in Brussels, the Count was angry with him because Queen Maria Christina had given this money only for Casals to attend the Brussels Conservatory. When Casals refused to go, he lost his stipend. The early years in Paris, with no stipend on which to depend, proved very, very difficult for Casals. And the other shock to his moral and ethical values was the Dreyfus Affair and its accompanying anti-Semitism. He could not fathom that France, a country noted for its liberalism, could entertain among its citizens such bigoted people.

Casals writes movingly of this episode:

For me, perhaps, the most frightful aspect of the Dreyfus affair was the fact that many people were against him because he was Jewish. And I found it almost unbelievable that in Paris—with all its culture and its noble traditions of the rights of man—that here in this city which was called *la ville lumière*, anti-semitism could spread like a foul plague. What words, indeed, are there to describe this disease, which would later infect a whole nation and rationalize the massacre of millions of men, women and children on the grounds that "Jewish blood" flowed in their veins? One's mind staggers at the monstrosity!

The very idea of hating Jews is incomprehensible to me. My own life has been so enriched by tender associations with Jewish fellow artists and friends. What people on earth have [sic] contributed more to human culture than the Jewish people? Of course they make wonderful musicians.[29]

Manuel de Falla, Catalan on his mother's side, took his first music lessons from her and moved to Madrid in the late 1890s to study with José Tragó, a pupil of George Mathias, himself a student of Chopin. (Mathias was on Viñes's jury at the Conservatoire.) He had already won a considerable number of prizes at the Madrid Conservatory, studied with Felipe Pedrell, the founder of Spanish musical nationalism, and had also launched a moderately successful career as a composer when, in 1907, he decided to head for Paris. De Falla comments that:

> . . . without Paris I would have remained buried in Madrid, done for and forgotten, laboriously leading an obscure existence, living miserably and keeping my first prize in a frame, like in a family album, with the score of my opera in a cupboard. To be published in Spain is worse than not being published at all. It's like throwing the music into a well.[30]

When he arrived, Falla took a room at the Hotel Kléber on the Rue de Belloy, the same hotel where his friend composer Joaquín Turina lived. He expected to make his name in the French capital with *La vida breve*. He played the score for Paul Dukas, who was so impressed that he announced it should be done at the Opéra-Comique. It was, but not until 1913, after Falla had already made the acquaintance of Debussy and Ravel.

Falla's first meeting with Debussy was a difficult one, apparently for both musicians. Neither said very much and finally, thinking about how to initiate a conversation, Falla announced that he had always liked French music. "I don't!" replied Debussy.[31] Steeped in the folk music of his native land, Falla wrote convincingly in an idiom that shows relationships with the Russians as well as the French. Another regionalist, he appealed to those who enjoyed the rhythm, melodies, phrasing, and nuances, particularly of Andalusian music. At the suggestion of Diaghilev, he transformed parts of his *Noches en los jardines de España*, a fantasy for piano and orchestra about which he consulted often with Viñes, into a ballet called *El Sombrero* (*Le Tricorne*, in French). It had its first performance in 1919 in London with designs by Picasso, and it is the most humorous of Falla's works.

One of Falla's single most important works was commissioned by Princesse Edmond de Polignac and first staged at her home in Paris in 1923. He set "El Retablo de Maese Pedro," taken from a chapter of *Don Quixote*, as a puppet opera with three main characters. A most unusual creation, it belongs with Schoenberg's *Pierrot Lunaire* and Stravinsky's *L'Histoire du Soldat* as an example of musical theater of reduced dimensions.

On the whole, Paris was kind to her émigrés. She nourished them and trained them and sent them forth on their way. All the foremost Spanish musicians who lived in Paris for any length of time praised the city's vitality and declared they could not have achieved what they did without this experience.[32] For some it became a second home; for others the pull of their homeland was too great to withstand. But as the American expatriates later would find subliminal "gallic accents" in their music, after having lived among the French, so, too, did the Spaniards, who caught some of the French delicacy and incorporated it into their more heavily accented native music.

9

The Russians in Paris, 1889–1914

When Serge Diaghilev and his troupe streaked across the artistic firmament of Paris in 1909, his dazzling achievement astonished even the sophisticated citizens of the French capital. No actor, no painter, no artist, no poet, no musician, no dramatist, not even an impresario when he started, Diaghilev was nevertheless able to surround himself with what was undoubtedly the foremost galaxy of artists ever assembled in any single enterprise. His accomplishments place him in the forefront of the artistic avant-garde of the twentieth century. For Diaghilev as for Wagner in the nineteenth century, his fantasies demanded a synthesis of the arts. "Perfect ballet," he is reported to have said, "can only be created by the fusion of dancing, painting and music." Practitioners of more than these three art forms, however, succumbed to Diaghilev's wizardry. Fashion, interior de-

Nijinsky in Afternoon of a Faun *depicted by the painter Valentine Gross-Hugo*

Diaghilev and his troupe streaked across the artistic firmament of Paris in 1909. He surrounded himself with what was undoubtedly the foremost galaxy of artists ever assembled in any single enterprise.

sign, stage settings, musical compositions, and, in a way, the cultural taste and artistic direction of two nations, France and later America, reveal the impact of his feverish activities. A bare half dozen years after Diaghilev's arrival on the Parisian scene in 1906, Proust wrote of the coming of the Russian dancers: "This charming invasion, against whose seductions only the stupidest of critics protested, infected Paris, as we know, with a fever of curiosity less burning, more purely aesthetic, but quite as intense, perhaps, as that aroused by the Dreyfus case."[1]

Diaghilev orchestrated his plans down to the last detail. His first French season found him represented at the Salon d'Automne in 1906 with an assemblage of works of art such as Paris nor any other European capital had yet seen. For 1907, he arranged a series of historical concerts aimed at demonstrating the wealth of talent kept under wraps in his native Russia.[2] The following year he prepared to introduce Modest Mussorgsky's *Boris Godunov* to the unsuspecting French, another first that was calculated to take them by surprise. And finally, with every artifice he could muster, and fortified with funds from friends and patrons[3]—throughout his career he was lavish with other people's money—he landed in the French capital with a troupe of dancers, scenic designers, choreographers, musicians, and artists who would change the course of dance in Western Europe.

In the twenty years of his reign in Paris, from 1909 to his untimely death in Venice in 1929 at the age of fifty-seven, Diaghilev controlled the destinies of his group much as a puppeteer manages his marionettes. An elitist and a cultural snob, he preferred to socialize with and perform for the upper classes. (His exalted opinion of himself was oddly affirmed by the size of his head, which was so large that he was obliged always to have his hats made to order.) While he gave the appearance of a dandy, his close friends insist that he had but one suit and one cape, both of which he wore until they were practically threadbare.[4]

Diaghilev was very superstitious. In 1913, after a fortune teller had told him he would die on the water, he refused to travel with his company when they left for South America. He remained behind; but his absence cost him dearly. While in Buenos Aires, Vaslav Nijinsky, Diaghilev's first protégé, married Romola de Pulszky, a Hungarian dancer in their corps de ballet. Diaghilev immediately sent off a cable firing the dancer, thereby snapping the tenuous thread that kept Nijinsky in touch with the real world. Within a few months, the great dancer was retired to a mental institution, and, except for a very few appearances, he never danced again.

With his hypnotic power over artists and patrons and even sovereigns, Diaghilev was unique, and it is doubtful that we shall ever again see his equal.

Most historians identify the appearance of Diaghilev and the Ballets Russes as the start of a new phase in the history of dance. But in fact, the phenomenon can be seen more as the culmination of a movement begun several decades earlier, with a Franco-Russian musical alliance that developed gradually in the late nineteenth century and carried into the early twentieth.

One of the most enlightening discussions of the Franco-Russian connection was written in 1953 by André Schaeffner for Pierre Souvtchinsky's *La Musique russe*.[5] In "Debussy et ses rapports avec la musique russe," Schaeffner covers the terrain of Russian music in Paris so carefully that any investigation of this phenomenon must begin with his analysis. He cites 1873 as the year that saw the beginning of new relations between France and Russia. Liszt was then at Weimar, where his ducal orchestra read numerous Russian works and made them known to many foreign visitors, among them Vincent d'Indy.[6] Years before, Adolphe Adam, after a visit to St. Petersburg, wrote of the extraordinary impact made on him by the Russian sacred music he had heard in the Imperial Chapel.[7] Berlioz, too, on the occasion of his first visit to Russia in 1847, marveled at the sonority of the basses who sang with the choir.[8] D'Indy, however, appears to have been among the first of the young Frenchmen in the latter part of the century to have heard live performances of this music—not merely to have read about them.[9]

In 1847, the Conservatoire in Paris received a package of twenty-seven scores, including almost all the orchestral works of Mikhail Glinka, *Sadko* and *The Maid of Pskov* of Rimsky-Korsakov, *Oprichnik* by Tchaikovsky, and various works by Alexander Dargomizhsky, César Cui, Alexander Serov, Alexei Verstovsky, and Anatoly Liadov, and also Mussorgsky's *Boris Godunov*.[10] (The presence of *Boris* among these scores makes the copy that Jules de Brayer left at Debussy's less important than had previously been believed.[11]) To this first packet of scores, the Russians added another hundred after the Universal Exposition of 1889 and still another fifty in 1893. Expositions, held in Paris in 1855, 1867, 1878, 1889, and 1900, eventually became the arenas for the presentation of new music of other nations. Exotic musical instruments, refreshingly new melodies, and novel approaches to rhythm, soon provided French composers with much-needed inspiration. At the Trocadéro, during the 1878 Exhibition, Nicholas Rubinstein conducted a series of four concerts that included pieces by Glinka, Tchaikovsky, Dargomizhsky, Serov and Mussorgsky.[12] César Cui contributed a series of explanatory articles on this music in the *Revue et Gazette musicale* from 12 May 1878 to 5 October 1880.[13]

Beginning in 1878, Louis Bourgault-Ducoudray, a French scholar and composer who had traveled to Greece to study ancient and popular music and had conducted similar research on the music of Brittany, started teaching music history at the Paris Conservatoire. In 1880, he first introduced his students to the music of Rimsky-Korsakov and Mussorgsky; in 1903 he offered an entire course on Russian music.[14] Like Berlioz before him, Bourgault-Ducoudray was much impressed with Mily Balakirev, with whom he began a lengthy correspondence.[15] Saint-Saëns, too, on his Russian visit, enjoyed the music of Balakirev, formed a good relationship with Tchaikovsky, and although he had heard much about Mussorgsky and his music, ended by disliking both with equal relish. (The Russian composer, for his part, felt the same about Saint-Saëns.[16]) Saint-Saëns also met with composer Sergei Tanaïev, when the latter came to Paris on tour in November 1876.[17]

Debussy visited Russia twice while in the employ of Madame von Meck, Tchaikovsky's celebrated patron, in the summer of 1881 and again in 1882.[18] At that time, however, the music of the "jeune école russe," as it was called by the French, did not receive many performances. The Russian establishment preferred the works of Tchaikovsky and Rubinstein, both of whom, being favored by the Tsar, were vigorously denounced by the younger musicians.

In the 1880s, Tchaikovsky was already widely known in Germany and in France, at least in the urban music centers. But the Russians, particularly the avant-garde, considered his structures too traditional and his style too Germanic, while the composer himself felt drawn to Paris and things French. In two letters (10 July 1880 and 5 July 1884) to Tchaikovsky, Madame von Meck mentions Debussy by name. In his reply, the Russian composer writes that he's very happy with "de Bussy's" [*sic*] success in achieving the Prix de Rome. And at the beginning of their relationship, when von Meck sent him a photo of Debussy, the older man even commented that Debussy had "something in his features and his hands that vaguely recalls Anton Rubinstein in his youth. May God grant that his destiny be as glorious as that of the King of pianists."[19]

Except in Russia, where his works were often performed, Rubinstein was far better known as a pianist than as a composer. And today, even his remarkable pianistic facility is long forgotten. (Most concertgoers think of Arthur, not Anton, when the name Rubinstein is mentioned. They are not related.) Nevertheless, his accomplishments remain a model of the nineteenth-century virtuoso's life style. From Russia, where he was born, he toured Poland, Germany, Holland, Belgium, France, Switzerland, Italy, Austria, Hungary, Denmark, Sweden, England, and crossed the Atlantic to perform in the United States and Canada as well. An incomparable virtuoso, he also wrote about a dozen operas, five oratorios on biblical subjects, a ballet, several piano concertos and piano sonatas, half a dozen symphonies, and more. He was not popular with the young Russian school and he knew it. To a friend he wrote: "The Jews regard me as a Christian; the Christians as a Jew; the classicists as a Wagnerian; the Wagnerians as a classicist; the Russians as a German, and the Germans as a Russian."[20]

Although Louis Laloy reports that Debussy met Rimsky-Korsakov, Balakirev, and Borodin, we cannot be certain that he did.[21] We have no evidence that Debussy heard any of Rubinstein's music. Nor do we know whether Debussy attended two concerts of Russian music that Rimsky conducted while Debussy was in Moscow.[22] He might have attended one of the presentations of the Rossignols de Koursk, a troupe of forty gypsies from Moscow who performed at the Trocadéro and the Orangerie during the Exposition of 1878.[23] Another friend of Debussy, Paul Vidal, describes the composer's enthusiasm for Tchaikovsky and Borodin[24] but says Debussy was not familiar with Mussorgsky's work.[25] Surely, the young composer—he was only sixteen in 1878—would have heard at least one of the six performances of Rimsky's *Sadko* either at the Exposition, which he visited often, or at one of Pasdeloup's numerous performances of the piece.[26] Schaeffner reports that from fall 1878 to spring 1902—excluding 1885–86, when Debussy was away in Rome and, oddly

enough, no Russian music of consequence was performed in Paris—
the following works were presented:

Prince Igor (Borodin)	13 performances
Sadko (Rimsky-Korsakov)	12 performances
In the Steppes of Central Asia (Borodin)	10 performances
Capriccio Espagnol (Rimsky-Korsakov)	9 performances
Antar (Rimsky-Korsakov)	7 performances
Thamar (Borodin)	6 performances
Sheherazade (Rimsky-Korsakov)	5 performances
Night on Bald Mountain (Mussorgsky)	2 performances
Second Symphony (Borodin)	2 performances[27]

Pasdeloup, Colonne, Lamoureux, and especially Chevillard, after
1897 when he took over from his father-in-law Lamoureux, offered
Russian music frequently on their programs. Lamoureux even included historian Bourgault-Ducoudray's *Cambodian Rhapsody* in a
concert of January 1889, and in June of that year, Rimsky-Korsakov
presented a series of concerts of Russian music.

Schaeffner's investigations virtually come to a halt with the production of *Pelléas et Mélisande* in 1902, and one must look elsewhere
for further information.

The fourth large-scale Universal Exposition, which took place in
1889, was also the year that French musicians made the pilgrimage
to Bayreuth *en masse*. The short voyage to the east of Germany
seems to have impelled those seeking new musical stimulation to
continue their quest for fresh melodic resources in Russia. Thereafter, by all indications, contact between French and Russian musical artists increased.

Le Guide musical, begun in 1855 and continued through 1917,
was first edited by Félix Delhasse in Brussels. Schott of Mainz published the weekly, which appeared every Thursday (and on Sundays,
beginning in 1894), and distributed it in Brussels and in Paris. By
1865, it could boast of correspondents in numerous European musical centers and between its pages one could find the thoughtful
comments of some of the finest musicians and critics of the day.
Advertisements for concerts, for instruments, for books about music, and for musical editions provided readers with considerable
information about musical activities in Europe and often in America

as well. Guest writers contributed essays; there were centenaries of composers' births or deaths, and a column featured obituaries of significant performers and composers; *nouvelles diverses* carried the kind of gossip about marriages and divorces always of more interest to women than to men.

A Russian influence was soon seen in its pages. In 1878, the publisher Pyotr Jurgenson announced a four-hand arrangement of Berlioz's *Harold en Italie*, nine years after the composer's death, by none other than Balakirev. By 1886, the first item in the journal is a piece on Borodin's Second Symphony. In the issue of 22 April 1886, a portrait of Anton Rubinstein accompanies an article on him that begins: "On dit de Rubinstein qu'il était le Michel-Anges de piano." (They say of Anton Rubinstein that he was the Michelangelo of the piano.) Maurice Kufferath, the Belgian Wagnerite who became editor-in-chief in 1887, was an early contributor.

In 1887, the journal's masthead listed an impressive array of music critics: Adolphe Jullien, Arthur Pougin, Georges Servières, Camille Bellaigue, and Michel Brenet of France; Edouard Evenepoel, Edouard de Hartog, Félix Delhasse, and Kufferath of Belgium, G. P. Harry from England, Egidio Cura from Italy, and César Cui from Russia.[28] They gathered news of musical interest to communicate to readers and subscribers in Europe; evaluated new productions of operas; provided critiques of vocal and instrumental performances; produced essays on significant musicians and performers; and, by and large, they raised the standards of musical journalism. A survey of materials published in *Le Guide musical* during the twenty-five year period from 1889 to 1914 helps shed light on the Franco-Russian exchanges that took place at this time.[29] While the following bibliographic essay differs stylistically from the others included here, the material in the *Guide* proved so rich that it merits inclusion.

1889

> *Prince Igor* is then, according to today's aesthetic, a decorative work. From this point of view, it is noteworthy and differs from other works of this genre through the picturesque or special color of the Russian school and, particularly, of Borodin. (*GM*, 21 February 1889, p. 63.)

Thus critic Marcel Rémy describes the newly published edition of Borodin's posthumous opera, completed by Rimsky-Korsakov and Glazunov from Borodin's own sketches.[30] Even taken out of context—a review of the edition and a summary of the plot—the two sentences encapsulate the French view of "la jeune école russe," who are dedicated to the reform of Russian music through the use of authentic Russian folk songs and colorful popular tunes and occasional references to the melodies of the Russian Orthodox Church, a revitalization along the lines that Wagner advocated for German music and that French Wagnerites, Catulle Mendès and others, prescribed for French composers. To lessen the impact of Wagner, French composers sought inspiration within their own ethnic and cultural roots. As the century drew to a close, German influence faded. After experiencing the delights of Russian music (as a result of the visits of Russian musicians and pianists at the Exposition of 1889), the French became more amenable to cultural contacts with their eastern neighbor.[31]

In July 1889, at the Trocadéro, two concerts of Russian music conducted by Rimsky-Korsakov and his young pupil Glazunov are well received by French critics, who deplore the absence of the public from the French capital at the time. They express the hope that Colonne, Lamoureux and Garcin will see fit to include works of these Russian masters on some of their winter programs. The critic Balthazar Claes reminds his readers that Mussorgsky's *Night on Bald Mountain* might conceivably be compared with Berlioz's "Witches' Sabbath" from his *Symphonie fantastique* and also with Saint-Saëns's *Danse macabre*. He recalls that the Saint-Saëns piece succeeded the Russian master's work—but all of them are indebted to Berlioz's orchestration and his descriptive style.

In autumn 1889, Gounod's forthcoming appearance for several concerts in St. Petersburg and Moscow is announced; the French pedagogue and pianist Louis Diémer is also expected there. On the fiftieth anniversary of Anton Rubinstein's professional debut, Countess Rostopchine, on behalf of the Russian colony and musicians of Paris, sends a congratulatory telegram. Signatories include A. Thomas, Gounod, Massenet, Saint-Saëns, Léo Delibes, and all the members of the musical section of the French Institute. The following week an extensive review of the celebrations accompanying Rubinstein's jubilee calls attention to "the contingents from New York, Chicago, Brussels, Antwerp, Berlin, Vienna, and Paris who have gathered to pay him homage." Countess Louise Mercy-Argenteau,[32] the celebrated Belgian Russophile and friend of Liszt, proffers her remarks in person.

1890

Maurice Kufferath, famous Belgian Wagnerite who became editor of the *Guide musical* heralds Rimsky's imminent arrival in Brussels, where he would conduct a concert devoted exclusively to Russian music. Roger Martin writes:

> The Russians seize every opportunity to express resoundingly their sympathy for French artists. They write us from Moscow that Edouard Colonne has just won an unprecedented success in that city. The concert he conducted at the Conservatoire was but one long ovation for our conductor and for French composers whose works preempted half the program. M. Colonne, whom the Muscovite society wanted to retain at all costs, was only able to leave Moscow by promising to return, next year, to give a series of concerts in Russia. (*GM*, 13 April 1890, p. 119.)

After the concert in Brussels, Kufferath remarks:

> I do not believe that there is currently in any country of Europe as interesting a group of artists, more knowledgeable about their craft and more completely equipped to bring before the public any newer or more original sensations. It is no longer young, this new Russian school. Two of its most eminent disciples, Borodin and Mussorgsky, are dead; still living are César Cui and Rimsky-Korsakov; Balakirev has attained the maturity of age and of talent. (*GM*, 20 April 1890, p. 125.)

Richepin's *Le Flibustier* with music by César Cui will be produced at the Opéra-Comique.

Rumor has it that the Tsar will establish in Paris an Academy for Russian artists and composers, the counterpart of the French Academy in Rome. It is well known how much the Russian government does for music: Tiflis, Warsaw, Karkov, Kiev, Moscow, St. Petersburg, and other cities all get substantial help. Would that the French government did likewise! (*GM*, 5 April 1891, p. 111.)

1891

In October, Colonne presents works of the Russian school. On 19 November he prepares once again to leave for St. Petersburg where the Russian papers list the following program: Beethoven's Fifth Symphony, Grieg's *Peer Gynt* Suite, three excerpts from Massenet's *Hérodiade*, Boccherini's *Minuet* and *Sicilienne*, and the Wedding March from *Lohengrin*. Vocalist Berthe Montalant will sing selections from Gluck, Saint-Saëns, Gounod, and Augusta Holmès. (*GM*, 25 October 1891, p. 270.)

1892

Publisher-impresario Belaïev[33] organizes two concerts of works by the new Russian school at St. Petersburg. Featured works include those by Rimsky-Korsakov, Mussorgsky, Sokolov, Liadov, and Glazunov, whose *Le Printemps* resembles Wagner's "Forestmurmurs" from *Siegfried*. (*GM*, 14 February 1892, p. 56.)

At the Trocadéro, La Société des Grandes Auditions Musicales gives a concert of Russian music, but includes not one piece by Mussorgsky, Sokolov, Liadov, Cui, Balakirev, or Dargomizhsky. They present four works by Tchaikovsky, the least Russian of these composers, and a chorus by the Czech composer Eduard Nápravník. And the most important work, Borodin's Second Symphony, is cut from the program. Are they afraid of tiring the audience? The Tchaikovsky concerto is played by Siloty [*sic*], a talented newcomer. (*GM*, 12–19 June 1892, p. 185.) Lamoureux is invited to St. Petersburg to conduct music by Richard Wagner [!] and works by composers of the young French school. (*GM*, 9 October 1892, p. 275.) The French Académie des Beaux-Arts appoints Tchaikovsky a correspondent member for music. (*GM*, 4 December 1892, p. 352.)

1893

The journal reports that Colonne has been far more successful in his Russian concerts than Lamoureux. (*GM*, 1 January 1893, p. 9.) Tchaikovsky, the most universally admired Russian composer, and Glazunov, the youngest musician of the new Russian school, both are the subject of articles. Advertisements for Tchaikovsky's newest pieces alert readers to their availability (*GM*, 8 January 1893, pp. 18–19.)

The visit of the Russian fleet to France has a musical counterpart, a Festival Russe organized by *L'Echo de Paris* at the Châtelet. A critic writes that Colonne is the best possible choice as conductor. Russian works already have an undeniable importance in Paris, although they are not so well-known as yet throughout France. Composers whose works are included are Glinka, Serov, Borodin, Cui, Rubinstein, Rimsky-Korsakov, Tchaikovsky, Mussorgsky, Dargomizhsky, Liadov, Glazunov, Nápravník, and Balakirev. The proximity of the Russians to the Orient has enabled them to study its rich melodies and modalities, and to leave behind the Italian music imported to their land in the eighteenth century. *L'Echo* has made careful plans for this festival, which will be attended by the Russian ambassador, significant members of the resident Parisian Russian colony, Sarah Bernhardt; several eminent singers—Bréval, Delma (of the Opéra-Comique), Divivier and Saleza—also either attend or perform. (*GM*, 22 October 1893, p. 409.)

Excitement associated with the visit of the Russian sailors permeates every musical event these past few weeks. From composers' pens flow new works that glorify the Russian Hymn or the Marseillaise. Excerpts from Glinka's *Life for the Tsar* are offered in a soirée at the opera.

Unfortunately, Gounod's death on 18 October interferes with the festivities and some concerts and recitals become memorials. (*GM*, 29 October 1893, p. 422.)

1894

Rémy reviews Cui's *Le Flibustier* at the Opéra-Comique and calls it boring—despite its illustration of the composer's precise theories expressed in his *Musique en Russie* (Paris 1880), where he calls for the exclusion of Italianisms and extensive patches of instrumental music in opera, along with the elimination of closed musical forms and the omission, as well, of duets, trios,[34] and so on. *Le Flibustier* is simply monotonous. (*GM*, 28 January 1894, p. 105.)

Tsar Alexander III died of kidney failure on 1 November. A long obituary praises this remarkable sovereign for his support of music. He had an excellent ear, played the cornet and bourdon [a bagpipe], and organized an orchestra of amateurs that gave benefit concerts and played at dinners and balls. He maintained a fine choir in his chapel under Balakirev and Rimsky-Korsakov. He had not cared for classical eighteenth-century music or Italian opera, preferring homegrown Russian opera. And although he disliked Anton Rubinstein's music, he backed the composer because he believed his work was good for Russia's cultural reputation. (*GM*, 18 November 1894, p. 906.)

The lead article in the *Guide musical* of 25 November 1894, is an obituary of Rubinstein by H. Imbert, who compares him favorably with Liszt. There is also an announcement that the Société des Concerts will present Rubinstein's works during the 1894–5 season. (*GM*, 25 November 1894, p. 923.)

1895

A season of French opera is announced by the Théâtre Korsch in Russia. The artistic efforts are due to M. Devoyod; the conductor will be Vianesi. The works included are *Les Huguénots*, *L'Africaine*, *Guillaume Tell*, *Charles VI*, *Hamlet*, *Faust*, *Rigoletto* [*sic*], *Mireille*, *Roméo*, *Lakmé*, *Werther*, *L'Attaque du moulin*, and *Carmen*. The occasion represents the first time that the French language will be sung at the Moscow opera house. (*GM*, 24 February 1895, p. 186.)

Siloti, who has lived for a long while in Paris, is leaving for a German tour on which he will perform piano compositions by the young Russian school. (*GM*, 27 October 1895, p. 811.)

1896

Scriabin, a young Russian pianist, will give a concert at the Salle Erard on 19 January. (*GM*, 12 January 1896, p. 29.)

An announcement notifies readers that at the Châtelet, at 2:00 P.M., Winogradsky, director of the Kiev Imperial Society of Music, will conduct a *grand festival de musique russe* at the Concerts Colonne. Works will include the following: the Overture to *Prince Kholsky* by Glinka; Tchaikovsky's *Pathétique* Symphony; *Roghneda* by Serov; Dargomizhsky's *Cosatchok*; *In the Steppes of Central Asia* by Borodin; Rubinstein's *Danses des Bayadères*; excerpts from Rimsky-Korsakov's *Snegourotchka*, Cui's *Berceuse*, and fragments from Mussorgsky's *Boris Godunov*. Berthe Montalant will be the vocalist. (*GM*, 8 November 1896, p. 739.)

Théodore Radoux, writing on *La Musique et les écoles nationales* most intelligently declares that the young Russian school derives from Berlioz and Liszt. After all, Berlioz was first recognized in Russia and certainly influenced Borodin. (*GM*, 15 November 1896, p. 743.)

1898

M. et Mme Scriabin will perform his works on 31 January. "We cannot forget the success he had here two years ago." (*GM*, 30 January 1898, p. 103.) A surprising series on Tolstoy and Nietzsche appears in the *Guide musical* in issues running from 28 August to 11 December. The author is Maurice Kufferath, who argues at length that philosophers are rarely so happy as when they can occupy themselves with discussions of the art of music. (*GM*, 4 December 1898, p. 935.)

1899

Glinka's *Life for the Tsar* is performed in St. Petersburg with Madame Gorlenko-Dorlina, a singer and impresario already known in Paris for her customary mastery in the role of Vania. Lamoureux and his son-in-law Camille Chevillard, who took over his orchestra in 1897, will each conduct a concert in St. Petersburg. Several French celebrities are invited. (*GM*, 29 October 1899, p. 805.)

1900

An advertisement cites the availability of works by Chabrier, Fauré, and Rubinstein (*GM*, 7 January 1900, p. 20.)

Ricardo Viñes, a young Catalan pianist, friendly with Ravel since 1888, begins to include works by the young Russians on his programs. (*GM*, 21 January 1900, p. 57.) At about the same time, conductor Camille Chevillard acquaints the French with the young Russians at the Concerts Lamoureux. (*GM*, 18 February 1900, p. 147.) The Russians complain of hearing too much Russian music. In Brussels, on the other hand, at the Théâtre de la Monnaie, audiences respond with enthusiasm to works by Glinka, Rimsky-Korsakov, Glazunov, Tanaïev, and Borodin. (*GM*, 25 February 1900, p. 184.) Colonne, received favorably in Russia in 1891 and 1894, returns and, under the direction of Gorlenko-Dorlina, performs music of Bizet, Saint-Saëns, and Berlioz with much success. (*GM*, 1 April 1900, p. 302.) Imbert raves about the Russian balalaika orchestras conducted by Andreëv at the Universal Exposition of 1900. (*GM*, 24 June 1900, p. 509.) An article on "L'Exotisme musical à l'exposition universelle" informs readers of a volume, *Les Musiques bizarres de l'Exposition 1889*, written by Louis Bénédictus, an intimate friend of Judith Gautier. (*GM*, 21 October 1900, p. 743.)

1901

Steinway announces that they make pianos for the Tsar of Russia and their advertisement cites endorsements from Rubinstein and other Russians. (*GM*, 5 May 1901, p. 430.) Marie Olénine [Maria Alexevna Olenina] sings Russian songs in Paris. Debussy, commenting on the performance, said she sang so well that Mussorgsky himself would have been pleased.[35] Without Pierre d'Alheim and his wife-to-be, Marie Olénine, Mussorgsky would have to wait a long time for recognition in France. (*GM*, 19 May 1901, p. 469.) Gustave Samazeuilh writes that Mussorgsky's *Nursery Songs* have been published in French translation at Froment, 40 Rue d'Anjou; and Marcel Boulestine, in the *Courrier musical*, has a penetrating study on them in an issue dedicated to Mussorgsky. (*GM*, 23–30 June 1901, p. 536.)

Samazeuilh remarks that French interest in the composer's music stems from the efforts of Pierre d'Alheim and several other musicians who don't wait for an artist to be accepted by "les snobs" before praising him. When critic Louis Laloy compared Ravel's *Histoires naturelles* to the Mussorgsky cycle in an article in the review *S.I.M.* (Société Internationale de Musique), Debussy took him to task. "I am dismayed," he wrote, "to find that a man of your taste deliberately sacrifices such a pure instructive masterpiece as the *Nursery* to the artificial Americanism of the *Histoires naturelles* of M. Ravel."[36] Lamoureux will give the first performance in Paris of Borodin's *Polovtsian Dances*. (*GM*, 20 October 1901, p. 751.)

1902

Gorlenko-Dorlina, soloist for the Russian Emperor, organizes the twelfth annual concert of French music conducted by Alfred Bruneau. All are warmly received by the Russian audience in St. Petersburg. Pianist Lucien Wurmser and violinist Jacques Thibaud are in the audience along with the Emperor's sister, Russian grand dukes, and the French ambassador. (*GM*, 19 January 1902, p. 68.) The indefatigable Colonne, in honor of the centenary of the birth of Victor Hugo, decides to mount a festival featuring writings by Hugo that have been set to music. He also organizes a Festival Russe on 23 March at the Châtelet Theater in Paris, at which Gorlenko sings excerpts from works by Arensky, Rimsky-Korsakov, Glazunov, and Rubinstein in a concert lasting four and a half hours! Gorlenko-Dorlina is acclaimed for her performance and the c-minor symphony by Glazunov, one of the young Russians whose music is most frequently heard, proves exceedingly attractive. (*GM*, 30 March 1902, p. 295.) Enthusiasm for the Russians extends to Belgium, where the distinguished lecturer Mademoiselle Biermé gives two lectures on "Russian Music since Peter the Great" at the Ecole de musique d'Ixelles. (*GM*, 25 May 1902, p. 472.)

Alfred Bruneau, sent to Russia by the French minister of public instruction and fine arts, offers the *Revue de Paris* the first of his studies on theaters, concerts, schools, churches, and music in general in Russia.[37] He analyzes the principal works of several great Russian composers, beginning with Glinka. He describes the generosity of Belaïev in his promotion of Russian music and Russian musicians, and reports that three theaters present Russian works, and that concerts are offered on early Russian instruments. Gorlenko-Dorlina organizes public performances at which Colonne, Chevillard, and Bruneau himself are given opportunities to conduct. (Alexander III had two orchestras, and he sometimes played cornet or bass tuba with the players.) The orchestra has a large building with an extensive library as well as an instrument museum. Bruneau is full of enthusiasm about the Rubinstein Conservatoire. (*GM*, 28 September 1902, p. 691.)

1903

The Franco-Russian musical alliance appears to have borne fruit in both nations. A report from Kiev indicates that every day French music acquires a larger audience in Russia. Conductor Winograd-sky, by now well known in Paris, is one of its principal promoters, since in concerts at Kiev and St. Petersburg, he successfully performed works by several composers previously unknown in Russia, including Lalo's Symphony in g-minor; Bruneau's Overture to *L'Ouragon*; the Prelude from *Armor* by Sylvio Lazzari; the *Enterrement d'Ophélie* by Bourgault-Ducoudray and the *Danse de Platée* by Rameau. Not content with offering French compositions, Winogradsky also engaged French artists Henri Marteau and Mademoiselle Emma Holmstrand to sing selections from Hector Berlioz, André Messager, and Gabriel Pierné. (*GM*, 8 February 1903, p. 133.)

During the entire concert season, Ricardo Viñes plays many selections of Russian piano music.

Alfred Bruneau's *Musique de Russie et Musiciens de France*, published by Fasquelle, gets good reviews, although the reviewer reminds us that the volume is really a compilation of several of his articles, many of which have already appeared in print. (*GM*, 12-19 July 1903, p. 544.)

Since the dawn of the twentieth century, many Russians have come to Paris. Today numbers of them are stranded without funds and without the guidance necessary to promote their careers and to help propagate their national gifts. Their needs will be met by the newly organized Union des Artistes Russes à Paris, which will promote events, concerts, and expositions. A large but select group, including the Russian Ambassador Ourousoff, will present a concert on 30 May at the Salle d'Athénée in Saint Germain, where the Schor, Krein, and Ehrlich Trio, celebrated in Russia, will perform in Paris for the first time. They will play Tchaikovsky's Trio composed in memory of Rubinstein, his teacher. Singer Georges Féderov of the

Opéra sang selections from *L'Africaine* and from Rubinstein's *La Nuit*. Mademoiselle Melgounoff appeared in selections from Borodin's *La Princesse endormie*, in the Bohemian song from Koreshchenko's *La Maison de glace*, and in Rubinstein's *La Russalka*; she also sang a song by Tanaïev. "Colonne should look to his laurels!" (*GM*, 14-21 June 1903, p. 491.) French pianist Raoul Pugno and Russian violinist Leopold Auer together tour Russia most successfully. (*GM*, 15 November 1903, p. 797.) Imbert complains about a performance of *La Juive*. "Why not mount some modern Russian operas, currently unknown in France?" he asks. (*GM*, 29 November 1903, p. 828.)

1904

At a meeting of Russian artists on 30 January, Bourgault-Ducoudray, with customary artistry, traces the history of Russian music and comments on current tendencies, pointing out similarities between the folk songs of Brittany and of Russia. In the midst of all these Russian students appears Bourgault-Ducoudray, a native of Brittany, who reveals a certain physical resemblance to Slavs. His words induce their youthful enthusiasm as they also warmly welcome the singer Lucien Berton and the lieder recitalist Madame Jeanne Arger, exquisite in blue tulle. Other Russian artists also perform, among them Mademoiselle M. Schmorgoner. The conference's organizer is Madame de Mouromzeff. (*GM*, 7 February 1904, p. 121.)

Arthur Pougin's monograph *Essai historique sur la musique en Russie* is published by the Paris firm of Fischbacher. In his review Imbert calls it a compilation of others' work, and "Pougin didn't have the decency to cite these references." Octave Fouque, G. Bertrand, Albert Soubies, César Cui, Anton Rubinstein, Alfred Bruneau, the Countess Mercy-d'Argenteau are among those from whom Pougin has lifted material [though he failed to cite Imbert's own essay on Tchaikovsky.] (*GM*, 17 April 1904, p. 369.) On 11 May, Russian pianist Ossip Gabrilovitsch will give a concert at the Salle Erard for the benefit of widows and orphans of Russian sailors lost on the battleship *Petropavlovsk*. [It was sunk by the Japanese at Port Arthur.] (*GM*, 8–15 May 1904, p. 444.)

1905

Calvocoressi gives the first of a series of lectures on Russian music at the Ecole des Hautes Etudes sociales. [He was born of Greek parents in Marseilles, studied music in Paris, and in 1916 settled in London. After learning Russian, he began to promote Russian music and musicians and wrote *La Musique Russe* in 1907; he also published monographs on Liszt, Glinka, Schumann, and Mussorgsky.[38]] He discusses works of Glinka, Serov, and Dargomizhsky. Mademoiselle Rabaïan [*sic*] from the Tiflis Conservatory illustrated some of the songs. (*GM*, 26 March 1905, p. 260.)

Viñes includes works by Balakirev in his series of historical piano recitals at Salle Erard. He plays Balakirev's *Islamey* and also Mussorgsky's *Tableaux* and repeats his program at the Université Populaire on the Rue du Faubourg Saint Antoine. Calvocoressi lectures on Russia and Mlle Babaïan illustrates the vocal works also at the Université Populaire (*GM*, 10 December 1905, p. 813), and the lead article in the *Guide musicale* is on Félia Litvinne, Russian soprano. (*GM*, 17 December 1905, p. 823.) Vassily Safonov, a pianist, conductor, and student of the celebrated maestro Theodor Leschetizky, conducts the Lamoureux orchestra in Paris. (*GM*, 24 December 1905, p. 851.)

1906

February is a big month for Russian music. Calvocoressi writes a two-part article (dedicated to the composer and pianist Joaquín Nin, Anaïs Nin's father) on the genius of "The Five"; their gifts are incorporated in Sergei Liapunov, whose *Etudes d'Exécution* he compares with those by Liszt. Debussy is indebted to Liapunov; Ravel and de Séverac owe much to Balakirev.[39] (*GM*, 11 February 1906, p. 105.) The Conservatoire and the Lamoureux orchestras feature music by Russian composers Borodin, Rimsky-Korsakov, Tchaikovsky, and Balakirev. Gabrilowitsch performs. Julien Torchet says that "Debussy [est] un impressioniste à la façon des peintres Monet et Sisley comme l'a dit si justement H. Imbert, d'un coloris séduisant sans ligne ni dessin, poète de l'irréel et du rêve." (*GM*, 18 February 1906, p. 128.)

Madame Olénine d'Alheim and M. Pierre d'Alheim offer their fifty-fourth recital devoted to works by Mussorgsky. Without this couple, the French would know nothing of Mussorgsky and his music. And nobody's works merit intimate study more than Mussorgsky's. Vincent d'Indy's *Tableux de voyage* and Gabriel Dupont's *Heures dolentes* show the impact of Mussorgsky's illustrative music. (*GM*, 10–17 June 1906, p. 438.)

Serge Diaghilev. "Perfect ballet," he is reported to have said, "can only be created by the fusion of dancing, painting, and music."

Rimsky-Korsakov (top), Borodin (middle left), and Mussorgsky (middle right), who together with Balakirev, and César Cui, were the most influential Russian composers of their day.

Anton Rubenstein, "the Michelangelo of the piano"

The Russians in Paris, 1889–1914

A concert of Russian music was given at the Grand Palais des Beaux Arts at the exhibit of contemporary and retrospective Russian art. Félia Litvinne sang; Selva and Pitsch performed Rachmaninoff's Sonata for Cello and Piano. Other works included Balakirev's *Islamey*, and excerpts from Glinka's *Life for the Tsar*, Serov's *Judith*, Tchaikovsky's *Onegin* as well as songs by Tchaikovsky and Borodin, and Rubinstein's *Le Voyageur dans la nuit*. (*GM*, 11 November 1906, p. 706.)

1907

The Lamoureux concerts conducted by Chevillard will present five programs of Russian music in May, 1907.

16 May: Glinka's *Russlan et Ludmilla*; Borodin's *Prince Igor*; Tchaikovsky's Second Symphony; Rimsky-Korsakov's *La Nuit de Noël*.

19 May: Excerpts from Rimsky's *Snegourotchka*; Mussorgsky's *Boris Godunov*; songs of Liadov and a symphony by Tanaïev.

23 May: Tchaikovsky's Fourth Symphony; a concerto by Scriabin; Borodin's First Symphony; and excerpts from Mussorgsky's *Boris Godunov*.

26 May: Glazunov's Second Symphony; a Rachmaninoff concerto and a cantata *Le Printemps*; excerpts from Mussorgsky's *Khovantschina* and Balakirev's *Thamar*.

30 May: Scriabin's Second Symphony; Liapounov's concerto; excerpts from Cui's *William Ratcliff* and Rimsky's *Sadko*.

Except for the fourth concert of May 26 when Chevillard will conduct, all the others will be led by Artur Nikisch. Singers include Litvinne, Chaliapin, Smirnov, and Zbrouiva. (*GM*, 21 April 1907, p. 319.) Henri de Curzon writes an article devoted to *Les Concerts historiques russes à Paris* and reveals the extent of Diaghilev's labors for Russian music in Paris. He comments on the preparations over the past decades for the extraordinary Franco-Russian musical alliance which has produced such fruitful exchanges of music, musicians, artists, and set designers. (*GM*, 2–9 June 1907, p. 419.)

1908

Under the Tsar's patronage, the Imperial Opera of St. Petersburg will give a series of ten Russian operas in Berlin from 20 May to 20 June and in Paris from 15 May to 15 June with two troupes. (*GM*, 1 March 1908, p. 196.) Marie Olénine d'Alheim, who has just written *Le Legs de Mussorgsky*, will give her 60th recital devoted to Mussorgsky's works. (*GM*, 21–28 June 1908, p. 479.) Louis Schneider,

Massenet's biographer, gives a lecture on Russian folk songs, after acknowledging the work of Soubies. "Particularly impressive is the *Chant hébraïque* of Rimsky-Korsakov," he says. (*GM*, 20 December 1908, p. 833.)

1909

The *Cercle artistique* devotes an evening to Russian music. Viñes plays works of Liapunov, Mussorgsky, Fyodor Akimenko (born Yakimenko), and Balakirev. (*GM*, 7 February 1909, p. 118.) Announcement that the Châtelet Theater will have a series of operas and ballets russes with Chaliapin, Litvinne, et al. (*GM*, 14 March 1909, p. 237.)

Henri de Curzon's piece on "La Saison russe à Paris" mentions the contribution of Diaghilev, Astruc,[40] and Nijinsky who, at eighteen, is so remarkable. They haven't seen his equal in fifty years. He enjoys particularly the *Pavillon d'Armide* (after Théophile Gautier), Benois's sets, and the conductor Tcherepnin. The choreography of Fokine and Petipa "de la famille française," the music of Glinka, Rimsky-Korsakov, Tchaikovsky, Glazunov, Mussorgsky all prove most successful. They have viewed these programs—the second offered Rimsky-Korsakov's celebrated *La Pskovitaine* (The Maid of Pskov)— but above all, de Curzon says, "it is the choreographic festival that overwhelms the public. The dances, the ballets-pantomimes, the dancing choruses, the first Russian scenes in their integral state, the sets, the costumes and all the various interpreters present the Parisian spectators with a most piquant and original attraction." De Curzon continues by citing Louis Schneider's excellently documented previous series of articles on the significance of the dance in the Russian theater. (*GM*, 23–30 May 1909, p. 434.)

1910

In a series on the history of the string quartet, the Quatuor Lejeune devotes five concerts to works by Russian composers at the Salle Pleyel. Dates are 22 December (1910) and 26 January, 23 February, 16 March, 13 April (in 1911). Nancy, Lyons, and Rouen are among other French cities now being exposed to Russian music. (*GM*, 2 January 1910, p. 10.)

The Concerts Lamoureux programs Rimsky-Korsakov's *Russian Easter Overture*, conducted by Chevillard. "What gorgeous hues! Bathed in incense. Countless number of candles. Divinely glorious chimes playing short themes of five notes, having certain affinities, it seems to me, with our old folk songs. And with it all, a furious virtuosity that surprises slightly. But what beauty!" (*GM*, 3 April 1910, p. 267.)

In July, the Russian season at the Opéra features Stravinsky's *Firebird*, whose plot is borrowed from Russian legend. Karsavina triumphs in this most significant work of the season. Fokine is responsible for the choreography; Pierné conducts. De Curzon proceeds to outline the plot: While hunting in the forest, Prince Ivan strays into the kingdom of the evil and immortal Kotschei. He captures the Firebird who wins her freedom by giving him one of her magic feathers with which the Prince may summon her in time of danger. A troupe of young girls, princesses, under the spell of Kotschei, enters the forest. Kotschei finds them and recognizes that Ivan has already fallen in love with one of them. When the two lovers fail to escape, Ivan calls up the Firebird who shows him where to find the egg that holds Kotschei's life. Ivan breaks the egg, Kotschei dies, his spell is broken, and in the final scene Ivan, with his bride beside him, is crowned and all the other princesses are united with the princes to whom they were formerly betrothed. Stravinsky is a pupil of Rimsky-Korsakov; this is his first ballet score. (*GM*, 3–10 July 1910, p. 507.)

Lamoureux plays Liadov's *Baba Yaga* and the critic calls it "le tableau musical le plus amusant, le plus spirituel qu'on puisse imaginer." As Gounod used to say, "Ce ne'st pas la musique à traverser le soir." (*GM*, 4 December 1910, p. 798.)

1911

Borodin, Mussorgsky, Rimsky-Korsakov, Liadov, Glazunov, Tchaikovsky are played by both Colonne and Lamoureux orchestras. Rimsky's *Antar* and *Shéhérazade* are favorites.

A lecture on *Félicien David et l'Orientalisme en musique* is given by M. Brancour at the General Psychological Institute. M. Paulet, a tenor, illustrates vocal selections.

The forthcoming season of the Ballets Russes, with Nijinsky dancing under Astruc and Diaghilev, will perform Stravinsky's *Petrouchka* and *Firebird*, Tcherepnin's *Narkis*, Rimsky-Korsakov's *Sadko*, Liszt's *Orphée* and his 4th Hungarian Rhapsody and Weber's *Spectre de la rose*. (*GM*, 5 March 1911, p. 189.)

The Russian Imperial Musical Society celebrated its fiftieth anniversary with more than sixty delegations from all over the world to honor Rubinstein's artistic enterprise. Works played include those by Rimsky-Korsakov, Tanaïev, Scriabin and Rachmaninoff. In its fifty years the Society has offered 670 symphonic concerts, 400 concerts of chamber music. More than 900 students have attended classes there, among them some who have become eminent in their field. (*GM*, 12 March 1911, p. 215.)

The Theater Sarah Bernhardt will open a Russian lyric season with Dargomizhsky's *Roussalka*, *La Fiancée du Tsar* and *May Night* of Rimsky-Korsakov, *The Demon* by A. Rubinstein, Tchaikovsky's *Pique Dame*, and *Eugène Onegin* with two casts, Russian and French. They will alternate languages in their performances. (*GM*, 30 April 1911, p. 352.)

1912

Before the close of the legislature, the Russian Ambassador, Isvolsky, and the French Minister of Foreign Affairs, M. de Selve, sponsor a law to protect literary and artistic works of France and Russia. (*GM*, 7 January 1912, p. 16.)

The Theater of the St. Petersburg Conservatory presents Saint-Saëns's *Samson et Dalila*, translated into Hebrew by a young student named Ravreb. The work is performed with much success before the top Jewish society of that city. (*GM*, 21 April 1912, p. 321.)

La Saison russe, organized by Serge Diaghilev at the Châtelet, becomes the third attraction of Gabriel Astruc's formal *grande saison de Paris*. After five symphonic concerts conducted by Felix Weingartner and several performances of [Belgian symbolist writer Verhaeren's] *Hélène de Sparthe* [with music by de Séverac], Diaghilev and Astruc have devoted the remaining weeks to the ballet. For four weeks, four works, each performed four times, will include the principal ballets of the repertoire. In this, their seventh season, they will feature, besides the usual *Firebird*, *Spectre de la rose*, and *Prince Igor*, Cocteau's *Le Dieu bleu* with music by Reynaldo Hahn. Principal dancers will be Karsavina and Nijinsky. Bakst has done the sets. Ingelbrecht and Monteux will alternate as conductors. (*GM*, 26 May–2 June 1912, p. 393.)

Balakirev's *Thamar* is added to the Russians' season. Three concerts are offered by Marie Olénine. The critic wonders why there are only three, noting that her voice is incomparable. Seven folk songs issued last year by her publishing house, Maison du Lied in Moscow, were not very interesting.

Professor Nathalie Aktzeri of the St. Petersburg Conservatory gives a recital covering the history of the *romance*, including works by Russian composers. (*GM*, 9–16 June 1912, p. 416.)

Madame Niktina of the St. Petersburg Opera gives a recital; Viñes, supposed to perform, falls ill. At this recital, Calvocoressi speaks about trends in Russian music and explains what the current crop of French musicians owe to the Russian Five. "Avec les penetrations des école russes, allemandes, et françaises, il est difficile de répondre à la question de M. Calvocoressi," says the journal's critic. "Où va l'école russe aujourd'hui?" (*GM*, 23–30 June 1912, p. 438.)

1913

In their eighth season in Paris, Nijinsky and the Ballets Russes have produced some works that are anti-artistic, according to Henri de Curzon. (*GM*, 25 May–1 June 1913, p. 420.)

Ravel's *Daphnis et Chloë* concludes the Russian season at the Châtelet, with Nijinsky and Karsavina as the principal dancers. (*GM*, 23–30 June 1913, p. 435.)

Next February, *Orphée*, with text and music by Roger-Ducasse will be choreographed at the Imperial Theater in St. Petersburg. (*GM*, 30 September–5 October 1913, p. 608.)

In 1914 *Le Guide musical*—until it temporarily ceased publication with the issue dated August 2–9—carried innumerable references to performances of Russian music in Paris, Brussels, and other capitals of Europe. The activities of Russian composers both within and outside of their native land, the visits of French musicians to Russia and performances of French music in Moscow and St. Petersburg continued to make the news.

In the United States, the venerable American music critic James Huneker had described the impact of the Russians before the turn of the century. He first heard the music of Mussorgsky and Rimsky-Korsakov at a Pasdeloup concert early in December in 1878.[41] Huneker often spoke of these concerts in the Philadelphia *Bulletin*, to which he contributed articles. On 29 January 1879,[42] commenting on the differences between the French and German approaches to music, he said, "To be successful in Paris, music has to be embellished with scenery, ballet and costumes, while the Germans, on the other hand, like music for its own sake." Later in 1915, his discerning essay, "A Musical Primitive: Modeste Moussorgsky", appeared in the magazine *Forum*.[43]

Before the outbreak of the war, Stravinsky, the young Russian composer who would emerge as the most significant musical representative of his country in the twentieth century—albeit mostly in exile—had established himself, as had Diaghilev and other nostalgic Russian émigrés in Paris. And after the conclusion of the war, came the Americans, engulfing the French capital with still another group of émigrés. Alfredo Casella in his quasi-autobiography, *Music in My Time*, commented most succinctly on the changed direction of French music: "However important German teaching may have been in [the] revival of French instrumental consciousness, it was evident by now that Germany had entered the descending parabola of her formidable musical cycle and that the light of the future must be sought elsewhere."[44]

10

The Legacy of Ida Rubinstein: Mata Hari of the Ballets Russes

On 4 June 1909, at the newly refurbished Châtelet Theater in Paris, an unknown dancer made her debut with the Ballets Russes in *Cléopâtre* and created a sensation. Just arrived in Paris, she was unknown not only to the audience, but also to her fellow dancers. She had rehearsed with them neither in her hometown of St. Petersburg nor in Paris, where they prepared for the opening. Instead, her mentor Michel Fokine had taught her privately. The ballet, originally known as *Nuits d'Egypte* and set to the music of Anton Arensky, had not been a success at the Maryinsky Theater where it premiered.[1] Diaghilev claimed he had disliked the Arensky music from the start.

So he changed the name of the ballet, retained some of Arensky's music as background, and for the rest substituted the music of Rimsky-Korsakov's *Mlada*, Glazunov's "Bacchanaie" from *The Four Seasons*, Glinka's Turkish dance from *Russlan and Ludmilla*, and Mussorgsky's Persian dance from *Khovanshchina*, and presented for the first time a new Cléopâtre in the person of Ida Rubinstein.[2]

Rubinstein would later figure in the composition and performance of many of the ballets of the first decades of the twentieth century; yet except for Michael de Cossart's recently completed but still unpublished biography dealing with her stage career and patronage,[3] no single book treats her life, her phenomenal energy, and her work in a manner that would bring her to the attention of today's dance-loving public. She has become as mysterious as Mata Hari, known to us only in the memoirs and reminiscences of luminaries of the Ballets Russes and biographies of contemporary composers.[4]

Born in 1885, Ida Rubinstein was the daughter of a wealthy Jewish banker, who died young, as did his wife. Orphaned early, Ida was raised by an aunt, a Mrs. Horowitz, who had a salon in St. Petersburg to which she regularly invited artists, writers, musicians, and dramatists. Stage-struck, but scarcely trained, young Rubinstein prevailed on her aunt to allow her to enroll at the Alexander Theater, where she studied drama with its director, M. Ozarovsky.[5] Within a short time Ida decided to produce Sophocles's *Antigone* with herself in the leading role. For the sets and costumes, she approached Léon Bakst. Because she had inherited considerable funds on the death of her parents, Rubinstein could easily pay the fees of those artists she wanted to hire. Bakst agreed to participate in her project, but advised her to limit herself to one act, which she should present before a private audience rather than as a commercial venture. Rubinstein took his counsel, and after two months of preparation she appeared ready to proceed.[6]

In 1905 she had her first success with *Antigone*. It spurred her to further efforts; and in December 1908 she staged Wilde's controversial *Salomé* to the music of Glazunov, not however, without surmounting numerous obstacles. Her family was shocked at the idea of her appearing nude in public. (She intended, in the famous dance of the seven veils, to remove them one by one until she appeared totally naked.) Rubinstein countered by marrying an agreeable cousin, thus establishing herself as an adult beyond the family's control.[7]

Official censors were another matter, and the Orthodox Church's Governing Synod outlawed the performance. Using her connections, Rubinstein managed to get permission to stage the work, provided she did not recite Wilde's original text. Bakst found the solution. Recognizing her expert gifts as a mime, he suggested she utilize this technique as a way of getting around the critics. The piece was performed in mime, and she achieved a spectacular success.[8]

The dancer Fokine, her private tutor, and Bakst became ardent boosters. When Diaghilev, at the time preparing to take his troupe to Paris for the opening season of the Ballets Russes, needed a replacement for Ludmilla Barach, his Cléopâtre, Fokine and Bakst prevailed on him to use Rubinstein.[9] Furthermore, inasmuch as she was a rich young woman, Diaghilev was convinced she would not be difficult about fees. Such an attitude represented, for him, a prime consideration; he was always short of funds.

Because they had discovered her, Bakst and Fokine felt a responsibility for her performance. They worked terribly hard—she was, after all, only an amateur dancer but with extraordinary stage presence and the kind of exotic beauty adored in the West—and her success in *Cléopâtre* exceeded their wildest dreams. Alexandre Benois described the scene as she gave herself up to a night of love:

> The disrobing took place to the beautiful but terrifying music of [Rimsky-Korsakov's] *Mlada*. Slowly . . . , one by one, the covers were unwound, disclosing the divine body omnipotent in its beauty. . . . When the slight figure emerged covered only by the wonderful transparent garment invented by Bakst, one experienced a feeling of awe. Here was not a pretty artiste appearing in frank *déshabillé*, but a real, fatal enchantress, in the tradition of the cruel and grasping Astarte.[10]

In fact, she won her audiences more with a set of poses than with her dances. Peter Lieven wrote: "Her long, youthfully slender, peculiarly angular body seemed to have just descended from an Egyptian bas-relief and her marvellous Eastern profile with narrow almond eyes was very appropriate to the role. . . ."[11] Jean Cocteau was so overwhelmed by those "vacant eyes, pallid cheeks, and open mouth . . . penetratingly beautiful, like the pungent perfume of some exotic essence," that he became a lifelong admirer: "Disposed as I was to admire Rimsky-Korsakov's music, Madame Rubinstein has fixed it in my heart, as a long blue-headed pin might impale a moth with feebly fluttering wings."[12] Count Robert de Montesquiou, dandy, aesthete, and arbiter of taste—Proust's model for Baron de Charlus—felt drawn to this mysterious, beautiful stranger and became a devoted follower, sitting through every performance of *Cléopâtre*. When the troupe closed in Paris, Rubinstein went on to England and America before going home to St. Petersburg.

The next year Diaghilev returned again to Paris and Rubinstein attained another legendary success, this time in *Shéhérazade*, with music from the first, second, and fourth movements of Rimsky-Korsakov's symphonic suite of that name. For days, Bakst, Benois, Fokine, and Diaghilev had deliberated over the appropriate gestures to go with the specific musical material. The idea for the piece originated with Bakst, and the magnificence of his sets and costumes surpassed anything he had done previously. For this ballet, he arranged for a startling array of colors and fabrics whose impact would eventually spill over into music halls and revues as well as into couturiers' collections. The sides of a large green tent enriched with gold and black encased and encircled the ladies' apartment, which was filled with a crowd dressed in orange, pink, and green clothes. They surrounded the single royal jewel, the Sultana Zobeïde [Rubinstein], a blue sapphire in a setting of rubies and emeralds.[13] (Bakst had coiffed her in a powder-blue wig.) Dance historian André Levinson remembers that "*Cléopâtre* had caused extraordinary surprise. *Shéhérazade* in 1910 surpassed everything. In recalling the annals of modern theater, it is scarcely possible to recollect any production that was given a similar reception. *Shéhérazade* represented Bakst's real Paris debut, *Cléopâtre* had been a revival."[14]

Because of her triumph, Rubinstein expected that the impresario would give her other roles in the future. When Diaghilev hesitated, she left him and began to work on her own. She made a few appearances at the Paris Olympia and then had one of her most brilliant inspirations: a plan for what became *Le Martyre de Saint-Sébastien*, in a collaboration with d'Annunzio and Debussy.

Sometime in 1910, the Italian poet, playwright, and soldier Gabriele d'Annunzio escaped from his creditors in Italy and settled in Paris. For several years he had contemplated a work on the martyrdom of St. Sebastian. His interest in the martyr was hardly religious; rather, he viewed the bleeding youth as a Christian transfiguration of the myth of Adonis. Like Cocteau and the Count de Montesquiou, he attended performances of *Cléopâtre* and *Shéhérazade* and immediately became an admirer of La Rubinstein. Were it not for her inspiration, he might never have written *Saint-Sébastien*. Her tall, slim, flat-chested body made him declare her the perfect interpreter of the young saint. He wanted to write for Paris and inasmuch as Rubinstein had no knowledge of Italian, he had additional reasons for setting this work in French.[15]

Two mystery plays on the saint's life—one from the fifteenth century and one from the sixteenth—already existed. D'Annunzio spent considerable time with the medievalist Gustave Cohen at the Bibliothèque Nationale and elsewhere in intense discussions of the setting, the customs, the appropriate text for such a piece. Imitating Wagner's approach, d'Annunzio took his historical material from a well-known source, *The Golden Legend*,[16] and added or revised at his pleasure. Many critics were displeased by his use of the French language. Cohen, on the other hand, announced that "Gabriele d'Annunzio possesses a prodigious verbal gift. His French vocabulary is no less rich than his Italian vocabulary."[17] And future statesman Léon Blum welcomed him saying, "French letters can now count one more great poet in its midst."[18]

Le Martyre de Saint-Sébastien comprises a prologue and five scenes: La Cour des lys, La Chambre magique, le Concile des faux dieux, Le Laurier blessé, and Le Paradis. Because these separate episodes lack direction and unity, it was hoped—in vain, as it turned out—that the music would provide the necessary cohesiveness.

Early in February 1911, Debussy wrote to his friend Robert Godet that he had been working on an Egyptian ballet for Maud Allan, the English dancer. At the same time, he said, "d'Annunzio asked me to write incidental music for his *Le Martyre de Saint-Sébastien*. I needn't tell you," he continued, "that the worship of Adonis is mingled in this work with the worship of Christ."[19] D'Annunzio had already written to Debussy on 25 November 1910, speaking of his admiration for the composer's music and asking if they could possibly meet.[20] Debussy had replied from Vienna, where he was rehearsing *La Mer*: "The mere thought of working with you sets up some sort of feverish excitement."[21] Debussy accepted the commission without having seen a word of the text. He had to work under terrible time pressure—Rubinstein and the impresario Gabriel Astruc had already selected a date for the premiere. Later, Debussy wished that he had had more time to familiarize himself with the material.[22] D'Annunzio, like Wagner, indulged himself to the utmost limits in luxury; Debussy's needs were relatively simple. Their collaboration boded no good.[23]

Despite several crises that left him on the verge of quitting, Debussy completed the score in two months, working from January to March 1911. He had delegated much of the orchestration to André Caplet, who conducted the first performance and, many believe, wrote the final chorus of the work. D. E. Inghelbrecht, chorus master under Caplet, reported that Caplet had said of Debussy, "He composed day and night, shut up at his home, sending off pages of the score one by one to the printer, with never a look back."[24] On 22 May 1911, *Le Martyre de Saint-Sébastien* was performed with a magnificent stage setting by Bakst, who had suffered considerable criticism from Diaghilev, the latter convinced that Bakst's obligations to Rubinstein were in conflict with his efforts for the Ballets Russes.[25]

The play was not a success. One writer, Boris de Schloezer, insisted that if it had lasted one hour, it might have been acceptable, but a five-hour performance proved too painful to contemplate.[26] The Catholic press and the Paris Archbishop, aware of pagan tendencies in the art of both Debussy and d'Annunzio, attacked it.[27] Apparently Rubinstein's poor pronunciation also contributed to its failure. Later versions of the work were more successful. In one revival at La Scala in 1926, Rubinstein appeared with Toscanini directing the orchestra. The text of the play first appeared in the theatrical supplement of *L'Illustration* of 27 May 1911, and a month later in book form from Calmann-Lévy. D'Annunzio dedicated it to Maurice Barrès who, arch-conservative that he was, hesitated to accept it. Not until 1941 did *Saint-Sébastien* win over the public—and then in a concert performance.[28]

Another d'Annunzio play with incidental music by Ildebrando Pizzetti, *La Pisanelle*, was written for Rubinstein and produced at the Châtelet in June 1913. It, too, failed.[29] The author and composer were Italian; the set designer and stage director Russian; Germans, Hungarians, and Poles participated in the venture; and the leading interpreter was the Jewish actress and dancer from the St. Petersburg Theater. The mélange spelled disaster in advance.

Neither d'Annunzio nor Rubinstein was discouraged. Both believed only circumstances and luck were against them. Astruc was nonplussed: "I don't understand it at all," he said. "I've united the greatest musician, the greatest poet, the greatest decorative artist

Ida Rubinstein was an amateur dancer, but with an extraordinary stage presence and the kind of exotic beauty adored in the West.

Costumes designed for the Ballets Russes by Léon Bakst. With the dancer Michel Fokine, he became one of Rubinstein's most ardent supporters.

Igor Stravinsky, the young Russian composer, would emerge as the most significant musical representative of his country in the twentieth century—albeit mostly in exile.

and the best choreography. And the work failed."[30] Nevertheless, the pagan spirit, initiated in the post-Wagner era by Sâr Péladan and others, remained alive in Parisian ballets: Stravinsky's *Le Sacre du printemps* and Ravel's *Daphnis et Chloë* followed soon afterward.

In Paris in 1914, Diaghilev once again turned to Rubinstein, after he had signed a contract with Richard Strauss's agent. She was assigned the role of Potiphar's wife in a ballet based on the biblical story of Joseph and his brethren. Diaghilev assumed she had consented to his request and telegraphed the news to Hugo von Hofmannsthal, who wrote to Strauss at Garmisch, congratulating him on his good fortune. Rubinstein, however, never took the role and insisted she had not agreed to it. Diaghilev staged the ballet without her; Nijinsky made Joseph one of his many celebrated roles.

Rubinstein persisted in her willful fashion, continuing to seek out composers from whom to commission new works. Arthur Honegger, one of the group of young composers dubbed "Les Six" by critic Henri Collet, composed in every conceivable medium: operas, oratorios, ballets, incidental music for plays, radio music, film music, choral works, orchestral pieces, chamber music for various combinations and even a work for ondes martenot, an electronic instrument. Like Milhaud, he often drew on classical legend and history. His handling of the voice, however, proved rather unusual. Speaking, screaming, whispering, murmuring, and humming all found a place in his works. Ida Rubinstein recognized his gift and as a result commissioned several works, the first as early as 1925.

She continued to generate works of various genres. Through her, Honegger met d'Annunzio and also Saint-Georges de Bouhélier.[31] For the latter's play *L'Impératrice aux rochers* (1925), he wrote incidental music. On commission from Rubinstein, he did the same for d'Annunzio's *Phèdre* and conducted its premiere in Rome in 1926.

Around the turn of the century, the poet Paul Valéry had suggested to Debussy that they collaborate on a ballet, *Amphion*. Later he proposed an opera on the same subject. Although Debussy was then seeking a classical subject, the piece never materialized. Years later, Honegger took on the challenge and in 1929 completed the ballet-melodrama *Amphion* to a text by Valéry.[32] Without Rubinstein's initiative, this work, too, would not have been completed. No sooner had the curtain fallen on *Amphion*, than Rubinstein ordered another mime-melodrama from Valéry for Honegger. *Sémiramis* opened at the Opéra on 11 March 1934, and Rubinstein again had a smashing success.[33] Instinctively she knew the kinds of works to commission and showed skill at matching poets with composers.

She introduced Honegger to Paul Claudel in 1934 and arranged for the two to collaborate on the oratorio *Jeanne d'Arc au bûcher*. At first Claudel would not consider the subject; it was too historical and too often quoted.[34] Through Rubinstein's persistence, the poet saw possibilities in the work and with time it became one of Honegger's most successful creations. The premiere took place on 12 May 1938 in a concert of the Basler Kammerorchester under Paul Sacher. Rubinstein starred in the title role; as narrator she was unequaled.

Too important to be overlooked, Stravinsky was the next musician to fire Rubinstein's imagination. As he completed work on *Les Noces*, the composer began to think seriously about writing incidental music for a staging of *Anthony and Cleopatra* in André Gide's translation. Rubinstein's agent, ever seeking out projects, wrote Stravinsky asking if he would accept a commission for this work. Bakst was promoting the venture, and Stravinsky was enthusiastic. Gide visited the composer and encouraged him. Stravinsky then sketched ten separate pieces of incidental music and, on 18 November 1917, telegraphed an associate of Rubinstein to ask if he should continue. Evidently, Rubinstein had failed to meet his financial demands. The project soon perished.

In December 1927, Rubinstein and Benois together devised a plan for Stravinsky to use Tchaikovsky's music as the skeleton of a new piece for ballet. She wrote to Stravinsky, who requested at least $6000 depending on the length and the exclusivity of the production. Between July and October 1928, after she agreed to his terms, Stravinsky composed *Le Baiser de la fée*, based on a story by Hans Christian Andersen. On 15 October, he wrote his close friend, the émigré Russian Gavril Païchadze, that he had finished the piano score and was sending it to him for the engraver. "Don't show it to Ida, Nijinsky or Benois," he cautioned. "It is necessary for people such as they are—not particularly initiated—that I play the music for them myself."[35]

On 27 November 1928, at the Paris Opéra, Stravinsky conducted the premiere. Although the work failed to attract admirers, Rubinstein arranged to present it again in Monte Carlo in January 1929.

Piqued that she allotted it only one performance and "that is hardly worth the expense to which she has gone," Stravinsky remarked that "no one in the artistic world is as mysteriously stupid as this lady."[36]

For some unexplained reason, *Le Baiser de la fée* marked the end of the friendship between Diaghilev and Stravinsky. The impresario suspected that Stravinsky, after his association with Rubinstein, would allow her to stage *Apollo*, a ballet that Diaghilev had presented first. When he asked the composer about it, Stravinsky replied enigmatically. With regard to this business of "my offer of *Apollo* to Ida Rubinstein, . . . I can tell you that Rubinstein, like many other theatrical entrepreneurs, has inquired from Païchadze about *Apollo*. I myself never offer my works to anyone, either directly or indirectly."[37] Presumably that stance removed him from any possible blame, should Rubinstein eventually present *Apollo*.

From Paris in January 1933, Païchadze wrote Stravinsky that the composer had erred in thinking that Paul Valéry would be his poet for another ballet, *Persèphone*. Païchadze related a long conversation with Ida Rubinstein, who, he said, "has André Gide in mind and he has written a remarkable piece for her; a classical text with chorus that should please you."[38] She wanted Gide to get in touch with Stravinsky as soon as possible, and Païchadze hoped that the financial terms would be the same as for *Le Baiser*. Tactfully, he cautioned the composer to act more diplomatically, less impulsively. Using Rubinstein as intermediary, because Stravinsky was on tour, Gide sent her his completed piece in late February. The debonair Harry Kessler confided to his *Diary* on 19 March 1933: "A visit from André Gide. He told me that he and Stravinsky are writing a ballet, *Persèphone*, for Ida Rubinstein."[39]

A month later Païchadze telegraphed Stravinsky that the contract with Rubinstein was signed and that he had sent the first payment of 25,000 francs on to the composer. Many points still needed to be settled. Rubinstein insisted on later dates for additional payments to the composer, and she wanted exclusive rights to concert as well as ballet performances so that concert performances would not interfere with the impact on the public of her ballet—that is, unless she herself arranged them. While Gide seemed eager at first to collaborate with the composer, their work did not proceed without problems. In the end, Stravinsky's setting did not please Gide who boycotted all three performances (30 April, 4 and 9 May in 1934).[40]

Four years after *Persèphone*, Rubinstein again appealed to Stravinsky, proposing Claudel as librettist. Unfortunately, the composer and the poet failed to agree on a subject, Stravinsky insisting it be Greek and Claudel that it be biblical. Despite Rubinstein's talents, collaborations between the artists creating her ballets did not always progress easily.

In 1927, when Rubinstein asked Ravel to write a ballet for her, he replied that he preferred orchestrating some of Albéniz's works instead. After Ravel's death, the composer Joaquín Nin, father of the writer and cult figure Anaïs Nin and of the composer-pianist Joaquín Nin-Culmell, recalled the genesis of *Boléro*, the piece that originated with Rubinstein's request.[41]

Nin and Ravel had known each other for many years—they were introduced by the composer Déodat de Séverac in 1903—and as they were traveling together from Monfort l'Amaury to St. Jean-de-Luz at the end of June 1928, Nin asked Ravel about his current projects. Ravel mentioned his intention to orchestrate several pieces from Albéniz's *Iberia* to be danced by Ida Rubinstein. He had already decided on a name: *Rondeña*. "I quickly told him," said Nin, "that Arbos had already orchestrated the entire work for a ballet for the dancer Argentina and that he held the copyright. There is no point in working on something that cannot be produced."

Ravel became very angry, wanting to know who Arbos was. Certainly the publishers, Max Eschig in Paris, would know the situation regarding copyright. After a call to Eschig and the realization that the copyright was firm, Ravel insisted, "The laws are idiotic. What am I going to tell Ida?" Nin proceeded to discuss other kinds of Spanish music with Ravel, who responded by citing the work of Rimsky-Korsakov, Debussy, even Meyerbeer, strangely enough, but "not d'Indy or Wagner."

Ravel left for Paris and a few weeks later a letter arrived announcing his involvement on a singular work: it had no real form, no development, almost no modulation, just a rhythmic insistence on a theme for orchestra, "of the same genre as Padilla, that vulgar author of *Valencia*." He first called it *Fandango*, and later changed the name to *Boléro*—although Spaniards declare it does not have the appropriate rhythm for a genuine bolero. (It is similar to the folk bolero as played in Majorca.) Ravel usually took a long while to incubate a piece, but the *Boléro* progressed quickly and on 20 November 1928 Rubinstein presented the premiere at the Opéra. *La*

Valse was on the same program and the two proved an excellent pair. Ravel gave Rubinstein exclusive rights to perform the piece for three years in the theater and one year in the concert hall.

Several years later Ravel confided to Rubinstein that he planned to turn *l'Histoire d'Ali Baba* into a drama: *Morgiane*, "full of blood and thunder."[42] Unfortunately, in 1932, Ravel was in an auto accident, as a result of which he suffered terribly in the last few years of his life. Disconsolate and unable to work, the composer longed to visit some of the places he had missed earlier. Rubinstein knew of his desire to see Spain and North Africa. With remarkable tact, she arranged and paid for him and his companion Léon Leyritz, a sculptor, to make the trip. At the Mamounia Hotel in Marrakech, the two gentlemen spoke at length about *Morgiane*. Sketches remain, but Ravel never completed it. After his accident, he wrote very little.[43]

An intense, domineering woman with inimitable panache, Ida Rubinstein created a sensation whenever she appeared in public, usually on the arm of a distinguished escort, such as the British beer magnate Guinness, the Parisian Baron de Montesquiou, or the Italian poet d'Annunzio. Her taste in clothes was faultless; when she wore black, she decorated her ensemble with white pearls and when she donned white, she sported black ones.[44] She spoke several languages, had a child's laugh, and the carriage of a goddess. Several contemporaries report that she lived on biscuits and champagne. Occasionally, she disappeared for a few weeks or months on jaunts to distant, exotic lands. She also hunted wild game, and a leopard cub and a panther were household pets. Once when Diaghilev entered her suite at the Meurice in Paris, the panther snarled at his frock coat, which the animal evidently disliked. Diaghilev jumped on a table, frightening the panther who proceeded to howl while he crouched in a corner. Rubinstein thought the whole affair hilarious. Not so Diaghilev, who arranged for the police to remove the animal as a threat to human safety.[45]

After 1925, when Rolf de Maré's Ballet Suédois disbanded and the Ballets Russes dominated the scene, Rubinstein reorganized her own troupe with the name Les Ballets Ida Rubinstein. (Diaghilev contemptuously called it Les Ballets Juifs.) She tried unsuccessfully to persuade Nicholas Nabokov, Diaghilev's cousin, to write for her. While he refused, most of those she invited to join her troupe accepted her offer with alacrity. Bronislava Nijinska, Nijinsky's sister, and Léonide Massine became her principal choreographers as she commissioned scores from Stravinsky, Ravel, Georges Auric and Florent Schmitt, and decors once more from Benois.

Ida Rubinstein was not an extraordinarily fine dancer, which makes us wonder all the more at her success. But her beauty, her stage presence, and her uncanny instinct to cast herself in appropriate roles—at least early in her career—catapulted her to fame.

Why did she slip into obscurity after making headlines during the first few decades of this century? Conceivably the roles she created have not survived her. We recall dancers who fashioned the roles of the faun in *L'Après-midi* or *Petrouchka* or even *Parade*. These roles are still popular today. On the other hand, *Cléopâtre* and *Shéhérazade*, ballets through which she achieved her earliest successes, are no longer in the repertory.

At a time when dance, particularly ballet, has attracted such a huge following, it seems appropriate to remember this woman who so skillfully commissioned and produced some of the foremost ballets of the century scored by some of the most celebrated international composers including Debussy, Ravel, Stravinsky, Honegger, Ibert, and Auric.

11

The Americans in Paris

Four decades prior to the American "invasion" of Paris in the 1920s, the French capital acted as a magnet to young American musicians. Few became as celebrated as the artists who arrived later, but they laid the groundwork for their successors. A continuous flow of ideas, commentaries, and criticism traveled back and forth across the Atlantic as Americans embarked for France and Frenchmen sailed to see the sights and sense the ambience of the New World. Not unexpectedly, much that transpired on the American musical scene from 1880 to 1914 reflected the prevalent attitude to France and French culture held by musicians, writers and artists of the time.

It was the age of the great American critics. Men like James Huneker (1860–1921), whose *patrie psychique*, as Van Wyck Brooks has said, would always be France.[1] Of his contemporaries—Philip Hale (1854–1926), Henry Krehbiel (1854–1923), William Apthorp (1848–1913), W. J. Henderson (1855–1937), Richard Aldrich (1863–1937), Henry Parker (1867–1937), and later Lawrence Gilman (1878–1939), Carl Van Vechten (1880–1964), and Olin Downes (1886–1955)—

some resembled Huneker in their love for the French; others, like Aldrich and Krehbiel, took every opportunity to castigate the native artists. For many, it was a love-hate relationship, as if the appeal of the place was so overwhelming it was frightening and had best be denied.

Few agreed with Longfellow that "all good Americans, when they die, go to Paris,"[2] or with Henry James, for whom France was "the mysterious home of art, the country who had given her inhabitants something called Taste, which distinguished them from other people."[3] Most agreed with Mark Twain, for whom the two great branches of French thought were science and adultery. "France," he said, "was a nation governed by prostitutes, a nation without winter, summer, or morals, a nation whose filthy-minded citizens were the connecting link between man and monkey." "A Frenchman's home," he quipped, "is where another man's wife is." And " 'Tis a wise Frenchman who knows his own father."[4] Such contrasting views by prominent American writers mirrored that of American musicians, whose reactions to French musicians proved just as varied.

By the mid-nineteenth century, Paris was an intellectual mecca for Americans. French criticism and French literary theory were the subject of numerous articles in scholarly American journals. From such diverse periodicals as *La France musicale*, *Revue et Gazette musicale*, *L'Illustration*, *Journal universel*, *Le Guide musical*, *Opinion nationale*, *Mireille*, and *Moniteur*, John Sullivan Dwight reported on French music in his *Journal of Music* published from 1852 to 1881.[5] Not surprisingly, many American musicians respectfully welcomed Alexandre Guilmant, Camille Saint-Saëns, Vincent d'Indy, the pianist Raoul Pugno, the musicologist Julien Tiersot, and the conductors Edouard Colonne and Charles Lamoureux on their arrival in the States. Arthur Foote remembers that in the nineties "we turned our steps towards Paris instead of Berlin, for Guilmant, in all his tours at that time, had made such an impression that students from all parts of the country began to go to him, as they have since to Widor, Bonnet, Vierne, and others."[6]

W. S. B. Mathews wrote in 1889 that most American singers spent a considerable part of their training period in Paris, studying with either Anna LaGrange or Mathilde Marchesi. But, he complained, "The most important defect of the ordinary American singers is their inability to sing artistically in their native tongue."[7] He recommended a national school as a possible remedy.

Rumors abounded. Every few years someone would come along with an idea for an American conservatory or news of its imminent establishment. As late as October 1912, the editors of the *Harvard Musical Review* quoted *The New York Times* regarding the efforts of several philanthropists to endow a national conservatory of opera with the official approval of our government. But the matter of government subsidy remained a debatable issue.

Offering their view of the Paris Conservatoire and the need for its counterpart in America, pianists Harold Bauer and Isidor Philipp argued that the Conservatoire alumni who had succeeded in their careers did so despite their training at that august institution. Bauer said:

> Certain characteristics of French nationalism are carefully cultivated: Clarity, elegance, proportion, logic, fluency, wit, and order. But it is quite possible that clarity may sometimes be opposed to imagination, that elegance may be antagonistic to sincerity, that academic canons of proportion may be cited to defeat the advancement of learning. . . . France has produced great artists, also possibly more mediocre ones than any other country, and it would not be unfair to suggest that this may be due to its national education methods.[8]

Earlier Philipp had pondered whether an institution like the Conservatoire could be established in America. He concluded that it neither could nor should be.[9] Nevertheless, the trend toward European training continued because local directors of music schools refused to entertain the idea of American teachers and persisted in hiring Europeans or European-trained musicians. Finally, Oscar Sonneck, in 1916, proposed an alternative: Americans should go to Europe only after substantial training at home, and after they had the opportunity to assimilate their own culture.[10]

Just as Americans voiced contradictory views of the French and what they owed them, Parisians expressed various opinions of Americans. In the winter of 1873, *L'Oncle Sam*, a new play by Victorien Sardou, was censored by the French government and then subsequently allowed to run. Enraged by the play's success, E. B. Washburne, the American minister to France, wrote:

> Although our country was one of the greatest customers of the French, and while 75 to 100 million dollars of our gold found its way to France every year, though our travellers filled all the hotels of Paris, crowded all the retail stores of the city, occupied the best apartments, and though

they comprised nearly a fifth part of the travellers on the great lines of railroads, the government and the people gave approbation to a national representation of the vilest character.[11]

But American culture began to be taken seriously. Three French operas of this period were based on American subjects. Jean Robert Planquette's *Rip Van Winkle* had its premiere in London in October 1882. Five years later his opera *Surcouf*, whose English version was altered to follow the lines of James Fenimore Cooper's *The Pilot*, enjoyed successful seasons in Paris and London. In 1911, Claude Terrasse's *Les Transatlantiques*, a musical comedy with scenes set in Newport and New York, opened in Paris.[12]

In 1896 S. C. de Soissons asks, "Why do Americans like minstrel shows? Honestly speaking, such taste is simply dreadful!"[13] But one of his compatriots did not agree, for two of Debussy's piano preludes, "Minstrels" and "General Lavine," derive their inspiration from this kind of American music.

Nonetheless, America was, at least in one sense, "the most musical country in the world" for de Soissons. "There is no other country," he marveled, "where there are so many pianos and players on them."[14] In his *Industrial History of the United States*, first published in 1877, Albert Bolles documents America's burgeoning piano industry. The annual production of pianos in the United States at that time was about 40,000, while all the European countries together manufactured only about 25,000. Bolles also reminds his readers that in the Universal Exposition in Paris in 1867, the American firms of Steinway and Chickering walked away with first prizes.[15] Historian William Peirce Randel offers the information that "in 1876, there were more pianos in America than bathtubs; they were second only to the kitchen range as a status symbol."[16]

In 1899, Albert Lavignac wrote that "though scarcely more than half a dozen American composers have achieved fame abroad, all Europe has resounded for a generation to her singers."[17] Whether or not they were meant for the profession, young American women went to Paris in droves. Among them were Clara Louise Kellogg, Anna Louise Cary, Minnie Hauk, Emma Thursby, Lillian Nordica, Emma Nevada, Mary Garden, and Geraldine Farrar.[18]

Male students included the singer Gaston Gottschalk (Louis's brother), violinist Albert Spalding, organists Seth Bingham, William

Crane Carl, and Wallace Goodrich, pianist Walter Rummel, and composers Chalmers Clifton, Henry Gilbert, David Stanley Smith, and Arthur Farwell who, after receiving a degree in engineering from the Massachusetts Institute of Technology, studied with Homer Norris in Boston and with Alexandre Guilmant in Paris. Norris may not be a familiar name, but he became one of America's more important Francophiles.

The American-born Norris graduated from the New England Conservatory and studied four years in Paris under Alexandre Guilmant, Théodore Dubois, Benjamin Godard, and Eugène Gigout, concentrating chiefly on composition and theory. He later was organist in several New England churches, finally becoming choirmaster and organist at St. George's in New York. In 1894 he published *Practical Harmony on a French Basis* in which he explained that he chose French methods because the French presented theories in an attractive as well as in a practical manner. "The Frenchman is instinctively an artist," he said. "Proof of this may be found in the many beautiful examples by eminent composers and theorists written expressly for this book. If one were not told, one would not expect that they were harmony exercises."[19]

In spite of the magnetism France began to exercise at mid-century, Germany was still the dominant cultural attraction for American students in the 1880s, when over two thousand of them studied at German universities.[20] But, by the nineties, France had begun to compete with her neighbor to the East as young people from the States began flocking to Paris, probably for more reasons than music. Not only did Americans visit France in greater numbers; French performers showed more interest in coming to the United States. Saint-Saëns, probably his country's most renowned musician at that time, made three visits. In 1892, he took part in the closing ceremonies of the World's Columbian Exposition in Chicago.[21] In 1906, under the sponsorship of the Knabe Piano Company, he performed with the New York Symphony under Walter Damrosch, as well as with the newly organized Minneapolis Symphony. His third visit was occasioned by the Panama Pacific Exposition held in San Francisco in 1915, where he served as good-will ambassador from war-torn France. For this event he composed a *Hymn to California* which, despite its rousing performance by the Sousa Band together with the Exposition Orchestra and an organist, was not particularly successful.

The French pianist Raoul Pugno, on a visit to the States, wondered how young Americans could succeed at all in view of the competition from foreigners invited to perform there.[22] Vincent d'Indy, beginning a three-week tour of the United States in 1905, admitted he was not acquainted with the works of American composers, especially the younger ones, although he planned to present pieces by several young Frenchmen during his American tour. Other French visitors that season included Marcella Sembrich, Pol Plançon, Marcel Journet, Julien Tiersot, and one hundred members of Mr. Charley's French Grand Opera Company bound for New Orleans.[23]

Among the more voluble French-speaking foreigners who crossed the Atlantic in the 1890s was the Belgian violinist Eugène Ysaÿe. In letters to his wife he described playing "all the important works, treating Americans with a respect to which they are unaccustomed." He declined to work there, however, because "though artists earn good money here, socially they receive little consideration." With a note of levity, he wrote that this country is full of beautiful women who enjoy being flattered. "I pay compliments to every woman as an artist," he tells his wife, "but I am quite prepared, should it ever become necessary, to seek safety in flight."[24]

The American critic Henry Krehbiel, who revised and completed the English edition of Thayer's *Life of Beethoven*, had a passion for the Germans and a genuine dislike of the French. He was concerned lest they corrupt the nation's morals. Reviewing the first performance of *Ruddigore* at the Fifth Avenue Theater in 1886, he wrote, "It is no small matter to furnish proof as Gilbert and Sullivan have furnished over and over again that comic operas can be written in English having all the artistic charms of the best French *opéras bouffes* without the indecency and vulgarity of subject and style which disfigure the latter as a rule."[25] He soon changed his tune.

Americans visiting Paris often went immediately to the famous cafés and theaters they had read about. Once café managers got wise, they did their best to satisfy them, lowering Parisian taste, as some said, to the level of the New Yorkers. Popular *café disants* featured entertainers like Yvette Guilbert, Aristide Bruant, and Louise Weber (better known as "La Goulue"). Guilbert's fame spread far beyond Paris's Divan Japonais and the Café Weber. Using the technique of half-spoken recitative, projecting her text so that it seemed addressed to each member of her audience, Guilbert played to and hypnotized large audiences in Brussels, London, and the United States.[26]

Among the first to introduce Parisians to American music was Frank van der Stucken, the Texas-born conductor of the Cincinnati Orchestra (founded in 1895). At the Paris Exposition of 1889, he presented a program of American works, including MacDowell's Second Piano Concerto, with the composer at the keyboard. In 1906 the Metropolitan Opera Company paid its first visit to Paris, unfortunately, without great success. Another American institution, the Sousa Band, fared much better, for in 1900 its sixty-three members took part in ceremonies marking the independence of both France and the United States, playing for the unveiling of the Lafayette monument on July 4th in Paris. After the ceremony the band marched through the main streets of Paris, escorted by units of the Garde Républicaine, regarded as one of the finest in the world. This band set a standard that John Philip Sousa tried to reach in the creation of his own ensemble.

A young American composer, Chalmers Clifton, found a friendly reception in Paris.[27] He won Harvard's Sheldon Travelling Fellowship in 1912 and studied for two years in France and in Russia; seven years later he returned to Paris to conduct the Paris Conservatoire Orchestra in an all-American program that aroused considerable interest.[28]

For several reasons, Franco-American relations intensified during the four decades from 1870 to 1914. Becoming a republic in 1870, France greatly appealed to Americans who were just celebrating their own centennial. Furthermore, French music and musicians had but recently found their own voice. Ten years after the establishment of the Société Nationale in 1871, young French composers, aided and encouraged by that organization, turned their attention to chamber music, instrumental works, and *mélodies*. They shunned the large operatic works because many felt impotent in the face of Wagner's colossal achievement and, more important, they recognized that the financial outlay necessary for opera precluded all but a very few from reaching production.

The members of the Société Nationale represented the avant-garde of their day. Most of them were talented musicians who had refused to accept the constraints of the Establishment—the Conservatoire and the Académie. A few of these dissidents, among them two of

César Franck's pupils, Charles Bordes and Vincent d'Indy, established the Schola Cantorum in 1894 to combat the stifling atmosphere of the Conservatoire. Ironically, the Schola Cantorum ultimately became more reactionary than the institution which it had opposed.

One of the positive effects of the teaching and orientation at the Schola Cantorum was its emphasis on French nationalism, its enjoinder to faculty and to students—paralleling Wagner's intentions—to explore their own musical backgrounds, to research their musical patrimony, and to build new works from these fresh musical resources.

There were similarities between the American Arthur Farwell and his Wa-Wan Press and the Schola Cantorum in Paris. Each was devoted to young composers unable to make their own way and each sought to revitalize national music. It is not inconceivable that Farwell, through his study with Homer Norris, was influenced by the French.

What began as a trickle of Americans who lived and studied in Paris during the final decades of the last century greatly expanded in the early part of the twentieth century as a result of the war and anti-German sentiment. Between 1910 and 1920, Harvard and Columbia universities both included on their staff French-trained musicians. Virgil Thomson insists that it was in France between 1890 and 1914 that the new century, foreseen by Emmanuel Chabrier and Gabriel Fauré, was realized in the work of Debussy, Ravel, Stravinsky, and Satie. Because French music had traditionally encouraged the absorption of exotic influences, it offered itself as a model for young American musicians to imitate. In his Harvard years, Thomson says, he identified with France "virtually all of music's glorious past, most of its acceptable present, and a large part of its future."[29]

Like their forebears, who had made the pilgrimage for almost four decades before the First World War, the new group of Americans in Paris was equally enthusiastic about their opportunities to live and learn and work in the French capital. And the French were delighted to have them.

Fortunately for the Americans, most of those active in the prewar era were still alive, some with their best work yet to come. Only Debussy and de Séverac were no longer on the scene. (Debussy died in 1918; de Séverac in 1921. Saint-Saëns, too, finally expired in 1921 at the age of eighty-one.) Still practicing their trade in Paris were Ravel, Fauré, Charles Koechlin, Paul Dukas, Henri Duparc (although he had stopped composing for many years already), Satie, and his group of disciples—Milhaud, Poulenc, Honegger, Auric, Durey, and Tailleferre—dubbed "Les Six." An even younger group shortly made its appearance, the School of Arceuil, named after the Paris suburb where Satie lived. These included Henri Cliquet-Pleyel (born 1894), Roger Desormière (born 1898), and Maxime Jacob (born 1906).

France's fortunes seemed at their lowest ebb when the United States entered World War I; the tide turned almost immediately afterward, and the French could not do enough for their conquering heros from across the sea. An American War Relief Clearing House and a French Heroes' Fund were but two institutions that helped cement Franco-American relations. Diplomats, politicians, military men, literary figures, and many distinguished musicians contributed to the French war effort.[30] Among the most significant musicians in the last group was the German-born American conductor, Walter Damrosch, who, with Pershing's aid, founded a school for American bandmasters in Chaumont, under the direction of Francis Casadesus.[31] It seems that the school resulted, in part, from a *faux pas* committed by the Americans in one of their first outdoor parades on the Champs Elysées as they celebrated the Fourth of July. At first they were welcomed by an enthusiastic crowd of Frenchmen, who then were horrified to see the Americans marching to a patriotic song, *Under the Double Eagle*, totally unaware of its German origin. The success of this first school led quickly to the founding of the most significant permanent music institution for Americans in France. American talents began to be nurtured in Paris through the auspices of Nadia Boulanger and her remarkable School of Fontainebleau.[32] Singlehandedly she trained and developed the foremost American musicians of the post-World War I era. George Antheil, Virgil Thomson, Aaron Copland, David Diamond, Roy Harris, and others would eventually reconfirm and reflect the essentially French base of their musical education.

Some Americans with good intentions were active in Paris even earlier. In 1908, fourteen American artists living in Paris formed the New Society of American Artists. Seeking the public recognition that had eluded them because they had adopted avant-garde styles, they flocked to the salons of Gertrude and Leo Stein, where they were introduced to the works of Van Gogh, Gauguin, Seurat, Cézanne, and Matisse. There they recognized that their own work was not so far out of the mainstream—the French mainstream. This group, the core of the New Society, included Daniel Putnam Brinley, Patrick Henry Bruce, Arthur B. Carles, Jo Davidson, Donald Shaw Mc-Laughlan, John Marin, Alfred Maurer, Edward Steichen, and Max Weber.[33]

The Steins, Leo and his sister Gertrude, until they separated in 1914, had the finest collection of modern art in Paris. Leo first noticed Picasso, and Gertrude, Matisse. But later Gertrude abandoned Matisse and befriended Picasso on a permanent basis. Matisse and Picasso met for the first time at the Steins and also made the acquaintance there of Henri Rousseau, André Derain, Georges Braque, Maurice de Vlaminck, Jules Pascin, Robert Delaunay, Marie Laurencin, and the Americans, Marsden Hartley, Alfred Maurer, and Maurice Sterne. The Steins were fortunate to be in Paris at the moment that these modern artists were working there together. They also, apparently, had the discerning taste that enabled them to build their collections with relatively small outlays of money. Two other family members lived in the city as well: Gertrude and Leo's brother Michael and his wife, Sarah. They, too, supported avant-garde artists through purchases, and eventually interested their friends Etta and Claribel Cone, spinsters from Baltimore, in buying works of art from both Picasso and Matisse.

The French, on the other hand, were slow to recognize the significance of the Impressionists; even the Post-Impressionists, Van Gogh, Toulouse-Lautrec, Gauguin, and Cézanne, did not win the admiration of their countrymen at the outset of their careers. Surprisingly enough, a record of their sales indicates that their first acceptance came in America.

In her preference for Picasso, Gertrude Stein revealed prescience. Picasso moved to Paris in the spring of 1904. He and Braque independently turned to cubism, and sometimes it is difficult to distinguish between them when it comes to their works of this period. For example, they both broke down the outlines and shapes of musical instruments. They presented them in diagrammatic form, dismantled, with parts seen from different aspects. Gertrude Stein's writing, in its own way, reflected what Picasso was doing in painting. She did "pen portraits" (short essays) of both Matisse and Picasso, and also of Apollinaire, writer Max Jacob, dealer Ambroise Vollard, Cocteau, Satie, Mabel Dodge, and other socialites. She also wrote sketches of Carl Van Vechten, Jo Davidson, Ernest Hemingway, Virgil Thomson, and Sherwood Anderson.

Sherwood Anderson, who influenced the earliest writing of William Faulkner and Ernest Hemingway, first visited Paris in 1921, at the age of forty-five. He claimed he was influenced by Notre Dame, the Louvre, the "Twillery" Gardens, people in the streets, and Gertrude Stein. In his notebook[34] he wrote that "Gertrude Stein has always been laughed at. Years ago, when her work first fell under my eyes and I was startled and profoundly stirred by its significants [*sic*] I made inquiry concerning her. Strange stories came out of Paris. She was a fat woman, very languidly lying on a couch, people came into the room and she stared at them with strange cold eyes. There was a strange power in her."[35] Young William Shirer, who went to interview her in 1926 for the *Paris Tribune* wrote:

> Miss Stein lived in a pavilion in a courtyard behind 27 Rue de Fleurus. I was ushered by a maid into a large studio salon. Though it was rather dark in the room I could make out the paintings, which already were famous and which occupied every inch of space on the walls. . . . The first things you saw were two canvases of [Picasso], a portrait of Miss Stein done before the Great War and his nude of the girl with the basket of flowers. I thought I also recognized a couple of Matisses and one or two by Juan Gris. . . . Then the author came in.
>
> She was so bulky that, as a note I jotted down reminds me, I thought she looked like a full-blown old Irish washwoman. But this first impression was soon changed. Above her heavyset body was a face that reminded you of a Roman emperor, masculine and strong and well chiseled, and her eyes were attractive and intelligent. Her hair was closely cropped, like Caesar's. She greeted me in a low, mannish but pleasant voice.[36]

In the 1920s, America produced a generation of composers born at the turn of the century or just a few years before. Many of them had received predominantly German musical training in their teens. New Jersey-born George Antheil, for instance, was a pupil of Ernest Bloch, but found there was not enough musical activity in the United States, despite the arrival in 1916, of French composer Edgar Varèse, who had organized in New York City an orchestra that played new music exclusively, and who, in 1921, as director of the International Composers' Guild, campaigned for contemporary music.[37] But Antheil was terribly impatient and, along with many other young American musicians, believed that to finish one's studies one had to go abroad, which meant, to Paris.

After World War I, the American Conservatory of Music (the Conservatoire américain, as they called it) was founded at Fontainebleau, as a summer school, with French teachers for American students. Walter Damrosch, who had gone to France in 1918 to train bandmasters for the American army, proposed the school together with General Pershing. In 1921 it opened its doors in a wing of the royal palace at Fontainebleau. Aaron Copland was the first to enroll, followed by Melville Smith and Virgil Thomson, who headed the unbelievably long list of Americans who studied with Nadia Boulanger between the wars. Aaron Copland wrote about her influence:

> In my own mind she was a continuing link in that long tradition of the French intellectual woman in whose salon philosophy was expounded and political history made. In similar fashion Nadia Boulanger had her own salon where musical aesthetics was argued and the musical future engendered. It was there that I saw, and sometimes even met, the musical greats of Paris: Maurice Ravel, Igor Stravinsky, Albert Roussel, Darius Milhaud, Arthur Honegger, Francis Poulenc, Georges Auric. She was the friend of Paul Valéry and Paul Claudel, and liked to discuss the latest works of Thomas Mann, of Proust, and André Gide. Her intellectual interests and wide acquaintanceship among artists in all fields were an important stimulus to her American students: through these interests she whetted and broadened their cultural appetites.[38]

Virgil Thomson describes the individual lessons:

> The lessons take place with the teacher at the piano, the student in a chair at her right. She reads the score before her silently at first, then little by little begins to comment, spontaneously admiring here and there a detail of musical syntax or sound, expressing temporary reservations about another. Suddenly she will start playing (and perfectly, for she is a fabulous sight-reader) some passage that she needs to hear out loud or that she wishes the student to hear as illustration to her remarks.[39]

After the Second World War, Boulanger went to the United States, where she taught at several colleges. She continued in her profession almost until her dying day.

On 5 May 1926, a concert of chamber music by American composers was given in Paris. It offered works by Copland, Thomson, Herbert Elwell, Theodore Chanler, Walter Piston, and Antheil. Except for Antheil, all had studied two or three years with Boulanger. Roy Harris's Concerto for Piano, Clarinet and String Quartet, written during his first year of study with Boulanger, had its premiere in Paris the following year. Harris said that "going to Paris was the best thing I ever did. I was just a truck driver then and had written my first works out of the fullness of my ignorance."[40] He had arrived in 1926. Later he wrote, "No words can express the nostalgia which oppressed me during my first year of return to America. . . ." He maintained that Americans could not understand composers, while Europeans understood how artists lived and worked among them.

Two women reigned supreme in the Paris of the 1920s. One was Gertrude Stein (1874–1944), and the other was Nadia Boulanger (1887–1979). Stein, the Mother Goose of Montparnasse, held court for the numerous French artists and writers who visited her at her residence on 27 Rue de Fleurus, where she lived with her longtime companion, Alice Toklas (1877–1967), from about 1907 (Toklas joined her in 1910) until 1938. Nadia Boulanger developed what was often dubbed the Boulangerie, teaching a mind-boggling array of American expatriates, most of whom expected to become professional musicians.

Stein had her supporters, many of them; but she also had her detractors. And they made fun of her, the fat lady languishing on her couch and making statements about art and literature and music with the authority of a Greek oracle. She was among the first to recognize the importance of the avant-garde paintings of Picasso and Matisse. She collected them when it was not yet fashionable to do so, but when they were eminently affordable. (Although her brother Leo insisted that he was the first of the clan to do so.)

Stein was an American expatriate who, remarkably enough, since she was Jewish (as was Toklas), remained in France during the Occupation and throughout the entire period of the Second World War. They had also survived the First World War in Paris. In 1939, however, they retreated to the south of France. Other Americans like the rich French-trained Natalie Barney, called "the Amazon" by Rémy Gourmont, also held salons. Barney did not collect art; she collected people. Djuna Barnes, an expatriate American poet and playwright was there, as was Sylvia Beach, the owner of the famous Paris bookstore, Shakespeare and Company, and *The New Yorker*'s Janet Flanner.

Nadia Boulanger was a born and bred Frenchwoman, who became the guiding genius of many French music students, but mainly of Americans. Supposedly, Leonard Bernstein was the last of her students to whom she spoke rationally a few days before her death. As Nadia used to say of herself: "There were three kinds of music students, the kind who had money and no talent, and those she took; the kind who had talent and no money, and those she took; and the kind who had money and talent and those she never got."[41]

Three years after her death at ninety-two in 1979 and close to sixty years after the start of her career as mentor to literally hundreds of young American and French musicians, Nadia Boulanger was described by Ned Rorem—probably the only living expatriate American composer who never studied directly with her—as the most influential teacher since Socrates.[42] "Myth credits every American town with two things," Rorem wrote, "a ten-cent store and a Boulanger student." Born to a venerable father, Ernest Boulanger, already twelve when Beethoven died in 1827, a composer and professor at the Paris Conservatoire, and the glamorous, much younger Russian Princess Raissa Myschetsky, her mother, Nadia absorbed her father's values—that music was a more natural part of life than literature or even sex—while remaining exceedingly close to her mother. At ten she entered the Paris Conservatoire, where she garnered first prizes in harmony, counterpoint, fugue, organ, and accompaniment (all aspects of score reading) and studied composition with Gabriel Fauré. Granted Second Grand Prix de Rome for her cantata *La Sirène* in 1908, she then left composition to her younger sister Lili who won the First Grand Prix five years later. From 1908 to 1918, Nadia Boulanger taught harmony at the Conservatoire, but was not named a full professor there until 1948, because the position was considered unsuited to a woman. Except for an opera to a libretto by Gabriele d'Annunzio—it was composed with her teacher, pianist Raoul Pugno, but never produced—Boulanger composed nothing after the deaths of Pugno in 1914 and Lili in 1918, devoting herself totally to teaching and to occasional performances as organist or conductor.

From the year it opened—1921—almost until she died, Boulanger was a fixture at the summer school for American students at Fontainebleau. She sweated out the Second World War in America, but apparently never really learned English, though she toured the country, gave lectures at numerous colleges, universities, and con-

Portrait of Gertrude Stein by Picasso. She was among the first to recognize the importance of the avant-gardistes Picasso and Matisse.

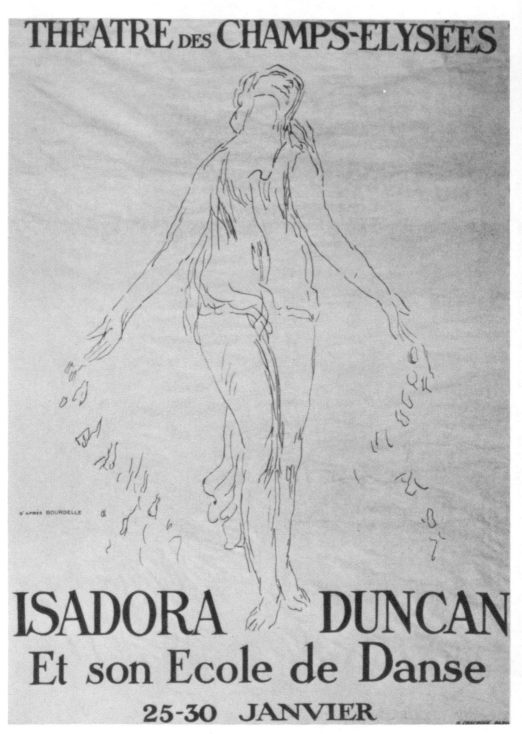

Isadora Duncan sensed dance as an expression of an inner urge or impulse. She rarely did the same movements twice in a performance.

servatories, and became the first woman to conduct both the Boston Symphony and later the New York Philharmonic. Her famous students are legion. Not only composers such as Aaron Copland, Virgil Thomson, Melville Smith, Herbert Elwell, Louise Talma, Roy Harris, Walter Piston, Elliott Carter, David Diamond, and Theodore Chanler, but also performers like Dinu Lipatti, Yehudi Menuhin, Maurice Gendron, Kathleen Ferrier, Noel Lee, and Nell Tangeman. Even in her late years, she often began her first lesson of the day at 7:00 A.M. and her last at midnight. Music came before everything else. Despite her anti-Semitism, a good many of her pupils were Jewish, "a condition," as Rorem says "she overlooked only when they were gifted or rich, whereas homosexuality was 'bad' only if it interfered with work."[43] For Boulanger, no woman could fulfill her role as mother and spouse at the same time as her role as artist, writer, or musician. Organist, conductor, musicologist, lecturer, and even for a short time a music critic for a newspaper, Nadia Boulanger was a one-woman source from which a stream of musical Americans—and some French, but not with the success of the Americans—flowed.

In a tribute in 1962, on the occasion of her seventy-fifth birthday, Virgil Thomson wrote in *The New York Times* (4 February 1962) that "if today there are fewer Americans than formerly in her immediate entourage, they have been replaced by fantastically gifted Turks, Iranians, Lebanese, Indians and Egyptians. Being midwife to developing musical nations would seem to be her basic role."[44] She told the first Americans who came to her that they would find no model in Western Europe for their growing pains, and very little sympathy. But she maintained that Americans in the 1920s were very much like Russians in the 1840s, bursting with inspiration but poorly trained. She set her sights on correcting the latter defect.

The only modern movement she never countenanced was twelve-tone composition. Somehow or other she found it within herself to justify Stravinsky's later attempts in that genre—and for her Stravinsky followed Bach in the pantheon of musical eminences. She even allowed Pierre Boulez his "dalliance" in that area owing to his phenomenal brilliance of mind and his impeccable musical ear. "She does believe, however," Thomson wrote, summarizing her position, "that serial dodecaphony is in general a musical heresy and that its influence risks creating as permanent a division among musicians in the West as the Protestant Reformation did among Christians."

* * *

Three other women played important roles in the impact of Americans on the French in Paris in the first quarter of the twentieth century: Loïe Fuller, Isadora Duncan, and Josephine Baker—"Bakayr," as the French called her. For thirty-five years, Loïe Fuller was the idol of Paris. She had started at the Follies at the age of twenty-two in 1892 and became the rage of Paris the following year when she danced at the Athenée. Although a great dancer herself, she accomplished more as an inspirer of the dance. She helped create the modern music hall, and found new uses for the limelight. The Folies-Bergère, the Moulin Rouge, the Casino de Paris, and the Palace all profited from her discovery of what electricity could do. Preparing the way for Isadora Duncan, she made her first appearances in Paris in the nineties. Soon after, the streets were crowded with little girls in white robes, long red cloaks, and white slippers. After she had curtailed her own performances, her pupils, the "petites Loïe Fullers" sustained her reputation.

Fuller actually got her exotic reputation by accident. One day a British officer gave her an East Indian dress of flowing silk. That evening while on stage she slipped, tearing her usual costume, and put on the Eastern robe. The light shone through the silk and the colors blended to dazzling effect, and she determined that this would be part of her act in the future. Georges Montorgeuil described her at this time: "She entered lightly, floatingly, giving the impression of a spirit which flies rather than walks. Her robe was so long that she found herself treading upon it. She held it in her two hands and raised her arms in the air. The audience cried 'A butterfly! a butterfly!' She pirouetted faster and faster. There was a fairy-like image of a flower and the audience cried 'An orchid, an orchid!' "[45]

Before long she was known everywhere in Paris for her "Fire Dance" and her "Serpentine Dance." Dumas *fils*, still writing when Fuller began to dance, raved about her. Rodin, Sarah Bernhardt, Flammarion, the astronomer, were enchanted with the way she managed light and color. Anatole France said she "evoked the lost movements of Greek music . . . interpreting the phenomena of nature and the metamorphoses of being." Poets and painters sang her praises. The symbolist Georges Rodenbach spoke of the "prelude in mauve expanding into lilac."[46] Poet Jean Lorrain, writing of her "Fire Dance," called her "the flame itself."[47] Mallarmé commemorated her in February 1893, when he went to the Folies-Bergère to see Fuller dance:

Her performance, *sui generis*, is at once an artistic intoxication and an industrial achievement. In that terrible bath of materials swoons the radiant, cold dancer, illustrating countless themes of gyration. From her proceeds an expanding web—giant butterflies and petals, unfoldings—everything of a pure and elemental order. She blends with the rapidly changing colors which vary their lime-lit phantasmagoria of twilight and grotto, their rapid emotional changes—delight, mourning, anger; and to set these off, prismatic, either violent or diluted as they are, there must be the dizziness of soul made visible by an artifice.[48]

During the war, she remained a true friend of France, working to promote intellectual and artistic exchanges between France and America. She helped found the Spreckels Museum in San Francisco's Golden Gate Park, and the Mary Hill Museum in Washington. This building was made possible through the generosity of Sam Hill, one of her friends from the early Paris days. Toulouse Lautrec's famous poster immortalized her.

Isadora Duncan, born to Irish parents in San Francisco, had her first music lessons from her mother. She studied ballet as a youngster, but soon broke away from conventional forms to express herself in her personal, spontaneous fashion. An unsuccessful Chicago debut in 1899 drew her to Paris for the 1900 Exposition, where Loïe Fuller, too, first enchanted the French. In the French capital she found her first really appreciative audiences. With little formal education, this self-taught young woman, whose arrival in Paris had been prepared by her toga-wearing, sandal-shoed brother Raymond, revolutionized traditional dance. She sensed dance as an expression of an inner urge or impulse and she sought that source in the solar plexus. She danced generally in a flowing tunic, as she was much influenced by Greece and Greek art, and she was the first Western dancer to appear barefoot on stage and without tights.

Duncan's Paris success led to engagements in Budapest, Berlin, Florence, and other European cities, and in 1904 she established her own school in Berlin. She revisited Russia both in 1907 and 1912 and also established schools in France, Germany, and the United States. She called what she did "free dance" as opposed to the formal type of ballets. In 1905, at her first appearance in Russia, Duncan created lasting controversy as the result of her dissent from the traditional ballet forms. Nevertheless, one of those whom she influenced was Michel Fokine, who later went on to become one of the principal choreographers of the twentieth century. Her kind of dancing was closer to pantomime; it was also mostly improvisatory. She rarely did the same movements twice. Because of that, it was hard for students to follow in her footsteps and after her tragic death—she was strangled by her scarf when it became entangled in the rear wheel of the car she was driving—few could imitate her movements.

Isadora Duncan danced for the last time in Paris in 1927 at the Théâtre Mogador. The theater was full, but Isadora at forty-nine had begun to show the effects of continual drinking, and her dancing had become more static than in former years. Critic Janet Flanner's first *New Yorker* profile appeared on 1 January 1927. Devoted to Isadora Duncan, it praised her innovative techniques: "Two decades before, her art, animated by her extraordinary public personality, came as close to founding an aesthetic renaissance as American morality would allow." The profile concluded that Duncan's

> ideals of human liberty are not unsimilar to those of Plato, to those of Shelley, to those of Lord Byron, which led him to die dramatically in Greece. All they gained for Isadora were the loss of her passport and the presence of the constabulary on the stage of the Indianapolis Opera House, where the chief of police watched for sedition in the movement of Isadora's knees.[49]

She inspired many artists of the century, particularly Rodin, Antoine Bourdelle, and Abraham Walkowitz. Along with only a few other American women in France at the turn of the century, she left an indelible impression.

Josephine Baker was born out of wedlock in 1906, the daughter of a domestic and a flashy drummer who played in St. Louis's black nightspots.[50] Shortly after the birth of a second child, the father abandoned the family. Josephine left home at twelve and moved in with the proprietor of a local ice-cream parlor, a man in his fifties. (Throughout her life she was always attracted to older men.) When the local "ethics committee" complained, she moved in with her grandmother and took a job as a waitress in a black nightclub. At thirteen, she was married for the first time, to a local foundry worker, but was soon separated. She joined the Dixie Steppers, a song-and-dance troupe, that was touring the South, although she had no apparent talent and no training. At fifteen, she married a railroad

For thirty-five years Loïe Fuller was
the idol of Paris. Mallarmé
described her performance as "at
once an artistic intoxication and an
industrial achievement. In that
terrible bath of materials swoons
the radiant, cold dancer, illustrating
countless themes of gyration."

For many, Josephine
Baker represented
the spirit of the jazz
age in Paris.

Young composers like George Gershwin began to see jazz and blues as components of serious music.

George Antheil climbing to his rooms above Sylvia Beach's Shakespeare and Company. His famous Ballet mécanique *threatened to eliminate the need for large orchestras for musical performance.*

porter, Willie Baker, and took his last name. They lived for a while in Philadelphia, but she left him the following year to enter a road company of *Shuffle Along*, a celebrated Broadway musical of the 1920s. Now the protégé of Eubie Blake, who was one of the authors of the show, she did everything possible to draw attention to herself, although she was only in the chorus. Baker thrilled to the applause of the audience and soon managed to get a featured role in Blake's next musical, *Chocolate Dandies*.

In 1925, she went to Paris and at nineteen appeared in a vaudeville production, *La Revue Nègre*, at the Théâtre des Champs-Elysées. There she became an overnight sensation and the toast of Paris. For opening night, she appeared in a pink flamingo feather, strategically placed, with feathers around her neck and ankles. Her most famous costume was a girdle of rhinestone-studded bananas. One year later, Alexander Calder did one of his first models in wire: Josephine Baker. Also in 1926, as American revues became the rage in Paris, the Cotton Club, from the corner of 142nd Street and Lenox Avenue in Harlem, arrived in Paris with the entire sixty-three-member show, including the "Blackbirds," the fifty copper-colored girls, comedians, and an orchestra.[51]

She had no children of her own, but adopted thirteen of different races and nationalities and tried to establish an international village of brotherhood on her estate, Les Milandes, in the Dordogne. For many Americans and many Frenchmen, Josephine Baker represented the spirit of the jazz age in Paris. A grand gala, celebrating Josephine Baker's fifty years in show business, was held on 9 April 1975. Guests included Princess Grace of Monaco, Sophia Loren, Jeanne Moreau, and others. President Giscard d'Estaing sent a telegram "in the name of a grateful France whose heart so often beat with yours." Baker died five days later. She had received the Légion d'honneur and the Médaille de la Résistance and on 15 April she was accorded the grandest funeral for an American ever witnessed in Paris. Josephine Baker became the only woman ever to receive a 21-gun salute.[52]

But while these women were a legendary part of the American presence in Paris, other individuals also had a lasting impact. Composer George Antheil, who felt he could not grow professionally in the States, produced his famous *Ballet mécanique* in Paris and threatened to eliminate the need for large orchestras. Speaking of the piece, he told representatives of the *Paris Tribune* that

> it begins at a high tension and stops suddenly at high tension, although thousands of notes go to form the body of the sound. The music changes every second just like the position of water in a whirlpool changes all the time, yet the mass of water remains the same, just as does the mass of music.[53]

On 21 January 1925 Antheil told Roger Fuller, a *Tribune* reporter, that "shortly all music for orchestral recitals will have to be produced mechanically, as you can get the most perfect reproduction of the original score in this manner. . . . It costs several thousand dollars to give a single recital with a symphony orchestra. With that money you could build a whole mechanical plant and still have money in hand and, what is more, have the composition perfectly rendered."[54] It's worth reporting that "the audience [for the premiere of the *Ballet mécanique*] was divided into two belligerent and opposing camps.[55] They made loud noises, whistled, and some put up their umbrellas and turned up their coat collars," while Ezra Pound shouted back "Silence, imbeciles!" The ballet lasted twenty-five minutes and was conducted by the American Charles MacKee. During the performance, a film of machinery—prepared by Fernand Léger, who also did some designs for the Swedish ballet that followed the Antheil work—added to the bizarre setting for the piece. Although Antheil did not know it immediately, his composition was selected because it was certain to draw an audience for the Ballets Suèdois that appeared on the same program.

Later, in 1930, Antheil's opera *Transatlantic* had one of the most brilliant successes in operatic history in Frankfurt.[56] Antheil and Pound also wrote violin compositions for Olga Rudge, a musician from Youngstown, Ohio, who was Pound's protégé. Although classically trained, she apparently was willing to devote her efforts to modern music. Rudge gave the premiere of Pound's first music for violin at the Paris Conservatoire in 1923. Her mother was Julia O'Connell, an American singer of note, who took Olga to Europe at the age of three to begin her musical education. She made many subsequent trips, but studied mainly with the French violinist Carambat. Since 1918, Rudge had been a European resident and had her first concert triumph in London, where she performed the premiere of Paul Paray's Violin Sonata, while Paray was still a prisoner of war in Germany.

On 11 March 1928 George Gershwin went to Europe with his brother Ira and sister-in-law Lee and his sister Frances. Stopping first in London, they arrived in Paris on 25 March, a Sunday, and settled into the Majestic Hotel. Six days later, Rhené-Baton (real name René Baton) conducted the Pasdeloup Orchestra in his *Rhapsody in Blue* at the Théâtre Mogador. He had already sketched *An American in Paris* and somehow managed to complete a whole section of it while in the hotel. (For that piece, he eventually bought French taxi horns in order to provide an authentic simulation of the sound of Parisian traffic.) On 16 April, at the Théâtre des Champs-Elysées, Gershwin was in the audience for the premiere of a new ballet, *Rhapsody in Blue*, choreographed by Anton Dolin, who had heard Gershwin play the piece at a party in Paris. On 29 May, Gershwin's Concerto in F had its premiere at the Paris Opéra with Vladimir Golschmann conducting the orchestra and Dmitri Tiomkin as soloist. The French critics were bowled over. Arthur Hoerée spoke of its "inexhaustible verve" and "the fascination of its flowing melodies" as well as the "composer's keen feeling for the orchestra." And Emile Vuillermoz wrote that "This very characteristic work made even the most distrustful musicians realize that . . . jazz might perfectly well exert a deep and beneficent influence in the most exalted spheres."[57] Gershwin was part of this young generation, but he came to serious music via Tin Pan Alley. Curiously enough, composers of serious music began at about this time—some started earlier—to see jazz as a possible component in their music. Indeed, while Americans learned much from the French in the decades between 1870 and 1914, the French began to import particular musical ideas, jazz and blues, from America soon afterward. Debussy, in his Preludes of 1910–13 was among the first to incorporate jazz elements. Milhaud had an extensive section in jazz in his *La Création du Monde* of 1923. (When he came to America, the first place he wanted to visit was the Apollo Theater in Harlem!) Ravel used the blues in his 1923 Sonata for Violin and Piano. The French composer very much admired Gershwin's music, even going so far as to ask the singer Eva Gauthier, who had given a birthday party for him on 7 March 1928, to arrange for him to hear and meet George Gershwin as his present. When

Gershwin asked Ravel about lessons, Ravel declined, insisting that the American had no need of lessons from him. Gershwin persisted for years, trying to secure one of the serious composers as his instructor—he even approached Stravinsky—but to their credit, each and every one refused, believing that Gershwin's own natural talents were more than sufficient.

Numbers of Americans continued to come to Paris to study and to launch their careers, but many lacked the talent to succeed.

On 17 May 1925, Irving Schwerke of the *Paris Tribune* summarized the situation of the American artists in Paris.

> The number of American "artists" actively engaged at the present time in an effort to convince Europe of their right to a place in the sun is by no means inconsequential, and it increases more rapidly than one would dare imagine. One after the other they come and go, the American artists—a recital here, a recital there, an operatic engagement or two, perhaps an orchestral, and then most of them disappear and are heard from no more. The careers of only a few run successfully from one season into the following. Not many of the Americans "who make themselves heard" on this side of the Atlantic are ready to assume the responsibilities a public life entails. Most of them (the truth is unpleasant but cannot be made known too quickly) give mediocre, unenlightened performances, and the unforgiving waves of the jealous musical sea are not slow to wash the names of these ill-advised persons from its sand.
>
> In Europe, as in America, the prerequisite to success is what is known in a certain expressive parlance as "the goods," only that Europe is less suddenly convinced. . . . Americans have provided European opera houses with some of their finest singers and singing, and the same is true of a number of our instrumentalists and teachers. But the positions these artists occupied (and still hold) in the Old World, were not won by the advertising, the bluff, the proclaiming-from-the-housetops business which, within recent years have come to characterize the artistic antics of so great a proportion of Americans abroad. They mounted by virtue of the quality of art they delivered.
>
> The interests of American artists in Europe can be completely advanced only when every American artist or would-be artist who performs here is so genuinely American that his *amour-propre* makes it impossible for him to offer Europe anything but the best. American aspirants to musical honors should become truer to the idealism of their country. Then they will never incur the risk of besmirching her musical record. . . . The mediocre may make it difficult beyond computation for the deserving few, and the great sorrow, so far as American interests in Europe are concerned, is that as yet no way has been found to keep our "second-raters" out of the European public eye.[58]

* * *

In the aftermath of the Second World War, the hegira began anew. During the halcyon days of the fifties, writers Irwin Shaw, A. J. Liebling, James Jones, Richard Wright, Carson McCullers, Theodore White, Art Buchwald and musicians Ned Rorem, Julius Katchen, David Amram, Julia Perry, and Dalton Baldwin represented but a few of the many Americans who once again called Paris home. It all "may have started with the reading of Dumas or Théophile Gautier or Balzac or a book by Fitzgerald or by seeing a movie about fighter pilots in World War I, or just by sensing something in the general climate of the time that made one feel that no artist could consider himself fully prepared for his life-work without eating a croissant for breakfast in the capital of France."[59]

12

Les Vingt

One of the most extraordinary avant-garde movements in the arts emerged in Brussels in 1883 and lasted until 1914. Very little has been written about the achievements of this diverse group of artists, musicians, and writers, who were guided mostly by the vision and encouragement of one man, an amateur painter and attorney at the appeals court in Brussels, Octave Maus. Were it not for the mammoth volume *Trente Années de Lutte pour l'Art*, published by his wife Madeleine in 1926, a few years after Maus's death, few today would be aware of the group's activities.[1]

The productivity of these artists separates easily into three distinct ten-year periods, from 1883-93, 1893-1903, and 1903-14. On the occasion of the twentieth anniversary of the founding of Les Vingt, on 1 March 1903, Maus summarized the movement's aesthetic credo for the revue *L'Art moderne*. He maintained that "to be of one's time [as an artist] is simply to be ahead of opinions held by contemporaries by ten, fifteen, twenty or even fifty years." He had envisaged, he said, the campaigns to come, campaigns whose perspective would suggest new ideas, and he was willing and ready to accept the challenge. The founding of Les Vingt, sometimes known simply as "Les XX," makes a fascinating story.

Les Vingt

Like France, Belgium in the late nineteenth century had an official body of so-called experts who represented the Establishment, the Academy, the voice of the Minister of Culture or Fine Arts. They judged the value of art works submitted to them, then exhibited them at an official salon. When a group of Belgian artists was insulted by a member of the official jury who refused to accept their works at the Salon, they were scornfully advised to "show at their own place." They proceeded to do just that, exhibiting their works in the halls of the Musée de Peinture, whose director agreed to give them the space, provided that one of their members assumed responsibility for the enterprise. That member was Octave Maus.

On 28 October 1883, the first Vingtistes (group of twenty) assembled around a table in the Taverne Guillaume and added their signatures to a petition which outlined the basis of their future association. On the reverse side of the sheet appeared the words "Rue de Berger, 27, Ixelles, O. Maus" and a list of twenty proposed guests. These were selected by the twenty artists and would remain independent despite their affiliation with the association. In other words, there were twenty permanent members of Les XX; their goal was to educate the public about avant-garde art of every sort. Each year, they would invite another twenty guests to exhibit with them. Among the better known founding artists—both native and foreign—were Félicien Rops, J. M. Whistler and Auguste Rodin. Each of the founders would have the right to show six canvases or pieces of sculpture—graphic works as well as plastic works were acceptable—and each guest might show one.

The group's activities commenced on 4 January 1884, with Octave Maus acting as official secretary. It was Maus who informed the press of the group's purpose and concerned himself with promoting the rights of individual artists. He also announced four lectures and two musicales which would take place in the Salon of the Palais des Beaux Arts on 2 February 1884. (The first three exhibitions were presented in the Palais des Beaux Arts of the Musée Ancien; subsequent ones were held at the Musée Moderne on the Place du Musée.)

It is difficult today to realize how unusual the group seemed to outsiders, although most members saw their work as evolutionary, not revolutionary. True, like many of the Impressionists in France, the painters among them experimented with the effects of light, but by and large they determined not so much to break with tradition as to *extend* it. Théo van Rysselberghe emerged as a leader among the painters; not far behind him stood Fernand Khnopff and James Ensor. Curiously, these painters discussed their works in musical terms; they spoke of blue "harmonies," of penetrating "symphonies." They were puzzled by the disdainful attitude of the critics. Maus, however, recognized that just in assuming a stance *as a group*, they offered a challenge to the establishment. He understood also that critics are capricious: "You can never tell what will exasperate them. It's all so unexpected," he remarked. The great liberal writer Emile Verhaeren, too, offered support and encouragement in the early years.

The distinguished roster of artists and lecturers who addressed the group's first exhibition included Edmond Picard, who spoke on *L'Art jeune*; Georges Rodenbach on *Les Jeunes Belgique*; Albert Giraud on *La Petite Presse en Belgique* and Catulle Mendès on *Richard Wagner*. Musicales were presented by Gustav Kefer's small group, the recently formed Union instrumentale; chamber music was played by violinist Emile Agniez and pianist Arthur de Greef. Compositions by Schubert and Mendelssohn, along with several Belgian works, figured on the programs; not until after 1888, with the "jeune école française" did genuinely modern music begin to be performed in a spirit that paralleled that of the fine arts exhibited.

From year to year, the composition of the group changed. Members died or, on occasion, resigned in protest against some stance taken by the group. The invited guests regularly changed, of course. Through constant renewal and expansion, sooner or later almost every artist, musician, and writer of significance had the opportunity to present his works at Les XX. Painters showed their newest pictures; musicians presented their most recent pieces; writers read from their current plays, poems, or essays. Probably the most productive aspect of their meetings was the interaction of creative artists from different disciplines.

In 1885, for example, Fantin-Latour, invited to exhibit from France, brought with him two lithos evoking Berlioz's *La Prise de Troie* and Wagner's *Parsifal*. The following year, Albert Besnard, Renoir, Monet, and Odilon Redon were the invited guests from France. A Dutch Jewish painter, Isaac Israëls, appeared on the scene a second time as the guest from Holland. Monet, apparently taking the invitation to exhibit very seriously, kept changing his mind about the pictures he proposed. He also disregarded the limit of one work per guest,

Octave Maus, founder of the extraordinary movement known at Les Vingt, maintained that "to be of one's time is simply to be ahead of opinions held by contemporaries by ten, fifteen, twenty, or even fifty years."

ANNÉE 1884

EXPOSANTS :

VINGTISTES :

A. Chainaye, F. Charlet, J. Delvin, P. Dubois,
J. Ensor, W. Finch, Ch. Goethals,
F. Khnopff, J. Lambeaux, P. Pantazis, D. de Regoyos,
W. Schlobach, F. Simons, G. Vanaise,
Th. Van Rysselberghe, G. Van Strydonck, P. Verhaert,
Th. Verstraete, G. Vogels, R. Wytsman.

The original members of Les Vingt. Each year, they would invite another twenty foreign guests to exhibit with them.

ANNÉE 1904

EXPOSITION DES PEINTRES IMPRESSIONNISTES

Préface par Octave Maus : *l'Art Impressionniste.*

EXPOSANTS :

Camille Pissarro (1830-1903);
Edouard Manet (1832-1883);
Alfred Sisley (1839-1899);
Berthe Morisot (1841-1895);
Paul Gauguin (1848-1903);
Vincent Van Gogh (1853-1890);
Georges Seurat (1859-1891);
H. de Toulouse-Lautrec (1864-1901);
Edgar Degas (1834);
Paul Cézanne (1839);
Claude Monet (1840);
Armand Guillaumin (1841);
Auguste Renoir (1841);

Mary Cassatt;
Henri-Edmond Cross (1856);
Maximilien Luce (1858);
Théo Van Rysselberghe (1862);
Paul Signac (1863);
Pierre Bonnard (1867);
K.-X. Roussel (1867);
Léon Valtat (1868);
Edouard Vuillard (1868);
Albert André (1870);
Maurice Denis (1870);
Georges d'Espagnat (1870);
Charles Guérin (1875).

CONFÉRENCES :

André Mellerio : *L'Evolution de l'Art impressionniste.*
Médéric Dufour : *Jules Laforgue et l'Impressionnisme.*
André Gide : *L'Evolution du Théâtre.*
Louis Laloy : *L'École contemporaine de musique française.*

CYCLE DE MUSIQUE CONTEMPORAINE

EMBRASSANT L'ÉVOLUTION PARALLÈLE A L'ESSOR DE L'IMPRESSIONNISME

PREMIER CONCERT

Mardi 1ᵉʳ mars 1904, à 2 heures et demie précises

1. Quatrième trio pour piano, violon et violoncelle.
   (En une seule partie.) . . . . César Franck.
   (1822-1890)
   Mˡˡᵉ M. Devos, MM. E. Chaumont et B. Hambourg.

2. A) *Sonnet mélancolique* (Armand Silvestre) . .
   B) *Le Bûcher* (Armand Silvestre) . . . . . } A. de Castillon.
   (1838-1873)
   M. Stéphane Austin.

3. *Estampes* pour le piano . . . . Claude Debussy.
   I. *Pagodes.* — II. *La Soirée dans Grenade.* — III. *Jardins sous la pluie.*
   M. R. Viñès.

4. A) *Cantique à l'Épouse* (Albert Jounet) . . . . Ernest Chausson.
   (1855-1899)
   B) *Épitaphe* . . . . P. de Bréville.
   M. Stéphane Austin.

5. A) *Pavane pour une infante défunte* . . . . . Maurice Ravel.
   B) *Loin des villes* . . . . D. de Séverac.
   I. *Coin de cimetière au printemps.* — II. *A cheval, dans la prairie.*
   M. R. Viñès.

6 Sonate pour piano et violon . . . . Henry Février.
   I. *Allegro risoluto.* — II. *Andante cantabile.* — III. *Allegretto moderato.* — IV. *Animato.*
   M. R. Viñès et E. Chaumont.

   Piano Erard.

A list of the participants in the program in 1904 includes some of the most important artists, musicians and painters of the early twentieth century.

no doubt believing that for him the committee would make an exception. James Ensor, a permanent member, submitted a painting entitled *La Musique russe*, and another permanent member, Fernand Khnopff, presented *En écoutant du Schumann*. Several painters took the opportunity to offer portraits of musicians, for instance Whistler's *Sarasate*.

In the third year of Les XX's existence, Berthe Morisot, Camille Pissarro and Georges Seurat joined the *invités* from France, while Walter Sickert arrived with his work from England. In 1888, Jacques-Emile Blanche, G. Caillebotte, Henry Cros, Toulouse-Lautrec, P. Helleu, Signac, and J. L. Forain contributed examples of their work and Villiers de l'Isle-Adam gave a lecture. That same year saw the first appearance of Vincent d'Indy who, with two other performers, played his Trio for Clarinet, Cello, and Piano. Madame Léontine Bordes-Pène, French pianist and sister-in-law of the composer Charles Bordes, gave the premiere of d'Indy's *Poème des Montagnes* for solo piano, dedicated to her by the composer, and she also offered works by Fauré and Alexis de Castillon. She concluded her program with another premiere, Franck's masterpiece, the Violin Sonata in A major, in which she was joined by its dedicatee, Eugène Ysaÿe. (She must have been a very fine pianist; Franck dedicated his *Prélude, aria et final* to her.) Fauré, himself made an appearance for an additional afternoon concert at which his c-minor Piano Quartet, several *mélodies*, and also *his* Violin Sonata in A major were performed. Antoine had recently founded his Théâtre-Libre in Paris and he and members of his troupe came to Brussels to help stir the Bruxellois out of their comfortable lethargy.

Concerts did not always play a part in the presentations of Les XX. But when they did, they featured the best composers and performers. Pierre de Bréville, Albéric Magnard, Ernest Chausson, Paul Vidal, Charles Bordes, and even père Franck all made appearances in Brussels during the first decade of the group's existence, keeping pace with the eminent artists and writers. No fees were offered, and all the artists seem to have come at their own expense, owing to the prestige of the invitation to participate.

Russian music appeared on a program first in 1891: pieces by Tchaikovsky, Rimsky-Korsakov and Borodin. Gauguin exhibited his pottery, and Les XX offered a retrospective exposition of the drawings of Van Gogh, only recently deceased. Indeed in the preceding months, the group had suffered grievous losses in the deaths of Van

Gogh, Seurat, and César Franck. Soon afterward, d'Indy wrote a letter to Maus in which he described the scandalous behavior of those at the Conservatoire who failed to appear at the services for the elderly composer who had taught there for many years. D'Indy, determined to right the wrong—even if it were in Brussels rather than in Paris, although he later established the Schola Cantorum in Paris in Franck's memory, too—arranged a memorial concert of Franck's music for Les XX.

Maus always insisted that it was d'Indy along with van Rysselberghe who enabled him to keep the group on an even keel. Still, Maus must have been an extraordinary man himself; in addition to his professional duties as an attorney, he was a "Sunday painter," played the piano, and conducted. Born 12 June 1856, he was guided and encouraged in the study of music by his cousin, Anna Boch, who played the violin and painted remarkably well. Louis Brassin, a disciple of Anton Rubinstein, taught Maus piano, helped him to acquire an excellent technique, and made him a confirmed Wagnerite, one of the earliest in Belgium. At twenty, he accompanied the first group of his countrymen to visit the Festival at Bayreuth. He returned transformed. In the course of a meeting of the Wagner Society of Brussels and on the occasion of several encounters at the home of Henri La Fontaine, he guided many uninitiated compatriots through the intricacies of the *Ring*. He also wrote a number of articles about Wagner for reviews of the period. Maus sought to promote a liaison among his artists. For example, he would compare the music of de Bréville to the painting of Seurat and then proceed to explain to the musician how he understood the difficulties of setting French text to music. Joseph Dupont, the great Wagnerian who also loved French music, approached Maus about providing time for Chausson's symphonic poem *Viviane* and the entr'acte from Chabrier's opera *Gwendoline*. Dupont knew that the public would have to be prepared for these novelties, and he urged Maus to "faire un peu de propagande," as he put it.

Early in 1892, painter Maurice Denis and composer Guillaume Lekeu entered the circle, replacing Van Gogh and César Franck. The following year, Paul Verlaine's lecture on contemporary poetry created a sensation and the Ysaÿe Quartet performed Franck's early Piano Trio, while other performers tackled Ernest Chausson's *Poème de l'Amour et de la Mer* and Vincent d'Indy's Suite in D. Between them, d'Indy and Maus programmed pieces by Fauré, de Bréville,

Chabrier, de Castillon and Lekeu, the circle of young composers who had surrounded and adored César Franck as their master. Then, unexpectedly, in November of 1893, the members of Les XX voted almost unanimously to dissolve their group at the end of the year. Maus said they feared that their avant-garde tastes might become stale with age. Their final exhibit, accompanied by a catalogue, would reveal how much they had accomplished for modern art.

After the dissolution of Les XX in spring 1893, Maus busied himself with the founding of another organization, La Libre Esthétique, whose aim would be similar to that of the earlier group, but whose structure would be different. To eliminate the rivalries that had previously existed among the different kinds of creative artists, the Libre Esthétique would have no artists, except for writers and poets. Enlightened amateurs, Belgian or foreign, joining out of a common desire to patronize new art, would be welcome. One annual salon would fuse together all aspects of art: lectures, concerts, painting, sculpture, graphics, and, for the first time, applied arts. Maus would coordinate everything. Aubrey Beardsley, James Ensor, Paul Gauguin, Fernand Khnopff, William Morris, Lucien and Camille Pissarro, Puvis de Chavannes, Redon, Renoir, Sisley, and Toulouse-Lautrec are but some of the artists who showed that year. Henri de Regnier and Henry van der Velde gave lectures, and works by Schubert and Beethoven joined those of d'Indy at concerts. On 1 March, the Libre Esthétique sponsored an all-Debussy program. Later that month, they even presented some Bach, not a great favorite in French-speaking countries.

In the following years, under Octave Maus's direction, the group introduced any number of new and little-known works to audiences made more responsive to them through his efforts.

The first Salon of the Libre Esthétique opened on 17 February 1894. It attracted a wide following. Art critics Gustave Geffroy, Roger Marx, and Camille Lemonnier all reported enthusiastically about the participants, their work, and the enlarged scope of the exhibitions. Not only did the artists themselves flock to Brussels, they brought their wives along with them, making the event a sumptuous affair. Evidently the women dressed to the nines, and might be said to have conducted their own fashion parade in combination with the arts show. From England came the papers and fabrics of William Morris, along with examples of his typography from the Kelmscott Press and samples of the work of the Bodley Head illustrators.

More than ever before, the exhibitors formed an international group. Again, Puvis de Chavannes, Eugène Carrière, Renoir, Gauguin, Redon, Sisley, Pissarro, Morisot, Signac, Denis joined several of the Belgian regulars and newcomers and artists from England in heated discussions of their works. The literary efforts of Mallarmé, Villiers de l'Isle-Adam, Edgar Allan Poe, and Henri de Regnier provided material for stimulating talks. Ysaÿe presented a historical series of chamber pieces, in an attempt to demonstrate their genuine links with the present and thus acquire approval for contemporary works. Pierre de Bréville offered two of his new pieces, a group of *Portraits de Musiciens* and a kind of pastiche based on the Tarnhelm motive from Wagner's *Rheingold*. An entire concert was devoted to works by Claude Debussy, a young composer for whom a promising career was predicted. Ysaÿe debated with himself about the sequence of pieces to be performed at that concert and settled finally on opening with Debussy's g-minor String Quartet in its first public performance. The composer then accompanied his fiancée, Mlle Thérèse Roger, in two of his *Proses lyriques*, before Ysaÿe returned to conduct the cantata *La Damoiselle élue*, in which Mlle Roger also sang the solo part. (Debussy, engrossed at this time in his work on *Pelléas et Mélisande*, had already completed his *Prélude à l'après-midi d'un faune*; he had set *Cinq Poèmes de Baudelaire*, one hundred fifty copies of which had been printed thanks to the generosity of Ernest Chausson; and his *Damoiselle* sported a cover lithograph by Maurice Denis. Nonetheless, his name was known only among the cognoscenti.)

The following year the number of exhibitors increased more than fivefold. Americans, British and Dutch painters joined those who had shown before. The Germans were noticeably absent. The French, more numerous than ever, had begun rounding up the younger generation. Pissarro, for example, arrived with his three sons, all of them painters: Lucien, Georges and Félix. (The last died a few years later.) Lecturers included writer Camille Mauclair and theatrical producer Lugné-Poë, who spoke on "Pour être un acteur d'aujourd'hui." Stressing the importance of the group rather than subservience to a single star, his talk provoked considerable discussion, along with requests from reporters for copies for distribution. (He would not provide them.) Examples of new Russian music by Glazunov and Sokolow appeared side by side with compositions by Chabrier, Magnard, Franck, d'Indy, Fauré, and Chausson. Mme

Georgette Leblanc, Maeterlinck's mistress, whom he intended for the role of Mélisande in Debussy's opera, sang the first performance of Henri Duparc's beautiful "L'Invitation au voyage," set to Baudelaire's poem.

Each year the number of exhibitors grew. In 1895, over 115 artists showed their works, some like the Daum brothers, Antoine and Auguste, Jules Chéret, Henri Lerolle, and Félix Vallotton for the first time. The following year, Mlle Frieda Lautmann sang several Brahms lieder at the second concert on 19 March, and the two Ysaÿe brothers, pianist Théo and violinist Eugène offered a Grieg violin and piano sonata in g-minor. Paul Gerardy, a poet from Liège, revealed to the assembled artists the beauty of the works of Hugo von Hofmannsthal and Stefan George. And in 1897, Gauguin exhibited his Tahitian works, Monet brought three of his Rouen cathedral paintings, and Verhaeren conducted a symposium devoted to Verlaine. Surprisingly, some writers, painters, even musicians promoted the works of their colleagues in a most comradely manner.

The tenor of the meetings became ever more dynamic, sometimes as the result of specific events of the preceding year, other times in the wake of the interactions of creative persons with different origins. Georges Espagnat, who did some fine group portraits of Ravel, de Séverac, Viñes, and others of their circle, exhibited in 1899 for the first time. Although there were no concerts given the following year, Tristan Klingsor offered a lecture on "Les Poètes mis en musique" and provided musical examples from the works of de Bréville, de Serres, Chausson, Samazeuilh, Fauré, and Duparc. André Gide presented a lecture, and the Belgian government itself finally began to purchase canvases shown by the group.

In the second year of the new century several younger members of d'Indy's Schola Cantorum achieved performances of their music: de Séverac, René de Castéra, Auguste Sérieyx, and Maurice Alquier. Maurice Denis showed his famous group portrait "Hommage à Cézanne," and many more of those involved in applied arts brought examples of their workmanship to the colloquia. Many of the artists, writers, and musicians carried on extensive correspondence with Maus. And as a founder and editor of *L'Art moderne*, he saw to it that several of the more significant letters found their way into the magazine's pages. In addition, he acted as his own public relations man and used the journal to inform the public about the avant-garde artists he was promoting.

Maus also sought variety in some of the musical programs. On 24 March 1903, for example, he presented a lecture recital on humor in music. The pieces he selected to illustrate his thesis might seem a bit unusual today, but he had an intriguing idea. Starting with Polyphemus's air from Handel's *Acis and Galatea*, he continued with "Le Jugement de Midas" and Columbine's aria, both by Grétry; "Pierrot," "Arlequin," "Eusebius," "Chopin," "Valse allemande," and "Paganini" from Schumann's *Carnaval*; two songs by Chabrier; and the four-hand piano version of Chabrier's "Joyeuse marche," which he performed with Emile Bosquet. Another interpretive artist whose name appears for the first time this year is that of the Catalan pianist Ricardo Viñes. He would soon give the premieres of most of the piano pieces of Debussy, Ravel, de Séverac, de Falla, Albéniz, and Granados among others. In this tenth anniversary year of the Libre Esthétique, Maus had already established patterns for correlating performances of musical works with the exposition of what he saw as related arts.

By 1914, at the threshold of the catastrophe that would see the end of civilization as he knew it, Maus had even arranged for performances of several German works by Gustav Mahler, Max Reger, and Joseph Marx. The Belgian government became an increasingly frequent purchaser of the arts on display, audiences achieved a measure of sophistication that even Maus had hardly thought possible, and creative artists from all over Europe vied with one another for invitations to exhibit. Maus could finally look back on his *Trente Années de Lutte pour l'Art* as an example of what one man, a determined and gifted amateur, could accomplish with superhuman motivation and devotion to a cause. No other single group, with the possible exception of the Secession and Jugendstil artists in Vienna at the turn of the century, had ever arranged such a successful mélange of initiators of the new art forms. Paris, it is true, became the cultural center of Europe in the years between the wars; but Brussels must receive credit for her contribution to the significant avant-garde movement of the new century.

13

Masterpieces of French Music 1870–1925

Several French scholars have written wise and witty essays on the characteristics of French music and how it differs from Italian and German music of the same period. But even the relatively uninitiated listener who finds himself drawn to the Gallic music of the period 1870–1925 will be able to discern those traits that establish it as genuinely French. Camille Saint-Saëns, recalling the Académie of Baïf, the operas of Jean-Baptiste Lully, and the instrumental pieces of the clavecinistes, utilized the entire landscape of French music beginning in the sixteenth century with the concern for *vers mesuré* and concluding with Vincent d'Indy and his ideas of music history, with many of which the elder statesman disagreed. Today's listeners need only bear in mind some of the observations Jean Chantavoine made many years ago in 1913 at a symposium on the general characteristics of French music.[1]

French music, he said, cannot be satisfied with pure Italian vocal orientation; its melody is not sufficiently pleasing for that. On the other hand, French melody seems too weak to nourish the development of a form. Thus, one observes that formal music has flourished above all in Germany. In philosophy . . . Germany is the country of the *chose en soi*, the *Ding an sich* while Cartesian France remains the country of the *Discours sur la méthode*, the country of the critique of knowledge. Between the music of the two countries there is the same difference as there is between their metaphysics. Formal music in which, from a pure melody, there issues the development of a whole work, without external help, recalls the philosophy of the *chose en soi*, the *Ding an sich* which, in a given material, claims to discover the form and substance of the whole universe. Such a role goes beyond the essence, the potentiality of French melody; just as French philosophy seeks explanations rather than constructions, and analysis rather than synthesis, French music is more concerned with expression than it is with formalism.

French music is linked by its origins and by constant tradition to the word, to thought, to an idea. A music whose melody has little vocal and symphonic richness will only rarely be able to be self-sufficient. Pure music seeks to support itself through a connection to the other arts and especially to literature. French literature is, moreover, so precocious in its formal perfection that it imposes itself quite naturally on music. In the Renaissance, the ambition of musicians was nothing more than to ornament worthily the poetry of a Marot, a Bellay, or a Ronsard; the whole of Lully's effort in the seventeenth century was to give music an equivalent of French classical tragedy, of the theater of Corneille and Racine; later, Romantic opera was inspired by an aesthetic which combines an imitation of both Victor Hugo and Alexandre Dumas, père; closer to the present . . . the influence of a poet like Stéphane Mallarmé manifests itself on a musician like Claude Debussy. . . . attempts at Symbolism are found in a lyric drama such as *Fervaal* by Vincent d'Indy. . . . The naturalism of Zola breeds that of composers Alfred Bruneau and Gustave Charpentier.

French music, seeking supports or models in the other arts, has always had to move in their wake; it has followed taste rather than formed it. It has taken up the tone set by poetry, dramatic art,

258

painting. A revolution at once dramatic and musical such as Wagnerism in Germany, accomplished by a musician, through music and for music, subordinating both drama and scenery to the sovereign demands of the music, would have been impossible in France. Rather than break the three unities of classical tragedy, French opera from Lully to Rameau turned from drama to spectacle and ballet.

French music, by dint of its relative melodic dryness, existing, moreover, alongside other arts in France whose apogees preceded its own, perpetually borrows from these arts types, models to imitate, subjects to treat, ideas to develop and expressive procedures. . . . A need to borrow certain Italianisms was necessary to correct, by means of vocal sensuousness, the excessively speech-like and intellectual qualities which French music owes to its origins and national traditions. . . . Later Russian music fulfilled that need and worked an analogous influence upon French art . . . an influence also noticeable in French literature . . . German song has more melancholy, more profundity; French has more vivacity. Mobile and alert, French melody is supple and diverse. Popular song obliges it to sing of everything: love, war, politics. French music needs a text or an action in which it shows itself, according to circumstances, in turn malign or eloquent, subtle or declamatory, austere or chatty, rigid or evanescent. . . . It does not ask to be evaluated for its own sake. It is the most faithful, the most exact interpreter of the French soul, the French spirit.

Certain specific characteristics call attention to the fact that the following pieces are of French origin. Whole tone scales vs. the German use of chromatic steps; modality and elements, particularly parallelism of chords, that recall Gregorian chant; a lean accompaniment of orchestration, with the exception of certain very luxuriant works; avoidance of melodic inevitability, one never knows exactly where or what the next note in a melodic line will be; a lack of rhythmic drive replaced by a kind of languor which keeps the listener in limbo—such are the traits of French music which distinguish it particularly from German or Italian music. The following very selective list of orchestral, chamber, and operatic music represents the masterpieces of French music of the years 1870-1925 that have survived in the repertory. It is hoped that these very brief discussions will motivate the listener to enjoy these works on his own.

BIZET

Carmen

Georges Bizet (1838–1875) was only thirty-six when he composed *Carmen*, but he already had six completed operas to his credit and at least seventeen projected or sketched (but destroyed, lost, or never realized). Without question *Carmen* is the finest lyric example of realism on the operatic stage. In its original state, with spoken dialogue (and without Guiraud's added recitatives), it offers a splendid example of a play set to music. Bucking the trend toward continuous music that began with Wagner, Bizet wrote a "number" opera; each of the separate musical pieces has a beginning, middle, and end and could be extracted or excerpted from the whole musical canvas. And what numbers they are! *Carmen* combines striking orchestration and remarkably original melodies and offers a story involving real people—not mythological or historical figures—that tightly grips the audience. The premiere took place at the Opéra-Comique on 3 March 1875.

Bizet was sensitive to critical pronouncements, and although he thought *Carmen* his best work, the critics did not. Anyone who reads contemporary reviews will recognize at once why he was disappointed by their remarks. Apparently Paul de Saint-Victor in *Le Moniteur*, Oscar Commetant in *Le Siècle*, and Arthur Pougin in *Le Ménestrel* wrote unfavorably about the premiere. Mina Curtiss provides an incomparable description of the first night audience in her splendid biography of the composer. "The audience, in short, was mixed, fashionable, replete with boulevardiers who, having been warned by the journalists in attendance to expect a scandalous work, were only too eager to be shocked and to condemn. The word 'immoral' was bandied about in the lobbies during the intermissions not merely by the ultra-bourgeois, but by members of the artistic and social worlds as well." The opera was not a failure, but it took some time before it became one of the most popular in the entire repertory. The other French realist opera that has held the stage, *Louise* (1900), by Gustave Charpentier, succeeded only in France. The most famous aria from this latter opera is "Depuis le jour," while the number of favorites from *Carmen* are just too many to list. (One of the librettists, Ludovic Halévy, was a first cousin of Geneviève, Bizet's wife.)

CHABRIER

España

Emmanuel Chabrier (1841–1894) held a position in the French civil service until his thirties, when he decided to devote himself full time to music. He visited Spain in 1882 and, like many other foreigners, particularly Frenchmen, he succumbed to her music, dances, and dancers. Chabrier described his reactions to Spain in letters to Edouard Moulle (Le Père Moulle), who had a famous piano shop in the Rue Blanche, and who collected and edited folk songs from Normandy and Spain. Chabrier composed *España* for the piano, but it cried out for orchestration and soon afterward he transcribed it himself. A rhapsody, based on two Spanish dances—the fiery, impetuous Jota and the slower, sultry Malagueña—*España*, heard in its orchestral version, the one generally performed, captivates most audiences. The Lamoureux Orchestra presented the premiere on 4 November 1883. The verve and passion and exhilarating *joie de vivre* that characterized Chabrier himself infuse *España* to an extraordinary degree.

A Wagnerite from the time he first visited Germany in 1879 with Henri Duparc and heard a performance of *Tristan und Isolde* at Munich, Chabrier later composed one of the most brilliant paraphrases of the opera, *Souvenirs de Munich*, a Quadrille for piano duet (four-hands). Chabrier was a friend of Verlaine as well as of Manet, and had extraordinary taste in painting. A cash gift his wife received in 1884 enabled Chabrier to purchase Manet's *Bar aux Folies-Bergère*, which, for the last ten years of his life, hung over the piano in his studio in the Avenue Trudaine. An auction on 26 March 1896, after his death, included the following oil paintings: one Cézanne; one Helleu; six Manets, plus the *Bar*; six Monets; three Renoirs; two Sisleys. Chabrier's collection also included pastels, watercolors, drawings, etchings, and lithographs by Forain, Helleu, Manet, Monet, and Renoir.

CHAUSSON

Concerto for Piano, Violin and String Quartet, Op. 21

Ernest Chausson (1855–1899) probably led the happiest life of any composer with the exception of Mendelssohn. Ironically, both these musicians who had everything to live for died young. Chausson had a charming wife, five beautiful children, and was extremely wealthy. He owned a home on the Boulevard Courcelles that was a veritable treasure house of art. He collected books and pictures, many by Degas, Albert Besnard, Puvis de Chavannes, and Eugène Carrière, and his home was always open to writers, musicians, and artists. He and the painter Henri Lerolle had married sisters, so it was only natural that the Chausson home be a meeting place for contemporary artists of all kinds.

A shy and modest man, Chausson, like many others of César Franck's pupils, was both an active member of the Société Nationale de Musique and a Wagnerian. His opera *Le Roi Arthus* reflects his interest in legendary forests and knights of the Round Table; and his *Poème de l'Amour et de la Mer* and *Chanson perpetuelle*, both for voice and orchestra, show the sensual side of his nature.

Between 1889 and 1891 Chausson composed the Concerto for Piano, Violin, and String Quartet, sometimes known as the Sextet. He dedicated it to the Belgian violinist Eugène Ysaÿe, who helped arrange its first performance in Brussels at the Salon des XX, where Octave Maus persistently promoted avant-garde art, music, and literature. Chausson was on the Riviera at the time and Vincent d'Indy took charge of rehearsals. At the last moment, the pianist in the group returned the score to Maus, insisting it was too difficult for him to handle. D'Indy was beside himself. If Chausson were disappointed again, d'Indy wrote Madeleine Maus, "it would be a disaster." Pierre de Bréville discovered the young pianist Auguste Pierret in Paris and the concert went on as scheduled on 4 March 1892. The performers were Auguste Pierret (piano), Eugène Ysaÿe (solo violin), and the Quartet Crickboom (comprising Crickboom, Biermasz, Van Hout, and Joseph Jacob). The work enjoyed an enthusiastic reception which pleased Chausson, who had not had an easy time with the critics. In Brussels his reception was much different.

The Concerto is in four movements: the first begins with a thirty-four-bar introduction and then proceeds in sonata form; the second movement, a Sicilienne, reveals the characteristic lyricism of Fauré, the third movement is a scherzo, and the finale is a set of variations rather than a sonata form. Like many of Franck's other pupils who followed in the direction their master had taken, Chausson conceived this work as a "cyclic" piece. D'Indy coined the term. It implies that a composition has acquired unity through repetition of specific musical materials or the transformation of material throughout several movements of a symphony, sonata, or quartet. Franck used this device first in 1841 in one of his piano trios; then used it in many later works, particularly in the d-minor Symphony, and it became a typical feature of French music of this era.

Symphony in B-Flat

The group of composers around Franck—Vincent d'Indy, Gabriel Pierné, Guillaume Lekeu, Guy Ropartz, and Henri Duparc—did not usually write many symphonies. Particularly after the Société Nationale had determined to promote works by French composers, most of them concentrated their creative energies on chamber music because shorter, less demanding works, which required fewer forces, would be more likely to achieve performances. Understandably then, symphonies by French composers of the period rarely appear on concert programs. Chausson's Symphony in B-flat is an exception. He completed this piece in 1890, and similar to Franck's great Symphony in d-minor, it is in three movements and it too incorporates a cyclical structure. The brief motto-theme that opens the Symphony reappears in a transformation in the beginning of the second movement, and recurs in the finale, the third movement. Chausson scored the Symphony for a large orchestra that includes two harps as well as expanded forces for brass and woodwinds.

DEBUSSY

Prélude à l'après-midi d'un faune

Claude Debussy (1862–1918) was born into a family of tradespeople. Nevertheless, he entered the Paris Conservatory at the age of eleven and won several prizes for his piano playing. In 1885, after submitting his cantata *L'Enfant prodigue* for the composition contest, the Conservatory awarded him the prestigious Prix de Rome, thus enabling him to spend two years in Rome at the Villa Medici with winners of other arts competitions. Like Berlioz, he disliked the

Roman experience and left before the two years had ended. During his sojourn in the Italian capital, however, he produced two fine works, the orchestral *Printemps* and *La Damoiselle élue* scored for two women soloists, female chorus, and orchestra.

He returned to Paris in 1887 and grew friendly with a group of avant-garde poets and writers, and in time became a regular visitor at the fourth-floor walk-up of Stéphane Mallarmé on the Rue de Rome. Here he met many of the future models and standards-setters of twentieth-century arts and letters. On winter evenings, Mallarmé would stand close to his porcelain stove in a dining room that served as his salon and, with a shawl wrapped around his shoulders, proceed to recite his musical, sensuous poetry. Despite the shabby appearance of his apartment, Mallarmé's salon boasted a Monet landscape, a Renoir head of the writer, Whistler's lithograph of Mallarmé, two Manet oils, a small Rodin cast, and a wooden statue sent from Tahiti by Gauguin.

Mallarmé composed his first version of his poem, *Monologue d'un faune*, in 1865. Curiously, he thought it might do well on the stage and for that reason brought it to the poet Théodore de Banville and the actor Constant Coquelin, hoping they would consider it for the Comédie-Française. They rejected it. Ten years later, Mallarmé submitted a second version, entitled *Improvisation du faune*, to the Parnassian poets (one of whom was Théodore de Banville) for an anthology. It, too, was rejected. The final version, the *Eglogue, l'Après-midi d'un faune*, appeared in 1876, in a slim volume with a line drawing by Edouard Manet. Mallarmé was accused of being dense, impenetrable, of aiming to confuse rather than enlighten. But within a few years the poem acquired unexpected celebrity. Huysmans cited it in *A Rebours*, and several of the Wagnerians decided that Mallarmé's symbolism complemented the composer's and invited him to contribute to the *Revue wagnérienne*.

Debussy had already set a Mallarmé poem, *Apparition*, in 1884 so he knew of the poet. When he returned from Rome in 1887 and joined Mallarmé's circle, he became more and more attracted to this new kind of poetry, where the words themselves made music. The *Revue indépendante* published the poem; Debussy bought at least one copy that he presented as a gift to his friend Paul Dukas.

Debussy began the composition of his *Prélude* about 1892, at a time when he certainly knew Mallarmé well enough to discuss with him the kind of music his poetry should evoke.

Georges Bizet (top left)

Emmanuel Chabrier
(top right)

Claude Debussy
(bottom)

Gabriel Fauré

César Franck

Charles Gounod

The text is the faun's monologue. He awakens in a forest and cannot recall whether or not he has dreamed about the visit of two beautiful nymphs or if they did indeed appear and then resist his embrace. As the day wears on, the temperature rises, the forest becomes more beautiful and the faun relaxes into sleep, his drowsiness blotting out his questions. Except for the familiar piano piece "Clair de lune," the *Prélude* is probably Debussy's best-known work.

The completed manuscript bears the date 1894—a facsimile exists—and the Société Nationale gave the first performances on 22 and 23 December under the conductor Gustave Doret. Debussy insisted on further changes, modifying sonorities throughout rehearsals. Doret worried about the reaction not only of the musicians to this new style and sonority, but also of the public, and pleaded with the players to do their best. As the flutist Georges Barrère unrolled his opening theme, Doret suddenly sensed, behind his back, a captivated audience. So enthusiastic were they that the orchestra broke precedent and immediately repeated the piece. The poem, with its sensuous symbolist language, its evanescent ambiguities, was totally and absolutely reflected in the music.

Nocturnes

Continuing along the path chosen by his painter and writer friends, the trend to dissolve language into a musically suggestive succession of words, to draw not specific objects but to evoke misty reminiscences, led Debussy to compose his three *Nocturnes*—*Nuages*, *Fêtes*, and *Sirènes*—between 1897 and 1899. They were first performed at a Lamoureux concert on 6 December 1900. (Camille Chevillard conducted the first two on that date and performed all three together on 27 October 1901.) At the time, Debussy is reported to have said, "The title *Nocturnes* is to be understood in a wider sense than that usually given to it, and should be regarded as conveying a decorative meaning. The form of the nocturne has not entered into consideration, and the term should be viewed as signifying all that is associated with diversified impressions and special lights." Of *Nuages*, he remarked on the "unchanging aspect of the sky, with the slow and melancholy passage of the clouds dissolving in a gray vagueness touched with white." For *Fêtes*, he pictured "the restless, dancing rhythms of the atmosphere, interspersed with abrupt scintillations. There is also an incidental procession—a wholly visionary pageant—passing through and blended with the argent revelry; but the background of uninterrupted festival persists: luminous dust participating in universal rhythm." The music evokes these images. The last piece, *Sirènes*, a wordless vocalise for women's voices with orchestra, reflects the white foam of the waves as they roll on to the shore. Few pieces better demonstrate Baudelaire's concept of *les correspondances* among the arts or Verlaine's comment *"de la musique avant toute chose"*.

La Mer: Three Symphonic Sketches

One year after the production of *Pelléas et Mélisande*, Debussy began work on his orchestral tone poem *La Mer*, which the Lamoureux Orchestra, under Camille Chevillard, first played in Paris on 15 October 1905. Some critics regard this piece and the three *Images* for orchestra (of which more on *Iberia*, No. 2 later) as the last of Debussy's great works. They are indeed his final expression in symphonic music, but numerous other masterpieces in different genres were yet to come, even during the last years when the composer was already suffering from the cancer that would eventually take his life.

La Mer has no program, but the titles of the separate sections— "De l'aube à midi sur la mer," "Jeux de vagues," and "Dialogue du vent et de la mer"—are so suggestive as to induce all kinds of fantasies in the minds of the listeners. Debussy calculated precisely the kind of impressionistic picture he wanted, and his music captures the colors, sounds, sights, the play of light and shadow, the rolling waves associated with the sea. "The sea has been very good to me," Debussy wrote to his publisher Jacques Durand before he had completed *La Mer*. "She has shown me all her moods." And he told André Messager, who had recently conducted the premiere of *Pelléas et Mélisande*, "You do not know, perhaps, that I was intended for the fine career of a sailor and that only the chances of life led me away from it. Nevertheless, I still have a sincere passion for it."

After the premiere of *La Mer*, the composer again wrote to Durand: "Here I am again with my old friend, the sea; it is always endless and beautiful. It is really the thing in nature which best puts you in your place. But people don't respect the sea sufficiently." Debussy insisted that the cover of this piece be a replication of Hokusai's famous color print of *The Wave*. The sea and water seem to have had a mystical hold on Debussy's creative imagination; many of his piano pieces also have titles associated with the sea.

Images

Like many other composers, Debussy was fascinated by numbers. Perhaps following the path of Bach or Chopin (the only composer to have been a dedicatee of any of his pieces, in this instance the Etudes) Debussy composed twenty-four Preludes and twelve Etudes and often fashioned his works in groups of three: three *Nocturnes* for orchestra, three symphonic sketches that comprise *La Mer*, and now three *Images* or pictures for orchestra. (He also wrote two sets of *Images* for piano, each comprising three pieces.) The second of the orchestral *Images, Iberia,* (which, incidentally, is in three sections—"Par les rues et par les chemins," "Les parfums de la nuit," and "Le Matin d'un jour de fête"—prompted the following remarks from Manuel de Falla: "[Debussy wrote Spanish music] without knowing intimately Spanish territory; though he was acquainted with Spain through books, through pictures, through songs and dances sung and danced by genuine Spaniards. . . . Permeated as he was by the musical language of Spain, Debussy created spontaneously, I might even say unconsciously, such Spanish music as might be envied him—who did not really know Spain—by many others who knew her only too well. Once only did he cross the frontier, in order to spend a few hours at San Sebastian and to see a bullfight." Undoubtedly, Debussy's friendship with Ricardo Viñes and his acquaintance with the music of Albéniz triggered his interest in the exotic melodies and the intricate rhythms of Spanish music.

He was not alone among non-Spaniards (Rimsky-Korsakov, Chabrier, Bizet, and Ravel) who found inspiration, particularly, in Andalusia. Debussy also interweaves French folk songs into his music. The piano piece *Jardins sous la pluie*, from *Estampes*, is a good example and so is the *Rondes de Printemps*, the third of the orchestral *Images* (The first of the *Images, Gigues*, evokes an English folk song; the second is the Spanish *Iberia*.) The composer originally conceived *Images* as a work for two pianos, but he soon realized that it demanded orchestration. Not all critics agreed with de Falla, but Ravel wrote enthusiastically to Debussy about the piece's "novel, delicate harmonic beauty [and] its profound musical sensitivity."

Jeux

Debussy composed the ballet *Jeux* for Diaghilev's Ballets Russes with choreography by Nijinsky. One of the most modern of Debussy's scores, it has been compared with such twentieth-century landmarks as Schoenberg's *Pierrot Lunaire* and Stravinsky's *Le Sacre du printemps*. A young man and two girls search for a lost tennis ball. They play "hide and seek" in various combinations, singly or as duos or trios. They quarrel and sulk and eventually embrace. Suddenly another tennis ball is mysteriously thrown onto the court. The young man and the girls disappear. Debussy apparently had some difficulty with the ending, which he did not want to be too abrupt. William Austin mentions that some critics have compared this example of Debussy's late work with various styles of painting—Rousseau's primitivism, Matisse's fauvism, Picasso's and Braque's cubism, Bonnard's intimism, and even André Breton's surrealism.

Jeux was the second ballet created by Nijinsky, the first being the *Prélude à l'après-midi d'un faune* (1912). Revolutionary in its choice of subject, it was revolutionary in its music as well. The American critic Carl Van Vechten wrote that he remembered *Jeux* for its opening glissando "as the tennis ball bounces across the stage followed by Nijinsky, who bounds across the broad stage of the Théâtre des Champs-Elysées in Paris in two leaps . . . triumphs of dexterity, grace of motion, and thrill."

Pelléas et Mélisande

Fortunately for posterity, Maurice Maeterlinck (1862–1949) and Claude Debussy were born in the same year and became intimately involved in one another's work at about the age of thirty. Maeterlinck's symbolist drama appeared in Brussels in 1892. Shortly after reading it, Debussy knew he had found the only kind of play he could set to music. (Later he made several unsuccessful attempts at writing a libretto and music to Poe's *Fall of the House of Usher* and *The Devil in the Belfry*.) Playwright and composer both saw people as relatively helpless creatures, functioning in a preordained manner, or, as Ernest Newman described it, "helpless corks on the sea of fate." There is no plot or story in the traditional sense in *Pelleas et Mélisande*. Instead, something of the pointlessness of all human endeavors is symbolically depicted by characters whose reality is always questionable.

Debussy used no middle man, no librettist. With suggestions from Maeterlinck, he cut and spliced where necessary and was thus able to fit the five-act play into a workable five-act opera. Some sections of Maeterlinck's text remained absolutely unaltered, despite being transplanted from play into opera. Three hundred years after Monteverdi, Debussy had achieved the goal of the originators of opera, a play set in music. The composer accepted for his libretto a text in which the author replaced traditional poetic construction with a kind of lyrical prose. (Many now feel that he borrowed some of his musical ideas from Mussorgsky, but Debussy resented any implication of that nature.) There are no arias, duets, or choruses. The vocal line alternates between recitative and arioso, a kind of speech song. Only very rarely does it sound like actual song, because musically, too, Debussy veers away from traditional set forms. He seeks plastic, ever-changing shapes. He overlaps phrases and sections and weakens traditional musical patterns of tension and release. He prefers streams of sound and veiled sonorities in which individual timbres stand out. Debussy's musical fabric was indeed an early example of modernism and very definitely avant-garde.

Unexpectedly, two weeks before the dress rehearsal of the opera, *Le Figaro* published an open letter from Maeterlinck denouncing Debussy and the work. The writer had expected that Georgette Leblanc, his common-law wife, would sing the title role. Instead, Debussy had selected the Scottish soprano Mary Garden for Mélisande. The premiere, conducted by André Messager, took place on 30 April 1902 at the Opéra-Comique, and the critics' response was mixed— as it still is today. But Debussy himself was certain he had created a landmark in the history of opera. On 27 January 1920, Maeterlinck, on his first visit to America, heard the opera in a performance by the Chicago Opera Company at the Lexington Theater in New York. Mary Garden continued in the role of Mélisande. Seventeen years and nine months after the original production that he had opposed so violently, Maeterlinck admitted his mistake. Without Debussy, his drama would soon have faded into oblivion.

String Quartet in g-minor

Debussy did not write much chamber music. Except for this remarkable quartet, on which he worked as he was just beginning to envision the possibilities for his opera *Pélleas et Mélisande*, he composed only three additional pieces that fit into this category: a cello and piano sonata (1915), a sonata for flute, viola, and harp (1916), and a violin and piano sonata (1917). Exquisite works, not frequently performed, they are all that he completed of an intended set of six sonatas *pour divers instruments*.

The g-minor String Quartet of 1893 bears the number "1"; but Debussy never wrote any others. He dedicated the piece to the Ysaÿe Quartet (Ysaÿe, Mathieu Crickboom, Van Hout and Joseph Jacob). Although not a member of Franck's circle, in this work Debussy borrows their cyclical approach to composition. Three of its four movements offer the seminal theme that opens the piece, a distinctly modal melody. (The modes are the scales used in the Middle Ages, long before the major and minor tonalities became the accepted means of composition. Playing the white notes on the piano, from D to D or E to E, without including any of the black notes, will produce the sound of some of the earlier modes.) The first performance took place on 29 December 1893 and it has retained a stellar place in the chamber music repertory since then.

DUKAS

L'Apprenti sorcier (The Sorcerer's Apprentice)

Paul Abraham Dukas (1865–1935), composer, critic, music editor, and teacher, set the highest standards for himself and his work and before his death destroyed every one of his pieces that he believed did not meet them. An intimate friend of Debussy, he also maintained close relationships with Bordes, d'Indy, and Edouard Dujardin, probably because of their mutual admiration for Wagner. Similar to Bizet, Dukas showed a remarkable gift for orchestration; and like Franck, he left several extraordinary works in different genres. Two piano pieces, the Sonata in E-flat, first performed by Blanche Selva on 10 May 1901(?) and the Variations on a theme by Rameau, first performed on 23 March 1901, stand out as masterpieces of French piano music. Twenty-five years after Dukas's death, his programmatic tone poem La Péri inspired Frederick Ashton's ballet of that name. Besides his opera Ariane et Barbe-bleu (based on Maeterlinck's drama), which the French regard as his masterpiece, the orchestral scherzo The Sorcerer's Apprentice, based on Goethe's ballad Der Zauberlehrling, is the work by which he is remembered today.

Goethe took the story of the sorcerer's apprentice from a tale originally written by the Greek satirist Lucian in the second century A.D. It was part of a dialogue entitled The Lie-Fancier in which its author intended to ridicule the magicians of his day.

A sorcerer has a magic formula for turning a piece of wood into a living servant who would perform all sorts of tasks for him. One day, during his master's absence, the sorcerer's apprentice, who has overheard his master mutter the formula, decides to try it himself. He too would like a servant, and so he transforms a broom into *his* apprentice. He orders the broom to fetch a pail of water from a nearby lake, which it proceeds to do unceasingly. When the house is filled with water, the apprentice discovers that he does not know how to stop the procedure and restore the broom to its natural state. As the house floods, he hacks the broom in two, but now both parts become apprentices and each continues to bring buckets of water into the house. Fortunately, the sorcerer himself finally returns to his home and states the appropriate formula for restoring order. Goethe wrote his ballad in 1796; Dukas wrote his musical composition in 1897. It was first performed by the Société Nationale on 18 May 1897, shortly after he had completed it.

FAURÉ

The music of Gabriel Fauré (1845–1924) is so essentially French that his works are not often performed outside his native land. He trained for the profession of chorusmaster at the Niedermeyer School of Religious Music, and in his composition leaned heavily in the direction of vocal music. When Saint-Saëns took over the piano class at the Niedermeyer in 1861, he introduced young Fauré to the music of Schumann, Liszt, and Wagner, thus broadening his musical horizons considerably.

A man of integrity and strong convictions, Fauré—in an unusual act for a musician—took part in the action to raise the siege of Paris in 1870. Shortly afterward, he substituted for Saint-Saëns at the organ in the Church of the Madeleine. When his engagement to Marianne Viardot (daughter of the singer Pauline Viardot) was broken, his inconsolable grief inspired several beautiful compositions: the First Violin Sonata, the First Piano Quartet, and the Ballade for piano. Although fascinated by the music dramas of Wagner, Fauré is one of the few French composers whose music does not reflect the German composer's influence. His personality, his innate modesty, and humility were so contrary to Wagner's that he could never promote himself or his music and for a long while even lacked a reputation in his native France. Fauré fantasized about writing large-scale works, but he had neither the time nor the inspiration—with the exception of his *Requiem*.

In Venice on vacation in the 1890s Fauré had a liaison with Emma Bardac, the future Madame Debussy. This affair inspired his song cycle *La Bonne Chanson*, which he dedicated to her. To her daughter Dolly he dedicated his four-hand *Dolly Suite*. (Dolly de Tinan, Debussy's stepdaughter, who died in 1985, was the last living link to the composer.) Fauré became chief organist at the Madeleine in 1896 and the same year succeeded Massenet as professor of composition at the Conservatoire. (His students included Ravel, Florent Schmitt, Charles Koechlin, Louis Aubert, Roger-Ducasse, Paul Ladmirault, Emile Vuillermoz, and Nadia Boulanger.) Understandably, he began to acquire a wider audience for his music. In England, under commission, he wrote incidental music for the English translation of Maeterlinck's play *Pelléas et Mélisande*; for the open air arena in Béziers, he composed his lyric tragedy *Prométhée*. From 1903 to 1921, Fauré wrote music criticism for *Le Figaro*, and in 1905 he succeeded Théodore Dubois as head of the Paris Conservatoire, remaining in the post until his retirement in 1920. In 1909, seeking a wider repertoire than that offered by the Société Nationale, of which he was a founding member, Fauré and his disciples withdrew from the organization and formed the Société Musicale Indépendante. Owing to his long life span, Fauré was born when Berlioz was engaged in writing *La Damnation de Faust* (1845) and lived until three years after Alban Berg had completed *Wozzeck*.

Requiem

Fauré was not a religious man, yet his *Requiem* is testimony to his compassion for his fellow human beings. It must communicate his deepest sentiments because it is far and away his most frequently performed work. Fauré most effectively reveals his feelings about death and the loss of a loved one in this *Requiem*. He revised it several times. The first version dates from 1877; the second from 1887–90. The final completed version stems from 1900. Scored for soloists, chorus, organ and orchestra, the *Requiem* is unique in that it has no musical or religious connection with any of the other famous requiems by Mozart, Brahms, Berlioz, or Verdi. It represents a plea for consolation from those who experience a loss rather than a theatrical *tour de force* meant to impress an audience by its powerful sonorities.

272

Sonata for Violin and Piano in A, Op. 13

Fauré composed two sonatas for violin and piano, the first Op. 13 in 1875, when he was thirty, and the second, Op. 108, when he was in his seventies. The warm, sensuous first sonata in A major anticipates by twelve years Franck's in the same key and compares favorably with that masterpiece. Saint-Saëns insisted that with this work Fauré had "defeated" the German school which, he agreed, had no rival in that area. The sonata respects the rules of classical form while at the same time projecting the very French personality of Fauré. The composer and Mademoiselle Marie Tayau presented the premiere of the piece on 27 January 1877 at a concert of the Société Nationale.

Piano Quartet in c-minor, Op. 15

Fauré composed two piano quartets and two piano quintets, all of which offer fine examples of his very personal style. In this first Piano Quartet, the piano writing reveals a variety of figurations; some seem to owe their inspiration to Schumann. The scherzo of this four-movement piece is usually the first to capture and hold the attention of the listener. Like the Sonata, the work is in four movements, with the slight difference that the andante follows the scherzo and precedes the finale. The premiere took place on 14 February 1880 in the Salle Pleyel, again at a concert of the Société Nationale. Afterward, the anonymous reviewer in the *Revue et Gazette musicale* of 22 February commented on the grace and delicacy of the scherzo movement.

FRANCK

Symphony in d-minor

Although he had begun his musical career as a child prodigy at the piano, César Franck (1822–1890) had no aspirations in that direction and remained an organist and teacher all his life. For thirty-two years, from 1858 until his death in 1890, Franck served as organist at Sainte Clothilde Church in Paris. His experience there left its mark on the orchestration of this symphony; the sonorities of the organ predominate in the musical texture. Franck composed his best works after the age of fifty, and he has left genuine masterpieces in several different genres: one symphony, one piano concerto, one piano quintet, and one string quartet.

The Paris Conservatory orchestra offered the first performance of the d-minor Symphony on 17 February 1889. It did not receive an enthusiastic reception, possibly owing to the composer's use of unusual instruments, some even in soloistic passages, for example, the English horn, to which Franck has given a prominent role; other instruments include a bass clarinet, two cornets (similar to a trumpet but with a shorter tube), and a harp, in addition to the usual complement of strings, woodwinds, and brass. The composer Gounod is reported to have said that the piece was "the affirmation of impotence carried to the point of dogma." Nevertheless, in time this symphony became as popular among instrumental works as Gounod's opera *Faust* was among operatic ones.

The Symphony is in three movements, each of which utilizes one or the other of two seminal motives. The first motive—it appears in the slow introduction to the first movement—is a replicate of a motive Beethoven, Liszt, and Wagner had already used in their works. Beethoven stated it in the finale of his last string quartet. He added the words "Muss es sein?" ("Must it be?") over his presentation of this three-note motive. Liszt uses it in the introductory section of his symphonic poem, *Les Préludes*; and Wagner's orchestra plays it constantly in the *Ring* operas, where it is the "fate motive." Franck's treatment of this motive, however, is totally original.

The second motive, longer and therefore more of a melody, appears in the development section of the first movement. Although the piece is in three movements, the second combines the functions of both a slow movement and a scherzo. The finale presents new material, but also utilizes the two motives of the first movement and the English horn's melody from the second movement. The composer also calls for a harp, which by this time seems commonplace in French music.

Symphonic Variations

Franck composed the *Symphonic Variations* in 1885 and pianist Louis Diémer presented the first performance at the Salle Pleyel in Paris on 1 May 1886. This one-movement piano concerto defies structural analysis. Some critics call it a work with an introduction, variations, and a finale; others simply cite the variations, as did the composer himself. According to the way Franck notated the work, it appears that there are eleven variations. The eighteen-measure theme appears in a dialogue between piano and strings at the start of the piece. The piano figurations, a delightful romp through pianistic patterns, reflect Franck's beginnings as a piano prodigy.

Piano Quintet in f-minor

Besides favoring a cyclical structure for his large works, Franck also uses a musical procedure known as "thematic transformation." Several themes, usually short ones, appear in transformation, that is in a slightly different form, throughout a work in order to unify an extended piece. (Franz Liszt, one of the first to discover this means of unification, incorporated the technique in many of his symphonic poems and also in his celebrated Sonata in b-minor for piano. Wagner borrowed the procedure for use with his leading motives, particularly in the *Ring* operas.) In most of his cyclical works, Franck not only presents his principal melodies as reminiscences throughout a piece—repeating material verbatim—but also serves them up to his listeners in thematic transformations. The Piano Quintet of 1878 is no exception.

The work is in three movements and again Franck favors a repeated-note theme that seems characteristic of many of his melodies. The Marsick Quartet gave the first performance of the piece at a concert of the Société Nationale de Musique on 17 January 1880 with Saint-Saëns as piano soloist. It is one of the first of Franck's later masterworks. A story associated with its premiere, long since forgotten, survives in W. W. Cobbett's *Cyclopedic Survey of Chamber Music*. Franck, who always enjoyed performances of his own music, regardless of the quality of the playing, was particularly pleased with Saint-Saëns's efforts. After thanking him, Franck continued: "Since you have interpreted my work so wonderfully, it is yours; accept my dedication of it and keep the manuscript in memory of this delightful evening!" Saint-Saëns turned on his heels, exited quickly and left the score on the piano. An employee of the firm of Pleyel later found it in a heap of trash.

Violin and Piano Sonata in A

In the Piano Quintet, the fifty-seven year old Franck revealed himself an unabashed Romantic. Six years later, in 1886, Franck wrote the magnificently lyrical Violin and Piano Sonata as a wedding present for his compatriot, the Belgian violin virtuoso Eugène Ysaÿe. In four movements, unlike most of his other pieces which are cast in three, it, too, has a cyclic structure. The most remarkable movement is the canonic finale where, in the coda, Franck combines the themes of the first and last movements in a contrapuntal setting that sustains the sensuous nature of the entire piece.

Vincent d'Indy, Franck's most devoted disciple, recounts an interesting story associated with this work. Ysaÿe and pianist Madame Bordes-Pène gave the first performance in the winter of 1886 at one of the concerts of Les Vingt at the Musée Moderne de Peinture in Brussels. It was the last work on the program, which had begun at three in the afternoon. The artists finished the first movement, but then, as it was rapidly growing dark, and they could barely see the music, they hesitated to continue. (Gas lights were not permitted because of the danger of a fire that would certainly destroy the canvases entrusted to them.) The enthusiastic audience refused to leave and so the duo proceeded with the succeeding three movements, playing them from memory with a fire and passion that overwhelmed the listeners.

GOUNOD

Faust

To many non-French listeners, Charles Gounod (1818–1893) is the archetypal French composer, a man who wrote more than sixteen operas, numerous oratorios and sacred vocal pieces, and many *mélodies*. Essentially, Gounod steered clear of instrumental music; a *Petite Symphonie* of 1885 very occasionally merits a performance, but not much more.

Gounod's father was a painter and his mother a pianist with whom he first took lessons. His musical education before entering the Conservatoire in 1836 was apparently so strong that he won the Second Prix de Rome in the following year, and in 1839 the Grand Prix. In Rome, where Gounod went to spend his obligatory two years, he met two women destined to be of great help to him: Mendelssohn's sister Fanny Hensel, who introduced him to the music of Bach, Beethoven, and her own brother—and also to Goethe's *Faust*, probably in Gérard de Nerval's 1827 translation—and Pauline Viardot, the singer who was the sister of the celebrated Maria Malibran.

Viardot was married to Louis Viardot, the director of the Théâtre-Italien, an excellent friend for a young composer to have. As a young man, Gounod wrote music for the church, but soon turned to opera. His sixth opera, *Faust*, premiered at the Théâtre-Lyrique on 19 March 1859 and became the most popular French work in the genre. It is still a number opera and Gounod fashioned it with the aid of those well-known librettists Jules Barbier and Michel Carré, who collaborated with him on several of his operas. Although the plot parallels Goethe's great drama, the Germans refuse to accept this French "version" of their classic and, as a result, *Faust* is always known as *Marguérite*, after its heroine, when it is produced across the Rhine.

D'INDY

Ardent Wagnerite and purveyor of German music to the French, Vincent d'Indy (1851–1931) was born to a patrician family of Vivarais, formerly a part of the Languedoc region of France. He determined to win his spurs as any other music student might do, through appropriate instruction from masters in the field. A prodigy at the piano, he studied with Diémer and Marmontel. Rather remarkably, considering his background, he served in the defense of Paris with the 105th Battalion of the National Guard during the Franco-Prussian War. With the War behind him, in 1871 he became one of the first to join the Société Nationale de Musique, where most of the premieres of his works took place. After Franck's demise, he became the *de facto* head of that organization. In his role as leading French Wagnerite, d'Indy hearkened to the call of Catulle Mendès, who suggested that instead of blindly imitating Wagner, the French should follow in his footsteps by applying his concepts to French music. In several compositions, d'Indy reveals the impact of Wagner, but he also demonstrates his own love of nature, particularly in such works as the symphonic ballad *La Forêt enchantée* (1878), the *Poème des Montagnes* for piano solo (1881), the *Tableaux de voyage* (1889) also for solo piano, *Jour d'été à la montagne* for orchestra (1905), and his two operas *Fervaal* and *L'Etranger*. He outdid Wagner in one specific area: his anti-Semitic writings are among the most vicious of any nineteenth-century artist. In his *Cours de Composition*, he even rewrote music history in order to avoid giving a Jewish composer like Salamone Rossi any credit for advanced ideas. He also described the years of the Empire, when Meyerbeer, Halévy, and Offenbach operas held the boards, as the "période judaïque," claiming that Jewish composers were never original, only borrowing from the host country in which they lived.

Symphonie cévenole (Symphony on a French Mountain Air)

For a long while, d'Indy was attracted to the Cévennes mountains, between Tortous and Bouchard. He found he could relax there, far away from the hassle of Paris. He was always a nature lover and because original melodies did not spring easily into his head, he sought folk tunes, often shepherd's songs, for inspiration. One of these is the melody he used for his *Symphony on a French Mountain Air*. The melody appears in the collection of *Chansons populaires du Vivarais* and Julien Tiersot included it in his *Histoire de la Chanson Populaire en France*, published three years after d'Indy's score had appeared.

This three-part orchestral piece for piano and orchestra depends for its structure on a recurrent French folksong. The tune undergoes thematic transformations, similar to a Wagner leading motive, common in a cyclical work. In no way, according to d'Indy, is this a concerto for piano and orchestra. Instead, the piano maintains its role as one among many other instruments, and the solo sections are not in bravura style. Franck heard and applauded the piece, which received its premiere by the Lamoureux on 20 March 1887. Madame Bordes-Pène (see above), the dedicatee, was the piano soloist. Like Lalo's *Symphonie espagnole* and Chabrier's *España*, this kind of folk-inspired composition emphasizes the nationalist spirit of French musicians, the return to their own musical heritage.

Harold Bauer was the pianist when the symphony was first performed on 5 April 1902 in Boston. In 1905, d'Indy conducted the Boston Symphony in several programs of French music and lectured on the subject at Harvard, that bastion of French-American music. Seth Bingham, David McK. Williams, Bruce Simonds, and Daniel Gregory Mason are among d'Indy's best-known American pupils.

LALO

Symphonie espagnole

Although born in France, Edouard Lalo (1823–1892) came of pure Spanish stock. He trained at the Conservatoire of Lille, where his family resided, but lived most of his life in Paris. Success as a composer came to him after the age of fifty, when no less a master than Peter Ilich Tchaikovsky raved about his extraordinary *Symphonie espagnole* in a letter of 15 March 1878 to Madame von Meck. Lalo dedicated the piece to the virtuoso violinist Pablo Sarasate, who played the premiere at a Colonne concert in Paris on 7 February 1875. The year before, he dedicated his Violin Concerto to Sarasate, who also presented its first performance.

Like Bizet, Lalo wrote captivating melodies. The *Symphonie espagnole*, which is really another violin concerto, projects such verve and passion that it has remained a favorite with audiences for more than a hundred years. In addition, for some time Lalo's opera *Le Roi d'Ys* of 1888 enjoyed considerable popularity on both sides of the Atlantic.

MILHAUD

Darius Milhaud (1892–1974) was born in Provence of an old Jewish family that had resided for centuries in Aix. His musical training began with the violin and he entered the Paris Conservatoire as a violin student, but soon turned to composition as his favorite metier. He enjoyed travel; he had many friends among writers and painters and both activities are reflected in his musical compositions. Writer Paul Claudel was a particularly close friend, and when in 1916 Claudel was appointed French Minister to Brazil, Milhaud followed him there as his secretary. The two years he spent in South America left an indelible impression that emerges later in certain of his works. At the close of the war, Milhaud became part of Cocteau's circle of writers, artists, and composers, many of whom would eventually collaborate wtih Diaghilev and his Ballets Russes. As a disciple of Satie, Milhaud belonged to the group known as "Les Six." A prolific composer, he went so far as to set a seed catalogue to music. On a tour of the United States in 1923, he had his first experience of

American jazz in a Harlem nightclub. Back home, Milhaud composed the ballet *La Création du monde* to a scenario by Blaise Cendrars.

La Création du monde

Milhaud's music has often provided the background for ballets: *L'Homme et son désir* for Les Ballets Suèdois in 1921; *Le Train bleu* for Bronislava Nijinska in 1924, and *La Rose des Vents* for Roland Petit as recently as 1958. The importance of *La Création du monde* (1923) lies in Milhaud's use of jazz in a serious musical composition. With decor by Fernand Léger and choreography by Jean Borlin, the composer describes a world of trees, animals, birds, insects, and finally the creation of man and woman. Ninette de Valois choreographed a new version in 1931 for the Camargo Society; it was eventually taken into the repertory of the Sadler's Wells Ballet. (*La Création*, with Stravinsky's *Ragtime* [1918], Poulenc's *Les Biches* ["The House Party," 1923], and Stravinsky's *Ebony Concerto* [1946] appeared at City Center on 7 December 1960 as the first of two "Jazz Evenings" of the New York City Ballet.)

OFFENBACH

Les Contes d'Hoffmann

Jacques Offenbach (1819–1880), the seventh of ten children, was the second son of a cantor at the Cologne synagogue, a man who had come originally from Offenbach am Main in about 1800. Young Offenbach—the townspeople called his father "Der Offenbacher," although his name was Isaac Juda Eberst—first studied the violin, but soon took up the cello and with his brother Julius, who played the violin, and his sister Isabella at the piano, formed a trio that played in several bars in Cologne. Their father took the two boys to Paris, where for a short time Jacob (who now was called Jacques) attended the Conservatoire. Impatient with school, Jacques left and continued further studies privately. He played with the orchestra of the Opéra-Comique and made a number of beneficial acquaintances. Later, as a cello virtuoso, after leaving the Opéra-Comique, he performed in Paris in 1841 with Anton Rubinstein and in 1843 in Paris with Liszt. He became a Roman Catholic, married and got started on what became a slow but steady road to success as a composer of operettas.

Offenbach achieved his greatest success with *La Belle Hélène* (1864), *Barbe-bleu* (1866), *La Vie parisienne* of the same year, *La Grande-Duchesse de Gérolstein* (1867), and *La Périchole* (1868). During the Exposition of 1867, his works filled three Parisian theaters, but after 1871 and the terrible year of the Commune, public taste changed and he lost favor. Offenbach spent time in London and Vienna and made a trip to America for the World Exhibition of 1876. He gave forty concerts in New York and Philadelphia and conducted performances of several of his works. Back in Paris, he published a book of his impressions of the United States.

From 1877 on, he was preoccupied with a work that he never completed, *Les Contes d'Hoffmann.*

It seems that in 1851 Offenbach conducted incidental music for a new play by Jules Barbier and Michel Carré, a well-known theatrical team. Over twenty-five years later, the composer remembered the play and thought he could refashion it into an opera, a serious opera that would reveal to the public he was good for more than just operettas. Carré had died by this time, so Barbier was obliged to work alone with the composer. The story is narrated by the celebrated writer, composer, and critic E. T. A. Hoffmann, who relates three incidents in his love life. He tells of the doll Olympia, the singer Antonia, and the courtesan Giulietta. Hoffmann had been in love with the prima donna Stella and only at the conclusion of the opera does the audience learn that each of the women portrays an aspect of Stella herself. Sometimes all three roles are tackled by one very gifted singer. In the end Hoffmann was able to transfer much of the vivacity, color, and melody that had earlier informed his operettas to this more serious opera. The premiere took place on 10 February 1881.

To complete his score, Offenbach had designated Guiraud, the composer who supplied Bizet's *Carmen* with recitatives.

For a long while, Guiraud's version was the one performed. Recently, conductor Antonio de Almeida found a set of orchestral parts in a closet of one of Offenbach's descendants. These parts had been used in a private performance, a kind of "backers audition" of the opera in Offenbach's living room on 18 May 1879, where his four daughters—he also had a son—and friends sang the principal roles. Almeida brought this material to the German musicologist Fritz Oeser who prepared the new edition in use today. Even so, many of the changes are open to question. (Unfortunately, a fire at the

Opéra-Comique in 1887 destroyed important manuscripts and performance instructions relating to the opera, so all versions are, in a way, conjectures.)

RAVEL

Boléro

Maurice Ravel (1875–1937) was born in Ciboure in the Pyrenees and his mother came of Basque parentage so it is not surprising that his compositions reveal the impact of Spain and Spanish music. Furthermore, his long and intimate friendship with the Catalan pianist Ricardo Viñes exposed him to this influence from childhood. Unlike many other families of composers, Ravel's family encouraged his interest in music. His father, an engineer, moved with the family to Paris, when it became evident that his son would select music as his profession. Ravel studied piano with Charles de Bériot, Viñes's teacher. Later he became a member of Fauré's composition class while studying counterpoint and orchestration with André Gedalge. He never received adequate recognition at the Conservatoire and when he was denied the Prix de Rome four times, the whole affair became a *cause célèbre* from which Ravel tried desperately to extricate himself.

Ravel, like Debussy, found the Exposition Universelle of 1889 a fascinating experience. He also followed with interest the concerts of Russian music given in the French capital by Rimsky-Korsakov. While Ravel enthused about the music of Wagner, Chabrier, Satie, and the Russians, in literature he favored the works of Baudelaire, Poe, Mallarmé, and Bertrand. Although his name is usually linked with that of Debussy as the *other* "impressionist" composer, his music reveals far more neo-classical elements than does Debussy's. He also favors music related to dance. A remarkably gifted orchestrator, Ravel often transcribed his own piano pieces for that medium. Also like Debussy, he wrote no symphonies, but he did not shy away from one-movement orchestral pieces. Fond of children, animals, nature scenes, and Spanish music, Ravel wrote many pieces reflecting these affinities.

A rhythmic *tour de force* that Ravel himself titled "an orchestral tissue without music," the *Boléro* was first presented as a ballet by

Edouard Lalo

Darius Milhaud

Jacques Offenbach

Charles Camille Saint-Saëns

Ida Rubinstein at the Paris Opéra on 22 November 1928. Walter Straram conducted; the Benois sets recalled a painting by Goya; Rubinstein exercised her hypnotic powers and the audience was overwhelmed. Rubinstein danced the solo in a scene that resembled a Spanish inn. The broad, round platform on which she danced was surrounded by men who followed her movements intensively. As she became more animated in her gyrations, they became more agitated. Finally, at a key moment, all erupted in a typical tavern brawl. The ballet was nothing less than a sensation; the first concert performance was given by the Lamoureux Orchestra in Paris on 11 January 1930.

Suites from *Daphnis et Chloë*

Boléro is not the only work of Ravel that shows his empathy with the dance. He composed another ballet, a kind of "choreographic symphony" entitled *Daphnis et Chloë* to a scenario by Fokine in 1910. Nijinsky and Karsavina played the title roles when Diaghilev's Ballets Russes performed it first at the Châtelet in Paris on 8 June 1912. Not the most popular of ballets, this work achieved its celebrity in the concert hall. Ravel derived two orchestral suites from the ballet; each consists of three movements. The sections of the first are "Nocturne", "Interlude", and "Danse guérrière"; those of the second are "Lever du jour", "Pantomime", and "Danse générale". The second suite is the favorite of both conductors and audiences.

La Valse

Another of Ravel's dance-related pieces is the choreographic poem *La Valse*. Ravel conceived the idea for this apotheosis of the Viennese waltz already in 1906, but not until the conclusion of World War I did he work on it in earnest and with much enthusiasm. He completed the orchestration in March 1920 and about a month later participated in a two-piano performance of the piece for Diaghilev, several members of his staff, Massine, Poulenc, and Stravinsky. When Diaghilev marveled at the piece but insisted it was not a ballet, Ravel grabbed his manuscript and exited in a huff. He broke permanently with Diaghilev that day. Chevillard conducted the Lamoureux Orchestra in the concert premiere of *La Valse* on 12 December 1920. Later, on 20 November 1928, Ida Rubinstein staged the work as a ballet at the Paris Opéra. Ravel had originally titled the work simply

Wien. When that was regarded as inappropriate so soon after the war, he changed it to *La Valse*.

Rapsodie espagnole

By 1905 Ravel had already composed his remarkable piano piece *Jeux d'eau*, in reality the first in the "impressionist" style, and his string quartet, along with many other pieces, when he turned his attention to Spain. He had just been rejected for the Prix de Rome for the fourth time and with the composition of two additional masterworks, the *Rapsodie espagnole* and the opera *L'Heure espagnole*, he seemed to thumb his nose at the juries who had spurned him. Manuel de Falla greeted this work as "genuinely Spanish," not like Rimsky-Korsakov's *Capriccio espagnol* which, he claimed, simply drew on folk elements and showed far less originality. Ravel had indicated an interest in Spanish music as early as 1895, in his Habañera for two pianos, part of the unpublished (until recently) *Sites auriculaires*. When Debussy produced several works with the performance instruction "dans le mouvement d'un habañera," the journalists had a field day trying to decide who had been first in demonstrating this Hispanic musical preference. The *Rapsodie* is one of Ravel's earliest works for full orchestra and it is divided into four sections: *Prelude, Malagueña, Habañera,* and *Feria*. The *Habañera* derives from that earlier one which comprised part of the *Sites auriculaires*.

Concerto for the Left Hand

Ravel wrote two concertos for piano and orchestra and he completed both in 1931. The Concerto for the Left Hand was commissioned by Paul Wittgenstein, a German pianist who lost his arm in the First World War. Ravel apparently was writing his Concerto in G-major when he received the commission, but decided he could work on the two together. The problem in writing for one hand is, of course, the necessity to produce the kind of texture that would make it difficult for the listener to realize that only one hand is engaged. Ravel more than surmounted this obstacle. The Concerto contains an extraordinary combination of scintillating pianistic figurations that defy the challenge confronted by the composer, but pose a more difficult one for the performer. Ravel divides this one-movement concerto into several sections: a lento, an allegro, and a section with a genuine blues movement. Wittgenstein played the premiere in Vienna on 27 November 1931.

Introduction et Allegro

For the listener, the *Introduction et Allegro* for harp, flute, clarinet, and string quartet bears comparison with Debussy's *L'Après-midi d'un faune*, although Arbie Orenstein, Ravel's biographer, describes it as a miniature harp concerto. It also serves as a fine introduction to Ravel's chamber music, particularly the String Quartet and the Piano Trio. Before joining Misia and Alfred Edwards on their famous yacht *Aimée*, Ravel completed this piece that had been commissioned by the Maison Erard. He dedicated it to Mr. A. Blondel, the director of the Erard Company, the organization that supplied the Conservatoire with harps and pianos. The *Introduction et Allegro* is in rather traditional sonata form, but Ravel inserted the cadenza in this quasi concerto *before* the recapitulation, rather than at the end, as was customary.

String Quartet in F

A twenty-seven year old Ravel dedicated his String Quartet "à mon cher maître Gabriel Fauré." He completed it in 1902, the year of the premiere of *Pelléas et Mélisande*. A four-movement work, with its opening movement in sonata form, the quartet contains within it evidence of Ravel's unique compositional approach to cyclical treatment. He often derives later themes from those stated earlier, thus linking sections and even movements—but subliminally. The derivations are so artfully maneuvered that it is difficult for all but the most sophisticated listeners to recognize them. Themes are so intertwined that on one occasion Ravel, performing his *Sonatine* for piano, inadvertently went from the end of the exposition of the first movement into the coda of the final, third movement. (The audience was unaware of the error fortunately, and when he concluded the composer greeted their applause with smiles.) Debussy and Ravel each wrote one String Quartet; both composers achieved masterpieces in this genre, but in no way do these pieces resemble one another. The Heymann Quartet gave the first performance of the piece on 5 March 1904 to mixed reviews.

Piano Trio

Already in 1908, Ravel contemplated writing a piano trio, but not until 1914 did he become intensely involved in its composition. Then the war broke out. Ravel worked fiendishly at completing the Trio before applying for military service. The first performance took place 28 January 1915 at a concert of the Société Musicale Indépendante, the organization founded by his teacher Fauré. (Alfredo Casella was the pianist.) Because of the political situation, few critics were on hand; those that were praised it highly. By the fall of that year, the composer was caring for wounded soldiers at Saint-Jean-de-Luz, but was still writing music.

The Trio has four movements, the first in sonata form. Ravel calls the second movement "Pantoum," possibly bowing to the exotic influences that had already had an impact on French composers (The rhythmic subtleties could have reminded him of the Malayan *pantun*). The third movement is a passacaglia, with one recurring melody that unifies the section; and the finale offers a virtuoso challenge, particularly to the pianist. This Trio represents one of Ravel's finest chamber works. Ravel also wrote an early violin and piano sonata and a violin and cello sonata, the latter (in 1920–1922) dedicated to the memory of Debussy.

SAINT-SAËNS

"Organist, pianist, caricaturist, dabbler in science, enamored of mathematics and astronomy, amateur comedian, feulletonist, critic, traveler, archaeologist" as Philip Hale described him, Charles Camille Saint-Saëns (1835–1921) is the perfect example of a polymath. A child prodigy whose feats might be compared to those of Mozart, he picked out tunes on the piano at the age of two and a half, could read at three, and shortly afterward wrote his first piece. Dated 22 March 1839, the manuscript rests today in the Paris Conservatoire. At five, Saint-Saëns started giving piano recitals and at seven he was reading Latin—he always regretted not having learned Greek—and becoming interested in science, particularly botany and lepidoptery. He started formal music lessons at seven and at ten made his official debut, at which time, as an encore, he offered to play any one of Beethoven's thirty-two sonatas from memory. Such were his beginnings. He lived a long time, long enough to make a number of enemies, particularly among those jealous of his gifts. A member of the avant-garde among composers, he was one of the principal founders of the Société Nationale de Musique in 1871, recognizing the need for a public forum for the works of native French composers. He introduced the works of Wagner, Liszt, and Schumann to the French, but later, when performances of German music threatened to overtake works by French composers, he withdrew his support of foreign musicians. That was when he lost out to Franck and particularly to d'Indy in the Société.

Saint-Saëns composed in every musical genre. A prolific musician whose extra-curricular activities seemed never to interfere with his principal vocation, he also found time to travel extensively and even made several tours of America in 1906 and 1915. Although his music reveals several conspicuously Gallic traits, even the French have not been kind to him in their estimates of his legacy. He apparently was too gifted, composed too readily, and demonstrated too much talent with too little effort. Several of his compositions rank with other masterpieces of this period.

Le Carnaval des Animaux (Carnival of the Animals)

Possibly Saint-Saëns's best-known work was composed in seventeen days in 1886 and published after his deaeth—because he felt it unworthy of publication. This "grand zoological fantasia" may have been withheld from the public because Saint-Saëns felt that at a time when the passion and sensuality of Wagner held sway over audiences, it was too much to expect them to display the sense of humor necessary for the enjoyment of this piece. The first public performance took place at a Colonne concert in Paris conducted by Gabriel Pierné on 25 February 1922, a year after Saint-Saëns's death. Walter Damrosch introduced it in New York the same year on 29 October. The *Carnaval* is a suite in fourteen movements for two pianos, two violins, viola, cello, double-bass, flute, clarinet, celesta, and xylophone. The animals include a lion, hens, and roosters, wild asses, tortoises, an elephant, kangaroos, a cuckoo, pianists (!) and a swan, among others. In this piece, Saint-Saëns was not above parodying Wagner, Berlioz, Mendelssohn, Offenbach, Rossini, and even himself.

Danse macabre

Again, one of the best-known of Saint-Saëns's works fits the description of his music offered by his detractors: "la mauvaise musique bien écrite" ("well-written bad music"). The third of his four symphonic poems, the *Danse macabre*, was composed in 1874 and displays Saint-Saëns's talents as an orchestrator. (He uses the xylophone to depict the rattling of bones in the cemetery.) The piece follows the pattern and form that Liszt originated in his thirteen symphonic poems: a one-movement work unified by thematic transformations. Here, one of the principal themes transformed is the medieval sequence *Dies Irae*. The poetry that inspired the composition, a type that Rossetti called "lively little ballads of the tomb," was written by a Frenchman, Henri Cazalis. It appears on a flyleaf of Saint-Saëns's score.

Saint-Saëns was one of the first composers to write music for films in the early decades of the twentieth century. The *Danse macabre* could readily serve to accompany any one of a number of the silent horror movies.

Piano Concerto No. 2 in g-minor, Op. 22

Saint-Saëns wrote five piano concertos. The fifth, the "Egyptian" Concerto of 1896 reflects his interest in exotic countries, to which he apparently traveled regularly. The second, composed almost thirty years earlier in 1868, has become the favorite of audiences today. The composer gave the first performance of this work in 1868 and except for some complaints that, like the so-called "Moonlight" Sonata of Beethoven, it lacked a first movement, the piece caught on. It opens with a free contrapuntal cadenza for piano and then offers a theme vaguely reminiscent of the eleventh of Schumann's *Etudes symphoniques*. (Schumann's piece, however, is in g sharp-minor.) Kettle drums introduce the second (scherzo) movement and the third movement allows for the irrepressible exuberance of the soloist. Saint-Saëns at his best! Besides the five piano concertos, Saint-Saëns also wrote three for violin and two for cello; the favorites of violinists, however, are not these concertos, but the spectacular virtuoso pieces known as the *Introduction et Rondo Capriccioso* for solo violin and orchestra (1863) and the *Havanaise* (again the Spanish/Cuban influence) for the same forces. Technical agility is as vital here to violinists as it is to pianists in the piano concertos.

Samson et Dalila

With more than a dozen operas to his credit, Saint-Saëns—in addition to composing so many instrumental works—was a prolific composer of operas as well. In 1877, Franz Liszt arranged for the premiere of his *Samson et Dalila*, based on the biblical story of the Hebrew hero. The three acts are peopled by the Hebrews and their oppressors, the Philistines, and the story follows closely that given in the Old Testament. After Dalila's blandishments, best illustrated by the most famous number in the score, "Mon coeur s'ouvre à ta voix," Samson is powerless. Deprived of his hair, the champion is overcome. When he prays to his God that he be allowed to give one final example of his extraordinary strength, he is granted his wish. With his mighty hands, he grasps the two pillars of the temple and brings the entire edifice crashing about his conquerors.

Symphony No. 3 in c-minor ("Organ" Symphony)

Saint-Saëns composed his "organ" symphony on commission from the London Philharmonic Society and he conducted its first performance in London on 19 May 1886. The composer prepared an analysis of the piece which was translated into English. It appears in its entirety in Philip Hale's *Boston Symphony Programme Notes*. Saint-Saëns reports essentially that this symphony comprises two parts which include the four sections of traditional symphonies: an adagio introduction, an allegro, and another adagio, which acts as the second movement (Part I). Part II consists of a scherzo and finale, thereby accounting for all the movements usually associated with the symphony, but avoiding, as the composer intended, many of the repeats. The organ and piano (four-hands) appear in the finale. Saint-Saëns later dedicated this piece to the memory of Franz Liszt, who had died in July of 1886.

SATIE

Mention of the granddaddy of the avant-garde, Erik Satie (1866–1925), still stirs controversy in some circles. There are those who recognize his impact on composers as varied as Debussy, Ravel, Poulenc, and John Cage, and others who believe he made a fetish out of composition, seizing upon bizarre titles and performance instructions to capture the attention of the public. Of mixed Scotch (his mother) and French (his father) parentage, Satie and his works essentially reflect the tongue-in-cheek attitude of many Frenchmen. Deemed lazy by his teachers, he was dismissed early from the Conservatoire and although he had, at the time, already composed a number of significant compositions, he later became a student of d'Indy at the Schola Cantorum from 1905 to 1908.

Satie's father had founded a music publishing business in the late 1880s and brought out the first of his son's published compositions. Young Satie completed his three *Sarabandes* in 1887—these may have influenced Debussy's piece of the same name in his *Pour le piano* suite—and in 1888, his *Gymnopédies*, later orchestrated by Debussy. After the Paris Exhibition of 1889, Satie produced his *Gnossiennes*, perhaps of oriental inspiration.

Satie began to show an interest in mysticism, the occult, and the group around Sâr Péladan, members of the Rosicrucian artistic movement. At the same time, he lost some of his characteristic restraints as he frequented Rudolphe Salis's café Chat Noir. To oblige Péladan, Satie wrote *Le Fils des étoiles* (a Chaldean pastorale for flutes and harps!) in 1891. About this time, perhaps at the Café, he met Debussy, with whom he remained on close terms for many years. He had a stormy love affair with the painter and one-time circus performer Suzanne Valadon, Utrillo's mother, and once he came to blows with Willy, Colette's husband, at a Colonne concert. His behavior was bizarre, to say the least, but he spoke his mind and made an impression on all those who knew him. His peculiar habits—he bought twelve identical gray velvet suits and always walked with an umbrella in one hand—marked him as an eccentric. He also—perhaps after his break with Debussy—took to choosing the oddest names for some of his piano pieces: *Trois Morceaux en forme de poire*, *Trois véritable préludes flasques (pour un chien)*, *Embryons désséches*, *Croquis et agaceries d'un gros bonhomme en bois*, among others. In 1913, pianist Ricardo Viñes included the recent Satie compositions, *Quatre préludes flasques*, in a recital. They became popular and several publishers requested his pieces. Then in April 1915, after a performance of the four-hand *Trois Morceaux* by Viñes and Satie together, Jean Cocteau took up the cudgels for Satie and overnight the composer became a celebrity.

Masterpieces of French Music 1870–1925

Parade

In May 1917 *Parade* almost started a revolution in the theater as Cocteau collaborated with Picasso, Massine, and Satie for Diaghilev's Ballets Russes. It certainly provoked several scandals. As a result of one—after Satie had sent an insulting card to a critic—the composer was given a suspended sentence for eight days in jail. Picasso fashioned cubist constructions as costumes and Satie wrote music to match, incorporating sounds of modern life such as typewriters, airplane propellers, and sirens. Apollinaire coined the term "surrealism" in his program notes for the ballet and later Braque, Derain, Dufy, Marie Laurencin, Matisse, and other French artists contributed their ideas and scenarios to the ballets while Milhaud, Poulenc, Honegger, and Auric composed the music. These four, together with Durey and Tailleferre, all partisans of Satie, eventually became known as "Les Six," dubbed by the critic Henri Collet.

Gymnopédies

In 1895, seemingly at the suggestion of Debussy, two of the three *Gymnopédies*—which Satie wrote in 1888—were published and the following year Debussy himself orchestrated two of them. At the beginning of 1911, at a concert of the Société Musicale Indépendante, Ravel performed Satie's three *Sarabandes* of 1887, and a couple of months later Debussy conducted his orchestrated version of two of the *Gymnopédies*. Satie was instantly regarded as a harbinger of the future. As a matter of fact, his success nettled Debussy, who had, after all, once called him a medieval musician who ventured by mistake into the twentieth century. As a mystic, interested in Gregorian chant, Gothic art, and the lives of saints, Satie did seem out of place in the new century. Even his titles, archaic in one way, sounded out of this world. Lean texture, clarity, and restraint characterize his compositions. Often he uses repetitive rhythmic figures and sometimes he absolutely eliminates bar lines, but most often he allows in his comments and performance instructions that his is a different, unusual kind of music.

While chamber and orchestral music represent the highlights of this period, several piano pieces and *mélodies* also deserve attention. Norman Demuth stated that "in no country have composers so sedulously cultivated the piano as have those in France." His comments may relate to his decision to write *French Piano Music* (London, 1959). Compared to the Germans, however, French composers of piano music do not hold center stage in the concert repertory. Unless a performer specializes in this music, he or she simply includes selections from the body of French piano music, while remaining basically faithful to German music of the period, particularly that of Brahms, who wrote more than enough to keep many a pianist busy. A short list of the most significant piano pieces by French composers of the period 1870–1925 follows.

Chabrier wrote a set of *Dix Pièces pittoresques* of which the scherzo/valse was a favorite of Arthur Rubinstein.

Paul Dukas, who conscientiously destroyed anything that did not meet his highest standards, wrote an extremely difficult and lengthy Sonata in b-flat minor, which he dedicated to Saint-Saëns.

Debussy's early piano pieces resemble those of Chopin and Schumann. A waltz, romance, and ballade fall into this category. Later, only slightly later, his *Suite bergamasque* (1890–1905), of which the "Clair de lune" has become a popular salon piece, and his suite *Pour le piano* have added immeasurably to the pianist's repertory. *Estampes*, the two books of *Images* with three pieces each, and the two books of *Préludes* and *Etudes*, dating from 1910–1913 and 1915 respectively, changed the course of piano music in the twentieth century. Debussy's extraordinary use of washes of sound, sonorities that had not been imagined earlier, coupled with his wonderful use of the pedal, anticipated the music of the future. *L'Isle joyeuse*, originally meant as part of the *Suite bergamasque*, stands on its own and relates to Watteau's painting *Embarquement pour Cythère*, representing Debussy at his sensual best. Finally, the *Children's Corner*, which Debussy wrote in 1906–1908 to entertain his daughter Chouchou, resembles those children's pieces by Schumann and others in that it has an attraction for grown-up "children" as well. Chouchou's English nanny must have told him about Jumbo the elephant, but Debussy misunderstood and it became "*Jimbo's* Lullaby." No such misunderstanding, however, regarding the parody of Wagner's *Tristan* in the "Golliwog's Cakewalk," a fine example of Debussy's use of American jazz. Elsewhere, in "Minstrels," from the *Préludes*, he also acknowledges his American friends from across the sea.

Fauré's *Barcarolle, Impromptus*, and *Nocturnes* have not fared well on the international stage, but the French love them. He is more or less a French Schumann. Harmonically experimental, most of the pieces are in a quasi-*ABA* design. Rubinstein, again, had some favorites.

As an organist, Franck wrote a considerable number of keyboard pieces for that instrument, but he did not completely neglect the piano. Many of his piano pieces, however, bear the mark of the organist. Even their titles give away their composer's source of inspiration. The *Prélude, Chorale and Fugue* is the best known of the piano works; the *Prélude, Aria, and Finale* and the *Prélude, Fugue and Variations* are two others worthy of study.

Vincent d'Indy, Franck's most devoted pupil, wrote a number of travel pieces, programmatic works in the manner of Liszt: a *Promenade*, the *Poème des montagnes*, *Helvétia*, and a *Tableaux de voyage*. One large-scale piano piece, the Sonata in e-minor, challenges the performer with its strenuous demands.

Darius Milhaud, one of "Les Six," accompanied Paul Claudel to Brazil for the latter's tour of duty there. The result was some very earthy pieces like the *Saudades de Brasil*. But the four-hand *Scaramouche* is the most popular of this composer's many works for piano. Another member of "Les Six," Francis Poulenc, contributed the *Mouvements perpetuels* to the piano repertory in about 1921.

Ravel, along with Debussy, wrote the most frequently performed piano pieces in the French repertory. A pianist himself and a good friend of Ricardo Viñes, the Catalan pianist who gave the premiere of so many of his works—*Menuet antique* and "Oiseaux tristes" from *Miroirs* are dedicated to him—Ravel is responsible for the first impressionist piano piece, the *Jeux d'eau*. Here he reveals precisely how he is descended from Liszt, just as Debussy derives from Chopin. The later *Sonatine, Miroirs, Tombeau de Couperin*, and the fiendishly difficult *Gaspard de la nuit*, an encyclopedia of pianistic figurations, show him veering ever more toward neo-classicism, with very precisely outlined structures. The *Valses nobles et sentimentales* reveal, once again, his feelings for the dance that he expressed so often in orchestral music. They portray the dying embers of Viennese romanticism, before the First World War, and they have often been used as the background for various ballets of the twentieth century. Ravel requires far less rubato than Debussy, even writing, in "Le Gibet" of *Gaspard*, "*sans expression*" to be sure that it is played correctly. Ravel was far better educated than Debussy, but more retiring and also less caustic. Unlike the older composer, he did not write regular music criticism and, except when asked, did not offer his opinions on the music of his contemporaries.

For some critics, Satie's eccentric and bizarre titles seem like camouflage for his relatively lean pieces. For others, he anticipates much of the twentieth century's piano works. He is one of the few French composers of his epoch who shows not one trace of Wagnerian influence. He is even anti-Debussy in that he wanted to reveal the absolute necessity of the separation of words and music—so that many of his titles are really tongue-in-cheek commentaries on those employed by his peers. He did not compose much, but he clearly influenced both Debussy and Ravel. Satirical, cynical elements characterize many of his languid piano pieces, along with several that show the impact of jazz. He did his best work *before* his personal insecurities led him to undertake a course of study with d'Indy at the Schola Cantorum. *Sports et divertissements* is worth more than a casual hearing.

Another graduate of the Schola, Déodat de Séverac was a regionalist, a musical painter of scenes in southwestern France, where he was born in Saint-Félix. Like Albéniz and Mussorgsky, the Baron de Séverac (he was a nobleman) described the countryside in three suites—*Chant de la terre*, *En Languedoc*, and *Cerdaña*. He wrote two charming groups of pieces for children or nostalgic adults in *En Vacances* and offered a tribute to his teachers, Bordes, Chabrier, and Albéniz in *Sous les Lauriers-Roses*. He presents a counterpart to Debussy's *L'Isle joyeuse* with his *Baigneuses au soleil*, which might even be a tribute to Renoir, one of the many artists he knew well.

Finally, a very brief glimpse of the short vocal pieces again celebrates the efforts of the same composers. Debussy wrote many more songs than Ravel, fifty-five to the latter's thirty-three. Each had a favorite "early" poet, Villon for Debussy, and Clément Marot for Ravel. Debussy confined himself to the art song, to the French *mélodie*, while Ravel often set selected ethnic tunes: Italian, Greek, even Hebrew. Debussy's settings of poems by Verlaine, Baudelaire, Mallarmé, and the composer's close personal friend Pierre Louÿs, particularly his *Chansons de Bilitis*, are his masterpieces. Debussy also wrote *mélodies* based on his own prose poems, the *Proses lyriques*, for example, and the touching "Noël des enfants qui n'ont plus de maisons."

Ravel's extraordinarily beautiful *Shéhérazade* for voice and orchestra to the very musical *vers libre* of Tristan Klingsor (note the Wagnerian influence in this pseudonym of Léon Leclerc) competes for attention with his settings of Jules Renard's prose poems, *Histoires naturelles*. Ravel, too, set the verse of Verlaine and Mallarmé along with several songs to his own texts.

Henri Duparc owes his fame to a mere fourteen songs that he wrote between 1868 and 1884. Several are very lush settings of Baudelaire, Gautier, Armand Silvestre, and Jean Lahor. At least six of the fourteen songs were later orchestrated by the composer himself. Unfortunately, Duparc was afflicted with a mental illness that precluded his musical activities after 1885—and he lived until 1933!

Fauré was the master craftsman for French *mélodies* of this era, writing over a hundred songs, many of them exquisite. In his songs, Fauré seems to have overextended himself. His song cycle *La Bonne Chanson*, set to poems of Verlaine and dedicated to Mrs. Emma Bardac (who became Debussy's second wife), remains the outstanding song cycle of the period.

Notes

1. THE DEATH OF BERLIOZ AND THE BIRTH OF THE SOCIÉTÉ NATIONALE DE MUSIQUE

1. In Paris, [died] 8 March, Mr. Louis-Hector Berlioz, born at Côte-Saint-André (Isère), 11 December 1803, composer and eminent critic. [Biographical] notice in Fétis's *Biographie universelle des musiciens et bibliographie générale de la musique* (Brussels, 1835–44), vol. 1, p. 362. See *Le Guide musical* of 11 March 1869. In the following issue of 18 March, Arthur Pougin devoted the lead article to Berlioz; he also cited two earlier ones that had appeared in the journal on 7 October 1858 and 19 November 1863. Pougin's opening words, "La vie de Berlioz a été une lutte perpetuelle" ("Berlioz's life has been a perpetual struggle") strike a note of truth.

2. See Jacques Barzun, *Berlioz and the Romantic Century* (Boston, 1950), vol. 1, p. 46. He did play the flute with reasonable proficiency, as well as the drum and guitar.

3. Quoted in Barzun, vol. 2, p. 230.

4. Anton Reicha (1770–1836), a Czech composer, knew Beethoven in Bonn and later in Vienna. He moved to Paris in 1799 and was appointed professor of counterpoint and fugue at the Conservatoire in 1818.

5. *Le Journal des Débats*, a famous daily paper, was founded in August 1789 as *Le Journal des Débats et Décrets*. At that time, it reported on discussions in the Assemblée Nationale and the Commune de Paris. In 1799, the brothers Bertin bought it for 20,000 francs, after which it became a leading journal with a circulation of 32,000. The Bertin family, particularly Armand Bertin, was very good to Berlioz.

6. Gaetano Donizetti's *Lucia di Lammermoor* and *Linda di Chamonix*, Michael Balfe's *The Maid of Honor* and Mozart's *Le Nozze di Figaro* were some of the operas Berlioz conducted in London. Louis-Antoine Jullien (1812–1860), the French conductor who was in charge of the opening season at the Drury Lane Theatre, had hired him. A dandy and a charlatan, Jullien never paid Berlioz for his labors, but, because the Revolution of 1848 had broken out in Paris at around this time, Berlioz was happy to be away. While in England, he also hoped to arrange a concert of his own music. See Hugh Macdonald's biographical essay in the *The New Grove Dictionary of Music and Musicians* (hereafter referred to as *New Grove*). (London, 1980), vol. 2, p. 588.

7. Berlioz met the Princess Carolyne zu Sayn-Wittgenstein in Russia in 1847; her liaison with Liszt had begun about this time. Berlioz corresponded with her from 1852 to 1867, and their letters are marked by mutual warmth and respect.

8. See particularly Berlioz's *Les Soirées de l'orchestre* (Paris, 1852; Eng. trans. 1956) and his *Mémoires de Hector Berlioz* (Paris 1870; Eng. trans. 1969).

9. The ophicleide, a large-sized keyed bugle, came into prominence in the second half of the nineteenth century. This brass instrument, later replaced by the tuba, was first used in Gaspare Spontini's opera *Olympie* (1819) and in Mendelssohn's overture to *A Midsummer Night's Dream* (1826).

10. An excellent source of information on Berlioz's *Symphonie fantastique* is the critical score, *Berlioz: Fantastic Symphony*, ed. by Edward T. Cone (New York, 1971). In the fifth movement, Berlioz uses an E-flat clarinet to imitate the strident sounds of Harriet Smithson in this "Dream of a Witches' Sabbath."

11. Rossini was born in a leap year, on 29 February 1792.

12. Information on Rossini derives mainly from Herbert Weinstock, *Rossini: A Biography* (New York, 1968).

13. Weinstock, p. 47.

14. Manuel del Popolo Vicente Garcia (1775–1832), a famous Spanish tenor, singing teacher, and composer, was a close friend of Rossini, with whom he is said to have collaborated on the characterization of Figaro in Rossini's *Il Barbiere di Siviglia*. He sired three celebrated musicians of the nineteenth century: Maria Garcia Malibran (1808–1836) and Pauline Garcia Viardot (1821–1910), two of the foremost sopranos of their day, and (at age 101!) a son, Manuel Patricio Rodriquez Garcia (1805–1906), a vocal coach and the inventor of the laryngoscope. Some speculate that Garcia, Sr., was a Marrano, a member of one of the Jewish families who went "underground" during the Inquisition.

15. Weinstock, p. 132.

16. See Stendhal [Henri Beyle], *La Vie de Rossini* (Paris, 1824; trans. Richard N. Coe, London and New York, 1957). See Ulrich Weisstein, *The Essence of Opera* (Glencoe, 1964), p. 191, for excerpts from Stendhal's book on Rossini, along with other interesting material.

17. Related in Francis Toye, *Rossini: A Study in Tragi-Comedy* (paperback ed., New York, 1963), p. 171.

18. Quoted in Weisstein, p. 182.

19. Eugène Scribe (1791–1861), a French dramatist who authored several hundred opera libretti. Scribe coined the phrase "the well-made play."

20. For the best sociological, political, and cultural essays on the French, see Theodore Zeldin, *France, 1848–1945* (Oxford, 1973–77), 2 vols.

21. An opera had to be sung in French; if the original language were other than French, it had to be translated. It usually consisted of five acts with a ballet at the beginning of the second act. The composer could not conduct his own opera. Italian operas generally appeared at the Théâtre-Italien; those produced at the Opéra had already been translated into French.

22. See Julien Tiersot, *Un Demi-Siècle de musique française, 1870–1919* (Paris, 1924), p. 6, and Martin Cooper, *French Music from the Death of Berlioz to the Death of Fauré* (Oxford, 1951), p. 10.

23. Jules-Etienne Pasdeloup (1819–1887), a piano student of Pierre Zimmerman at the Conservatoire, became a celebrated French conductor. He organized the Société des jeunes élèves du Conservatoire (1851) at the Cirque d'Hiver. This pioneer series of good, inexpensive concerts was a popular success from the start. Pasdeloup lost his audience to Colonne and Lamoureux and ended the series in 1884, but revived it in 1886–87, shortly before his death.

24. Pasdeloup played the works of Beethoven, Mendelssohn, and Schumann. See Cooper, p. 11.

25. These three composers, along with Edouard Lalo, continued to write chamber music, expecting that this kind of music would have a better chance of being performed! They also composed sacred music, a longstanding French tradition.

26. After the defeat of France in 1870, he also wrote a *Lamentation*. See Tiersot, p. 11.

27. For more on the Société Nationale de Musique, see material in books by Tiersot and Cooper already cited. See also Romain Rolland, *Musicians of Today*, trans. Mary Blaiklock (New York, 1915), pp. 265ff.

28. Several of these men participated in chamber music groups that specialized in the classics, rather than the music of contemporary French composers. Among the French chamber music societies of the nineteenth century were the Société Alard Franchomme (1848), the Société des Derniers Quartets de Beethoven (1851), the Société de Musique de Chambre Armingaud, where Lalo played second violin (1856), Lamoureux's Séances Populaires de Musique de Chambre (1859) and the Société de Musique de Chambre Jacoby-Vuillaume (1864). See Cooper, p. 10.

29. Edouard (real name Judas) Colonne (1838–1910), a violinist and French conductor, founded the Concert National (1873), which later gained renown as the Concerts du Châtelet and then became the Concerts Colonne. At the Concerts Colonne he played many of the larger Berlioz works, along with scores by contemporary German and French composers. In 1878, he conducted the official Exposition con-

certs (see Chapter 4). He was a visiting conductor in England, Russia, Portugal and even, in 1905, in the United States with the New York Philharmonic. During the Occupation, 1940–1945, the Nazis removed Colonne's name from the concert series owing to his Jewish origin.

2. WAGNER IN FRANCE AND FRANCE IN WAGNER

1. Romain Rolland, *Musicians of Today*, trans. Mary Blaiklock (New York, 1915), pp. 66–67.
2. *Ibid.*, pp. 252–53.
3. Robert W. Gutman, *Richard Wagner, The Man, His Mind, and His Music* (New York, 1968), p. 2.
4. Quoted in Gutman, p. 80.
5. Gutman, p. 185.
6. *Ibid.*, p. 332.
7. Ernest Newman, *The Life of Richard Wagner*, vol. 1 (New York, 1933), p. 245.
8. Martine Kahane and Nicole Wild, eds. *Wagner et la France* (Paris, 1983), p. 150.
9. Newman, p. 221.
10. *Ibid.*, pp. 99–100.
11. *Ibid.*, pp. 71, 225.
12. Richard Wagner, *My Life*, authorized translation from the German, no translator's name given (New York, 1911), p. 179.
13. Newman, p. 178; see also Wagner's article "Aus Magdeburg" in the *Gesammelte Schriften*, ed. W. Golther, vol. 12 (Berlin, 1913). The article appeared in the *Neue Zeitschrift* of 3 May 1836. It is not in the English translation of the prose works.
14. Gutman, p. 66.
15. *Ibid.*, p. 67.
16. Gutman, *loc. cit.*
17. Gutman, *loc. cit.*
18. Newman, p. 279.
19. *Ibid.*, pp. 290, 291.
20. *Ibid.*, p. 283.
21. *Ibid.*, p. 280.
22. Gutman, pp. 72–73.
23. Newman, pp. 292, 297.
24. *Ibid.*, p. 286.
25. Newman, *loc. cit.*
26. Gutman, p. 72.
27. Kahane and Wild, p. 151.
28. Gutman, p. 81.
29. See "Parisian Amusements" and "Parisian Fatalities for the Germans" in *Richard Wagner, Prose Works*, trans. William Ashton Ellis, vol. 8 (New York, 1966; repr. from London, 1899), pp. 70ff, 87ff.
30. Kahane and Wild, p. 151.
31. Kahane and Wild, *loc. cit.*
32. *Ibid.*, p. 152.
33. Gutman, p. 193; Newman, vol. 2 (New York, 1937), pp. 593–94.
34. Kahane and Wild, p. 153.
35. See also Newman, vol. 3, p. 110.
36. Kahane and Wild, *loc. cit.*
37. Newman, vol. 3 (New York, 1941), p. 5.
38. Kahane and Wild, p. 153.
39. Wagner, *My Life*, pp. 758–65.
40. *Ibid.*, pp. 716–17.
41. See W. Golther, ed. *Richard Wagner und Mathilde Wesendonck: Tagebuchblätter und Briefe 1853–1871* (Leipzig, 1904; Eng. trans. 1905).

42. See Maxime Leroy, *Les Premiers Amis français de Wagner* (Paris, 1925).

43. See Julien Tiersot, ed. *Lettres françaises de Richard Wagner, recueillies et publiées par J.T.* (Paris, 1935), and Kahane and Wild, p. 153. See complete letter on p. XX.

44. Kahane and Wild, p. 153.

45. Wagner, *My Life*, pp. 750–51. See also Elaine Brody, "The Jewish Wagnerites," *The Opera Quarterly*, vol. 1, no. 3, 1983.

46. Wagner, *My Life*, pp. 756–64.

47. Kahane and Wild, p. 39.

48. D. Ollivier, ed. *Correspondance de Liszt et de sa fille Madame Emile Ollivier* (Paris, 1936).

49. See A. W. Raitt, "Richard Wagner" in *Villiers de L'Isle-Adam et le mouvement symboliste* (Paris, 1965), p. 105.

50. Kahane and Wild, p. 155.

51. Kahane and Wild, *loc. cit.*

52. Recalled and quoted by L. de Fourcaud in the *Revue international de musique*, 1 March 1898.

53. *La France musicale*, 30 May 1869.

54. Kahane and Wild, p. 58; see also J. Herlihy, *Catulle Mendès, critique dramatique et musical* (Paris, 1936).

55. See Newman, vol. 4, p. 277.

56. *Le Ménestrel*, 1875–76, p. 351.

57. See Brody, "The Jewish Wagnerites."

58. Kahane and Wild, pp. 50–52.

59. *Ibid.* p. 68.

60. Rollo Myers, *Emmanuel Chabrier and His Circle* (London, 1969), p. 26.

61. Letter printed in *Renaissance musicale*, 21 May 1882.

62. Gutman, p. 417; see also Newman, vol. 4 (New York, 1946), pp. 667–68.

63. Kahane and Wild, p. 56.

64. Kahane and Wild, *loc. cit.*

65. Kahane and Wild, *loc. cit.*

66. *Ibid.*, p. 59.

67. *Ibid.*, p. 60.

68. Unpublished journal of Richardo Viñes is in the possession of the author.

69. See Paul Dukas, "L'influence wagnérienne," *Wagner et la France*, special number of *La Revue musicale*, 1 October 1923, pp. 3–4.

70. André Suarès, "Sur Wagner," *Wagner et la France*, pp. 10–18.

3. LE JAPONISME ET L'ORIENTALISME

1. See Colta Feller Ives, *The Great Wave: The Influence of Japanese Woodcuts on French Prints* (New York, 1974) pp. 7 and 13. For further reading, see Yvonne Thirion, "Le Japonisme en France dans la seconde moitié du XIX siècle, à la faveur de la diffusion de l'estampe Japonaise" in *Cahiers de l'Association Internationale des Etudes Françaises*, vol. 13 (Paris, 1961) pp. 117–130; Henri Focillon, *L'Estampe Japonaise et la Peinture en Occident dans la seconde moitié du XIXe siècle* (Paris, 1921); and the more recent book by Lucille R. Webber, *Japanese Woodblock Prints: The Reciprocal Influence Between East and West* (Provo, Utah 1984).

2. Ives, p. 12.

3. Cited in Ives, p. 7.

4. See Edward Lockspeiser, *Debussy: His Life and Mind*, vol. 2 (London 1965) p. 24. For innumerable references to Hokusai in Goncourt's *Journal*, see George G. Becker and Edith Philips, eds. and trans. *Paris and the Arts, 1851–1896, from the Goncourt Journal* (Ithaca, 1971). See also, in this book, the "Afterword on Japanese Art and Influence" by Hedley H. Rhys, pp. 327ff.

5. See Becker and Philips, p. 229.

Notes

6. *Ibid.*, p. 254. In 1891, Edmond de Goncourt also wrote *Art japonais du XVIIIe siècle: Outamaro*, the first of a series on Japanese art.

7. See Braquemond's "Rousseau Table Service," pictured in the Brooklyn Museum's catalogue for the exhibit entitled *From Courbet to Cézanne, A New 19th Century, Preview of the Musée d'Orsay in Paris*, compiled by Guy Cogeval, trans. Domingo Barbiery and James Mayor (Paris, 1986), cat. no. 116. See also Ives, p. 8.

8. Ives, p. 8.

9. Cited in Lockspeiser, p. 25.

10. Apparently, the avant-garde in literature and art sponsored Wagner as well as Japanese art, a curious pair.

11. Lockspeiser, p. 23.

12. See H. Borgeaud, ed. *Correspondance de Claude Debussy et Pierre Louÿs* (Paris, 1945).

13. See Eric Walter White, *Stravinsky, the Composer and His Works* (Berkeley, 1966) p. 180.

14. See James Harding, *Saint-Saëns and His Circle* (London, 1965) p. 119.

15. Both empires were greater in extent than any since the Mongols or Rome. Britain, at her height, ruled 20% of the world's population and 25% of the world's land area.

16. Joseph Arthur, Comte de Gobineau (1816–1882), a French diplomat and essayist, is remembered today specifically for his *Essai sur l'inégalité des races humaines* (1853–1855). He believed that only the white, the "Aryan" race, the creator of civilization, possessed the supreme human virtues: honor, love of freedom, qualities which could be perpetuated only if the race remained pure. While he was not particularly anti-Semitic, he insisted that the Latin and Semitic peoples had degenerated in the course of history through various racial intermixtures. Only the Germans had preserved their "Aryan purity." Richard Wagner was one of Gobineau's foremost admirers.

17. See E. Robert Schmitz, *The Piano Works of Claude Debussy* (New York, 1950), pp. 181–82. For more on the impact of exoticism and orientalism on Debussy, see *Segalen et Debussy*, compiled and edited by Annie Joly-Segalen and André Schaeffner (Monaco, 1961).

18. See *Pour la Musique française: Douze Causeries avec une préface de Claude Debussy* (Paris 1917). The essays printed in this volume derived from papers presented from March to June in 1915 at Lyons by some friends of French music. Victor Loret, of the Faculty of Letters, presumably of Lyons, contributed an essay entitled "L'Orientalisme dans la musique française," pp. 135–73.

19. *Djamileh* is the story of Harun, a Turk from Cairo, who tires of the wine, women, and gambling in which he indulges regularly. He listens to the song of the Nile boatmen and laughs when his steward Spendiano accuses him of being a spendthrift. (He sends away each slave girl, when he's tired of her, laden with gifts. His style of living has begun to be too costly.) Djamileh, one of his "girls," adores him. When he recognizes several unusual features about her, he revokes his gift and frees her. When she refuses to accept her freedom, he turns again to gambling. That night, the slave dealer brings Harun a new girl, who is veiled. Spendiano, at Djamileh's insistence, has allowed her to pass as the "new" girl. Delighted with this new lover, Harun removes her veil and discovers that she is none other than Djamileh. When she confesses she would rather be his slave than be free, she awakens strong passions in Harun who then decides to claim her as his own. For more information see Rana Kabbani *Europe's Myths of the Orient* (Bloomington, Indiana 1986).

20. See Dorothy Veinus Hagan, *Félicien David, 1810–1876* (Syracuse, 1985). See also "Orientalism" in Frits Noske, *French Song from Berlioz to Duparc*, trans. Rita Benton (Dover repr., New York, 1970).

21. See *Pour la Musique française*, p. 151.

22. For more on Nouguès, see Elaine Brody, "A Selection of Letters from Déodat de Séverac," *Canadian University Music Review*, no. 6 (1985), pp. 284–92.

23. For plot summaries of some of the more obscure operas, see Frederick H. Martens, *A Thousand and One Nights of Opera* (New York, 1926).

24. See *Pour la Musique française*, p. 159.
25. Richard Buckle, in *Diaghilev* (New York, 1979), p. 314, says that "perhaps Diaghilev thought that all the best Spanish music was written by French composers." He is probably quoting S. L. Grigoriev, *The Diaghilev Ballet, 1909–1929* (London, 1953) p. 123. See also *L'Exotisme musical français*, a special issue of the *Revue internationale de musique française*, no. 6 (November 1981), pp. 47ff.

4. MUSIC AT THE GREAT EXHIBITIONS

1. Cited in John Allwood, *The Great Exhibitions* (London, 1977), p. 7.
2. Cited in Julian Barnes, *Flaubert's Parrot* (New York, 1984), p. 36.
3. Cited in Norma Evenson, *Paris: A Century of Change, 1878–1978*, p. 2.
4. *Ibid.*
5. Paraphrase of quotation in Evenson, p. 5.
6. Allwood, pp. 10, 33.
7. See Henry Fougère, *Les Délégations ouvrières aux expositions sous le Second Empire* (Montlucon, 1905).
8. Richard D. Mandell, *Paris 1900: The Great World's Fair* (Toronto, 1967), p. 13.
9. Allwood, p. 44.
10. *Ibid.*, p. 48.
11. *Ibid.*, p. 43. As a liberal, Victor Hugo bitterly opposed the reactionary repression of Napoleon III in the 1850s. That he wrote by government commission in 1867 is a sign of reconciliation.
12. In *L'Exposition Universelle de 1867 illustrée*, an extensive section on Oriental exhibits appears in issue 3, pp. 38–39. A glowing account of the Egyptian exhibit is featured in issue 4, pp. 53–60; this issue also contains a description of a Moorish café that features Moroccan music.
13. See Oscar Comettant, *La Musique, Les Musiciens et les Instruments de Musique chez les différents peuples du monde* (Paris, 1869). The author here describes all the official documents relating to music, the composition of the various juries, and the words of the specially written cantatas and hymns. See pp. 20–51.
14. Rossini had written a hymn for this exposition and Comettant wanted to publish it. He asked the composer's permission but did not receive any response. On 14 November 1867, Madame Olympe Rossini wrote to him, explaining that her husband's poor health prevented him from replying sooner. Whereas Rossini would not give permission for the entire hymn to be reprinted, he did allow Comettant to publish excerpts. See pp. 133–35.
15. Comettant actually describes—as an ethnomusicologist might attempt to do —the most ancient African and Asian instruments and their function in the society in which they were used. See pp. 517–76.
16. See Comettant, p. 602.
17. Monsieur,

   Je viens d'entendre les magnifiques instruments que vous nous avez apportés d'Amérique et qui sortent de vos ateliers. Permettez-moi de vous complimenter pour les belles et rares qualités que ces pianos possèdent. Leur sonorité est splendide et essentiellement noble, et de plus vous avez trouvé le moyen d'affaiblir, au point de la rendre presque insensible, la terrible resonance de septième mineure qui se faisait entendre sur les huit ou neuf cordes graves, au point de rendre cacophoniques les accords les plus simples et les plus beaux. C'est un grand progrès, entre autres, que vous avez apporté dans la fabrication du piano; un progrès dont tous les artistes et amateurs doués d'une oreille delicate vous sauront un gré infini.

   Recevez, je vous prie, avec mes compliments, mes salutations empressées.

   Votre devoué,

   Hector Berlioz

Notes

Comettant, pp. 605ff. Later, on p. 613, he asks: "Why haven't the Americans sent us their *banjo?*"

18. Comettant, p. 613.
19. Allwood, p. 63. See also George Augustus Sala, *Paris Herself Again* (London, 1880), 2 vols.
20. See the *Rapport administratif sur l'exposition universelle de 1878 à Paris*, vol. 2, pp. 248–49.
21. See *Rapport*, vol. 2, pp. 240–44.
22. *Ibid.*, p. 412.
23. *Ibid.*, pp. 411–15.
24. *Ibid.*, p. 413.
25. Mandell, p. 14.
26. Allwood, p. 75.
27. *Ibid.*, p. 77.
28. Mandell, p. 19.
29. Allwood, p. 77.
30. *Ibid.*, p. 78.
31. See Paul Marguerite, "Le Sourire à l'Exposition," *L'Exposition à Paris de 1889*, 28 September 1889, p. 311.
32. See Charles Rearick, *Pleasures of the Belle Epoque: Entertainment and Festivity in Turn-of-the-Century France* (New Haven, 1985), p. 121. The Galerie des Machines covered nearly 15 acres.
33. This was the first exposition to recognize the use of electricity as a possible practical servant, not just as a curiosity. See Mandell, p. 21, and A. Morillon, "Les résultats de l'Exposition," *Correspondant*, vol. 157, no. 5, 10 December 1889, p. 801.
34. See Rearick, p. 134, where he quotes the Goncourts. Edmond says: "At bottom, it's too big, too immense, there are too many things and one's attention, diffused, attaches itself to nothing."
35. Théodore Dubois, César Franck, Garcin, Godard, Gounod, Guiraud, Joncières, Edouard Lalo, Lamoureux, Lecomte, Lenepveu, Massenet, Pessard, Rety, Reyer, and Saint-Saëns participated.
36. Diémer's concert may have been one of the first of his recitals devoted to early music.
37. Information about this competition of exotic music appears in issue 15 of *L'Exposition de Paris (1889) publiée avec la collaboration d'écrivains spéciaux.*
38. See issue 16, p. 126.
39. See issue 74, pp. 268–69.
40. Julien Tiersot, *Musiques Pittoresques: Promenades musicales à l'Exposition de 1889* (Paris, 1889), p. 4.
41. *Ibid.*, pp. 24ff.
42. *Ibid.*p. 52. See also *Le Ménestrel*, 21 July and 6 October 1889.
43. *Ibid.*, p. 75. He probably means the *Capriccio espagnol*.
44. Quoted in Edward Downes, *The New York Philharmonic Guide to the Symphony* (New York 1976) p. 757. The premier of the Capriccio espagnol took place on 31 October 1887 at the Imperial Russian Opera House, St. Petersburg. At the first rehearsal, players applauded after they concluded each section. The composer, touched by their obvious admiration, dedicated the work to them.
45. In Neuilly, Buffalo Bill and his troupe competed with the exposition. With his 200 cowboys, cowgirls and Indians, 150 horses and 20 buffaloes, Buffalo Bill offered a fascinating picture of the "Wild West." See Rearick, p. 130, and Tiersot, pp. 99, 101.
46. Tiersot, p. 116.
47. See Brian N. Morton, *Americans in Paris* (New York, 1986), pp. 72–73.
48. More and more of the lower classes came to the fairs as the century progressed. The number of visitors increased to 16 million in 1878, half again more than in 1867; 32 million in 1889, and more than 50 million in 1900. (Rearick, p. 89).
49. Rearick, p. 120.

50. *Ibid.*, p. 127. See also Alfred Picard, *L'Exposition de Paris 1889*, especially 12 October 1889.

51. Rearick, p. 139.

5. CAFÉS CONCERTS, CABARETS, AND MUSIC HALLS

1. Although it is dated, by far the most informative essay on the music in the café-concerts and cabarets appears in L. Rohozinski, *Cinquante Ans de Musique française, 1874–1925* (Paris, 1926), vol. 2, chapter 9, "La Chansonnette et la Musique au Café-Concert," pp. 227–70. See also Jules Bertaut, *Les Belles Nuits de Paris* (Paris, 1927), Bettina L. Knapp, "The Golden Age of the Chanson," *Yale French Studies*, vol. 32 (May 1964), pp. 82–98.

2. See Rohozinski, vol. 2, p. 227.

3. Quoted in Joanna Richardson, *La Vie parisienne, 1852–1870* (New York, 1971), p. 152.

4. Rohozinski, vol. 2, p. 245.

5. Lisa Appignanesi, *The Cabaret* (New York, 1976), p. 9.

6. François Caradec and Alain Weill, *Le Café-Concert* (Paris, 1980), p. 7.

7. See *ibid.*, pp. 11–12, for Berlioz's comments on Darcier.

8. *Ibid.*, pp. 12ff; see also the illustrations here.

9. *Ibid.*, pp. 14–15. The café-concerts had become so numerous that by the turn of the century there were an estimated 264 in Paris. See Charles Rearick, *Pleasures of the Belle Epoque* (New Haven, 1985), p. 83. Jules Claretie, Director of the Comédie-Française called them the "democratized theater," the theaters of the poor, according to André Chadbourne. See his *Les Cafés-Concerts* (Paris, 1889), p. 368.

10. The market for new songs was so great that Paris "consumed" twelve to fifteen thousand songs a year in the 1890s. See Rearick, p. 75. See also Bettina L. Knapp, "The Golden Age of the Chanson," *Yale French Studies*, vol. 32, (May 1964), pp. 82–98.

11. Rohozinski, p. 235.

12. *Ibid.*, pp. 234–35.

13. Appignanesi, p. 11.

14. See Appignanesi, p. 11; Rearick, p. 55. See also Jules Lévy, *Les Hydropathes* (Paris, 1928), pp. 5–15.

15. Appignanesi, p. 17. See also Rearick, p. 60.

16. See George Auriol, "Rudolphe Salis et les deux 'Chat Noir'" in *Mercure de France*, vol. 9 (1926), pp. 321ff.; Edmond Deschaumes, "Le Cabaret du Chat Noir," in *Revue encyclopédique*, 16 January 1897, pp. 43–45. Music at the Chat Noir was represented by Charles de Sivery, Verlaine's brother-in-law. See Philippe Jullian, *Montmartre*, trans. Anne Carter (New York, 1977), p. 74.

17. Appignanesi, p. 19; Jullian, p. 86. Jouy, like other members of the *Hydropathes* (see footnote 14), drank heavily, particularly the "green fairy" absinthe. He eventually died of it.

18. The journal *Chat Noir* had a run of fifteen years.

19. See Rearick, p. 58; Appignanesi, p. 19.

20. Appignanesi, p. 20.

21. *Ibid.*, pp. 21–23.

22. See Bettina L. Knapp, *Le Mirliton: A Novel Based on the Life of Aristide Bruant* (Paris, 1968); also Appignanesi, p. 26. Rearick comments that Bruant and Jouy "sang of prostitutes and pimps, rogues and felons, the hungry and the homeless suffering in the reign of the smug bourgeoisie; tenderness toward the poor mixed with venomous anti-Semitism and bitter scorn for capitalist exploiters and the clergy." See Rearick, p. 26.

23. Caradec and Weill, pp. 95ff.

24. Appignanesi, p. 28.

25. See Yvette Guilbert, *La Chanson de ma vie* (Paris, 1928) and *Autres temps, autres chants* (Paris, 1946).

26. Jacques-Charles, *Cents Ans de Music-Hall* (Geneva, 1956), pp. 94ff. See also Rearick, chapter 4, "The Music Halls: A New Democratic Culture?"
27. Rearick, p. 78; Caradec and Weill, pp. 108–9.
28. Jacques-Charles, p. 41.
29. *Ibid.*, pp. 97–104.
30. Caradec and Weill, p. 128. See also Paulus, *Trente Ans de café-concert* (Paris, n.d.).
31. For an interesting commentary on the public of the Folies-Bergère, see J. K. Huysmans, "Les Folies-Bergère en 1879," *Croquis parisiens* (Paris, 1880).
32. See Léon de Bercy, *Montmartre et ses chansons* (Paris, 1902). See also Philippe Jullian, *Montmartre*.
33. Jacques-Charles, p. 137. The largest music hall was the Casino de Paris in the Rue de Clichy, but Lautrec preferred Le Divan Japonais.
34. See Bettina Knapp and Myra Chipman, *That Was Yvette* (London, 1966), p. 70.
35. See Jacques-Charles, *Cents Ans de Music-Hall* (Geneva, 1956), p. 129. When the Germans occupied Paris in the early 1940s, Yvette Guilbert did not fare too well. Because of her marriage to Dr. Max Schiller, an American chemist who was also Jewish, the Nazis suspected that she, too, might be Jewish. Constantly harassed, their apartment "burglarized" by the Gestapo, the couple finally moved to Aix-en-Provence, where Yvette died on 2 February 1944.
36. *Ibid.*, pp. 150ff.

6. MUSIC AND ART

1. See *Lettres de Claude Debussy à son éditeur* (Paris, 1927); letters of August, n.d., 1903, 21 August 1903, 27 July 1905, and 7 January 1907, among others. A fine introductory article that surveys original graphic designs for printed music is James J. Fuld and Frances Barulich, "Harmonizing the Arts: Original Graphic Designs for Printed Music by World-Famous Artists," *Notes*, vol. 43, no 2 (December 1986), pp. 259–71.
2. See Romain Rolland, *Musicians of Today*, trans. Mary Blaiklock (New York, 1915), p. 254.
3. *Ibid.*, p. 253.
4. Poet Paul Verlaine (1844–1896) declared, "De la musique avant toute chose," in *Art poétique*. See "Paul Verlaine and Stéphane Mallarmé" in O. B. Hardison, Jr., ed., *Modern Continental Literary Criticism* (New York, 1962) 174–88.
5. For more information on the salons, see Alphonse Jacobs, ed., *Gustave Flaubert–George Sand Correspondance* (Paris, 1981). See p. 36 in the Flaubert chronology and p. 572 in the index of names. Princess Mathilde's name appears in many of the letters. See also the Goncourt Journals for more information on the period.
6. See T. J. Walsh, *Second Empire Opera: The Théâtre Lyrique, Paris, 1851–1870* (New York, 1981).
7. The nineteenth century also witnessed the rise of the bourgeoisie, many of whom would seek to imitate the nobility and start to purchase paintings, attend concerts, and, owing to increased literacy, read newspapers, journals, and books. See "Music, Patronage, and the Public" in Leon Plantinga, *Romantic Music* (New York, 1984) pp. 5ff.
8. See Rosaline Bacou, *Odilon Redon*, vol. 1 (Geneva, 1956), p. 243.
9. See E. Dujardin, "La Revue wagnérienne," *Revue musicale*, October 1923.
10. The letter is dated 17 February 1860. See Julien Tiersot, *Lettres françaises de Richard Wagner recueillies et présentées par J.T.* (Paris, 1935), pp. 198ff. See translation of complete letter on page xx.
11. See Emeric Fiser, *Le Symbole littéraire* (Paris, n.d.), part 2, *Présymbolisme de Wagner*.
12. See Théodore de Wyzewa, *Essai sur l'interpretation esthétique de Wagner en France* (Paris, 1934), p. 13.
13. See the account of the July 1869 visit of the Mendès couple and Villiers de

l'Isle-Adam to Wagner and Cosima at Tribschen in Elaine Brody, "La Famille Mendès: A Literary Link between Wagner and Debussy," *The Music Review*, vol. 33, no 3 (August 1972), pp. 177–89.

14. See Odilon Redon, *A Soi-même, Journal, 1867–1915* (Paris, 1922), p. 56; see the English translation, *To Myself, Notes on Life, Art, and Artists* by Mira Jacob and Jeanne L. Wasserman (New York, 1986).

15. See letter of 15 June 1894 to Ed Picard, cited in Bacou, *Redon*, p. 249.

16. See letters of 26 November 1903 and 5 February 1904 to A. Bonger, cited in Bacou, *Redon*, p. 250.

17. See Edward Lucie-Smith, *Henri Fantin-Latour* (New York, 1977), plate 20.

18. Jean Delville (1867–1953) often incorporated musical associations in his paintings. See also his "Orpheus" (1893), plate 79, in Robert Rosenblum and W. H. Janson, *19th-Century Art* (New York, 1984).

19. See Jacques-Emile Blanche, *Portraits of a Lifetime: The Late Victorian Era— The Edwardian Pageant, 1870–1914*, trans. Walter Clement (New York, 1938).

20. *Ibid.*, 304. Rebecca West in *1900* (New York, 1982), p. 101, writes that "in 1890 French portraiture had fallen into the hands of one Jacques-Emile Blanche, an engaging party who looked like a sheep, and he gives an idea of what his times were up to, more or less. If one looks at the collection of his portraits in the art gallery at Rouen, one will discern his findings. There they all are: the sages, the ones with spiritual difficulties, the ones that had chosen instead to have difficulties with Algerian youths, the ones who had both kinds of trouble, and all the rest of the people who moved in Paris as goldfish in a bowl."

21. Marcel Guicheteau, *Paul Serusier* (Paris, 1976), p. 41.

22. See Alfred H. Barr, Jr., "Cézanne, après les lettres de Marion à Morstatt," *Gazette des beaux-arts*, January 1937. Morstatt later became director of the Music School at Stuttgart. Marion became professor of zoology at the University of Marseilles and director of the Natural History Museum there.

23. See Georges Rivière, *Renoir et ses amis* (Paris, 1921), p. 71.

24. See Jean Renoir, *Renoir, My Father*, trans. Randolph and Dorothy Weaver (London, 1962), p. 170.

25. *Ibid.*, p. 169.

26. *Ibid.*, p. 172.

27. See John Rewald, *Georges Seurat* (New York, 1946), p. 59. See also G. Kahn, *Les Dessins de Georges Seurat, 1859–1891* (Paris, 1928), and D. Sutter, "Les Phénomènes de la vision," six articles published in *L'Art*, vol. 99 (1880).

28. Blanche, *Portraits*, p. 85. When French and English Wagnerites Theodore de Wyzéwa and H. S. Chamberlain opened a bookstore in the Chaussée d'Antin, they also had a picture gallery, where they showed the work of Seurat, Lautrec, Van Gogh, and Whistler.

29. See Maurice Denis, *Henri Lerolle et ses amis* (Paris, 1932), and Suzanne Barazzetti-Demoulin, *Maurice Denis* (Paris, 1945).

30. See Charles Oulmont, *Musique de l'amour: Ernest Chausson et la bande à Franck* (Paris, 1935), p. 94.

31. See Maurice Denis, *Journal*, vol. 1 (Paris, 1957), p. 132.

32. *Ibid.*, p. 224.

33. Denis, *Journal*, vol. 2, p. 109. See also Barazzetti-Demoulin, particularly the chapter "Maurice Denis et les musiciens."

34. Robert Descharnes and Jean-François Chabrun, *Auguste Rodin* (Paris, 1967), p. 62.

35. Judith Cladel. *Rodin: Sa Vie glorieuse, sa vie inconnue* (Paris, 1936), pp. 253ff.

36. Jacques de Caso and Patricia B. Sanders. *Rodin's Sculpture* (San Francisco, 1977), p. 307.

37. Auguste Rodin, *Art: Conversations with Paul Gsell*, trans. Jacques de Caso and Patricia B. Sanders (Berkeley, 1984), p. 70.

38. John L. Tancock. *The Sculpture of Auguste Rodin* (Philadelphia, 1976), p. 532.

39. Victor Frisch and Joseph T. Shipley. *Auguste Rodin: A Biography* (New York, 1939), p. 438.

40. Edward Lockspeiser, *Debussy: His Life and Mind*, vol. 2 (New York, 1965), p. 107, note 2. Apparently, the Rodin Museum in Paris has three busts of Mahler, in marble (listed as a head of Mozart, according to Lockspeiser), in bronze, and in plaster.

41. Robert McCameron, "Auguste Rodin: His Life and Work with a Consideration of the Proposed Rodin Room in the Metropolitan Museum of Art," *Town and Country*, 4 February 1911, p. 19.

42. See Carter Ratcliff, *John Singer Sargent* (New York, 1982), p. 57.

43. See Ethel Smyth, *What Happened Next* (London, 1940), and James Lomax and Richard Ormond, *John Singer Sargent and the Edwardian Age* (London, 1979), p. 74, and Richard Ormond, *John Singer Sargent* (London, 1970).

44. See David McKibbin, *Sargent's Boston* (Boston, 1956), p. 56.

45. See Sir George Henschel, *Musings and Memories of a Musician* (London, 1918), p. 333. Henschel was a conductor, composer, and singer who founded the London Symphony concerts in 1886.

46. See Denys Sutton, *Nocturne: The Art of James McNeill Whistler* (London, 1963), p. 55, and *James McNeill Whistler* (London, 1966).

47. See Edgar Allan Poe's *Essay on the Poetic Principle*, quoted in Sutton, *Norturne*, p. 56.

48. See James W. Lane, *Whistler* (New York, 1942), p. 20.

49. See Sutton, *Nocturne*, p. 140.

50. Debussy's *Reflets dans l'eau*, Ravel's *Jeux d'eau*, and de Séverac's *Sur l'étang* are but a few examples.

51. See, for example, Debussy, "The Snow is Dancing" from *Children's Corner*; "Des pas sur la neige," "Le Vent dans la plaine," and "Ce qu'a vu le vent d'ouest" from the *Préludes I*; and "Cloches à travers les feuilles" from *Images*, set 2.

52. See de Séverac's *En Languedoc* and *Cerdaña*.

53. See Debussy's *Children's Corner*, Ravel's *Ma Mère l'Oye* for piano 4-hands, Fauré's *Dolly*, also for 4-hands and de Séverac's *En vacances* and *Le Soldat de plomb*, another 4-hand piece.

54. See Debussy's "Minstrels" and "General Lavine" in the first and second book of *Préludes* respectively.

55. See Debussy's "Iberia" from the orchestral *Images*, and the piano pieces "La Soirée dans Grenade," "La Sérénade interrompue," and "La Puerta del vino," as well as Ravel's early "Habañera," his "Alborada del gracioso" from *Miroirs*, and the orchestral *Rapsodie espagnole*.

56. "Pour l'Egyptienne" is the fifth of the *Six épigraphes antiques*.

57. See Vuillermoz, *Claude Debussy* (Paris, 1920).

58. See Judith Cladel, *Aristide Maillol* (Paris, 1937), p. 117.

59. See Henri Frère, *Conversations de Maillol* (Paris, 1956).

60. *Ibid.*, p. 218.

61. *Ibid.*, p. 253.

62. See Alfred H. Barr, Jr., *Picasso: Fifty Years of His Art* (New York, 1946), p. 262, for note to p. 110; see also Fernande Olivier, *Picasso et ses amis* (Paris, 1933), p. 153.

63. See Pierre Cabanne, *Pablo Picasso: His Life and Times*, trans. Harold J. Salemson (New York, 1977), p. 187.

64. See Judith Cladel, *Rodin*, p. 254.

7. MUSIC AND LITERATURE

1. The music included the Overture to *Der fliegende Holländer*, the Prelude to *Tristan und Isolde*, and fragments of *Tannhäuser* and *Lohengrin*. See also Elaine Brody, "La Famille Mendès: A Literary Link between Wagner and Debussy," *The Music Review*, vol. 33, no. 3 (1972). Baudelaire's letter to Wagner, excerpts of which have been printed in various biographies of the composer, appears here complete, from Kahane and Wild, *Wagner et la France*, pp. 30–31.

Vendredi, 17 février 1860

Monsieur,

Je me suis toujours figuré que si accoutumé à la gloire que fut un grand artiste, il n'était pas insensible à un compliment sincère, quand ce compliment était comme un cri de reconnaissance, et enfin que ce cri pouvait avoir une valeur d'un genre singulier, quant il venait d'un français, c'est-à-dire d'un homme peu fait pour l'enthousiasme et né dans un pays où l'on ne s'entend guères plus à la poësie et à la peinture qu'à la musique. Avant tout, je veux vous dire que je vous dois la plus grande jouissance musicale que j'aie jamais éprouvée. Je suis d'un âge où on ne s'amuse plus guères à écrire aux hommes célèbres, et j'aurais hésité longtemps encore à vous témoigner par lettre mon admiration, si tous les jours mes yeux ne tombaient sur des articles indignes, ridicules, où on fait tous les efforts possibles pour diffamer votre génie. Vous n'êtes pas le premier homme, Monsieur, à l'occasion duquel j'ai eu à souffrir et à rougir de mon pays. Enfin l'indignation m'a poussé à vous témoigner ma reconnaissance; je me suit dit : Je veux être distingué de tous ces imbéciles.

La première fois que je suis allé aux Italiens, pour entendre vos ouvrages, j'étais assez mal disposé, et même, je l'avouerai, plein de mauvais préjugés; mais je suis excusable; j'ai été si souvent prétentieux. Par vous j'ai été vaincu tout de suite. Ce que j'ai éprouvé est indescriptible, et si vous daignez ne pas rire, j'essaierai de vous le traduire. D'abord il m'a semblé que je connaissais cette musique, et plus tard en y réfléchissant, j'ai compris d'où venait ce mirage; il me semblait que cette musique était la mienne, et je la reconnaissais comme tout homme reconnait les choses qu'il est destiné à aimer. Pour tout autre que pour un homme d'esprit, cette phrase scrait immensément ridicule, surtout écrite par quelqu'un qui, ccomme moi, ne sait pas la musique, et dont tout l'éducation se borne à avoir entendu (avec grand plaisir, il est vrai) quelques beaux moreaux de Weber et de Beethoven.

Ensuite le caractère qui m'a principalement frappé, ç'a été la grandeur. Cela représente le grand, et cela pousse au grand. J'ai retrouvé partout dans vos ouvrages la solennité des grands bruits, des grands aspects de la Nature, et la solennité des grandes passions de l'homme. On se sent tout de suit enlevé et subjugué. L'un des morceaux les plus étranges et qui m'ont apporté une sensation musicale nouvelle est celui qui est destiné à peindre une extase religieuse. L'effet produit part l'Introduction des invités et par la Fête nuptiale est immense. J'ai senti toute la majesté d'une vie plus large que la nôtre. Autre chose encore : j'ai éprouvé souvent un sentiment d'une nature assez bizarre, c'est l'orgueil et la jouissance de comprendre, de me laisser pénétrer, envahir, volupté vraiment sensuelle, et qui ressemble à celle de monter dans l'air ou de rouler sur la mer. Et la muqiue en même temps respirait quelquefois l'orgueil de la vie. Généralement ces profundes harmonies me paraissaient resembler à ces excitants qui accélèrent le pouls d l'imagination. Enfin, j'ai éprouvé aussi, et je vous supplie de ne pas rire, des sensations qui dérivent probablement de la tournure de mon esprit et de mes préoccupations fréquentes. Il y a partout quelque chose d'enlevé et d'enlevant, quelque chose aspirant à monter plus haut, quelque chose d'excessif et de superlatif. Par exemple, pour me servir de comparaisons empruntées à la peinture, je suppose devant mes yeux une vaste étendue d'un rouge sombre. Si ce rouge représent la passion, je le vois arriver graduellement, par toutes les transitions de rouge et de rose, à l'incandescence de la fournaise. Il semblerait difficile, impossible même d'arriver à quelque chose de plus ardent; et cependant une dernière fusée vient tracer un sillon plus blanc sur le blanc qui lui sert de fond. Ce sera, si vous voulez, le cri suprême de l'âme montée à son paroxysme.

J'avais commencé à écrive quelques méditations sur les morceaux de Tannhoeuser *et de* Lohengrin *que nous avons entendus; mais j'ai reconnu l'impossibilité de tout dire. Ainsi je pourrais continuer cette lettre interminablement. Si vous avez pu me lire, je vous en remercie. Il ne me reste plus qu'à ajouter que quelques mots. Depus le jour où j'ai entendu votre musique, je me dis sans cesse, surtout dans les mauvaises heures : Si au moins, je pouvais entendre ce soir un peu de Wagner! Il y a sans doute d'autres hommes faits comme moi. En somme vous avez dû être satisfait du public dont l'instinct a été bien supérieur à la mauvaise science des journalistes. Pourquoi ne donneriez-vous pas quelques concerts encore en y ajoutant des morceaux nouveaux? Vous nous avez fait connaître un avant-goût de jouissances nouvelles; avez-vous le droit de nous priver*

Notes

du rest?—Une fois encore, Monsieur, je vous remercie; vous m'avez rappelé à moi-même et au grand, dans de mauvaises heures.

Ch. Baudelaire.

Je n'ajoute pas mon adresse, parce que vous croiriez peut-être que j'ai quelque chose à vous demander.

2. See Ernest Newman, *The Life of Richard Wagner*, vol. 3 (New York, 1941), p. 9.

3. Balzac, for example, knew nothing about music; Théophile Gautier, although a writer and critic of musical events, was hardly very knowledgeable.

4. Newman, *loc. cit.*

5. On 10 May 1861, Baudelaire wrote to Liszt about Wagner. He dedicated his "Thyrse" from *Petits poèmes en prose* to the composer. Baudelaire had read Liszt's *The Gypsy in Music*, and Liszt interested him from the point of view of the material on gypsies and also because the virtuoso impressed him as a dandy. The interest was mutual. On 7 July, 1861, Liszt wrote to his daughter Blandine in Paris to send him two copies of Baudelaire's brochure on Wagner. When he had not received them, he wrote again on 27 July. See *Correspondance de Liszt et de sa fille, Madame Emile Ollivier*, ed. Daniel Ollivier (Paris, 1936), pp. 288–91.

6. See Jonathan Mayne, ed. *Baudelaire: The Painter of Modern Life and Other Essays* (New York, 1970), pp. 139–46.

7. See G. Servières, *Wagner jugé en France* (Paris, 1887), p. 57.

8. See Philip Ouston, *The Imagination of Maurice Barrès* (Toronto, 1974), p. 9.

9. *Ibid.*, p. 130.

10. *Ibid.*, p. 225.

11. See Barrès, *Mes Cahiers*, vol. 14, p. 133, cited in Ouston, p. 230.

12. See Paul Valéry, *Pièces sur l'art* (Paris, 1936), p. 51; see also R. Gibson, *Modern French Poets on Poetry* (Cambridge, 1961), p. 182.

13. Ouston, p. 233.

14. See M. Raimond, *La Crise du roman: Des Lendemains du naturalisme aux années vingt* (Paris, 1967), pp. 403–4.

15. See Edouard Schuré, "Baudelaire et le Wagnérisme à la *Revue des deux mondes* d'après un document inédit," *Bulletin Baudelairien*, vol. 16, no. 1 (Summer 1980), pp. 11–12; see also Maxime Leroy, *Les Premiers Amis français de Wagner* (Paris, 1925), particularly the chapter "Comment A. Gasperini, Léon Leroy, Baudelaire, Schuré sont devenus wagnériens."

16. See David J. Niederauer, ed., *Henri de Regnier: Lettres à A. Gide, 1891–1911* (Geneva, 1972), p. 35, letter of 25 August 1892.

17. See G. Jean-Aubry, ed., *Jules Laforgue: Lettres à un ami 1880–1886* (Paris, 1941).

18. See Laforgue's *Moralités légendaires*, ed. Daniel Grojnowski (Paris, 1980).

19. See Pierre Menanteau, *Tristan Klingsor*, (Paris, 1965); see also Lester J. Pronger, *La Poésie de Tristan Klingsor, 1890–1960* (Paris, 1965).

20. See François Coppée, *Oeuvres complètes*, ed. L. Hébert (Paris, 1892); (?) *Poésie*, vol. 3, 1888.

21. See Helen Trudgian, *L'Esthétique de J.-K. Huysmans* (Paris, 1934); see also Lucien Descaves, "Huysmans et Villiers de l'Isle-Adam," *Le Magazine littéraire*, 12 June 1930.

22. See Jean Chalon and Paul Bernard, eds., *Max Jacob, Lettres à Liane de Pougy* (Paris, 1980).

23. See Colette, *Oeuvres complètes*, ed. Claude Pichois with Robert Forbin (Paris, 1973).

24. Several of Séverac's letters are in the possession of the author. See Elaine Brody, "Un Choix de lettres de Séverac" in *Revue de musique des universitées canadiennes*, no. 6 (1985), pp. 284–92.

25. See Edward Lockspeiser, *Debussy: His Life and Mind*, vol. 1 (London, 1962), p. 191.

26. Lockspeiser, *loc. cit.*

27. *Ibid.*, p. 201.

28. *Ibid.*, p. 177. The comment, coming as it did before the infamous Dreyfus affair, highlights the prevalence of anti-Semitism.

29. See Linda Laurent with Andrée Tainsy, "Jane Bathori et le Théâtre du Vieux-Colombier, 1917–1919," *Revue de musicologie*, vol. 70, no. 2 (1984), pp. 229–57; see also the same author's New York University dissertation, *The Performer as Catalyst: The Role of the Singer Jane Bathori (1877–1970) in the Careers of Debussy, Ravel, Les Six, and Their Contemporaries in Paris, 1904–1926* (New York, 1982).

30. See Rollo Myers, *Ravel: Life and Works* (London, 1960), p. 125.

31. *Ibid.*, p. 34.

32. *Ibid.*, p. 31.

33. *Ibid.*, p. 203.

34. See James Harding, *Saint-Saëns and His Circle* (London, 1965), p. 118.

35. Harding, p. 88.

36. See James Harding, *Erik Satie* (New York, 1975), p. 52.

37. The dictionary definition of "Dada" is *cheval d'enfant*, or "hobby horse," but the tag was really chosen at random.

38. See Robert Orledge, *Gabriel Fauré* (London, 1979), p. 10.

39. Orledge, p. 18. According to Jann Pasler, in a paper presented at the 1986 American Musicological Society meeting in Cleveland, the following salons were the most significant:

Comtesse Greffulhe's, which featured Robert de Montesquiou, Proust, and Fauré from 1890 to the early years of the twentieth century.

Pierre Louÿs's where all young writers, particularly those involved in the *Revue Blanche*, mingled with Debussy; this salon existed at the same time as the Comtesse Greffulhe's.

Madame de Saint-Marceaux's, which boasted most of the celebrated musicians of the day: Messager, Reynaldo Hahn, d'Indy's students Ravel and de Séverac, along with Colette, her husband Willy, painters and sculptors, the Princesse de Polignac, Jules Lemaître, Pierre Louÿs, and d'Annunzio. This salon existed from about 1890 to 1914.

The Godebskis', which included Ravel, his friends the Apaches, Valéry, Gide, and painters Bonnard and Redon; this salon lasted from about 1900 to 1914.

Madeleine Lemaire's, where, at the beginning of the century, Proust, Hahn, Rodin, Degas, pianist Alfred Cortot, composers Inghelbrecht, Massenet, and Saint-Saëns, Isadora Duncan, Robert de Montesquiou, and the Comtesse Greffulhe were frequent visitors.

40. *Ibid.*, 42. Orledge quotes Lockspeiser's article on the songs in the *Monthly Musical Record* (1945), pp. 79–84.

41. *Ibid.*, p. 118.

42. *Ibid.*, p. 87.

43. *Ibid.*, p. 46.

44. Quoted in Noske, p. 88. The original is in Fernand Divoire, "Sous la musique, que faut-il mettre? De beaux vers, de mauvais, des vers libres, de la prose?" in *Musica* no. 101-102 (February-March 1911), pp. 38–40, 58–60.

Gaston Calmette of *Le Figaro*, invited Fauré to be music critic in 1903. Unlike many of his peers, Fauré felt that this was forced labor, sometimes a real torment. Conscientious as always, Fauré performed his duties in this role, but he was not happy doing so.

45. See Rollo Myers, *Chabrier and His Circle* (London, 1969), p. 144.

46. See Pierre Lalo, *De Rameau à Ravel* (Paris, 1947), p. 151.

47. See Jean-Pierre Barricelli and Leo Weinstein, *Ernest Chausson: The Composer's Life and Works* (Norman, Oklahoma, 1955), pp. 74, 131.

48. *Ibid.*, p. 64.

49. See Louis Reynaud, *L'Influence allemande en France au XVIIIe et au XIXe siècle* (Paris, 1922), pp. 274ff.

50. Quoted in Frits Noske, *French Song from Berlioz to Duparc*, trans. Rita Benton

Notes

(repr. New York, 1970), p. 72. De Musset's review appeared in the *Revue des deux mondes*, 4th ser., vol. 17, (1 January 1839), p. 111.

51. Barricelli and Weinstein, p. 72.

52. *Ibid.*, p. 192.

53. Painters included Albert Besnard, Eugene Carrière, Odilon Redon, Edouard Manet, Pierre-Auguste Renoir, Edgar Degas, the sculptor Auguste Rodin; writers, Stéphane Mallarmé, de Regnier, Henri Gauthier-Villars, Colette, André Gide, Camille Mauclar, and Maurice Bouchor; among musicians and performers, César Franck, Emmanuel Chabrier, Henri Duparc, Vincent d'Indy, Gabriel Fauré, conductor Camille Chevillard (Lamoureux's son-in-law and successor), Sylvio Lazzari, Raymond Bonheur, Guy Ropartz, Albéric Magnard, Charles Koechlin, Gustave Samazeuilh, Erik Satie, Charles Bordes, Claude Debussy, Paul Dukas, Eugène Ysaÿe, Jacques Thibaud, Armand Parent, and Alfred Cortot.

54. See Martin Cooper, "Massenet," *New Grove* (London, 1980) vol. 11, p. 801.

55. See Jules Massenet, *My Recollections*, trans. H. Villiers Barnett (repr. New York, 1970), p. 226.

56. *Ibid.*, p. 245.

57. See James Harding, *Massenet* (New York, 1970), p. 123.

58. Massenet, *Recollections*, p. 208.

59. *Ibid.*, p. 101.

60. *Ibid.*, p. 16.

61. *Ibid.*, p. 205.

62. Charles Koechlin and Florent Schmitt, a most prolific composer, were also his students, but they did not write operas.

63. Darius Milhaud, *Notes Without Music*, trans. Donald Evans, ed. Rollo H. Myers (New York, 1952, 1953), p. 252.

64. *Ibid.*, p. 247.

65. *Ibid.*, p. 56.

66. Milhaud, *loc. cit.*

67. See Christopher Palmer, "Milhaud" *New Grove* (London, 1980) vol. 12, p. 307.

68. Pierre Bernac, *Francis Poulenc: The Man and His Songs*, trans. Winifred Radford (New York, 1977), p. 38.

69. Quoted in Bernac, p. 39.

70. Bernac, *loc. cit.*

71. Henri Hell, *Francis Poulenc*, trans. Edward Lockspeiser (London, 1959), p. 81.

72. The Greek poet Jean Moréas (1856–1910), whose real name was Iannis Pappadiamantopoulos, first used this term to describe the movement in *Le Figaro* on 18 September 1886.

73. Besides the three writers already mentioned, Henri de Regnier, Jules Laforgue, Tristan Corbière, and Villiers de l'Isle-Adam also belonged to the group. They founded several reviews, one of which, *La Mercure de France*, still exists. Others include *Le Décadent*, *La Revue blanche*, *La Revue indépendante*, and *La Revue wagnérienne*. Mallarmé's poetry for this last journal was subject to considerable criticism because its density made it all but impenetrable to readers. The two foremost Symbolist critics were Marcel Schwob and Rémy de Gourmont; Huysmans's *A Rebours* is a good example of a Symbolist novel.

74. See Stéphane Mallarmé, "Poetry as Incantation," quoted in "Crisis in Poetry," in R. Ellmann and C. Feidelson, Jr., eds., *The Modern Tradition: Backgrounds of Modern Literature* (Oxford, 1965), pp. 111–12.

75. Rhené Ghil, *Traité du Verbe*, 2nd. ed. (Paris, 1889), cited in Suzanne Bernard, *Mallarmé et la Musique* (Paris, 1959), p. 16.

76. Anna Balakian, *The Symbolist Movement: A Critical Appraisal* (New York, 1977), p. 60.

77. Balakian, p. 63.

78. Balakian, p. 86.

79. Geneviève Mallarmé in *Nouvelle Revue française* (November 1926), p. 521, cited in Bernard.

80. Valéry, p. 82. See also note 12 above.

81. See Madame Louise Faure-Favier, *Souvenirs sur Guillaume Apollinaire* (Paris, 1945). At the "Journées Apollinaire" held in Stavelot in August 1965, the theme of the colloquium was "Apollinaire et la musique." See *Actes du colloque* (Stavelot, 1967).

82. See James R. Lawler, "Music in Apollinaire," *The Language of French Symbolism* (Princeton, 1969), p. 219.

83. See Apollinaire's letter to Martineau, published in *Le Divan*, March 1938.

84. Lawler, p. 223. Lawler contends that Apollinaire's recitation is reminiscent of the psalmody that he heard as a boy at the Collège de Saint-Charles in Monaco. He comes to this conclusion from something said by Max Jacob and cited in *Présence d'Apollinaire* (Paris, 1944).

85. Lawler, p. 228.

86. See G. Jean-Aubry "André Gide on Music," *Music and Letters*, vol. 22 (1941), pp. iii, 264.

87. Quoted in *ibid.*, p. 268. Gide made the remark in reply to an inquiry launched by the *Berliner Tageblatt* on the twenty-fifth anniversary of Wagner's death. He reproduced it many years later in his *Journal*.

88. Quoted in *ibid.*, p. 269, from the entry in the *Journal* of 31 July 1928, p. 887.

89. Quoted in Denise Mayer, *Marcel Proust et la musique*, special no. of *La Revue musicale* (1978), p. 51. Letter derives from Philip Kolb, ed., *Correspondance générale de Marcel Proust*, vol. 6, *Lettres à Madame Strauss*, letter 100, p. 189.

90. See Emile Bedriomo, *Proust-Wagner et la Coincidence des arts* (Paris, 1984).

91. Louis Gautier-Vignal, *Proust connu et inconnu* (Paris, 1976), pp. 73–74.

92. Gautier-Vignal, *loc. cit.*

93. Gautier-Vignal, p. 76.

94. Valéry, pp. 76–77.

95. See Paul Verlaine, "Art poétique," in O. B. Hardison, Jr., ed., *Modern Continental Literary Criticism* (New York, 1962), pp. 175–76.

96. See Maurice Marc LaBelle, *Alfred Jarry: Nihilism and the Theater of the Absurd* (New York, 1980), p. 89.

97. Valéry, p. 84.

98. See Mallarmé, "Poetry as Incantation" in note no. 74, p. 112 above.

99. See Aimé Patri, "Mallarmé et la musique du silence," *La Littérature française et la Musique*, special no. of *La Revue musicale* (1952), pp. 102–3.

100. See H. Bouiller, *Victor Segalen* (Paris, 1961), particularly Chapter 3, "Segalen et la Musique," pp. 110–126.

101. These ideas stem from Bouiller, *op. cit.*

102. See Philip Kolb, ed., *Correspondance: Marcel Proust*, vol. 1, 1880–1895 (Paris, 1970); letter 239 to Reynaldo Hahn, dated May (?) 1895, pp. 381–82.

103. *Correspondance: Marcel Proust*, vol. 5, 1905; letter 5, to Paul Grunebaum-Ballin, dated 6 January 1905, pp. 25–28.

104. Stéphane Mallarmé, "Music and Literature" in O. B. Hardison, Jr., ed., *Modern Continental Literary Criticism* (New York, 1962), p. 181.

105. *Correspondance: Marcel Proust*, vol. 2, 1896–1901; letter 309, to Saint-Saëns, dated 14 December 1895, p. 493.

106. Quoted in John Cruikshank, "French Literature Since 1870," in D. G. Charlton, ed., *France; A Companion to French Studies* (New York, 1972), p. 400.

107. Jean-Aubry, "André Gide on Music," *Music and Letters*, vol. 22 (1941), pp. iii, 276.

108. See Louis Emié, *Dialogues avec Max Jacob* (Paris, 1954), p. 74.

109. Quoted in Jean-Aubry, p. 268.

110. Jean-Aubry, *loc. cit.*

8. THE SPANIARDS IN PARIS

1. Singer Victoria de los Angeles, pianist Alicia de Larrocha, guitarist Andrés Segovia, cellist Pablo Casals, painter Pablo Picasso, and architect-sculptor Antonio Gaudì, along with Viñes, are among the better-known gifted Catalan artists.

Notes

2. G. Jean-Aubry, *French Music of Today*, trans. Edwin Evans (London, 1920), p. 218.

3. Julius Schulhoff (1825–1898), Czech pianist and composer, who lived in Paris and gave concerts under the patronage of Chopin, to whom he dedicated his first composition.

4. The numbers in parentheses refer to the particular arrondissement in Paris.

5. At that time, the exchange rate was five French francs to one American dollar. In 1784, it cost Thomas Jefferson twelve francs a month to rent a piano.

6. Marmontel, still alive when Viñes arrived in Paris, was a brilliant student of the legendary Pierre-Joseph Zimmerman. He succeeded Zimmerman at the Conservatoire in 1848 and retired in 1887, the year Viñes enrolled. Ernest Guiraud, a French composer and pedagogue, was born in New Orleans in 1837 and died in 1892 in Paris, where he had lived for most of his life. He wrote the recitatives to Bizet's *Carmen* and completed the orchestration of Offenbach's *Contes d'Hoffmann*. Among his students were Debussy, the theorist André Gédalge (1856–1926), and the American composer Charles Martin Loeffler (1861–1935). See Debussy's very interesting "Conversations with Ernest Guiraud," a record of which was made by Maurice Emmanuel. It appears in Edward Lockspeiser, *Debussy: His Life and Mind* (London, 1962) vol. 1, appendix B., pp. 204ff.

7. Composer-pedagogue Ambroise Thomas (1811–1896) held the directorship of the Conservatoire from 1871, when Auber died, until 1896. He was succeeded by Théodore Dubois (1896–1905) and then by Fauré (1905–1920).

8. Charles-Marie Widor (1844–1937), like Louis Vierne (1870–1937) was one of the foremost organists of the French organ school of the late nineteenth century. Vierne counted Nadia Boulanger (see Chapter 11) among his pupils.

9. Composer-violinist Benjamin Godard (1849–1895) was obliged to demonstrate the importance of ensemble work to his piano students in particular. Most of them preferred spending their time practicing the piano.

10. Albert Lavignac (1846–1916), French musicologist and pedagogue, is best known for his celebrated *Encyclopédie de la musique et dictionnaire du Conservatoire*, which he edited from 1913 until his death. His theoretical works and his book *La Voyage artistique à Bayreuth* (1897) provided him with considerable visibility. *Le Voyage* was translated into English in 1898 as *The Music Dramas of Richard Wagner*.

11. Auguste-Joseph Franchomme (1808–1884), a celebrated cellist, studied and taught at the Paris Conservatoire. An intimate of Chopin, he also organized chamber-music evenings in Paris along with Charles Hallé (1819–1895) and Alard (1815–1888).

12. Albéniz traveled often to Brussels, London, Madrid, and Barcelona; he was very much involved in the production of his operas *The Magic Opal* (1893), *Henry Clifford* (1895), and *Pepita Jiménez* (1896). The English titles of two of these operas derive from the fact that Albéniz had a British sponsor, banker Francis Burdett Money-Coutts.

13. It is important to remember that there were no telephones, and Viñes spent a lot of time going back and forth to different people's homes, leaving his calling card and hoping to find them at some point.

14. An excellent source for a diagram of the interior seating plan of the Opéra is Charles Nuitter, *Le Nouvel Opéra* (Paris, 1875). It includes the numbers of the boxes as well as the numbers of the individual seats in the orchestra and parterre. The boys, Maurice and Ricardo, sat in the third row, seats 188 and 190.

15. The move cost 13.50 francs!

16. Notice Viñes's incredible ability to remember precisely where the applause occurred, despite the tension that normally accompanies a performance.

17. French custom in this matter differs considerably from American tradition. Following the recent successful New York debut of a young French pianist, he phoned the author to ask whether or not it was appropriate to write a letter of thanks to his reviewer, who had praised him highly. After having been told it is not done in America, he replied that he had asked because it *is* done in Paris.

18. Thus it was Viñes who first called Ravel's attention to these prose poems by Louis (also called Aloysius) Bertrand (1807–1841). Bertrand wrote them in about

1830, and they were published posthumously, probably owing to Baudelaire's efforts, in 1842. Ravel wrote his three piano pieces of *Gaspard de la nuit* in 1908.

19. French baritone Victor Maurel (1848–1923) created the role of Iago in Verdi's *Otello* (Milan, 1887) and the title role in *Falstaff* (Milan, 1893).

20. Reported by Viñes in his journal.

21. See Elaine Brody, "Viñes in Paris: New Light on Twentieth-Century Performance Practice," *A Musical Offering: Essays in Honor of Martin Bernstein*, ed. by Edward H. Clinkscale and Claire Brook (New York, 1977), pp. 45–62.

22. See the review *S.I.M.* (Société Internationale de Musique) of 1 December 1913.

23. See Edgar Istel, "Isaac Albéniz," *The Musical Quarterly*, vol. 15 (1929), p. 143.

24. In a more formal vein, Jankélévitch comments: "Albéniz follows less the discursive order of development than the cumulative order of the great variation; his subject matter is not of the rhetorical-dialectical type, but much rather of the biological-biographical type. To plead like Cicero, to preach like Bourdaloue [a Jesuit priest of the seventeenth century], to hold forth like Victor Cousin [a philosopher of the nineteenth century]—there is the ideal of a music which aspires to both the profundity of the philosopher and the eloquence of the lawyer or preacher. . . . The music of Albéniz, like that of Rimsky-Korsakov, has no other ambition than that of narrating, of singing and of dancing: and in that it reveals a rhapsodic spirit." See the chapter on Albéniz in Vladimir Jankélévitch, *La Rhapsodie: Verve et improvisation musicale* (Paris, 1955), particularly p. 151.

25. Istel, p. 118.

26. See Pablo Casals and A. E. Kahn, *Joys and Sorrows* (London, 1970), p. 106.

27. *Ibid.*, p. 133.

28. See Suzanne Demarquez, *Manuel de Falla* (Philadelphia, 1968) p. 12.

29. Casals and Kahn, p. 95.

30. Demarquez, p. 34.

31. *Ibid.*, p. 48.

32. Albéniz reportedly said: "The French public presents [us with] a particular psychology; it is refined, eclectic in its tastes, sensitive to beauty and artistic emotion, generous and enthusiastic." Quoted in Jacqueline Kalfa, *Inspiration hispanique et écriture pianistique dans "Iberia" d'Isaac Albéniz*, musicology thesis at the Sorbonne (Paris, 1982), pp. 453–54.

9. THE RUSSIANS IN PARIS

1. Marcel Proust, *Remembrance of Things Past* (New York, 1932), vol. II, 544.

2. The following excerpt appeared in *The Musical Courrier, A Weekly Journal* on 12 June 1907, vol. LIV, no. 24, p. 9. Americans, too, were interested in the events in Paris. This report helps us to understand why.

> It is possibly no exaggeration to state that no place except this city is capable at any one time to bring in personal contact so many universal celebrities as one could see within a few days within the cirucmference of a small circle— say, the distance comprised in New York in the block from Broadway and 34th Street to the Waldorf—for they were all seen in that sized territory and among them were Nikisch, Chaliapine [sic], Godowsky and Mrs. Godowsky, Kubelik, Ysaye, Pugno, Carouso, Smirnov, Sarasate, Farrar, Raoul Gunsburg, Rimsky-Korsakov, Harold Bauer, Kreisler and Mrs. Kreisler, Blumenfeld (conductor at St. Petersburg), Kussewitzsky, Vance Thompson, Dazian, the friend of the late Maurice Grau, Sickesz and about a thousand more . . .

See also Alfredo Casella, *Music in My Time*, trans. and ed. by Spencer Norton (Norman, Oklahoma, 1955) 75ff.

3. Arnold L. Haskell, *Diaghilev: His Artistic and Private Life* (New York, 1935), p. 142.

4. See John J. O'Connor on "TV: Diaghilev on Cable Arts Channel" in *The New York Times*, 12 July 1982, C15. Balanchine, Tamara Geva, Alexandra Danilova and others describe their experiences with Diaghilev in a documentary shown on television's CBS Cable during the summer of 1982.

Notes

5. André Schaeffner, "Debussy et ses rapports avec la musique russe" in Pierre Souvtchinsky, ed. *La Musique russe* (Paris, 1953), pp. 95–138.

See also Andreas Liess, "Claude Debussy und die 'Fünf' " in *Neue Zeitschrift für Musik* CXXXCII/2 (Feb. 1967), p. 9ff; Roman Pelinski, "Musikexotismus um 1900: Claude Debussy" in *Weltkulturen und moderne Kunst*, ed. Siegfried Wichmann (München, 1972) p. 412–425.

6. Léon Vallas, *Vincent d'Indy: la jeunesse* (Paris, 1946), pp. 150–159.

See Liszt's letters to the Belgian Countess de Mercy-Argenteau in *Franz Liszts Briefe*, vol. II, pp. 371–2 and 375, letter of 24 October 1884 and 20 January 1885.

7. *France musicale*, juillet 1840, cited in Arthur Pougin *La Musique en Russie* (Paris, 1904), p. 14.

8. Hector Berlioz, *Les Soirées de l'orchestre*, deuxième edition (Paris, 1854), "Vingt et unième soirée," pp. 268ff. Berlioz, like Schumann, wrote glowingly of Alexei Lvov (1798–1870), a Russian violinist and composer, and author of the Russian national hymn under the Tsars. His comments may be found in *Les Soirées de l'orchestre*, in the same twenty-first evening. Oddly enough, another curious article on Lvov appeared in the *Revue et Gazette musicale* of 11 October 1840 by none other than Richard Wagner. Wagner did not visit Russia until 1863, but he may have heard Lvov in Leipzig.

9. Schaeffner, "Debussy et la musique russe" in Souvtchinsky, *op. cit.*, pp. 104ff.

See also report of an interview conducted by Henri Malherbe on "Russian Music and French Composers" in *Excelsior*, 9 March 1911.

10. Bibliothèque du Conservatoire de Paris: nos. 17844 to 17870; *Boris* is registered as no. 17866. This information appears in Schaeffner, *op. cit.*, p. 108, footnote 1.

11. Robert Godet in *En marge de Boris Godounof* (Paris, 1926), pp. 502–504, along with several other writers, has cited Saint-Saëns's copy of the score of *Boris Godounov*, which he loaned to the organist Jules de Brayer and which that gentleman left with Debussy, as the link between Debussy and Mussorgsky. It now seems that de Brayer could not have obtained the score before 1876, because Saint-Saëns, in Russia between December 1875 and January 1876, did not return until then. De Brayer's letter about *Boris* to Pierre d'Alheim, another Russophile whom we will meet later, claims incorrectly that he had the score in 1874. Schaeffner, p. 109.

Debussy entered the Paris Conservatoire in 1872, at the age of ten. By 1877, he was already using the library. He could well have stumbled upon the score of *Boris Godounov* shortly thereafter. If so, it would mean that the copy of the score he received from de Brayer was the second one available to him.

12. These concerts were presented on 9, 14, 21, and 27 September 1878.

13. Cui, whose father had been a soldier with Napoleon's army in Russia, became one of the more forceful promoters of the Franco-Russian musical alliance. The essays written for the *Revue et Gazette musicale* appeared as *La Musique en Russie* (Paris, 1880); the volume was dedicated to Franz Liszt.

14. A summary of this course, written by one Mlle Daubresse, appears in the *Courrier Musical* of 1902 in the issues of 15 April, 15 May, 1 and 15 June, 1 August and 1 October. Curiously, Maurice Emmanuel and Louis Laloy, both friends of Debussy, succeeded Bourgault-Ducoudray in his post as teacher of music history at the Conservatoire; both were entranced with the melodies of the East.

15. Edward Garden, *Balakirev: A Critical Study of His Life and Music* (London, 1967), p. 116.

16. James Harding, *Saint-Saëns and His Circle* (London, 1965), p. 142.

17. M. D. Calvocoressi and Gerald Abraham, *Masters of Russian Music* (New York, 1936), p. 440.

18. Edward Lockspeiser, "Debussy, Tchaikovsky et Mme von Meck" in *La Revue Musicale*, November 1935; also Lockspeiser's "Claude Debussy dans la Correspondance de Tchaikovsky et de Mme von Meck" in *La Revue Musicale*, October 1937.

19. This letter dates from 14 October 1880, when Debussy was eighteen.

See also Catherine Drinker-Bowen and Barbara von Meck, *Beloved Friend* (London, 1937).

315

In another letter to Mme von Meck (17 February 1883) Tchaikovsky writes: "In the modern French composers, you do not find that ugliness in which some of our composers indulge in the mistaken idea that originality consists in treading underfoot all previous traditions of beauty." Cited in Edward Lockspeiser, "Tchaikovsky the Man" in G. Abraham, ed. *Tchaikovsky: A Symposium* (London, 1945), p. 20.

See also VI. Féderov, "Cajkovskij et la France" in *Revue de Musicologie*, vol. LIV, no. 1 (1968) pp. 19–65.

20. Quoted in Pougin, *op. cit.*, p. 127.

This Rubinstein quote is similar to something Albert Einstein said in 1919, when awaiting experimental confirmation of his ideas on general relativity. "If my theory turns out to be correct, the Germans will hail me as a German, the French as a Swiss Jew. Should my theory be disproven, the Germans will call me a Swiss Jew, and the French will call me a German."

One sign of the times, in the 1880s, was a trend towards historical recitals. In 1885, Anton Rubinstein presented a series of seven historical concerts of piano music comprising 193 works by 31 different composers. He played these works both in St. Petersburg and in Moscow in the space of seven weeks. On the morrow of each public concert, he repeated the concert gratis for students at the respective conservatories. All works were played from memory.

21. Louis Laloy, *Claude Debussy* (Paris, 1909), p. 15.

22. Rimsky-Korsakov, *My Musical Life*, trans. Judah A. Joffe from the rev. 2nd ed. (New York, 1935), p. 192.

23. *Revue et gazette musicale*, 23 June 1878, p. 198; also Vallas, *op. cit.*, p. 19.

24. Paul Poujaud, another friend, had in his possession a copy of Borodin's songs on which Debussy had written in a French translation of the Russian text. Léon Vallas, *Claude Debussy et son temps* (Paris, 1932), p. 17.

25. Schaeffner, *op. cit.*, p. 117. See François Lesure, ed. "Correspondance de Claude Debussy et de Louis Laloy" in the special Debussy issue of the *Revue de musicologie* (July–December 1962).

26. Rimsky's *Sadko* was performed at the 1878 Exposition. It was also presented by Pasdeloup on 1 and 29 December 1878; on 1 February 1880, 19 February 1882 and 12 May 1883. At the performance of 19 February 1882, a concert devoted to Franco-Russian music, Ernest Guiraud's *Danse persane* was included among the French pieces. Inasmuch as Guiraud was Debussy's teacher at the Conservatoire, the younger composer may have attended this concert. Schaeffner, *op. cit.*, footnote 1, p. 118.

27. Schaeffner, *op. cit.*, footnote 2, p. 118.

28. Cui's review of Verdi's *Otello* today sounds rather amusing. "Il n'y a presque pas d'inspiration; on pouvait même dire presque pas de musique." He claims that Verdi has copied his Iago from Gounod and Boito's Mefistopheles!

29. I have translated and summarized most of the material. Occasionally, I have chosen to leave quotations in French, in order to capture the flavor of the original. "GM, 21 February 1889, p. 63, " for example, refers to the *Guide musical*, the issue of 21 February 1889, p. 63. Readers wishing a more detailed list, may consult Elaine Brody, "The Russians in Paris (1889–1914) " in *Russian and Soviet Music: Essays for Boris Schwarz*, ed. Malcolm H. Brown (Ann Arbor, 1984), pp. 157–191. This article also contains information on French music and musicians in Russia in a supplement prepared by Claudia Jensen under Elaine Brody's supervision.

30. He complains, however, of the misuse of the *leit-motif*, and uses that exact term. "In so many pseudo-Wagnerian works," he says, "the means is taken for the ends, the container for the contents."

31. We might do well to note here two significant historical events: first the enthusiastic French response to the visit of the Russian Admiral Avellan who, with his bearded soldiers, had anchored at Toulon in 1893; and second, the Parisian visit of Tsar Nicholas II and his Tsaritsa Alexandra in October 1896, an event that reassured the French they were no longer alone vis-a-vis the Germans.

32. Countess Louise de Mercy-Argenteau, who promoted Russian music and musicians particularly in Belgium, wrote a biography of César Cui in 1888.

33. Mitrofan Belaïev (1835–1904) came from a wealthy family in the timber business. After his father's death in 1888, Belaiev decided to enter the field of music publishing. He had his printing done in Leipzig. Actively promoting concerts of Russian music in St. Petersburg, he arranged for ten symphonic concerts and four chamber music recitals each season. Belaïev's editions proved vital in the development of Russia's national music. See M. Montagu Nathan, "Belaïev, Maecenas of Russian Music" in *The Musical Quarterly* (July, 1918), pp. 450–465.

34. Cui condemned Rubinstein and Tchaikovsky for imitating the Germans and not being sufficiently original. Ironically, Cui's own operatic subjects derived from Heine (*William Ratcliff*), Victor Hugo (*Angelo*), and Dumas (*Sarrasin*). He was against the customary repetition of text, closed musical forms and any kind of ensemble—very much à la Wagner. See Pougin, *op. cit.*, pp. 168–169.

35. See François Lesure, *Debussy on Music*, trans. Richard Langham Smith (New York, 1977), p. 21.

36. See Debussy's article on the *Nursery* songs in *Revue Blanche*, 1901. Quoted in Lesure, *op. cit.*, pp. 24–25.

37. See Alfred Bruneau's *Musiques de Russie et Musiciens de France* (Paris 1903).

38. See also Bruneau's *Music and Ballet* (London, 1933) and *Musical Criticism* (London, 1923).

39. Ravel and some friends, who called themselves the Apaches, adopted as their identifying motto, a tune from Borodin's Symphony in b minor. See Hans Stuckenschmidt's *Maurice Ravel* (New York, 1968), p. 55. Stuckenschmidt says that his compositions were affected by the nationalist Russian school, particularly Borodin. (Stuckenschmidt, *op. cit.*, p. 185.) See also his piano piece *A la manière de Borodine* (1913) and his orchestration of Mussorgsky's *Pictures at an Exhibition* (1922).

40. Gabriel Astruc was a French-Jewish music publisher and impresario who founded La Société Musicale to promote new music. He convinced the Countess Greffulhe to become its president. The Countess, daughter of Prince Caraman-Chimay, the Belgian foreign minister, was the original of Proust's Princesse de Guermantes. Astruc handled—or at least tried to manage—Diaghilev's financial affairs.

41. Arnold T. Schwab, *James Gibbons Huneker: Critic of the Seven Arts* (Stanford, 1963), p. 24.

42. The *Philadelphia Evening Bulletin*, 29 January 1878, p. 2.

43. James Gibbons Huneker, "A Musical Primitive: Modeste Moussorgsky," in *Forum* vol. LIII (February 1915), pp. 275ff.

44. Alfredo Casella, *Music in My Time* (Norman, Oklahoma, 1955). Casella was here referring to the year 1900. However, the stimulation of *la jeune école russe* had, for some time, been nourishing *une nouvelle jeune école française*. For still another contemporary account of the Russians in Paris, see *Les Ecrits de Paul Dukas* (Paris, 1948) pp. 129ff. His piece of October 1893 proves most enlightening.

10. THE LEGACY OF IDA RUBINSTEIN

1. Much of the material concerning Rubinstein's origins, her early years, and her subsequent rivalry with Diaghilev derives from Michael de Cossart's fine article "Ida Rubinstein and Diaghilev: A One-Sided Rivalry," *Dance Research*, vol. 1, no. 2 (Autumn 1983). See also Louis Thomas, "Le Peintre Bakst parle de Madame Ida Rubinstein," *Revue critique des idées et des livres*, no. 221 (January 1924), pp. 87–104.

2. See Richard Buckle, *Diaghilev* (New York, 1979), p. 128.

3. De Cossart reports the completion of his book in a letter to the author dated 2 January 1985.

4. Among the books I consulted are the following:

Alexandre, Arsène. *The Decorative Art of Léon Bakst*, with notes on the ballets by Jean Cocteau. Translated by Harry Melvill. London, 1913; repr. New York, 1972.

Buckle, Richard. *Diaghilev*. New York, 1979.

———, *Nijinsky*. New York, 1971.

Fokine, Michel. *Memoirs of a Ballet Master*. London, 1961.
Grigoriev, Serge. *The Diaghilev Ballet, 1909–1929*. London, 1960.
Kochno, Boris. *Diaghilev and the Ballets Russes*. Translated by Adrienne Foulke. New York, 1970.
Krasovskaya, Vera. *Nijinsky*, translated by John E. Bowlt. New York, 1979.
Levinson, André. *Bakst: The Story of the Artist's Life*. London, 1923; repr. New York, 1971.
Lieven, Prince Peter. *The Birth of the Ballets Russes*. London, 1936.
Lifar, Serge. *Serge Diaghilev: His Life, His Work, His Legend*. New York, 1940.
Percival, John. *The World of Diaghilev*. London, 1971.
Propert, W. A. *The Russian Ballet in Western Europe, 1909–1920*. New York, 1972.

5. The Alexander Theater in St. Petersburg was the equivalent of the Comédie-Française in Paris.

6. See De Cossart, p. 4 (cited in note 1).

7. *Ibid.*

8. Alexandre Benois, *Reminiscences of the Russian Ballet* (London, 1941), p. 296.

9. Prince Peter Lieven, *The Birth of the Ballets Russes* (London, 1936), p. 53. See also Boris Kochno, *Diaghilev and the Ballets Russes* (New York, 1970), p. 12, and Alexandre Benois, *Memoirs*, vol. 2, trans. Moura Budberg (London, 1964), p. 243.

10. Benois, p. 296.

11. Lieven, p. 97.

12. Jean Cocteau, "Notes on the Ballets" in Arsène Alexandre, *The Decorative Art of Léon Bakst* (London, 1913), p. 28. See also Cocteau's comments as cited in Kochno, pp. 36–37.

Alexandre Benois, p. 241, says: "Of all the press notices, the one that pleased me most was the one by Robert de Montesquiou. He did not miss a single performance. But he showed an even greater admiration for Ida Rubinstein, who drove all Paris crazy and put even Pavlova in the shade. The latter, so it was said, was so vexed that she refused to take part in Diaghilev's next season. It was not, however, to her dancing that Ida owed her triumph; she did not dance, in fact she walked. But how she walked, with what a regal bearing, with what beauty of movement."

13. Michel Fokine, *Memoirs of a Ballet Master* (London, 1961), p. 155. Jacques-Emile Blanche painted a large portrait of Rubinstein lying on a couch dressed in her *Shéhérazade* costume. And a Moscow friend, the painter Serov, did a portrait of her, also on a couch but in the nude. Oddly enough, she posed for these portraits in a building in the Boulevard des Invalides that had once been a monastery. See Lieven, p. 119.

14. Levinson, *Bakst: The Story of the Artist's Life* (New York, 1971), p. 144.

15. The material on d'Annunzio derives from Giovanni Gullace, *Gabriele d'Annunzio in France: A Study in Cultural Relations* (Syracuse, 1966), pp. 84–90. See also Edward Lockspeiser, *Debussy: His Life and Mind* (London, 1965), vol. 2, pp. 158–67; *Le Martyre de Saint-Sébastien. De La Création en 1911 à la reprise à l'Opéra en 1957*, a special issue of *La Revue musicale* (1957); Robert Orledge, *Debussy and the Theatre*, (Cambridge, England, 1982); Guy Tosi, ed., *Debussy et d'Annunzio, correspondance inédite* (Paris, 1948).

16. *The Golden Legend* is a popular collection of saints' lives written in the thirteenth century by Jacobus de Voragine; it was originally entitled *Legenda sanctorum*.

17. "Gabriele d'Annunzio possède un prodigieux don verbal. Son vocabulaire français n'est pas moins riche que son vocabulaire italien." Quoted in Gullace, p. 86.

18. "Les lettres françaises comptent un grand poète de plus." Quoted in Gullace, p. 86. Marcel Proust, too, commended d'Annunzio for his command of the French language, but, curiously, he admits to spending most of his time admiring the beautiful legs of La Rubinstein. See Lockspeiser, *Debussy*, p. 165. See also Philip Kolb, ed., *Marcel Proust: Lettres à Reynaldo Hahn*, (Paris, 1956), p. 206, letter 131, 23 May 1911, in which he gives his impressions of *Le Martyre*. See also Philip Kolb, ed., *Marcel Proust: Correspondance*, vol. 1, p. 231. Another unusual account of *Le Martyre* appears in Marguerite Long, *Au Piano avec Claude Debussy* (Paris, 1960), pp. 155–

69. It seems that Rubinstein had presented Madame Long with a gift of several letters that d'Annunzio had written to her at the time of the creation of *Le Martyre*.

19. See Debussy's letter quoted in Lockspeiser, *Debussy*, p. 153.

20. See d'Annunzio's letter to Debussy, also in Lockspeiser, *ibid.*, p. 158.

21. Debussy wrote from the Hotel Krantz in the Austrian capital. See his letter of 30 November 1910, also quoted in Lockspeiser, *Debussy*, p. 159.

22. See Gullace, p. 87. Gabriel Astruc, a Jewish impresario of Central European origin (although he bears a well-known Sephardic name), built the Théâtre des Champs-Elysées in 1913. He dedicated it "to the glory of Bourdelle [who executed reliefs for the Theater] and to Debussy." See Lockspeiser, *Debussy*, p. 267. A festival of French music, conducted by Debussy and others, opened the Theater; yet Astruc was regarded as sufficiently cosmopolitan in his tastes for the Theater to be dubbed *Astruckisches Musikhaus*.

23. Debussy really created both Maud Allan's ballet *Khamma* and d'Annunzio's *Saint-Sébastien* as the result of a dire need for funds to support his new wife and child. His daughter Chou Chou was born in 1905; he married her mother Emma Bardac in 1909. See Orledge, pp. 128ff.

24. See Lockspeiser, *Debussy*, p. 164, note 1.

25. Diaghilev, always terribly jealous, fought with all his intimates over their attention to or work for others. He particularly resented Rubinstein, who had started her own troupe in 1915 and who, because of her financial reserves, could engage any artist or composer she fancied.

26. See Boris de Schloezer, "Le Martyre de Saint-Sébastien à l'Opéra," *Nouvelle Revue française*, 2 September 1922, p. 245.

27. Gullace, p. 87.

28. *Ibid.*, p. 91.

29. A curious commentary on Rubinstein and this ballet appears in Ferruccio Busoni, *Letters to His Wife*, trans. Rosamond Ley (London, 1938), p. 224. In a letter from Paris dated 23 June 1913, Busoni writes:

Now I am going to the Châtelet, to Pisanelle, or "la mort parfumée." I shall see Mlle Rubinstein, of whom it is said by one that she cannot speak but can dance; by another that she has a beautiful body, but cannot dance; by a third, that her body is not womanly, therefore not beautiful. She is just like St. Sebastian, pierced with arrows by all.

30. Lockspeiser, *Debussy*, p. 163.

31. Saint-Georges de Bouhélier (pseudonym of Stéphane-Georges de Bouhélier-Lepelletier, 1889–1942) was a poet and dramatist whose verse promoted ideals of universal brotherhood and indicated a resentment of social injustice.

32. For Paul Valéry and *Amphion*, see Huguette Laurenti, *Paul Valéry et le Théâtre* (Paris, 1973), pp. 456ff.

33. Marcel Delannoy, *Honegger* (Paris, 1953), p. 132.

34. Willy Tappolet, *Arthur Honegger* (Zurich, 1954), p. 140.

35. Vera Stravinsky and Robert Craft, *Stravinsky in Pictures and Documents* (New York, 1978), p. 285.

36. *Ibid.*, p. 286.

37. *Ibid.*

38. *Ibid.*, p. 315.

39. Harry Kessler (1868–1937) was an art patron and book publisher, diplomat and cosmopolitan, nobleman and radical democrat. Raised trilingually in France, Germany, and England, he befriended many of the foremost artists of his time. At his Cranach Press in Weimar, Kessler published the works of Aristide Maillol, George Grosz, Eric Gill, André Gide, Hugo von Hofmannsthal, and Paul Valéry. He knew Shaw, Cocteau, and Brecht, Hauptmann, Diaghilev, and Einstein. He hated the Nazis and left Berlin for Paris in 1933. His diaries are among the richest documents covering Europe in the 1920s. See *In the Twenties: The Diaries of Harry Kessler*, trans. Charles Kessler (New York, 1971), p. 450.

40. A musical excerpt from *Persèphone*, with a dedication "Pour vous, Ida Svovna, ce 'Chant du merle', votre I Str 27 oct 33," brought 150,000 French fancs in an auction at the Drouot on 3 July 1985.

41. The complete account of Ravel, Rubinstein, and the creation of the *Boléro* appears in Joaquín Nin's contribution to a special issue of *La Revue musicale, Hommage à Maurice Ravel* (December 1938), pp. 211–13. All cited quotations appear in this article, entitled "Comment est né le *Boléro* de Ravel". See also Arbie Orenstein, *Ravel, Man and Musician* (New York, 1975), pp. 98–99, and Hélène Jourdan-Morhange, *Ravel et Nous: L'Homme, L'Ami, Le Musicien* (Geneva, 1945), pp. 163ff.

42. Orenstein, p. 103.

43. R. Chalupt and M. Gerar, ed., *Ravel au miroir de ses lettres* (Paris, 1956), p. 243.

44. Keith Lester, "Rubinstein Revisited," *Dance Research*, vol. 1, no. 2 (Autumn 1983), p. 22. See also Philippe Jullian, *Prince of Aesthetes: Count Robert de Montesquiou 1855–1921*, trans. John Haylock and Francis King (New York, 1965), pp. 222–28.

45. See Thomas (cited in note 1), p. 103. See also, for a more recent reminiscence of Ida Rubinstein, Diana Vreeland, *D.V.*, eds. George Plimpton and Christopher Hemphill (New York, 1985), pp. 22–23. For this last reference, I am indebted to Asya Berger.

11. THE AMERICANS IN PARIS

1. Van Wyck Brooks, *The Confident Years: 1885–1915* (New York, 1952), p. 3.

2. Christopher Campos, *The View of France from Arnold to Bloomsbury* (London and New York, 1965), p. 108.

3. *Ibid.*, pp. 117–18.

4. Justin Kaplan, *Mr. Clemens and Mark Twain: A Biography* (New York, 1966), p. 222.

5. See Marcia Wilson Lebow, *A Systematic Examination of the "Journal of Music and Art" Edited by John Sullivan Dwight, 1852–1881, Boston, Massachusetts* (Ph.D. diss., UCLA, 1969). For French criticism and French literary theory in American journals see Howard Mumford Jones, *The Age of Energy, Varietes of American Experience 1865–1915* (New York, 1970), pp. 220 ff.

6. Arthur Foote, "A Bostonian Remembers," *The Musical Quarterly*, 23 (1937), pp. 37 ff.

7. W.S.B. Mathews, *100 Years of Music in America* (Chicago, 1889), p. 169.

8. Harold Bauer, "The Paris Conservatoire: Some Reminiscences," *The Musical Quarterly*, 33 (1947), pp. 535–40.

9. Isidor Philipp, "The French National Conservatory of Music," *The Musical Quarterly*, 4 (1920), pp. 214–26.

10. Oscar Sonneck, *A Survey of Music in America* (New York, 1913; repr. New York, 1969), p. 139.

11. E. B. Washburne, *Recollections of a Minister of France* (New York, 1889), p. 300.

12. Harold Earle Johnson, *Operas on American Subjects* (New York, 1964), pp. 83–94.

13. S. C. de Soissons, *A Parisian in America* (Boston, 1896), p. 187.

14. *Ibid.*, p. 186.

15. Albert Bolles, *Industrial History of the United States*, 3rd. ed. (Norwich, Conn., 1881; repr., New York, 1966), p. 537.

16. William Peirce Randel, *Centennial, American Life in 1876*, (Philadelphia, 1969), p. 345.

17. Albert Lavignac, *Music and Musicians*, trans. H. E. Krehbiel (New York, 1899), p. 491.

18. Oscar Thompson, *The American Singer* (New York, 1937; repr., New York, 1969), pp. 185–87.

19. Homer Norris, *Practical Harmony on a French Basis* (Boston, 1894), p. iii.

20. A. M. Schlesinger, *The Rise of the City 1878–1898* (New York, 1933), p. 211.

21. See John Henry Mueller, *The American Symphony Orchestra, A Social History*

of Musical Taste (Bloomington, Ind., 1951), pp. 121, 262 and *passim*; also Rose Fay Thomas, *Memoirs of Theodore Thomas* (New York, 1911; repr., Freeport, N.Y., 1971), p. 404.

22. *Musical America* (Nov. 25, 1905), p. 5.

23. *Musical America* (Nov. 18, 1905), p. 9.

24. A. Ysaÿe and Bertram Ratcliffe, *Ysaÿe, His Life, Work and Influence* (London, 1947), pp. 75–76.

25. H.E. Krehbiel, *Review of the New York Musical Season*, 2, 1886–87 (New York, 1887), p. 116. He was on the jury for musical instruments at the 1900 Paris Exhibition and received the Croix de Légion d'Honneur in 1901.

26. During World War I, she remained in New York and taught at the Mannes School. After the war, determined to promote what she described as the "interpenetration of the arts," she opened a school of her own at New York's Hotel Majestic on 72nd Street and Central Park West.

27. See Elaine Brody, "Letters from Judith Gautier to Chalmers Clifton" *The French Review*, vol. 58, no. 5 (April 1985).

28. Walter R. Spalding, *Music at Harvard* (New York, 1935), pp. 100–1.

29. Virgil Thomson, *Virgil Thomson* (New York, 1966), p. 51.

30. Leonie Rosenstiel, *Nadia Boulanger, A Life in Music* (New York, 1982), p. 139.

31. *Ibid.*, p. 137.

32. As early as 1915, Lili Boulanger, Nadia's younger sister, whose illness and untimely death cut short what promised to be a remarkable musical career, had, with Nadia, formed the Comité Franco Américain du Conservatoire National de Musique et Déclamation under the patronage of American architect Whitney Warren. The organization listed two groups on its letterhead: an honorary committee composed of Saint-Saëns, Fauré, Dubois, Emile Paladilhe, Gustave Charpentier, Charles Widor, and Paul Vidal, and an active committee of the group's two vice-presidents, Widor and Vidal, and their treasurer Blair Fairchild, an American diplomat-composer. Nadia and Lili were the only women in the organization, and they were among the most active members. Money was sent to Fairchild; letters of inquiry, clothing, and food packages were directed to the Boulangers. See Rosenstiel, pp. 128, 136.

33. See *The New York Times*, 5 April 1986, p. 14.

34. See Michael Fanning, ed. *Paris Notebook, 1921* (Baton Rouge, Louisiana 1976).

35. Quoted in William Saroyan's review of the Fanning book in *The New York Times*, 15 August 1976.

36. Brian N. Morton, *Americans in Paris* (New York, 1986), pp. 79–80.

37. Later, the Copland-Sessions Concerts did likewise from 1928 to 1931. See Carol J. Oja, "The Copland-Sessions Concerts and Their Reception in the Contemporary Press," *The Musical Quarterly*, vol. 45, no. 2, pp. 212–29.

38. For the Copland quotation on Boulanger, see George Wickes, *Americans in Paris* (New York, 1969), p. 197.

39. Morton, p. 14.

40. *Ibid.*, p. 198.

41. Rosenstiel, p. 412.

42. See The *New York Times Book Review*, 23 May 1982, p. 1.

43. *Loc. cit.*

44. See Virgil Thomson, "The Greatest Music Teacher—at 75," *The New York Times Magazine*, 4 February 1962, p. 24; see also Aaron Copland, "Copland Salutes Boulanger" in *The New York Times*, 11 September 1977.

45. See Nigel Gosling, *The Adventurous World of Paris 1900–1914* (New York, 1978); see also Charles Rearick, *Pleasures of the Belle Epoque* (New Haven, 1985), pp. 132 and 189. See Clare de Morinni, "Loïe Fuller, the Fairy of Light," *Dance Index*, vol. 1, no. 3 (March 1942), pp. 42ff; also *Loïe Fuller, Fifteen Years in a Dancer's Life*, Introduction by Anatole France in *Dance Horizons* (New York repr. of 1913 first edition), p. 44.

46. See Frank Kermode, "Poet and Dancer before Diaghilev," *What to Dance?* ed. Copeland and Cohen (New York, 1983), p. 153.

47. *Ibid.*, p. 152.

48. Kermode, p. 155.

49. Morton, p. 36.
50. See the review of Lynn Haney's biography of Josephine Baker, *Naked at the Feast*, by James R. Mellow in *The New York Times Book Review* of 29 March 1981.
51. Morton, p. 86.
52. *Ibid.*, pp. 76, 125.
53. See Hugh Ford, ed. *The Left Bank Revisited: Selections from the Paris Tribune 1917–1934* (University Park, Pa., 1972), p. 213.
54. Ford, *loc. cit.*
55. Ford, p. 220.
56. "Transatlantic" is the name of one of the little magazines that Ford Madox Ford edited.
57. Quoted in David Ewen, *George Gershwin, His Journey to Greatness* (Englewood Cliffs, New Jersey, 1970), p. 131. In another biography of Gershwin by Edward Jablonski and Lawrence D. Stewart, *The Gershwin Years*, 2nd ed. (New York, 1973), Ira Gershwin's account of the first performance of the *Rhapsody in Blue* with the Pasdeloup Orchestra conducted by Rhené-Baton deserves to be quoted here. It comes from Ira Gershwin's journal.

> I alternately giggled and squirmed during this performance. It was at times almost unbelievably bad. The solo part had evidently proved too hard for M. Wiener [probably Jean Wiener], the premier soloist, so he got an assistant to oompah. Some of the fast tempi were taken at a funereal pace, and the rhythms were terrible in spots. A banjo played the same chord almost all through the piece. The middle theme couldn't be spoiled, of course, and came like a violet ray on a bald spot. And yet I realized that since probably 95% of the audience had never heard it before they might take the occasional sour notes as a true reading and find it all interesting. Sure enough, at its conclusion that (sic) was real spontaneous applause all over the house. (Jablonski, p. 133.)

58. Ford, p. 214.
59. Irwin Shaw and Ronald Searle, *Paris! Paris!* (New York, 1977), p. 3.

12. LES VINGT

1. The material for this chapter derives principally from Madeleine Octave Maus's *Trente Années de lutte pour l'art, 1884–1914* (Brussels, 1926). Two other sources are Albert Vander Linden's *Octave Maus et la vie musicale belge, 1875–1914* (Brussels, 1950), particularly for information about Maus, and *Lettres de Vincent d'Indy à Octave Maus*, annotated by Albert Vander Linden, a bound offprint from the *Revue belge de musicologie*, vol. 15 (1961), fasc. 1-4. For further information, see also E. Evenepoel, *Le wagnérisme hors d'Allemagne* (Paris and Brussels, 1891), Ch. Oulmont, *Musique de l'amour* (Paris, Brussels, n.d.) 2 vols., and C. Mauclair, *Histoire de la musique européenne, 1850–1914* (Paris, 1914).

Several years ago, the Brooklyn Museum featured a show of the work of these fin-de-siècle artists in Belgium. Grace Glueck, in the *New York Times* of 25 April 1980, commented: "The mystical Symbolist movement flourished there, Art Nouveau permeated the decorative arts, and the Pointillist theories of Georges Seurat, little known in his native Paris, were adopted by avid followers after showings of his work in Brussels in the late 1880s." She continued: "Les Vingt and La Libre Esthétique were by no means doctrinaire. Artists of every stripe belonged, and an even wider variety of artists were annually invited to the group exhibitions." The museum published an excellent catalogue, with essays on Les Vingt, Seurat, the Symbolists, and other topics.

Selected Bibliography

Abraham, Gerald, ed. *Tchaikovsky, A Symposium*. London: 1945.
Ackere, Jules van. *L'Âge d'or de la musique française 1870–1950*. Paris: 1966.
Aguettant, Louis. *La Musique de piano des origines à Ravel*. Paris: 1954.
Alldritt, Keith. *Eliot's "Four Quartets": Poetry as Chamber Music*. London and Totowa, N.J.: 1978.
Allwood, John. *The Great Exhibitions*. London: 1977.
Anderson, David L., ed. and comp. *Symbolism: A Bibliography of Symbolism as an International and Multi-Disciplinary Movement*. New York: 1975.
Andrieux, Françoise. *Gustave Charpentier: Letters inédites à ses parents: la vie quotidienne d'un élève du Conservatoire 1879–1887*. Paris: 1984.
Antoine, A. P. *Antoine, père et fils*. Paris: 1962.
Appia, Adolphe. *Music and the Art of the Theatre*. Translated by Robert Corrigan and Mary Douglas Dirks, foreword by Lee Simonson, edited by Barnard Hewitt. Coral Gables, Fla.: 1962.
Appignanesi, Lisa. *The Cabaret*. New York: 1976.
Applebaum, Stanley, ed. and trans. *French Satirical Drawings from "L'Assiette au Beurre."* New York: 1978.
Arnoult, Léon. *Les Grands imprécistes du 19e siècle: Turner, Wagner, Corot*. Paris: 1930.
Arntzen, E., and Rainwater, R. *Guide to the Literature of Art History*. Chicago: 1980.
Arsène, Alexandre. *The Decorative Art of Léon Bakst*. Translated by Harry Melvill. London: 1913. Reprint, New York: 1972.
Austin, William W. *Music in the 20th Century From Debussy Through Stravinsky*. New York: 1966.
Axsom, Richard H. *"Parade": Cubism as Theater*. Ann Arbor, Mich.: 1974.

Bablet, Denis. *Esthétique générale du décor de théâtre de 1870 à 1914*. Reprint, Paris: 1975
——— *The Revolutions of Stage Design in the 20th Century*. Original lithographs by Joan Miró; book design by Jacques Dopagne. Paris and New York: ca. 1977.
Bacou, Rosaline. *Odilon Redon*. Geneva: 1956.
Bailbé, Joseph-Marc. *Le Roman et la musique en France sous la monarchie de juillet*. Paris: 1969.
Bailly, E. *Le Pittoresque musical á l'Exposition*. Paris: 1900.
Balakian, Anna. *The Symbolist Movement: A Critical Appraisal*. New York: 1977.
——— *The Symbolist Movement in the Literature of European Languages*. Budapest: 1982.
Baldick, Robert, ed. and trans. *Pages from the Goncourt Journal*. Reprint, Oxford: 1978.
Barazzetti-Demoulin, Suzanne. *Maurice Denis*. Paris: 1945.
Barnes, Julian. *Flaubert's Parrot*. New York: 1984.
Barr, Alfred H., Jr. *Picasso: Fifty Years of His Art*. New York: 1946.
Barrès, Maurice. *Mes Cahiers*. Edited by Philippe Barrès, 14 vols. Paris: 1929–[57].

Barricelli, Jean Pierre, and Leo Weinstein. *Ernest Chausson: The Composer's Life and Works*. Norman, Okla.: 1955.
Barthes, Roland. *The Eiffel Tower and Other Mythologies*. Translated by Richard Howard. New York: 1979.
Barzun, Jacques. *Berlioz and the Romantic Century*. Boston: 1950.
——— *Darwin, Marx, Wagner: Critique of a Heritage*. Boston: 1941.
Baumann, Emil. *Les Grandes Formes de la musique. L'Oeuvre de Camille Saint-Saëns*. 2 ed. Paris: 1905.
Beckson, Karl, ed. *The Memoirs of Arthur Symons: Life and Art in the 1890s*. University Park, Pa.: 1977.
Bedriomo, Emile. *Proust-Wagner et la coïncidence des arts*. Paris: 1984.
Bellaigue, Camille. *Notes brèves, première série*. Paris: 1911.
——— *Notes brèves, deuxième série*. Paris: 1914.
Bénédictus E. *Les Musiques bizarres à l'Exposition*. Paris: 1889.
Benjamin, Paul Henri (Baron d' Estournelles de Constant). *Les Etats-Unis d'Amérique*. Paris: 1913.
Benois, Alexandre. *Memoirs*. Translated by Moura Budberg. London: 1964.
———. *Reminiscences of the Russian Ballet*. London: 1941.
Benstock, Shari. *Women of the Left Bank: Paris 1900–1940*. Austin, Tex.: 1986.
Bercy, Léon de. *Montmartre et ses chansons*. Paris: 1902.
Berlioz, Hector. *Mémoires de Hector Berlioz*. Paris: 1870.
———. *Les Soirées de l'orchestre*. Paris: 1852.
Bernac, Pierre. *Francis Poulenc: The Man and His Songs*. Translated by Winifred Radford. New York: 1977.
———. *The Interpretation of French Song*. Translated by Winifred Radford. London: 1970.
Bernard, Robert. *Albert Roussel: sa vie, son oeuvre*. Paris: 1948.
———. *Les Tendances de la musique française moderne*. Paris: 1947.
Bernard, Suzanne. *Mallarmé et la musique*. Paris: 1959.
Bertaut, Jules. *Les Belles Nuits de Paris*. Paris: 1927.
———. *Paris 1870–1935*. 1936. Reprint. New York: 1973.
Bertier de Sauvigny, G. de. *La France et les français vus par les voyageurs américains 1814–1848*. Paris: 1982.
Bienaymé, G. *Le Coût de la vie à Paris à diverses époques*. Paris: 1900.
Billy, André. *L'Epoque 1900*. Paris: 1951.
Bizet, Georges. *Lettres à un ami*. Introduction by Edmond Galabert. Paris: 1909.
Blanche, Jacques-Emile. *Portraits of a Lifetime: The Late Victorian Era—The Edwardian Pageant 1870–1914*. Translated by Walter Clement. New York: 1938.
———. *More Portraits of a Lifetime 1918–1938*. Edited and translated by Walter Clement. London: 1939.
Body, Albin. *Le Théâtre et la musique à Spa*. Brussels: 1885.
Bolles, Albert. *Industrial History of the United States*. 3d ed. Norwich, Conn.: 1881. Reprint, New York: 1966.
Bonnerot, Jean. *Camille Saint-Saëns, sa vie et son oeuvre*. Paris: 1914.
Bonnet-Roy, Flavien. *La Vie musicale au temps romantiques: salons, théâtres et concerts*. Paris: 1977.
Bordes, Charles. *De l'Opportunité de créer en France*. Paris: 1906.
Borgeaud, H., ed. and coll. *Correspondance de Claude Debussy et Pierre Louÿs, 1893–1904*. Paris: 1945.
Boschot, Adolphe. *Chez les musiciens*. 2e série. Paris: 1924.
Bouiller, H. *Victor Segalen*. Paris: 1961.
Bouissac, Paul. *Circus and Culture: A Semiotic Approach*. Bloomington, Ind.: 1976.
Boulanger, Nadia. *Lectures on Modern Music*. Houston, Tex.: 1921.
Boulet, Paul. *Richard Wagner et le douanier Edmond Roche*. Paris: 1951.
Bouvery, A. *Les Musiciens célèbres du second empire, jugés par leurs contemporains*. Paris: 1911.
Bouvet, Charles. *Massenet*. Paris: 1929.

Selected Bibliography

Bowie, Malcolm. *Mallarmé and the Art of Being Difficult*. Cambridge, 1978.

Bowler, Thomas Gibson. *The Defence of Paris: Narrated as it was Seen*. London: 1871.

Brancour, René. *Massenet*. Paris: 1922.

Brauns, D. *Traditions japonaises sur la chanson, la musique et la danse*. Paris: 1890.

Bredin, Jean-Denis. *The Affair: The Case of Alfred Dreyfus*. Translated by Jeffrey Mehlman. New York: 1986.

Brinton, Crane. *The Americans and the French*. Cambridge, Mass.: 1968.

Brody,, Elaine. "The Piano Works of Déodat de Séverac: A Stylistic Analysis." Ph.D. diss., New York University, 1964.

Broido, Lucy, ed. *French Opera Posters, 1867–1930*. New York: 1976.

Brooks, Van Wyck. *The Confident Years: 1885–1915*. New York: 1952.

Broome, Peter, and Chesters, Graham. *The Appreciation of Modern French Poetry*. Cambridge, 1976.

Brown, Frederick. *Theater and Revolution: The Culture of the French Stage*. New York: 1980.

Browse, Lillian. *Forain, the Painter 1852–1941*. London: 1978.

Bruneau, Alfred. *Bruneau-Zola: A l'ombre d'un grand coeur. Souvenirs d'une collaboration*. Paris:

————. *Massenet*. Paris: 1935.

————. *Musique de Russie et musiciens de France*. Paris: 1903.

Buckle, Richard. *Diaghilev*. New York: 1979.

————. *Nijinsky*. New York: 1971.

Burchell, S. *Imperial Masquerade: The Paris of Napoleon III*. New York: 1971.

Burnand, Robert. *La Vie quotidienne en France de 1870 à 1900*. Paris: 1947.

Busoni, Ferruccio. *Letters to His Wife*. Translated by Rosamond Ley. London: 1938.

Cabanne, Pierre. *Pablo Picasso: His Life and Times*. Translated by Harold J. Salemson. New York: 1977.

Calvocoressi, M.-D. *Music and Ballet: The Recollections of M.-D. Calvocoressi*. London: 1933.

————. *Musical Criticism*. London: 1923.

————. *La Musique russe*. Paris: 1907.

————, and Gerald Abraham. *Masters of Russian Music*. New York: 1936.

Campos, Christopher. *The View of France from Arnold to Bloomsbury*. London and New York: 1965.

Canteloube, Joseph. *Déodat de Séverac*. Beziers: 1984.

Caradec, François, and Alain Weill. *Le Café-Concert*. Paris: 1980.

Caron, François. *An Economic History of Modern France*. London: 1979.

Casals, Pablo, and A. E. Kahn. *Joys and Sorrows*. London: 1970.

Casella, Alfredo. *Music in My Time*. Translated and edited by Spencer Norton. Norman, Okla.: 1955.

Casso, Jacques de, and Sanders, Patricia B. *Rodin's Sculpture*. San Francisco: 1977.

Castle, Charles. *La Belle Otéro: The Last Great Courtesan*. London: 1981.

Catalogues des objets japonais exposés à l'Exposition Universelle de 1867. Paris: 1867–68.

Chadbourne, André. *Les Cafés-Concerts*. Paris: 1889.

Chalon, Jean, and Bernard, Paul, eds. *Max Jacob, Lettres à Liane de Pougy*. Paris: 1980.

Chalupt, R., and Gerar, M. *Ravel au miroir de ses lettres*. Paris: 1956.

Chamberlain, H. S. *Richard Wagner: Vues sur la France*. French translation by Robert Pitrou, commentary by Gustave Samazeuilh. Paris: 1943.

Champfleury, Jules. *Grandes Figures d'hier et d'aujourd'hui: Balzac, Gérard de Nerval, Wagner et Courbet*. Paris: 1861.

Chantavoine, Jean. *De Couperin à Debussy*. Paris: 1921.

Chapman, J. M. *The Life and Times of Baron Haussman: Paris in the Second Empire*. London: 1957.

Charle, Christophe. *Les Hauts Fonctionnaires en France au XIXe siècle*. Paris: 1981.

Charlton, D. G., ed. *France, A Companion to French Studies*. New York: 1972.

Charpentreau, Simonne. *La Chanson*. Paris: 1960.
Chase, Gilbert. *America's Music*. 2d ed. New York: 1966.
———. *The Music of Spain*. 1941. 2d ed., rev., New York: 1959.
———, ed. *The American Composer Speaks*. Baton Rouge, La.: 1966.
Chassiron, Le Baron Ch. de. *Notes sur le Japon, la Chine, et l'Inde, 1858–1860*. Paris: 1861.
Chavignerie, Bellier de la. *Dictionnaire général des artistes de l'école française*. 2 vols. Paris: 1882–85.
Cladel, Judith. *Aristide Maillol*. Paris: 1937.
———. *Rodin, sa vie glorieuse, sa vie inconnue*. Paris: 1936.
Clark, T. J. *The Absolute Bourgeois: Artists and Politics in France 1841–1951*. Princeton: 1982.
———. *The Painting of Modern Life: Paris in the Art of Manet and His Followers*. New York: 1985.
Clive, H. P. *Pierre Louÿs 1870–1925: A Biography*. London: 1978.
Cobb, Richard. *French and Germans, Germans and French: A Personal Interpretation of France Under Two Occupations 1914–1918/1940–1944*. Waltham, Mass.: 1983.
———. *Promenades: A Historian's Appreciation of Modern French Literature*. New York: 1980.
———. *The Streets of Paris*. London: 1980.
Cocteau, Jean. *Le Coq et l'arlequin*. Paris: 1918.
Coeuroy, André. *La Musique française moderne*. Paris: 1922.
———. *Panorama de la musique contemporaine*. Paris: 1928.
———. *Wagner et l'esprit romantique. Wagner et la France. Le wagnérisme littéraire*. Paris: 1965.
Cogeval, Guy, and Lesure, François, eds. *Debussy e il simbolismo*. Rome: 1984.
Cohen, H. Robert. *Les Gravures musicales dans "L'Illustration."* Quebec: 1985.
Colette, Maurice Delage, Léon-Paul Fargue, et al. *Maurice Ravel par quelques-uns de ses familiers*. Paris: 1939.
Colling, Alfred. *César Franck, ou le concert spirituel*. Paris: 1952.
Comettant, Oscar. *La Musique, les musiciens et les instruments de musique chez les différents peuples du monde*. Paris: 1869.
Cone, Edward T. *Berlioz, Fantastic Symphony: Critical Score*. New York: 1971.
Cooper, Dougles. *Picasso Theatre*. New York: 1967–68.
Cooper, Martin. "Aleksandr Skryabin and the Russian Renaissance." *Studi Musicali*, Anno I, 1972.
———. *French Music from the Death of Berlioz to the Death of Fauré*. London: 1951.
———. *Georges Bizet*. Oxford: 1938.
Cortot, Alfred. *French Piano Music*. Translated by Hilda Andrews. 3 vols. London: 1930, 1932, 1934.
Cossart, Michel de. *The Food of Love: Princesse Edmond de Polignac (1865–1943) and Her Salon*. London: 1979.
Cozanet, Albert. *L'Art du lied et les mélodies de Massenet*. Paris: 1931.
Curtiss, Mina. *Bizet and His World*. London: 1959.
Curzon, Henri de. *L'Oeuvre de Richard Wagner à Paris et ses interprètes, 1850–1914*. Paris: n.d.

Daix, Pierre, and Rosselet, Joan. *Picasso, The Cubist Years 1907–1916, A Catalogue Raisonné of the Paintings and Related Works*. New York: 1979.
Danckert, W. *Claude Debussy*. Berlin: 1950.
Dandelot, A. *La Société des Concerts du Conservatoire 1828–1923*. Paris: 1923.
Daubresse, Mathilda. *Le Musicien dans la société moderne*. Paris: 1914.
Daumard, Adeline. *Les Bourgeois de Paris au dix-neuvième siècle*. Paris: 1970.
———. *Maisons de Paris et propriétaires parisiens au XIXe siècle*. Paris: 1965.
Davies, Laurence. *César Franck and His Circle*. Boston: 1970.
———. *The Gallic Muse*. London: 1967.

Selected Bibliography

———. *Ravel Orchestral Music. BBC Guide.* Seattle, Wash.: 1971.

Dawes, Francis Edward. *Debussy Piano Music. BBC Guide.* London: 1969.

Dean, Winton. *Georges Bizet: His Life and Work.* London: 1965.

Deane, Basil. *Albert Roussel.* London: 1961.

Debussy, Claude. *Lettres de Claude Debussy à son éditeur.* Paris: 1927.

———. *Monsieur Croche antidilettante.* Paris: 1921. 2d ed. 1926; English trans. of 2d ed., 1962.

Debussy, Claude, and Poe, Edgar Allan. *Documents inédits recueillis et presentés par Edward Lockspeiser.* Preface by André Schaeffner. Monaco: 1961.

Delannoy, Marcel. *Honegger.* Paris: 1953.

Deldevez, Edouard M. E. *La Société des concerts, 1860 à 1885.* Paris: 1887.

Delevoy, Robert L. *Symbolists and Symbolism.* Translated by Barbara Bray, Elizabeth Wrightson, and Bernard C. Swift. New York: 1978.

Delville, Olivier. *Jean Delville, Peintre.* Brussels: 1984.

Demarquez, Suzanne. *Manuel de Falla.* Philadelphia: 1968.

Demuth, Norman. *Albert Roussel, A Study.* London: 1947.

———. *César Franck.* London: 1949.

———. *Introduction to the Music of Gounod.* London: 1950.

———. *Ravel.* New York: 1962.

———. *Vincent d'Indy.* London: 1951.

Denis, Maurice. *Henri Lerolle et ses amis.* Paris: 1932.

———. *Journal.* vol. 1, 1884–1904; vol. 2, 1905–1920; vol. 3, 1921–1943. Paris: 1957–59.

Desaymard, J. *Emmanuel Chabrier d'après ses lettres.* Paris: 1934.

Descharnes, Robert, and Chabrun, Jean-François. *Auguste Rodin.* Paris: 1967.

Dietschy, Marcel. *La Passion de Claude Debussy.* Neuchâtel: 1962.

Digeon, Claude. *La Crise allemande de la pensée française, 1870–1914.* Paris: 1959.

Dill, Marshall, Jr. *Paris in Time.* New York: 1975.

Donington, Robert. *Wagner's "Ring" and Its Symbols: The Music and the Myth.* London: 1963.

Downes, Edward. *The New York Philharmonic Guide to the Symphony.* New York: 1976.

Drinker-Bowen, Catherine, and von Meck, Barbara. *Beloved Friend.* London: 1937.

Dujardin, Edouard, ed. *Revue wagnérienne.* Paris: 1885–88.

Dukas, Paul. *Chroniques musicales sur deux siècles 1892–1932.* Preface by Jean-Vincent Richard. Paris: 1948, 1980.

Dukas, Paul. *Les Ecrits de Paul Dukas.* Paris: 1948.

Dumas, Alexandre *fils. La Princesse de Bagdad.* Paris: 1881.

Dumesnil, Maurice. *Claude Debussy.* Binghampton, N.Y.: 1940.

Dumesnil, René. *La Musique contemporaine en France.* 2 vols. Paris: 1930.

———. *La Musique en France entre les deux guerres, 1919–1939.* Geneva: 1946.

———. *La Musique romantique française.* Paris: 1944.

———. *Portraits de musiciens français.* Paris: 1938.

Eames, Emma. *Some Memories and Reflections.* New York: 1927.

Eckart-Backer, Ursula. *Frankreichs Musik zwischen Romantik und Moderne.* Regensburg: 1965.

Edwards, Stewart, ed. *The Communards of Paris, 1871.* Ithaca, N.Y.: 1973.

Ellmann, R., and C. Feidelson, Jr., eds. *The Modern Tradition: Backgrounds of Modern Literature.* Oxford: 1965.

Emié, Louis. *Dialogues avec Max Jacob.* Paris: 1954.

Evenepoel, E. *Le Wagnérisme hors d'Allemagne.* Paris and Brussels: 1891.

Evenson, Norma. *Paris: A Century of Change, 1878–1978.* New Haven, Conn.: 1979.

Ewen, David. *George Gershwin, His Journey to Greatness.* Englewood Cliffs, N. J.: 1970.

L'Exposition Universelle de 1867 illustrée.

Falla, Manuel de. *Escritos*. Introduction and notes by Federico Sopeña. Madrid: 1947.
Fanning, Michael. *Paris Notebook, 1921*. Baton Rouge, La.: 1976.
Fargue, Léon-Paul. *Portraits de famille. Souvenirs*. Paris: 1947.
Farwell, Beatrice. *French Popular Lithographic Imagery, 1815–1870*. Lithographs and Literature, vol. 1. Chicago: 1981.
Faure, Elie. *History of Art: Modern Art*. New York: 1937.
Fauré, Gabriel. *Opinions musicales*. Paris: 1930.
Faure-Favier, Madame Louise. *Souvenirs sur Guillaume Apollinaire*. Paris: 1945.
Fauré-Fremiet, Philippe. *Gabriel Fauré*. Paris: 1929. Rev. ed. 1957.
Favre, Georges. *L'Oeuvre de Paul Dukas*. Paris: 1969.
Fétis, François-Joseph. *Biographie universelle des musiciens et bibliographie générale de la musique*. Brussels: 1835–44.
Finck, Henry. *Massenet and his Operas*. New York: 1910.
Finke, Ulrich. *French 19th-Century Painting and Literature with Special Reference to the Relevance of Literary Subject Matter to French Painting*. New York: 1972.
Fiser, Emeric. *Le Symbole littéraire: Essai sur la signification du symbole chez Wagner, Baudelarie, Mallarmé, Bergson et Marcel Proust*. Paris: 1941.
Fokine, Michel. *Memoirs of a Ballet Master*. London: 1961.
Ford, Hugh, ed. *The Left Bank Revisited: Selections from "The Paris Tribune" 1917–1934*. University Park, Pa.: 1972.
———. *Published in Paris: American and British Writers, Printers, and Publishers in Paris, 1920–1939*. New York: 1975.
Fougère, Henry. *Les Délégations ouvrières aux expositions sous le Second Empire*. Montluçon: 1905.
Fowlie, Wallace. *A Reading of Proust*. Chigago: 1975.
Fraguier, Marguerite M. de. *Vincent d'Indy*. Paris: 1934.
Frankenstein, Alfred. *A Modern Guide to Symphonic Music*. New York: 1966.
Freedman, William. *Laurence Sterne and the Origins of the Musical Novel*. Athens, Ga.: 1978.
Fregnac, Claude, and Andrews, Wayne. *The Great Houses of Paris*. New York: 1979.
Frejaville, G. *Au Music Hall*. Paris: 1923.
French Painting, Second Half of the 19th to Early 20th Century. The Hermitage Museum. Leningrad: 1977.
Frère, Henri. *Conversations de Maillol*. Paris: 1956.
Frisch, Victor, and Shipley, Joseph T. *Auguste Rodin: A Biography*. New York: 1939.
Fuller, Loïe. *Fifteen Years in a Dancer's Life*. New York: 1913.
Garden, Edward. *Balakirev, A Critical Study of His Life and Music*. London: 1967.
Garnier, Jacques. *Forains d'hier et d'aujourd'hui: Un Siècle d'histoire des forains, des fêtes, et de la vie foraine*. Paris: n.d.
Gauthier, André, ed. *Debussy, Documents iconographiques*. Geneva: 1952.
Gautier, J. *Les Musiques bizarres à l'Exposition de 1900*. Paris: 1900.
Gautier, Judith. *Richard Wagner et son oeuvre poétique depuis "Rienzi" jusqu'à "Parsifal."* Paris: 1882.
———. *Le Second Rang du collier*. Paris: 1903.
———. *Le Troisième Rang du collier*. Paris: 1909.
Gay, Peter. *Art and Act, On Causes in History—Manet, Gropius, Mondrian*. New York: 1976.
Gay, Peter, and Webb, R. K. *Modern Europe*. New York: 1973.
Gedo, Mary Mathews. *Picasso: Art as Autobiography*. Chicago: 1980.
Ghil, Rhené. *Traité du verbe*. 2d ed. Paris: 1889.
Gibson, R. *Modern French Poets on Poetry*. Cambridge, 1961.
Gilman, Lawrence. *Orchestral Music: An Armchair Guide*. Edited by Edward Cushing. New York: 1951.
Godet, Robert. *En marge de Boris Godounof*. Paris: 1926.
Golther, W., ed. *Richard Wagner und Mathilde Wesendonck: Tagebuchblätter und Briefe 1853–1871*. Leipzig: 1904.
Goncourt, Edmond de. *Manette Salomon*. Paris: 1881.

Selected Bibliography

Gordon, Robert, and Forge, Andrew. *Monet*. New York: 1984.
Gosling, Nigel. *The Adventurous World of Paris 1900–1914*. New York: 1978.
———. *Nadar*. New York: 1976.
Gounod, Charles François. *Autobiographical Reminiscences, with Family Letters and Notes on Music*. Translated by W. Hely Hutchinson. London: 1896. Reprint. New York: 1970.
Gray, Nicolete. *Nineteenth-Century Ornamented Type Faces*. Berkeley, Calif.: 1975.
Green, Christopher. *Léger and the Avant-Garde*. New Haven, Conn.: 1976.
Gregor-Dellin, Martin, and Mack, Dietrich, eds. *Cosima Wagner's Diaries*. 2 vols. Translated and introduction by Geoffrey Skelton. New York and London: 1978, 1977.
Gribenski, Jean. *French Language Dissertations in Music: An Annotated Bibliography*. New York: 1979.
Griffiths, Paul. *A Concise History of Modern Music, From Debussy to Boulez*. London: 1978.
Grigoriev, Serge. *The Diaghilev Ballet 1909–1929*. Baltimore, Md.: 1960.
Grun, Bernard. *The Timetables of History*. New York: 1975.
Guérard, Albert. *French Civilization in the Nineteenth Century*. London: 1914.
Guichard, Léon. *La Musique et les lettres au temps du romantisme*. Paris: 1955.
———. *La Musique et les lettres au temps du wagnérisme*. Paris: 1963.
Guicheteau, Marcel. *Paul Serusier*. Paris: 1976.
Guilbert, Yvette. *Autre temps, autres chants*. Paris: 1946.
———. *La Chanson de ma vie*. Paris: 1928.
Guimet, Emile. *Promenades japonaises*. Paris: 1880.
Gullace, Giovanni. *Gabriele d'Annunzio in France: A Study in Cultural Relations*. Syracuse, N.Y.: 1966.
Gutman, Robert W. *Richard Wagner, the Man, His Mind and His Music*. New York: 1968.

Hackett, C. A. *Rimbaud: A Critical Introduction*. Cambridge, 1981.
Halle, C. E., and Halle, M. *Life and Letters of Sir Charles Halle*. London: 1896.
Handlin, Oscar. *This Was America*. Cambridge, 1949.
Haney, Lynn. *Naked at the Feast: A Biography of Josephine Baker*. New York: ca. 1981.
Hardeck, Erwin. *Untersuchungen zu den Klavierliedern Claude Debussys*. Regensburg: 1967.
Harding, James. *Erik Satie*. New York: 1975.
———. *Folies de Paris: The Rise and Fall of French Operetta*. London: 1979.
———. *Gounod*. New York: 1973.
———. *Massenet*. New York: 1970.
———. *Saint-Saëns and His Circle*. London: 1965.
Hardison, O. B., Jr., ed. *Modern Continental Literary Criticism*. New York: 1962.
Haskell, Arnold, with Nouvel, Walter. *Diaghileff: Artistic and Private Life*. 1935. Reprint. New York: 1977.
Haussmann, Baron Georges-Eugène. *Mémoires du Baron Haussmann: Grands Travaux de Paris*. Reprint. Paris: 1979.
Hell, Henri. *Francis Poulenc*. Translated by Edward Lockspeiser. London: 1959.
Hemmings, F. W. J. *Culture and Society in France 1848–1898*. New York: 1971.
———. *The Russian Novel in France, 1884–1914*. London: 1950.
Henderson, John A. *The First Avant-Garde, 1887–1894: Sources of the Modern French Theatre*. London: 1971.
Henschel, Sir George. *Musings and Memories of a Musician*. London: 1918.
Herlihy, J. *Catulle Mendès, critique dramatique et musical*. Paris: 1936.
Hertz, David Michael. *The Tuning of the Word: The Musico-literary Poetics of the Symbolist Movement*. Carbondale, Ill.: 1987.
Hill, Edward B. *Modern French Music*. New York: 1924.
Hillairet, Jacques. *Dictionnaire des rues de Paris*. 2 vols. Paris: 1963.
Hoeree, A. *Albert Roussel*. Paris: 1938.

Hoffmann, Stanley et al. *In Search of France*. Cambridge, Mass.: 1963.
Holloway, Robin. *Debussy and Wagner*. London: 1979.
Holt, Richard. *Sport and Society in Modern France*. London: 1981.
Huddleston, Sisley. *In and About Paris*. London: 1927.
———. *Paris Salons, Cafes, Studios*. Philadelphia and London: 1928.
Hueffer, Francis. *Correspondence of Wagner and Liszt*. Translated and preface by Hueffer. 2d ed. Revised by W. Ashton Ellis. New York: 1973.
Hugo, Jean. *Avant d'oublier 1918–1931*. Paris: 1976.
Hull, A. E. *Dictionary of Modern Music*. London: 1924.
Huschke, Konrad. *Musiker, Mahler und Dichter als Freunde und Gegner*. Leipzig: 1939.
Hyman, Paula. *From Dreyfus to Vichy: The Remaking of French Jewry 1906–1939*. New York: 1979.
Hyslop, Francis. *Henri Evenepoel, Belgian Painter in Paris, 1892–1899*. University Park, Pa.: 1975.

Imbert, Hugues. *Profils d'artistes contemporains: Alexis de Castillon Paul, Lacombe, Charles Lefebvre, Jules Massenet, Antoine Rubinstein, Edouard Schuré*. Paris: 1897.
———. *Profils de musiciens*. 3 vols. Paris: 1888, 1892, 1897.
d'Indy, Vincent. *Catalogue des partitions et livres provenant de la bibliothèque de Vincent d'Indy*. Paris: 1933.
———. *César Franck*. Translated by Rosa Newmarch. Rev. ed. New York: 1965.
———. *Emmanuel Chabrier et Paul Dukas*. Paris: 1920.
———. *Richard Wagner et son influence sur l'art musical français*. Paris: 1930.
Inghelbrecht, Germaine, and Inghelbrecht, D. E. *Claude Debussy*. Paris: 1953.
Ives, Colta Feller. *The Great Wave: The Influence of Japanese Woodcuts on French Prints*. New York: 1974.

Jablonski, Edward, and Stewart, Lawrence D. *The Gershwin Years*. 2d ed. New York: 1973.
Jacobs, Alphonse, ed. *Gustave Flaubert–George Sand Correspondance*. Paris: 1981.
Jacobson, Anna. *Nachklänge Richard Wagners im Roman*. Heidelberg: 1932.
Jacques-Charles. *Café Conc'*. Paris: 1966.
———. *Cents Ans de Music-Hall*. Geneva and Paris: 1956.
Jankélevitch, Vladimir. *Debussy et le mystère*. Paris: 1949.
———. *Debussy et le mystère de l'instant*. Paris: 1976.
———. *Fauré el l'inexprimable*. Paris: 1974.
———. *Gabriel Fauré et ses mélodies*. Paris: 1938. 2d ed. 1951 as *Gabriel Fauré, ses mélodies, son esthétique*.
———. *Maurice Ravel*. Paris: 1939. 2d ed., enlarged, *Ravel*. Paris: 1956.
———. *La Musique et l'ineffable*. Paris: 1961.
———. *Le Nocturne: Fauré, Chopin et la nuit: Satie et le matin*. Paris: 1957.
———. *La Rhapsodie; Verve et improvisation musicale*. Paris: 1955.
———. *La Vie et la mort dans la musique de Debussy*. Neuchâtel: 1968.
Jarocinski, Stefan. *Debussy: Impressionism & Symbolism*. Translated by Rollo Myers, with preface to the French edition by Vladimir Jankélévitch. London: 1976.
Jean-Aubry, G. *French Music of Today*. Translated by Edwin Evans. London: 1920
———, ed. *Jules Laforgue: Lettres à un ami 1880–1886*. Paris: 1941.
Jean Cocteau and the French Scene. A collection of essays by diverse authors published by Abbeville Press, copyright French American Foundation. New York: 1984.
Joanne, Adolphe. *Paris illustré en 1870 et 1877*. Paris: n.d.
Johnson, Douglas. *A Concise History of France*. New York: 1971.
———. *France and the Dreyfus Affair*. London: 1966.
Johnson, Harold Earle. *Operas on American Subjects*. New York: 1964.
Jones, Howard Mumford. *The Age of Energy, Varieties of American Experience 1865–1965*. New York: 1970.
Jourdan-Morhange, Hélène. *Ravel et nous: l'homme, l'ami, le musicien*. Geneva: 1945.

Selected Bibliography

Jullian, Philippe. *Prince of Aesthetics: Count Robert de Montesquiou 1855–1922.* Translated by John Haylock and Francis King. New York: 1965.
Jullien, Adolphe. *Hector Berlioz.* Paris: 1888.
———. *Musiciens d'aujourd'hui.* Paris: 1892.
———. *Paris dilettante au commencement du siècle.* Paris: 1884.
———. *Richard Wagner, Sa Vie et ses oeuvres.* Paris: 1886.

Kahane, Martine, and Wild, Nicole, eds. *Wagner et la France.* Paris: 1983.
Kahn, G. *Les Dessins de Georges Seurat 1859–1891.* Paris: 1928.
Kaplan, Justin. *Mr. Clemens and Mark Twain: A Biography.* New York: 1966.
Kellner, Bruce. *Carl van Vechten and the Irreverent Decades.* Norman, Okla.: 1968.
Kessler, Harry. *In the Twenties: The Diaries of Harry Kessler.* Translated by Charles Kessler. New York: 1971.
Knapp, Bettina L. *Le Mirliton: A Novel Based on the Life of Aristide Bruant.* Paris: 1968.
——— and Myra Chipman. *That Was Yvette.* London: 1966.
Kochno, Boris. *Diaghilev and the Ballets Russes.* New York: 1970.
Koechlin, Charles. *Debussy.* Paris: 1927.
———. *Gabriel Fauré.* Translated by Leslie Orrey. Rev. ed. Paris: 1949.
Koehler, E. Edmond, and Goncourt, Jules. *Die Begründer des Impressionismus: eine Stilgeschichtliche Studie zur Literatur und Malerei des 19 Jahrhunderts.* Leipzig: 1912.
Kolb, Philip, ed. *Correspondance, Marcel Proust.* Paris: 1970.
———. *Marcel Proust, Lettres à Reynaldo Hahn.* Paris: 1956.
Kracauer, S. *Offenbach and the Paris of His Time.* London: 1937.
Kramer, Lawrence. *Music and Poetry: The Nineteenth Century and After.* Berkeley, Calif.: 1984.
Krasovskaya, Vera. *Nijinsky.* Translated by John E. Bowlt. New York: 1979.
Krehbiel, H. E. *Review of the New York Musical Season.* New York: 1887.
Kris, Ernst, and Kurz, Otto. *Legend, Myth, and Magic in the Image of the Artist.* New Haven, Conn.: 1981.

LaBelle, Maurice Marc. *Alfred Jarry: Nihilism and the Theater of the Absurd.* New York: 1980.
Labracherie, Pierre. *La Vie quotidienne de la bohème littéraire au XIXe siècle.* Paris: 1967.
Lalo, Pierre. *De Rameau à Ravel.* Paris: 1947.
Laloy, Louis. *Claude Debussy.* Paris: 1909.
———. *La Musique retrouvée 1902–1927.* Paris: 1928.
Landormy, Paul. *La Musique française de la Marseillaise à la mort de Berlioz.* Paris: 1944.
Landowski, Wanda Alice. *Maurice Ravel, sa vie, son oeuvre.* Paris: 1950.
Lane, James W. *Whistler.* New York: 1942.
Lang, Paul Henry. *One Hundred Years of Music in America.* New York: 1961.
Large, David C., and Weber, William. *Wagnerism in European Culture and Politics.* Ithaca, N.Y.: 1984.
Lasalle, A. de. *La Musique pendant le siège de Paris.* Paris: 1872.
Laurencie, Lionel de la. *Le Goût musical en France.* Paris: 1905.
Laurenti, Huguette. *Paul Valéry et le théâtre.* Paris: 1973.
Lavignac, Albert. *Music and Musicians.* Translated by H. E. Krehbiel. New York: 1899.
Lebow, Marcia Wilson. "A Systematic Examination of the *Journal of Music and Art* edited by John Sullivan Dwight, 1852–1881, Boston Massachusetts." Ph.D diss. University of California at Los Angeles, 1969.
Legouvé, E. *Soixante ans de souvenirs.* Paris: 1886.
Leguy, Jean. *Répertoire bibliographique des ouvrages en français sur la musique.* Chambray-les-Tour: 1975.

Lehmann, A. G. *The Symbolist Aesthetic in France, 1885–1895*. Oxford: 1950.
Lehrmann, C. *L'Elément juif dans la littérature française*. Zurich: 1941.
Léon-Martin, Louis. *Le Music-Hall et ses figures*. Paris: 1928.
Le Roux, Hugues. *Les Jeux du cirque et la vie foraine*. Paris: 1889.
Leroy, Maxime. *Les Premiers amis français de Wagner*. Paris: 1925.
Lesure, François, ed. *Claude Debussy: Lettres 1884–1918*. Paris: 1980.
———, ed. *Debussy on Music*. Translated and edited by Richard Langham Smith. New York: 1977.
———, ed. *Gabriel Fauré*. Paris: 1963.
Lesure, François, and Cogeval, Guy, eds. *Debussy e il simbolismo*. Rome: 1984.
Lethève, Jacques. *Daily Life of French Artists in the Nineteenth Century*. Translated by Hilary E. Paddon. New York: 1968.
Levinson, André. *Bakst, The Story of the Artist's Life*. London: 1923. Reprint. New York: 1971.
Lévy, Jules. *Les Hydropathes*. Paris: 1928.
Liess, Andreas. *Claude Debussy: Das Werk im Zeitbild*. 2 vols. Leipzig: 1937.
Lieven, Prince Peter. *The Birth of the Ballets Russes*. London: 1936.
Lifar, Serge. *Serge Diaghilev: His Life, His Works, His Legend*. New York: 1940. Reprint. 1976.
Linden, Albert van der. *Lettres de Vincent d'Indy à Octave Maus*. Brochure of "Revue Belge de Musicologie," vol. 15, 1961, fasc. 1–4.
———. *Octave Maus et la Vie musicale belge 1875–1914*. Brussels: 1950.
Lipschutz, Ilse Hempel. *Spanish Painting and the French Romantics*. Cambridge, Mass.: 1972.
Liszt, Franz. *Lohengrin et Tannhüser de Richard Wagner*. Leipzig: 1851.
Lockspeiser, Edward. *Debussy: His Life and Mind*. 2 vols. London: 1962–65.
———. *Music and Painting: A Study in Comparative Ideas from Turner to Schoenberg*. New York: 1973.
Lomax, James, and Ormond, Richard. *John Singer Sargent and the Edwardian Age*. London: 1979.
Lona, Toussaint. *Atlas statistique de la population de Paris*. Paris: 1873.
Long, Marguerite. *Au Piano avec Claude Debussy*. Paris: 1960.
———. *Au Piano avec Gabriel Fauré*. Paris: 1963.
———. *Au Piano avec Maurice Ravel*. Paris: 1971. English translation. 1973.
Loti, Pierre. *Fantôme d'Orient*. Paris: 1892.
———. *Japonneries d'automne*. Paris: 1889.
———. *Le Mariage de Loti, par l'auteur d'Aziyade*. Paris: 1880.
Louÿs, Pierre. *Une Ascension au Venusberg*. Paris: 1896.
Lucas, Edward V. *A Wanderer in Paris, 1914*. New York: 1926.
Lucie-Smith, Edward. *Henri Fantin-Latour*. New York: 1977.
Lueders, Edward. *Carl Van Vechten and the Twenties*. Albuquerque, N. M.: 1955.

Macdonald, Nesta. *Diaghilev Observed by Critics in England and the United States 1911–1929*. London: 1975.
Malino, Frances, and Wasserstein, Bernard, eds. *The Jews in Modern France*. Hanover, N. H.: 1985.
Mandell, Richard D. *Paris 1900: The Great World's Fair*. Toronto: 1967.
Marek, George R. *Cosima Wagner*. New York: 1981.
Marguerittes, Julia (Granville). *The Ins and Outs of Paris or Paris by Day and Night*. Philadelphia: 1855.
Marmontel, A. *Conseils d'un professeur sur l'enseignement, technique et l'esthétique du piano*. Paris: n.d.
Marnold, Jean. *Musique d'autre fois et d'aujourd'hui*. Paris: [1912].
Marrus, Michael R., and Paxton, Robert O. *Vichy France and the Jews*. New York: 1981.
Martens, Frederick H. *A Thousand and One Nights of Opera*. New York and London: 1926.

Selected Bibliography

Martin, Benjamin F. *The Hypocrisy of Justice in the Belle Epoque*. Baton Rouge, La.: 1984.

Martin, Michael Rheta. *A Graphic Guide to World History*. Consulting editor Geoffrey Brun. New York: 1959.

Martineau, René. *Emmanuel Chabrier*. Paris: 1919.

Massenet, Jules. *My Recollections*. Translated by H. Villiers Barnett. Paris: 1912. Boston: [1919]. Reprint. New York.

Mathews, W. S. B. *100 Years of Music in America*. Chicago: 1889.

Mauclair, Camille. *Histoire de la musique européenne 1850–1914*. Paris: 1914.

———. *La Religion de la musique*. Paris: 1919.

Mauner, George. *Manet, Peintre-Philosophe, A Study of the Painter's Themes*. University Park, Pa.: 1975.

Mauriac, François, and Blanche, Jacques-Emile. *Correspondance, 1916–1942*. Paris: 1976.

Maus, Octave. *Trente années de lutte pour l'art*. Brussels: 1926.

Mayne, Jonathan, ed. and trans. *Baudelaire, The Painter of Modern Life and Other Essays*. New York: 1965.

McKibbin, David. *Sargent's Boston*. Boston: 1956.

Mehlman, Jeffrey. *Legacies of Anti-Semitism in France*. Minneapolis, Minn.: 1983.

Meister, Barbara. *Nineteenth-Century French Song: Fauré, Chausson, Duparc and Debussy*. Bloomington, Ind.: 1980.

Menanteau, Pierre. *Tristan Klingsor*. Paris: 1965.

Mendès, Catulle. *Richard Wagner*. Paris: 1886.

Milhaud, Darius. *Notes Without Music*. Edited by Rollo H. Myers, translated by Donald Evans. New York: 1952, 1953.

Miller, Michael B. *The Bon Marché: Bourgeois Culture and the Department Store 1869–1930*. London: 1981.

Mitchell, Allen. *The German Influence in France after 1870: The Formation of the French Republic*. Chapel Hill, N. C.: 1981.

Monnier, Adrienne. *The Very Rich Hours of Adrienne Monnier: An Intimate Portrait of the Literary and Artistic Life in Paris Between the Wars*. Translated and with an introduction and commentaries by Richard McDougall. New York: 1976.

Montarlot, Gérard. *Le Jazz et ses musiciens*. Paris: 1963.

Morton, Brian N. *Americans in Paris: An Anecdotal Street Guide to the Homes and Haunts of Americans from Jefferson to Capote*. New York: 1984, 1986.

Moser, R. *L'Impressionisme français. Peinture, littérature, musique*. Geneva: 1952.

Moulin-Eckart, Richard Count du. *Cosima Wagner*. 2 vols. Translated by Catherine Alison Phillips, introduction by Ernest Newman. New York: 1930.

Mueller, John Henry. *The American Symphony Orchestra: A Social History of Musical Taste*. Bloomington, Ind.: 1951.

Munro, Thomas. *The Arts and Their Interrelations*. Revised and enlarged edition. Cleveland, Oh.: 1969.

Musée-Jacquemart, André. *La Vie parisienne au temps de Guy Nadar*. Paris: 1959.

Myers, Rollo H. *Emmanuel Chabrier and His Circle*. London: 1969.

———. *Erik Satie*. New York: 1968.

———. *Ravel: Life and Works*. New York: 1960.

Nadar. *L'Atelier Nadar et l'art lyrique*. Paris: 1975.

Nattiez, Jean-Jacques. *Proust Musicien*. Paris: 1984.

Nectoux, Jean-Michel. *Fauré*. Paris: 1972.

———. *Gabriel Fauré: His Life Through His Letters*. Translated by J. A. Underwood. London and New York: 1984.

Nerval, Gérard de. *Journey to the Orient*. Selected, translated and with an introduction by Norman Glass. London: 1985.

Newman, Ernest. *The Life of Richard Wagner*. 4 vols. London: 1933–46.

———. *The Wagner Operas*. New York: 1959.

Niederauer, David J., ed. *Henri de Regnier: Lettres à André Gide 1891–1911*. Geneva: 1972.
Nori, Claude. *French Photography from its Origins to the Present*. Paris: ca. 1980.
Norris, Homer. *Practical Harmony on a French Basis*. Boston: 1894.
Noske, Frits. *French Song from Berlioz to Duparc*. Translated by Rita Benton. Reprint. New York: 1970.
Nuitter, Charles. *Le Nouvel Opéra*. Paris: 1875.

Olivier, Fernande. *Picasso et ses amis*. Paris: 1933.
Ollivier, D., ed. *Correspondance de Liszt et de sa fille Madame Emile Ollivier*. Paris: 1936.
Orenstein, Arbie. *Ravel, Man and Musician*. New York: 1975.
Orledge, Robert. *Debussy and the Theatre*. Cambridge, 1982.
———. *Gabriel Fauré*. London: 1979.
Ormond, Richard. *John Singer Sargent*. London: 1970.
Oulmont, Charles. *Musique de l'armour. Ernest Chausson et la bande à Franck*. Paris: 1935.
Ouston, Philip. *The Imagination of Maurice Barrès*. Toronto and Buffalo: 1974.

Pachter, Marc, and Frances Wein, eds. *Abroad in America: Visitors to the New Nation 1776–1914*. Reading, Mass.: 1976.
Papich, Stephen. *Remembering Josephine*. Indianapolis, Ind. and New York: 1976.
Parent, Hortense. *Répertoire encyclopédique du pianiste*. Paris: 1926.
Park, Julian, ed. *The Culture of France in our Time*. London: 1954.
Paulus. *Trente ans de café-concert*. Paris: n.d.
Percival, John. *The World of Diaghilev*. London: 1971.
Peter, René. *Claude Debussy*. Paris: 1931. 2d ed. 1944.
Petitfils, Pierre. *Verlaine*. Paris: n.d., ca. 1981.
Pierrot, Jean. *The Decadent Imagination 1880–1900*. Translated by Derek Coltman. Chicago: 1982.
Pincherle, Marc. *Musiciens peints par eux-mêmes. Lettres de compositeurs écrites en français 1771–1910*. Paris: 1939.
Piroue, Georges. *Proust et la musique du devenir*. Paris: 1960.
Pistone, Danield, ed. *L'Exotisme musical français*. Vol. 6 of *Revue internationale de musique française*. Geneva and Paris: November 1981.
———, ed. *La Musique en France de la Revolution à 1900*. Paris: 1979.
———, ed. "Wagner à Paris." In *Revue Internationale de Musique Française*, no. 1 (February 1980).

Pitrou, Robert. *Dew Gounod à Debussy*. Paris: 1957.
Plantinga, Leon. *Romantic Music*. New York: 1984.
Plimpton, George, and Hemphill, Christopher. *D.V. Diana Vreeland*. New York: 1985.
Polunin, Vladimir. *The Continental Method of Scene Painting*. Edited by C. Beaumont. London: 1927.
Ponchie, Jean-Pierre. *French Periodical Index, Repertoriex*. Westwood, Mass.: 1980.
Pontecoulant, A. de. *La Musique à l'Exposition de 1867*. Paris: 1868.
Poueigh, Jean. *Musiciens français d'aujourd'hui; notice biographiques, suivies d'un essai de bibliographie et accompagnées d'un autographe musical*. Paris: 1921.
Pougin, Arthur. *Essai historique sur la musique en Russie*. Paris: 1904.
———. *Le Théâtre à l'Exposition Universelle de 1889: Notes et description, histoire et souvenirs*. Paris: 1890.
Pougy, Liane de. *Mes Cahiers bleus*. Paris: 1978.
Poulenc, Francis. *Emmanuel Chabrier*. Paris: 1961.
Pour la Musique française: Douze Causeries, avec une préface de Claude Debussy. Paris: 1917.
Propert, W. A. *The Russian Ballet in Western Europe 1909–1920*. New York: 1972.

Selected Bibliography

Proust, Marcel. *Remembrance of Things Past*. 2 vols. Translated by C. K. Scott Moncrieff. New York: 1924–32.
Putnam, Samuel. *Paris was our Mistress*. Carbondale and Edwardsville, Ill.: 1947.

Quinn, Patrick F. *The French Face of Edgar Poe*. Carbondale, Ill.: 1954.

Raitt, A. W. *Life and Letters in France*. Vol. 3. *The Nineteenth Century*. London: 1965.
Ramus, Charles F., ed. *Daumier: 120 Great Lithographs*. New York: 1978.
Randel, William Peirce. *Centennial, American Life in 1876*. Philadelphia: 1969.
Ratcliff, Carter. *John Singer Sargent*. New York: 1982.
Rearick, Charles. *Pleasures of the Belle Epoque: Entertainment and Festivity in Turn-of-the-Century France*. New Haven, Conn.: 1985.
Redon, Odilon. *A Soi-même, Journal 1867–1915*. Introduction by Jacques Morland. Paris: 1922. English edition, *To Myself: Notes on Life, Art, and Artists*. Translated by Mira Jacob and Jeanne L. Wasserman. New York: 1986.
Reff, Theodore. *Modern Art in Paris 1855–1900, Two Hundred Catalogues of the Major Exhibitions Reproduced in Facsimile in Forty-Seven Volumes*. New York: 1981–.
Renieu, Lionel. *Histoire des théâtres de Bruxelles*. Paris: 1928.
Renoir, Jean. *Renoir, My Father*. Translated by Randolph and Dorothy Weaver. London: 1962.
Rewald, John. *Georges Seurat*. New York: 1946.
Reynaud, Louis. *L'Influence allemande en France au XVIIIe et au XIXe siècle*. Paris: 1922.
Reynolds-Ball, E. A. *Paris in Its Splendor*. Boston: 1900.
Richardson, Joanna. *Colette*. London: 1983.
———. *Judith Gautier*. London: 1987.
———. *La Vie parisienne 1852–1870*. New York: 1971.
Rimsky-Korsakov, N. *My Musical Life*. Translated by Judah A. Joffe. New York: 1935.
Ritter, Frederic Louis. *Music in America*. New York: 1890. Reprint. New York: 1970.
Rivière, Georges. *Renoir et ses amis*. Paris: 1921.
Robert, Gustave. *La Musique à Paris 1897–1898*. Paris: 1898.
Rodin, Auguste. *Art: Conversations with Paul Gesell*. Translated by Jacques de Casso and Patricia B. Sanders. Berkeley, Calif.: 1984.
Rogers, W. G. *Ladies Bountiful*. New York: 1968.
Rohozinski, L. *Cinquante ans de musique française 1824–1925*. Paris: 1926.
Roland-Manuel. *Maurice Ravel*. Translated by Cynthia Jolly. London: 1941.
Rolland, Romain. *Musicians of Today*. Translated by Mary Blaiklock. New York: 1915.
Rosenblum, Robert, and H. W. Janson. *19th-Century Art*. New York: 1984.
Rosenfeld, Paul. *Musical Chronicle 1917–1923*. New York: 1923.
Rosenstiel, Leonie. *Nadia Boulanger, A Life in Music*. New York: 1982.
Rousiers, Paul de. *American Life*. Translated by Herbertson. Paris: 1982.
Rudorff, Raymond. *The Belle Epoque: Paris in the Nineties*. New York: 1972.
Russell, Frank, ed. *Art Nouveau Architecture*. London: 1980.
Rutz, Hans. *Claude Debussy, Dokumente seines Lebens und Schaffens*. Munich: 1954.

Saalman, Howard. *Haussmann: Paris Transformed*. New York: 1971.
Sagardia, Angel. *Isaac Albéniz*. Plasencia: 1951.
St. James, Ashley. *Valloton: Graphics*. London: 1978.
Saint-Saëns, Camille. *Outspoken Essays on Music*. Translated by Fred Rothwell. London: 1922. Reprint. 1969.
Sala, George Augustus. *Paris Herself Again*. London: 1880.
Samazeuilh, G. *Un Musicien français, Paul Dukas*. Paris: 1913.
Sauvigny, G. de Bertier, and Pinckney, David. *History of France*. Revised and enlarged edition, trans. by James Friguglietti. Arlington Heights, Ill.: 1983.
Schlesinger, A. M. *The Rise of the City 1878–1898*. New York: 1933.
Schmitz, Elie Robert. *The Piano Works of Claude Debussy*. Foreword by Virgil Thomson, edited and designed by Merle Armitage. New York: 1950.

Schnapper, Dominque. *Jewish Identities in France: An Analysis of Contemporary French Jewry*. Translated by Arthur Goldhammer. Chicago: 1983.
Schneider, Louis. *Massenet*. Paris: 1926.
———. *Massenet, l'homme, le musicien*. Paris: 1908.
Schneider, Pierre. *Matisse*. Translated by Michael Taylor. New York: 1984.
Schoolfield, George C. *The Figure of the Musician in German Literature*. Chapel Hill, N. C.: 1956.
Schwab, Arnold T. *James Gibbons Huneker: Critic of the Seven Arts*. Stanford, Calif.: 1963.
Schwab, R. *La Littérature française et la musique (1900 à nos jours)*. Paris: 1952.
Séché, Léon. *Les Annales romantiques*. 11 vols. Reprint. Geneva: 1967.
Seigel, Jerrold. *Bohemian Paris: Culture, Politics, and the Boundaries of Bourgeois Life, 1830–1930*. New York: 1986.
Selva, Blanche. *Déodat de Séverac*. Paris: 1930
Selz, Peter. *Art in our Times: A Pictorial History 1890–1980*. New York: 1981.
Séré, O. *Musiciens français d'aujourd'hui*. Paris: 1911.
Serieyx, Auguste. *Vincent d'Indy*. Paris: 1913.
Serra (Crespo), José. *Senderos espirituales de Albéniz y Debussy*. Mexico City: 1944.
Servières, Georges. *Emmanuel Chabrier*. Paris: 1912.
———. *La Musique française moderne*. Paris: 1872.
———. *Wagner, jugé en France*. Paris: 1887.
Seurat, Georges. *The Drawings of Georges Seurat*. Introduction by Gustave Kahn. New York: 1978.
Shattuck, Roger. *The Banquet Years: The Arts in France, 1885–1918*. New York: 1961.
Shead, Richard. *Music in the 1920s*. London: 1976.
Shikes, Ralph E., and Harper, Paula. *Pissarro, His Life and Work*. London: 1980.
Sieburth, Richard. *Instigations: Ezra Pound and Rémy de Gourmont*. Cambridge, 1978.
Silver, Kenneth E., and Golan, Romy, et al. *The Circle of Montparnasse: Jewish Artists in Paris 1905–1945*. New York: 1985.
Slonimsky, Nicolas. *Music Since 1900*. 4th ed. New York: 1971.
Smith, Edward-Lucie. *Fantin Latour*. Oxford: 1978.
Smyth, Ethel. *What Happened Next*. London: 1940.
Soissons, S. C. de. *A Parisian in America*. Boston: 1896.
Solenière, Eugène de. *1800–1900: Cent années de musique française*. Paris: 1901.
Sonneck, Oscar. *A Survey of Music in America*. 1913. Reprint. New York: 1969.
Sopena, F. *Joáquin Turina*. Madrid: 1945.
Souvtchinsky, Pierre, ed. *La Musique russe*. Paris: 1953.
Spalding, Walter R. *Music at Harvard*. New York: 1935.
Les Spectacles à travers les âges: Théâtre, cirque, music-hall, cafés-concerts, cabarets. Preface by Denis Amyel. Paris: 1931.
Stasov, Vladimir. *Selected Essays on Music*. Translated by F. Jonas. London: 1968.
Stein, Jack. *Richard Wagner and the Synthesis of the Arts*. Detroit, Mich.: 1960.
Stendhal (Henri Beyle). *La Vie de Rossini*. Translated by Richard N. Coe. Paris: 1824. Reprint. London and New York: 1957.
Stimpson, Brian. *Paul Valéry and Music: A Study of the Techniques of Composition in Valéry's Poetry*. Cambridge, 1984.
Stokowski, Olga Samaroff. *An American Musician's Story*. New York: 1939.
Stoullig, Eduard. *Les Annales du théâtre et de la musique*. Paris: 1910.
Stravinsky, Vera, and Craft, Robert. *Stravinsky in Pictures and Documents*. New York: 1978.
Suarès, André. *Musique et póesie*. Paris: 1928.
Sutton, Denys. *James McNeill Whistler*. London: 1966.
———. *Nocturne: The Art of James McNeill Whistler*. London: 1963.

Taine. Hippolyte Adolphe. *Parisian Culture and Society 1830–1849, Notes on Paris*. Translated by John A. Stevens. New York: 1899.

Selected Bibliography

Tancock, John L. *The Sculpture of Auguste Rodin*. Philadelphia: 1976.
Tannenbaum, Edward R. *1900: The Generation Before the Great War*. New York: 1976.
Tappolet, Willy. *Arthur Honegger*. Zurich: 1954.
Templier, Pierre Daniel. *Erik Satie*. 2d ed. Cambridge, Mass.: 1969.
Thomas, Rose Fay. *Memoirs of Theodore Thomas*. New York: 1911. Reprint. Freeport, N. Y.: 1971.
Thompson, Oscar. *The American Singer*. New York: 1937. Reprint. New York: 1969.
———. *Debussy, Man and Artist*. New York: 1937.
Thomson, Virgil. *American Music Since 1910*. New York: 1970.
———. *Virgil Thomson*. New York: 1966.
Thoumin, Jean. *Bibliographie retrospective des périodiques français de la littérature musicale 1870–1954*. Paris: 1957.
Thuillier, Guy. *Bureaucratie et bureaucrates en France au XIXe siècle*. Paris: 1981.
Tiénot, Yvonne, and O. d'Estrade-Guerra. *Debussy: L'homme, son oeuvre, son milieu*. Paris: 1962.
Tiersot, Julien. *La Chanson populaire et les écrivains romantiques*. Paris: 1931.
———. *Un Demi-siècle de musique française: 1870–1919*. 2d ed. Paris: 1924.
———. *La Musique aux temps romantiques*. Paris: 1930.
———. *Musiques pittoresques et promenades musicales à l'Èxposition de 1889*. Paris: 1889.
———, ed. *Lettres françaises de Richard Wagner recueillies et publiées par Julien Tiersot*. Paris: 1935.
Tilley, A. *Modern France*. Cambridge: 1922
Tombs, Robert. *The War Against Paris 1871*. Cambridge, 1982.
Tosi, Guy, ed. *Debussy et d'Annunzio, correspondance inédite*. Paris: 1948.
Toye, Francis. *Rossini: A Study in Tragi-Comedy*. New York: 1963.
Trigano, Shmuel. *La République et les juifs*. Paris: 1982.
Trudgian, Helen. *L'Esthétique de J.-K. Huysmans*. Paris: 1934.

Uzanne, L. O. *La Française du siècle, modes, moeurs-usages*. Paris: 1886.

Valéry, Paul. *Pièces sur l'art*. Paris: 1938.
Vallas, Léon. *César Franck*. Translated by Hubert Foss. London: 1951.
———. *Claude Debussy: His Life and Works*. Translated by Maire and Grace O'Brien. London: 1933.
———. *Claude Debussy et son temps*. Paris: 1932.
———. *The Theories of Claude Debussy*. Translated by Maire O'Brien. London: 1929.
Vandam, A. D. *An Englishman in Paris*. London: 1893.
———. *My Paris Note-book*. Philadelphia: 1894.
Van Vechten, C. *The Music of Spain*. London: 1920.
Vasili, Paul. *Society in Paris*. New York: 1890.
Vignal, Louis Gautier. *Proust connu et inconnu*. Paris: 1976.
———. *Vincent d'Indy: La Jeunesse, 1851–1886*. Paris: 1946.
———. *Vincent d'Indy: La Maturité, la vieillesse, 1886–1931*. Paris: 1950.
Villar, Rogelio. *La Musica y los musicos españoles modernos*. San Sebastian.
Villoteau, Pierre. *La Vie parisienne à la Belle Epoque*. Paris: 1968.
Vizetelly, Ernest Alfred. *Paris and Her People under the Third Republic*. ca. 1921. Reprint. New York: 1971.
Vollard, Ambroise. *Recollections of a Picture Dealer*. Translated by Violet M. Macdonald. 1936. Reprint. New York: 1978.
Vuillemin, Louis. *Albert Roussel et son oeuvre*. Paris: 1925.
Vuillermoz, Emile. *Claude Debussy*. Paris: 1920.
———. *Gabriel Fauré*. Philadelphia: 1969.

Wagner, Richard. *My Life*. Edited by Mary Whittall, translated by Andrew Gray. Cambridge: 1983.

————. *Richard Wagner's Prose Works*. Translated by William Ashton Ellis. London: 1899. Reprint. New York: 1966.

Wagner et la France. Special number of *La Revue musicale*. Paris: 1923.

Walsh, T. J. *Second Empire Opera: The Théâtre Lyrique, Paris 1851–1870*. New York: 1981.

Washburne, E. B. *Recollections of a Minister of France*. New York: 1889.

Weber, Adna Ferrin. *The Growth of Cities in the Nineteenth Century: A Study in Statistics*. Ithaca, N. Y.: 1963.

Weber, Edith. *Debussy et l'évolution de la musique au XXe siècle*. Paris: 1965.

Weber, Eugen. *France, Fin de siècle*. Cambridge, Mass.: 1986.

Weber, Johannes. *La Situation musicale et l'instruction populaire en France*. Leipzig: 1884.

Wechsler, Judith. *A Human Comdey: Physiognomy and Caricature in 19th-Century Paris*. London: 1982.

Weinstock, Herbert. *Rossini: A Biography*. New York: 1968.

Weisberg, Gabriel P., et al. *Japonisme: Japanese Influence on French Art 1854–1919*. Cleveland, Oh.: 1975.

Weiss, J. J. *Les Théâtres parisiens*. Paris: 1896.

Weisstein, Ulrich. *The Essence of Opera*. Glencoe, Ill.: 1964.

Weld, John. *Young Man in Paris*. Chicago: 1985.

West, Rebecca. *1900*. New York: 1982.

Whistler, James A. McN. *Selected Etchings of James A. McN. Whistler*. Selected and introduced by Maria Naylor, technical note by Elizabeth Lunning. New York: 1975.

Whitford, Frank. *Japanese Prints and Western Painters*. London: 1977.

Who's Who in France. Editions Jacques Lafitte, Paris.

Wichmann, Siegfried. *Japonisme*. Paris: 1982.

————, ed. *Weltkulturen und moderne Kunst*. Munich: 1972.

Wickes, George. *The Amazon of Letters: The Life and Loves of Natalie Barney*. New York: 1977.

————. *Americans in Paris 1903–1930*. New York: 1969.

Wiéner, Jean. *Allegro Appassionato*. Paris: 1978.

Wild, Nicole. *Affiches illustrés 1850–1950*. Vol. 2 of *Les Arts du spectacle en France*. Paris: 1977.

Wilhelm, J. *La Vie à Paris sous le Second Empire et Troisième République*. Paris: 1947.

Williams, G. *La Vie de Bohème*. Paris: 1913.

Wilson, Stephen. *Ideology and Experience: Antisemitism in France at the Time of the Dreyfus Affair*. London: 1982.

Wiser, William. *The Crazy Years: Paris in the Twenties*. New York: 1983.

Woon, Basil Dillon. *The Paris That's Not in the Guide-books*. New York: 1926.

Wormser, Georges. *Français Israelites*. Paris: 1963.

Wright, Gordon. *France in Modern Times*. 3rd ed. New York: 1960, 1974, 1981.

Ysaÿe, A. and Ratcliffe, Bertram. *Ysaÿe, His Life, Work and Influence*. London: 1947.

Zeldin, Theodore. *France 1848–1945*. Oxford: 1973–1977.

Index

Index

Index

Index

ILLUSTRATIONS